AF478136

Gender in Focus

Andreea Zamfira
Christian de Montlibert
Daniela Radu (eds.)

Gender in Focus

Identities, Codes, Stereotypes and Politics

Barbara Budrich Publishers
Opladen • Berlin • Toronto 2018

A CIP catalogue record for this book is available from
Die Deutsche Bibliothek (The German Library)

© 2018 by Barbara Budrich Publishers, Opladen, Berlin & Toronto
         www.barbara-budrich.net

     ISBN   978-3-8474-2183-2
     eISBN   978-3-8474-1211-3

Die Deutsche Bibliothek – CIP-Einheitsaufnahme
Ein Titeldatensatz für die Publikation ist bei der Deutschen Bibliothek erhältlich.

Verlag Barbara Budrich 🅑 Barbara Budrich Publishers
Stauffenbergstr. 7. D-51379 Leverkusen Opladen, Germany

86 Delma Drive. Toronto, ON M8W 4P6 Canada
www.barbara-budrich.net

Jacket design by Bettina Lehfeldt, Kleinmachnow – www.lehfeldtgraphic.de
Image © www.lehfeldtmalerei.de
Technical editing: Anja Borkam, Jena – kontakt@lektorat-borkam.de

TABLE OF CONTENTS

The Interplay between Identities, Codes, Stereotypes and Politics in Studying Gender in Western and Non-Western Societies

Andreea ZAMFIRA, Christian de MONTLIBERT and Daniela RADU

1. Argumentum

'Science is totally opposed to opinion, not just in principle but equally in its need to come to full fruition. If it happens to justify opinion on a particular point, it is for reasons other than those that are the basis of opinion; opinion's right is therefore always to be wrong. Opinion thinks badly; it does not think but instead translates needs into knowledge. By referring to objects in terms of their use, it prevents itself from knowing them. Nothing can be founded on opinion: we must start by destroying it. Opinion is the first obstacle that has to be surmounted. It is not enough for example to rectify opinion on specific points, so maintaining provisional common knowledge like some kind of provisional morality. The scientific mind forbids us to have an opinion on questions we do not understand and cannot formulate clearly. Before all else, we have to be able to pose problems. And in scientific life, whatever people may say, problems do not pose themselves. It is indeed having this sense of the problem that marks out the true scientific mind. For a scientific mind, all knowledge is an answer to a question. If there has been no question, there can be no scientific knowledge. Nothing is self-evident. Nothing is given. Everything is constructed.'

(Bachelard 2002: p. 25)

In social sciences, in order to deconstruct and explain individual identities, and traditional and modern configurations of the feminine and/or masculine universe, gender is to be considered similarly to other topics, regardless of personal presuppositions, everyday opinions and even of what is stated as common truth by the academic community. Although one may find this to be a commonplace assertion, gender studies seems to attract more and more researchers who are convinced that the social construction of the feminine/masculine categories cannot be appropriately studied by the opposite gender. Nevertheless, by invoking such an argument, the uniqueness of personal experience and its importance in understanding a given issue, may call into question a very large part of research in philosophy, history, cultural studies, anthropology, sociology or political science. In practice, codes usually used in the mental mapping of femininity and masculinity could fundamentally hinder the understanding of gender-related issues. Therefore, the reference to Bachelard's thesis on scientific mind (2002) is nothing less than an invitation to put gender into study the way we proceed with all other research objects in social sciences.

From this perspective, the study of gender does not need particular natural prerequisites. Instead, it requires a *savoir-faire* that scholars who are aware of gender-related biases in conceptualizing, problematizing, operationalizing, analyzing and interpreting could benefit from. In the end, both types of outlooks – self-oriented and hetero-oriented – bring to light important multi-faceted aspects of gender identities, codes used for socially constructing the feminine and masculine categories, stereotypes influencing couple/family configurations, and social and political constraints on men and women (with all the inequalities resulting from here). Completing the gender theoretical puzzle is also inconceivable without approaching the issues related to (and also raised by) sexual minorities, to those in-between categories that are extremely challenging for academic research.

2. From Questioning Biology to Studying Gender and Gender Identities

In the 50s and 60s, American clinical psychologists such as John Money and Robert Stoler reported accounts of dissociation between patients' anatomical structure and the accustomed configuration of their identity. Since the 70s, various theoretical models have described and explained the *male/female* syntagm as a natural, biological given, and the *masculine/feminine* one as a cultural construct defined as a result of individuals' interactions within social and micro-political spaces (see Elisabeth Badinter, Pierre Bourdieu, Michel Foucault, Thomas Laqueur, Anne Oakley and others). This turning point not only brought more conceptual clarity regarding gender but also the necessity of developing a new well-ordered system of thought – gender studies. Thus, starting in the 80s, gender became a useful instrument in understanding, constructing and deconstructing the male-female relation, and gender studies generously offered a wide interdisciplinary field for specific approaches such as juridical and political philosophy, history of religions, postcolonial studies, cultural anthropology, social psychology, political sociology, and so on.

The premises of gender studies are shaped around the idea that an attributed biological status does not represent more than the primary material that is subsequently transformed by values and norms, through the process of primary or secondary socialization, into *masculinity* and *femininity*. The cultural and social construction of masculinity and femininity is the result of an intellectual exercise of associating the biological and cultural/social dimensions, but also offers the possibility to reconsider the terms of this association. Researchers in gender studies find their objects of study all around them: migration, the labor market, discrimination within professional or home milieus, lack of access to resources, public spaces, stereotypes in everyday life, traditional subordination relations, role conflicts and confusing identities, human rights and politically (in)correct discourses, for example.

From an epistemological point of view, gender studies encounter two main obstacles. The first obstacle is that of clearly defining and integrating the demarche within a particular field of study. It comes down to the researcher to skillfully deal with the existing plurality of disciplinary perspectives and, thereby, to enrich and strengthen the originality of his/her work. The second obstacle or challenge for researchers in the field of gender studies is related to the operationalization of concepts and the selection of indicators. Measuring gender inequalities, for instance, could prove to be a difficult task, since they are historically rooted in the relations of cultural and social domination.

3. From Questioning Social Inequalities Related to Gender to Studying Symbolic Domination and Political Stances

A significant part of research on gender addresses, both specifically and in general, the issue of social inequalities and symbolic domination – in other words, the effects of the interplay between identities, codes, stereotypes and politics. Living in gendered societies makes it necessary to take into account the influence of specific power stakes on individual values, beliefs, attitudes, in-group and out-group relations, and on social structure. The social effects of gendering processes are easily to recognize in our daily lives. An extraordinary number of performative acts, produced in real-time, are worth analyzing more attentively. In order to demonstrate this, let us take a glance with Christian de Montlibert at some phenonema that might seem to be unlike each other, but that help us to formulate coherent meanings for the observed events.

In 2015, visiting Bucharest, Montlibert noted that this is a city that experiences considerable traffic congestion, but in order to explain this it does not suffice to speak of influxes of vehicles and scarce tramrails or bus lines. Instead, we would understand the situation a little better if we saw what a sociologist who is somewhat curious about the effects of *male domination* notices immediately: men use their cars, whereas women wait at public transportation stations. To exert power over space with the automobile remains a male privilege.

During his very first research project in 1964-1965, Montlibert was confronted with issues of gender. He was surveying some employees who, after their working day, attended evening classes to prepare for a diploma which would give them access to a more qualified job, and he was amazed to find that out of 120 students randomly selected there were only four women, and these were all single and childless. They explained to him that some of their colleagues wanted to follow the same curriculum, but the time constraints of the double workday imposed by the household and the care of their children prevented them from undertaking it. Meeting these potential female candidates he understood that, besides their workloads, their very self-definition in the social world was at stake. This was not perceived and defined in the same manner by men and women: all conditions being similar, the men he met were not satisfied with their social place, while the women resigned themselves to it.

A few years later, around 1974-1975, he was asked to teach sociology to a group of social workers. Here the sex ratio was reversed. The student population was overwhelmingly female, as if the care and assistance provided to others through social work could be put into practice only by a woman, or as if help was inherent in the feminine nature. This is to say, that the conventional partition which requires women to take care of the family and the subjective realm, while men are in the public arena, was internalized to the point of guiding the choices of female and male students. The functioning of social structures insidiously contributed, in the professional world and even among the graduates Montlibert studied, both men and women, to the reproduction of the conventional distribution of activities between the masculine and the feminine.

These examples allow us to see that the list of the concepts needed to ponder over gender effects is a long one: 'time constraints', 'inequalities and discriminations', 'socialized nature', 'self-definition' in the social world, 'internalization', 'social reproduction', and 'male domination'. Thus a number of developments would be justified, each one referring to a history of the social sciences, and would deserve a place in the biographies of the authors who contributed to its elaboration.

Dealing with gender also allows us to attempt to solve the central problems of sociological research. In the first instance, the study of gender effects raises questions about the manner in which the social world influences individuals; in short, how the social world is incorporated to the point of shaping the body and internalized to the point of structuring desires and representations. Everything indicates that the social world becomes a constitutive part of each individual. Secondly, the investigation of gender leads us to ask ourselves how such a social partition can maintain its permanence while it suffers constantly concomitant variations and transformations of social structures, and especially while it is the subject of harsh and tenacious criticism. More precisely, it is as if the institutions of power were able to strengthen in a specific manner the models and representations of the gendered division of labor which they disseminate by adapting them to various situations.

4. Origins of Male Domination

We shall refer here only very briefly to three accounts of the origins of male domination, insofar as the question of origins is not a main issue. We believe three major theories can be detected here.

The first one is essentialist and claims that this domination is rooted in women's biological data: childbirth and breastfeeding force women to limit themselves in a dominated world. These theories may even seek to justify male domination by certain properties of the female body, which is seen as less able to perform not only multiple kinds of heavy work, but is also less capable of conducting complex intellectual operations. The second theory makes men's strength and violence an argument to explain the will of men to oppress the female workforce to their advantage, both in terms of production and sexuality. The third, more historical theory, emphasizes the role of women in the organization of capitalist bourgeois society, and particularly in the social division of labor at the stage of the primitive accumulation of capital.

The first theory stumbles due to the study of ethnology, prehistory, and archaeology, which have demonstrated the lack of universality of biological effects. Childbirth, maternity, and breastfeeding do not everywhere and always isolate women in the world of the home; there are societies where children are weaned early and are fed by the community, and lots of archaeological evidence shows that in certain prehistoric European societies women were excluded neither from production or war (Testard 2014).

These biological data have stimulated quite various kinds of research, which helped develop a second theory underpinned by individuals' biological data: masculine strength, for example, was explained by the repeated effects of food over long periods of time. That is, let us suppose that men used to appropriate the most nourishing victuals, which in the long term enabled them to become bigger and more muscular. In the same manner, Durkheim ([1897] 2008), in his time, had underlined the existence of a segregation between men and women in the most primitive societies (chronologically speaking) – the differentiation of genders in languages appeared to him as a relic of that same segregation. He argued that the fear of menarche, menstrual blood, and the blood of parturition in many societies transformed women into a group both impure – for which reason women were considered inferior – and linked to the sacred – which earned them the appellation of sorceresses and witches (Durkheim 2008). Thus he claimed that from this point various mythologies of male/female relationships developed which survived in the unconscious. Françoise Héritier (2007), whose work we significantly schematize here, emphasizes the role of myths in male domination, which, in her opinion, results from a 'cognitive bias' that finds its expression in the categories of binary thinking ('active'/'passive' or 'hard'/'soft'). She says that women, belittled by all myths, are ultimately reduced to childbirth and that the violence they experience traces its origin in the fact that they must 'make children' for men. Moreover, as the author points out, they produce children of both sexes, a completely abbhorent fact in the eyes of men. This being the case, the 'differential valence of the sexes' is universal and crosses historical periods.

The third theory, without denying the more ancestral forms of male domination, is more interested in those modern characteristics which are to be found in the organization of the bourgeois society. Durkheim ([1913] 1975: pp. 129-130) wrote:

'From the moment the Roman law made its influence felt, the husband became "lord and master" of the community's goods; he could dispose of them "at his pleasure and will"; women, on the contrary, were struck by a radical inferiority and inability' (our translation).

The implementation of this subordination is well documented in the work of historians. Georges Duby (1996) states that at the end of the Middle Ages the appropriation of fiefdoms, and the transfer of property thus constituted, were accompanied by a transformation of kinship which subjected women to their husbands, alongside a disinheritance of other offspring in favor of the eldest son. To sum up, the advent of the bourgeoisie as a social force led not only to social violence in the sphere of work in general (assigning to each person a place he/she has not chosen and depriving him/her of rights), but it also led to social violence against women. Marxist sociologists and anthropologists (particularly those of the Anglo-Saxon school) have underlined this historical explanation. Recently Silvia Federici (2014), in a very stimulating book, Caliban and the Witch, developed a thesis according to which the primitive accumulation of capital has led to a debasement of women's situation and to the confinement of women in the world of both physical reproduction (childbirth and early education) and symbolic reproduction (educational work with a view to inculcating submission to the symbolic order) of the work force[1]. But this confinement could not be put into effect unless it was substantiated to the point of becoming legitimate, something for which the Catholic Church strove unrelentingly. Jack Goody (1985), in his book *The Evolution of the Family and Marriage in Europe*, was interested in the

---

1   The accumulation and reproduction of capital requires that the physical and symbolic reproduction of the workforce is not renumerated, and confines women to these chores. Thus, capitalism pays but one half of reproduction (actually less, since the State provides another part of this work of the reproduction and preservation of the labor force).

symbolic work of the Christian Church and showed that, in order to consolidate its power and increase its chances of receiving donations (especially money and properties) from the deceased, it transformed the institution of kinship and organized the family accordingly. As widows often bequeathed their property to the Church, it was important to prevent them from having children again, and therefore from remarrying, hence dispossessing them of their sexuality, and compelling them to be obedient and submitted. The hunt for 'witches' who were supposed to be acquainted with contraceptive methods (Riddle 1997) helped expedite female submission – by sending them to the stake. In short, marriage and household work became the true vocation of women. The largest number of women were kept within the bounds of the most discredited menial work: they were domestic servants, farm workers, spinners, knitters, and washers. Everything pushed the woman into the house[2] and kept her away from the public square[3]. Symbolic organization accompanied this forced confinement.[4] This great transformation divided the nascent proletariat and gave men compensation for the submission that the new social structures of nascent capitalism required of them (Delphy 1998; Scott 1990: pp. 2-15), thus allowing the emergence of a new model of the woman: an ideal, passive, thrifty, hardworking and chaste housewife. This model, internalized, would leave indelible traces in the female psyche.

5. Gendered Thinking: Men's Outside World and Reason versus Women's Inner World and Affectivity

Regardless of the origins of 'male domination' it actively exerted itself in the nineteenth century, as well as throughout the twentieth century and even at the beginning of the twenty-first century. The new discipline of sociology has recognized it since the late nineteenth century. Durkheim ([1897] 1930) described women's condition as marked by discriminations and inequalities. A woman's lot was exclusively the economy of the home, subject to marital

---

2   Worried about the development of factories, male artisans drove women away from the workshops, because they competed with them, and were paid less.

3   Under these conditions prostitution increased until it was criminalized: women no longer had the right to occupy the street (Le Roy Ladurie 1969). And in sixteenth century France, simultaneously to the strengthening of State power, women lost the right to enter and appear in court.

4   The nobility resisted these changes longer, as shown in the early seventeenth century by the revolt of the Fronde led by a princess, 'La Grande Mademoiselle'. Even by the middle of the eighteenth century the women of the high nobility still did not raise their children themselves. But the Catholic Church and the State power endeavored to reduce any resistance (Ariès 1973).

power. Women were locked in their marital sex life more than men were, and were deprived of the right to manage their own goods, were excluded from the control of economic capital, denied the right to vote, and, for some of them, subject to the worst living conditions (for example, the prostitution of young women coming from rural areas and migrating to big cities). This situation has structured a socioeconomic partition between the outside world limited to men, and the world of the house as a woman's domain, and a psychological partition that could be characterized as 'masculine reason against feminine affectivity'.

This partition and this domination generate certain kinds of psychological reactions that are observed and captured in literature, theatre, journalism, and even psychoanalysis, and which describe as a fact of nature the emotional dimension which characterizes women. Durkheim ([1897] 1930) was echoing it when he wrote that women, as perceived at the end of the nineteenth century, are more 'instinctive', that their sexuality largely depends on 'the requirements of their body', that 'their mental life is less developed', and that 'their sensitivity is more rudimentary than very developed'. But unlike many writers of the time, Durkheim saw this characteristic as not natural, but the result of a social situation, historically created[5]. If at the end of the nineteenth century women were more emotional, it was because they 'live outside the common life' (Ibid.) and, for this reason, were less impregnated with sociability or, in other words, less bounded by social interactions. Everything happened as if men had managed to build a world which, internalized and somatized by women, inhibited their mental and emotional development. Indeed, if the intensity of social exchanges lead to an increasingly pronounced individualization, if society created the individual and individual mental complexity and if, conversely, the lack of interdependence engenders anomie (socialization and asociality have inhibitory effects on personal development), we understand that at the end of the nineteenth century, women, barred from the public space, were more emotional or more instinctive than men. Thus Durkheim ([1901] 1975: p. 131) states that 'gender equality can only become greater if the woman mingles more with outer life' (our translation).

---

5   Durkheim ([1897] 1930) states that the individual is a social production: first of all from the historical point of view, because society allowed its emergence, and then from the psychological viewpoint, since the 'ways of doing, acting, thinking' of each individual are actually socially constructed. That being so, even somatic characteristics depend on social situations and living conditions. Everything happens as if a double determination were operating: that of almost invisible social conditions, effective in the objectivity of things and bodies, and the more visible one of the inculcations of social representations, effective in the subjectivity of thoughts and emotions.

6. The Effects of Feminism

In the twentieth century feminism transformed women's status (Beauvoir 1949), but it would be an error to believe that this critical movement is the only one responsible for these transformations: it had a significant impact mainly because morphological social changes allowed and supported it. The decline of the 'family business' that had implied the indivisibility of the family was rapid and noticeable. The appropriation of company profits by the ruling classes did not limit this ownership to men but extended it to the women of the dominant classes by allowing them to occupy senior positions and be part of the leadership. Seeing its income increase, the middle class could invest in more years of schooling for its daughters, which had numerous effects on female employment. These three dynamics have entailed not only a transformation of the way of viewing the world, but they also resulted in a change of the Law (Lenoir 2003). The women of the working classes have, in their turn, led many battles for improving their living conditions and related rights[6]. Certain authors often linked to the socialist movement or the anarchist movement, ever since the end of the nineteenth century, have initiated struggles which have not remained without effects. Finally the invention of modern contraceptives and, concomitantly, the changes in sexual representations and practices contributed to these transformations.

These morphological transformations – related in particular to the sharing of the benefits of economic growth (Lenoir 1985) – which accompanied feminism, and the increasingly high educational level of girls, concurrently transformed numerous representations of women's status so as to contribute to their return to the public arena (for example, law on the representation of women in politics). After the struggles of women's movements, the State was forced to institutionalize measures favorable to women[7]. Although male domination continued to exert itself, under the pressure of very heterogeneous feminist groups, the State condescended to allow an improvement of the social status of women. In addition the State, by

---

6   In 1955, in France, *Antoinette*, the newspaper for women of the General Confederation of Labor (CGT, close to the Communist Party), appeared. It highlighted the issue of women's working conditions; the 'sick children' leave days or the lengthening of pregnant women's leave were all obtained through the struggles of female workers (Gallot 2015).

7   In France, for example: provisions eliminating the legal incapacity of women (1938); the right to vote and eligibility (1944); legalized contraception (1967); legalization of the right of the mother to transmit her nationality where necessary; autonomy in the management of her property by the wife (1975); widened and softened divorce measures; decriminalization of abortion and the IVG (voluntary termination of pregnancy); abolished control of the wife's correspondence by the husband (1975), and replaced paternal and marital authority by joint authority (1993).

extending schooling and developing personal assistance services, also contributed to boost the morphological changes from which women benefited. Moreover, certain exceptional historical circumstances allowed, at least for a while, the dissipation of inhibitions, as was the case in France, for example, with the strong participation of women in political debates during the 1789 Revolution (Michaud 1960), their active presence in the debates of the Commune, their involvement in the struggles of the female pacifist teachers against the First World War, their resistance against the Nazi occupation or the social regression desired by the dictatorship of the 'French State'.

7. Inequalities Persist through Habitus, Languages and Practices

Certainly, the access of women to the world of work – between 1968 and 1975 more than two million women were recruited in France, for example – called into question the Bourdieusian principles of 'vision and division' of the social world and led to disputes. But the women who were hired held positions which transposed the traditional responsibilities of women (education, health, care of others, domestic administration, etc.) into the world of work; in other words, women were performing in the outside world the functions they previously had exercised inside their homes and which the family had lost. For example, women who specialized in domestic sewing were thus more likely to become textile workers. They were subject to more binding working conditions than men (for instance, among other things, women workers are more monitored). Nowadays, women of low educational level frequently become a home help or a childminder. The care of others offers them employment which continues the domesticity of the past and/or transposes household chores into professional terms.

As for women members of boards of directors, they more often than not owe their presence in these leading positions to the capital owned by their family, while those who rise to positions of senior managers through their studies rarely hold managerial positions. Furthermore, in the business press, highly educated women journalists are editorial managers more seldom than men. Suffice it to say that the symbolic partition feminine/masculine pushes women to be responsible for sections of the newspaper regarded as more feminine (textiles, luxury consumption of households, loans...); the other way around, more than 95% of automotive columns are written by men (Montlibert 2007).

Actually, everything seems to indicate that women have easier access to social positions which are rather disregarded, or lose the benefits they had before, the reason for this being that men relinquish them in order to move towards other more remunerative and more valued jobs.

Moreover, the symbolic transformations brought about by feminism touch but marginally the model of the 'good mother' and 'good housewife', which was exalted in the literature of the nineteenth century (Grimaud 1924). In France, for instance, this model was promoted vigorously during Pétain's dictatorship, between 1940 and 1944 (Muel-Dreyfus 1996). The institutional changes (such as the mandatory presence of women on candidate lists in elections) only slightly improved the presence of women in the National Assembly (to the point that it was necessary to impose a male/female binomial in the last regional elections of 2015 in France to be sure that women gained the same percentage as men in the elections). The laws on family, marriage, inheritance, and attribution of parenthood remain under the spell of the dominant representations. Yet parents have the opportunity to give their newborn double names (both the name of the father and the name of the mother), or only the name of the mother, although this possibility is rarely used, most couples preferring to give their children the father's surname. Moreover, married women continue to shun their own names, taking their husband's. It is as if marriage and unmarried cohabitation were a 'market' that obeys the rule of social homogamy. Finally we should underline that the use of contraceptives varies directly with the level of education, as evidenced by the early pregnancy of young women belonging to the popular class. Social class prevails, its homogeneity is preserved.

Additionally, the celebration of the body and of the psychological characteristics ascribed to women persist: high-level sportswomen are always referred to as having feminine aesthetic qualities, especially in sports that imply a strong musculation, or in combat sports; for example, '[she won such and such competition] yet she is still beautiful' (Mennesson 1995).

Finally, physical and psychological violence against women remains: just note the number of women murdered or abused by their husbands or partners, and the number of women raped or sexually assaulted, in order to understand the persistence of this phenomenon. It could be said that sexual violence increases as women gain benefits in other fields, as if it acted as a reminder of an inescapable order. The exercise of physical violence undoubtedly has the effect of facilitating the internalization of threat prior to submission.

If discriminations and inequalities continue to manifest themselves, it is because they are inscribed in the *habitus* of each and every one of us, not only men but also women, in *languages* (particularly in injunctions) and *modalities* (spatial and temporal organization), as well as in the *practices* of the social institutions and structures which form and reinforce these habits constantly. Durkheim (1938: p. 16) observed:

'In each of us, according to variable proportions, there is something of the man of yesterday; and it is even the man of yesterday who, by force of circumstance, prevails in us, since the present is but very little compared to that long past during which we were formed and from which we stem. Only we do not feel this man of the past, because it is ingrained in us; it forms the unconscious part of ourselves' (our translation). '

This sexed habitus is engraved on the body and is constantly reactivated by garments and cosmetics[8]. But more fundamentally it is in bodies, in heads and in hearts. It is in the symbolic universe, in the language, in representations (TV, cinema, magazines, urban advertisements, pictorial traditions...). It shapes tastes and dislikes, preferences and aversions, seduction strategies, values and ethical guidelines. It is the product of an explicit and implicit pedagogical work of the 'feminization of women', as Simone de Beauvoir said, and the 'masculinization of men', as Pierre Bourdieu (1998) added. Thus, despite all the measures aiming at equality, divisions tendentiously persist. Nothing shows this better, all other conditions being equal, than the distribution of readings of books between men and women (Mauger & Pauliak, 2000) or the dietary injunctions addressed to women and men (Bordo 1995), or the choices of the topics of papers among female and male students (Montlibert 2001). The former deal with the family (in all its forms) or the body, while the latter deal with work or politics. Furthermore, men use the word 'method' quite frequently, while women talk about 'images'. This difference is rooted in women's position in the market of symbolic goods in which the family (regardless of the form under which it is constituted) holds an essential place. In fact, as Bourdieu (1998: pp. 55-56) wrote:

'The dominated apply categories constructed from the perspective of the dominant to the relations of domination, thus making them appear as natural. ...Symbolic violence is instituted... when the patterns she applies in order to perceive and appreciate herself, or to perceive and appreciate the dominant...are the product of the incorporation of the...classifications of which her social being is the product' (our translation).'

Under these conditions, we shall admit that the perceptions and practices stemming from a dominated habitus are not those – as Bourdieu put it so well – of that kind that one can suspend through an effort of the will issued from a liberating awareness. And this is all the more so since the gendered differentiation is part of one of the most perennial institutions, the family. The fact that the family escapes a little more from marriage, regardless of the fact that in many cases it is recomposed after having been decomposed, changes but little the strategies that develop in the bosom of the family.

---

8   Observe the prominence given to the female body in newspaper and magazine advertising (Goffman 1977).

24

8. The Family: A Place of Reproduction of Gender Effects

If investments in and within the family are so great, the reason is that it is the place where the internalization of those habitus which contribute to the two most important operations of any society are played out: the social reproduction of social divisions and the sexual division of work. The family is organized around the reproduction of the place it occupies in social divisions and differentiations: undoubtedly a material place, but also social and symbolic place. This reproduction is itself subject to the sexual division of social labor which obeys the almost universal rule of male domination. These two processes, which are variously combined, contribute to the transmission of culture by shaping the masculine and feminine, and the dominant and dominated habitus.

The family is the place of reproduction of the resources necessary to maintain or improve one's place in the social division of labor, i.e., the reproduction of economic capital. But it is also the place of reproduction of cultural capital (a resource of which Durkheim in the early twentieth century and Weber some ten years later thought would determine and influence professional and social trajectories), as well as of symbolic capital, a mixture of honour, prestige, reputation, respect, and esteem, for example; all things that do not exist in themselves but which are recognized as essential at a given moment.

Bourgeois families who perhaps attain them more easily than others, develop *economic and patrimonial strategies* (important purchases, financial investments, constitution of collections, etc. belong to this category). *Matrimonial strategies* are closely intertwined: milieu of origin, meeting places, and cultural level favors the union of peers[9]. Everything happens as if social reproduction required social homogamy[10]. Yet in order to facilitate homogamy, it is also necessary that young men and young women of the same milieu find the opportunity to meet; the families possessing the most important resources know how to do it.

The requirements of reproduction of the social classes also lead to *fertility strategies*: the fertility of men from the better-off classes is higher than that of the men from the working classes. It is true that some have a name, a heritage, and symbolic, cultural and economic capital to bequeath,

---

9   Michel Bozon (2002) was interested in homosexual couples and obtained similar results.

10   See Alain Girard (1964) *Le choix du conjoint. Une enquête psycho-sociologique en France,* Paris: Presses Universitaires de France – about 'social homogamy': Marriage remains rare for unemployed members of the working classes (the unemployed are not marriageable) and, if marriage does take place, it tends to impoverish couples who take out a loan for the organization of the ceremony, while in the upper classes all the gifts and donations offered enrich the young couple and offer them opportunities to expand their network of relationships.

while the legacy of others is reduced to a minimum. The men of the ruling classes are inserted into networks of social practices that favor the family, which is not the case for men of other classes, not only symbolically speaking. All this is to say that a logic of social reproduction of inequalities is at work in the family.

The family is the scene of *cultural and educational strategies* which are so important in a world where educational and cultural capitals play such an important role in the allocation of places. They organize themselves from the earliest age and women play a major role in this matter. In a world of increased competition, due to the opening of high schools to a greater number of pupils, the families most endowed with cultural capital have been able to make larger investments to safeguard their advances, and nowadays they do not hesitate to make additional financial investments in order to increase the chances of their offspring (Montlibert 2002). But we should also talk about the *strategies for the accumulation of social capital* (maintaining relations with distant relatives and managing contacts, for example), and *prophylactic strategies* (the proliferation of gyms, fitness halls, and relaxation rooms in the beautiful neighborhoods of Paris and other European cities followed the installation of the offices of company managers). The choice of holidays, food, etc. depends on these strategies, which are mainly reserved for women.

All these strategies contribute in varying degrees to the *strategies of accumulation of symbolic capital* (from the choice of first names to the valorization of all that is linked to what is seemly and pleasing (cosmetics, clothing, maintenance, and home decoration, for example) which are largely reserved for women, including the management of 'honor'. All these strategies contribute, at least, to avoid a deterioration of types of capital and, at best and if possible, to increase their volume. The participation of families in social reproduction thus contributes to the stratification of society into social classes or, to put it more simply, to the unequal distribution of various types of capital. This being so, it must be emphasized that the implementation of these different functions varies considerably from one social group to another.

But the fact remains that this system of reproduction of the social status works only within the framework of a sexual division of labor. If the family is the place of social reproduction, it is also the place of reproduction of the division between masculine and feminine. It is the place where the masculinization of boys and the feminization of girls develop, strongly contributing thereby to male domination, which is the second invariant that characterizes the family. Certainly, the emergence of women into the world of work has called into question the Bourdieusian principles of 'vision and division' and has lead to contestations. But men, whether in the popular or dominant classes, continue to dominate the public space and the field of power, while women are ousted to the extensions of the domestic universe and the extensions of the universe of social capital management, which are both symbolic universes. These transformations touch only marginally the model of the 'good mother of the family', which has been exalted for such a long time and which animates many debates. The laws on family, marriage, inheritance and attribution of kinship remain under the sway of dominant representations. Of course the variations are important from one social class to another, but the same discriminations can be found at all levels.

But for these capital reproduction strategies to work there still must be heirs who accept the inheritance. This involves the internalization of dispositions, which Bourdieu called a habitus. If discriminations and inequalities persist the reason is that they are inscribed in the habitus of everyone, not only of men but also of women. This sexed habitus is in bodies, heads and hearts. Women, as mothers, contribute significantly to its formation. Thus, in spite of all the measures tending towards equality, divisions show a tendency to persist. It will be objected that *things change*, whereupon I will reply that as Bourdieu (1998: p. 125) wrote: 'In work as in education, the progress of women must not hide the corresponding advances of men, as in a handicap race where the structure of the gaps is maintained' (our translation).

The fact remains that even if there is *'permanence in and through change'* (Bourdieu 1998), women's access to the labor market, sexual freedom gained through contraception and abortion, the slightest family control due to the implementation by the State of the extension of schooling and due to the material and symbolic consumption, and the recognition of homosexuality, all contributing to the weakening of family ties (divorce, blended families, single parenthood), leads to a social effervescence that could somewhat partake in a redefinition of female status, and at the same time male status. Sociology can contribute to it. As Durkheim said more than a century ago, in a sentence with which we agree completely, sociology would not be worth an hour of painstaking work if it had not a social utility. This is also regarding the discriminations and inequalities faced by women; it could contribute to *re-historicizing by de-naturalizing* those conceptions which, in specific historical circumstances, were *de-historicized and then, due to this operation, naturalized and thereby eternalized* by the institutions of power (Bourdieu 1998: p. 156). To make a long story short, sociology can give to culture that which pretends to be nature.

9. Brief Description of the Volume's Scope and Content

This volume is mainly based on papers presented at the 2015 LUSEEC Conference on Humanities and Social Sciences in Bucharest, entitled

Perspectives on Gender in a Global World, organized by the University of Bucharest and the Lumina University of South-East Europe in Bucharest. It also includes papers subsequently gathered through open call and rigorously selected in order to form a coherent collective work. This volume aims to scientifically address the gender balance encompassing various approaches in philosophy, anthropology, cultural studies, sociology, law, history and political science.

Both the authors and the editors come from quite distinct academic backgrounds. Andreea Zamfira comes from the Lucian Blaga University of Sibiu. She is a Romanian political and social scientist, and a member of the Francophone research centers CEVIPOL (Center for the Study of Political Life, Brussels) and CEREFREA Villa Noël (Centre Régional Francophone de Recherches Avancées en Sciences Sociales, Bucharest). She has dedicated the majority of her work to social representations and political behaviors in multicultural communities. Christian de Montlibert is a French sociologist, Professor Emeritus at the Marc Bloch University of Strasbourg, researching the structuralist-constructivist perspective initiated by Pierre Bourdieu, and particularly interested in explaining the different forms of social and symbolic domination. Daniela Radu holds a Ph.D. in International Relations (with an important teaching experience in this field). She is also a practitioner of Human Rights (within projects of the United Nations Office in Geneva and the University of Geneva), mainly concerned with the situation of the vulnerable categories of the population in Africa (women and children). Having in common an interest in cultural anthropology, social psychology and political sociology, and the social construction and reproduction of differences related to ascriptive factors (such as gender or ethnicity), the editors have pursued the main goal of assembling a multidisciplinary volume on gender issues. This collective work focuses on the manner in which identities, codes, stereotypes and politics are structured and structure contemporary social relations.

The first part of the volume, entitled *Sexual Bodies and Gender Identities Around the World*, opens up an interesting debate about the multiplicity of gender identities, the influence particular cultures and local traditions have on perceiving and living gender, and the different discourses (the academic one included) on these matters.

The case studies included in this first part also reveal practices of crossbreeding mysticism and religious belief in the symbolical investment of the gendered human body with supernatural attributes. Imagining sacred beings or satanic beings, and afterwards socially interacting with them, is still part of life for some Asian indigenous people, reminding us of how sophisticated the construction of gender and of gender identities can be. In her chapter 'Speaking to the Spirits: Thinking Comparatively about Women in Asian Indigenous Beliefs', Barbara Watson Andaya discusses the genuine interplay between religion, gender and age, and the evolution through time of the ritual roles attributed to post-menopausal women in Asia. The author scientifically reports the attitudes and beliefs related to older women (considered spirit mediums) within urban-based ritual communities, on the one hand, and rural cults on the other. This distinction is extremely important for correctly understanding the changes that globalization has inflicted upon traditional Asian communities. Although senior women still fulfill old ritual roles and interrelated practices survive (or, in some cases, even flourish), sedentary lifestyle and urbanization, global communication and the advance of world religions and of mobility have been weakening more and more the traditional belief systems across Asia. The opposition of Christianity and Islam to spirit veneration have certainly undermined the role of mysticism and old rituals in countries like Indonesia, Japan, Korea, Malaysia, Vietnam, etc. However, this constitutes just a turning point in rethinking and symbolizing the communication with spirits and, also in redefining images and identities for women.

The second chapter, 'The *Bissu*: Study of a Third Gender in Indonesia', continues the discussion about indigenous beliefs, sexual bodies and gender identities in Asia. In this chapter, Leonard Y. Andaya invites us to discover a double gendered category of people in Indonesia. This interesting case study draws our attention to the cultural construction of a particular third gender (the *bissu* of South Sulawesi, regarded by the Bugis society to be both sexually male and female). The author, aiming to contribute to the debate on sexed bodies and gender identities, historicizes *bissu* and places it within a larger panoply: *figapa* (meaning 'like a woman', a category including children, premenopausal women, postmenopausal women who have had two or fewer children, and old men); *kakora* ('like a man', a category of postmenopausal women who have given birth to three or more children and are believed to be defeminized); *bayasa* (male priests characterized by being effeminate); *balian* and *basir* (or 'someone who becomes another', believed to represent the deity); *sida-sida* (eunuchs); *hijra* ('other worldly people', impotent men, and some even castrated, who have become ascetics and religious mendicants), etc. Though an important number of these gender categories have been undermined or even suppressed by Islamic fundamentalism and modernity (*bissu* is also affected by such forces), people continue to use old references to hybrid genders in non-Western societies.

As has been emphasized in the chapters by Barbara Andaya and Leonard Andaya, an important number of factors related to urbanization and globalization are at the origin of massive changes in defining and living gender. Modern cultures and discourses ineluctably urge indigenous and local communities to re-think and re-write their specific identities, habitus and practices. Relevant evidence in this sense is also to be found in Sarah Murru's research on 'How Globalization and the Neoliberal Turn Are

Shaping Gender Relations in Hanoi'. The author is particularly concerned with documenting and explaining the effects of *Doi Moi* (the opening up of a global economy in Vietnam), the consumerism of gendered practices, such as the increasing number of extra-marital sexual relations, and single moms and new family configurations (in spite of the still dominant Confucian and patriarchal values). Sarah Murru also presents interesting observations on the influence of the Vietnamese State and its essentialist discourses on women with respect to motherhood, sexuality and gender relations, over time.

The fourth chapter, 'Gender and Asexuality in Academic Sources', is given over by Petra Filipová to a specific type of gender category, constructed around non-feminine and non-masculine elements. The author, principally interested in establishing the genealogy of this (somehow unusual) subject of academic study in the Western world, is first led by bibliographical data to the psychiatric discourse of the nineteenth century as a starting point in scientifically describing, explaining and (de)stereotyping asexuality. In her chronological account, Filipová turns back to Richard von Krafft-Ebing's *Psychopathia Sexualis* (1886), a reference book of psychiatry, based on several cases of patients reporting absence of sexual feeling (*anaesthesia sexualis*); she continues her research by exploring various discourses about asexuality (the medical view, the psychiatric approach, and the legal practices of the nineteenth century) that preceded the academic discourse of the twentieth century, and which is largely still in use today. This academic discourse was practically launched through the Kinsey Reports (1948, 1953), which advanced, for the first time, a scale of human sexual orientation, and other similar relevant scientific works interrogating the nature of asexuality. Relying on this diachronic analysis of the definitions of asexuality (as sexual orientation/sexual dysfunction/mental illness, etc.). Filipová's Foucauldian study attentively examines the controversial relation between sexuality and ethics, the medicalization and criminalization of sexuality, and the relation of asexuality to questions of masculinity and femininity.

The first part of the volume provides important insights into the dynamics of gender identity around the world and its dependency on local beliefs, central structures and dominant discourses. The second part, entitled *Codes Within Women's Auto- and Hetero-Representations*, is designed to highlight the way in which the codes for representing women and female nature are constructed and usually used in written literature and television productions. In order to do this, the authors included in this section propose interesting discussions around some relevant oeuvres.

The fifth chapter, dedicated to three representative Romanian female poets of the 70s and 80s ('the ethical and heretical Ileana Mălăncioiu and Mariana Marin, the intimist-visceral Marta Petreu') by Daniela Moldoveanu, draws our attention to an ideological-cultural opposition. This dual relation

30

proves to be particularly useful in understanding how the politics of representation and metaphor regimes disputed the expression of personal and social identity during those years. This opposition, described in 'The Communist Dictatorship vs. Romanian Women Poets' Discourse of Resistance in the 70s and 80s', occupied a meritorious place within the economy of dissidence the writing of that epoch. Moldoveanu offers us solid arguments in this regard as she analyses different and complex ways of resistance to the illnesses of the century (conformism, Communist doctrine, and the imagination) and of encoding (in verse) the depths of their tormented minds and souls. Moldoveanu offers her readers important insights into what she calls 'the feminine reflection upon the self and the world' in Communist Romania. She also foregrounds the female fight for freedom from the communist regime and for liberating the self.

If the poetry written in the 70s and 80s in Romania is infused with 'an inborn dose of autofiction', as Moldoveanu argues in her chapter, women become 'the true creators of a literary new genre called autofiction' after the revolution against communism in 1989, the *annus mirabilis*. This idea is amply developed in Florina-Elena Pîrjol's chapter, 'Corporeality and Sexuality in Women's Autofictions: A Few Romanian Examples'. From the 90s onwards, Romania has witnessed an authentic rebirth of women's literature in terms of form and content. Self-reflexivity and free reflection on formerly taboo subjects (body, sexuality, birth, abortion, rape, loss of child, etc.) replace auto-censorship and sublimation. To analyze women's literature within this specific temporal context is to apprehend the fundamental cultural and ideological changes experienced by Romanian society after Communism. Pîrjol is manifestly dedicated to this mission of offering new explanations and findings in this field.

The seventh chapter, 'Diffused Gender Codes and Transcultural Outcomes in Jhumpa Lahiri's *The Lowland*', constitutes further evidence provided by cultural studies regarding the importance of literature in mirroring feminine life. Adriana Elena Stoican invites us to take a look at the South Asian American writer Jhumpa Lahiri's *The Lowland* (a novel with a presumed autobiographical source of inspiration). Her paper challenges readers to discover ways in which normative traditional gender codes influence nomadic women's subjectivity and objective experiences. A significant number of Stoican's observations are to be taken into account as useful theoretical tools concerning the nomadic women's life: the healing function of mobility as peregrination after personal traumatic events; the liberating function of detaching from conventional norms (i.e., the gender roles prescribed by the Hindu culture) vs. the anomic effects of deconstructing personal gender identity; and personal metamorphosis along individualistic lines as a strategy of transgressing the East-West divide (a divide broadly explained in famous books such as Edward Said's

Orientalism, Vesna Goldwsorthy's *Inventing Ruritania*, etc.). 'Transculturality' represents another concept that Stoican attentively examines. The author's outlook offers a key theoretical notion for understanding both the transformations engendered by the encounter between tradition and modernity, and the major changes related to globalization, also discussed in the first part of the volume.

At the end of the second part of the volume, the reader is guided to pass from the study of literary works to those of television productions. As the title of her chapter ('The Politics of the Feminine Body: A Manifesto and Three TV Series') indicates, Viorella Manolache chooses to talk about representations of the feminine body (and, implicitly, about representations of the feminine) with reference to three popular TV series (*The Bridge*, *Bron/Broen* and *The Tunnel*). Placing her study within a critical perspective, and combining methods of philosophical analysis and psychoanalysis, Manolache aims to solve gender code puzzles incorporated within the given TV drama series. Similarly to all audio-visual productions, the selected cases are undoubtedly 'generators of worlds' (Soulages 2007: pp. 17-18). Therefore, examining images from the series, and the related figurativization process of the feminine subject/object, Manolache also points out the way media culture and different politics of representation (feminist, postmodern, etc.) interlace. By overlapping, they translate the social universe into images and fabricate new televisual and social representations of the feminine body and, more broadly, of feminine/masculine existences. Depicting the anatomical-visual structures presented in the three TV series, this author practically illustrates the place and cultural forms women occupy in the social imagination. As she writes, 'the hypostasis of body/corpse from/on the border/bridge/tunnel, uniting two halves belonging to two different women' is somehow a 'formula for diagnosing social, cultural, economic, attitudinal-psychological or political halves within two distinct spaces' (where 'space' is defined in a Foucauldian-heterotopological manner).

The third part of the volume, *Gender Stereotypes, Couple/Family Configurations and Reproduction* opens the door for discussions on private, domestic, social, legal, and ideological/political matters related to living together within gendered frames.

With her opening chapter on 'Gender Stereotypes in Emmanuel Lévinas's Concept of Subject', Marzena Adamiak problematizes the very relation between femininity and female gender by revisiting the French philosopher's work *Totality and Infinity: An Essay on Exteriority* (1979). Adamiak departs from Lévinas's ontological and ethical considerations on objectivity and subjectivity in human relationships, pointing out the prominence of gender stereotypes even in notorious theories on feminine and masculine categories. Associating femininity with weakness, docility, fearfulness, animality, carnality, Eros, and Thanatos, and masculinity, on the contrary, with vitality, activity, enjoyment, freedom, egoism, and atheism, Lévinas plunges into an essentialist approach, epistemologically acceptable only through recourse to a separation from empiricism. Lévinas's work displays with forethought the well-known myths and images of femininity (seen as 'the absolute Otherness') and masculinity (as 'the subject' par excellence). Nevertheless, the phenomenologist philosopher does not critically analyze them. Implicitly, he does not succeed in challenging the cultural stereotypes deeply responsible for the real state of inter-gender relations.

The tenth chapter, 'The Division of Labor within the Family and Altruism: A Feminist Critique of Becker's Models', continues the analysis of limits in theoretically explaining inter-gender differences, as well as the reproduction of gender-related stereotypes and social discrimination. With this research, Oana Crusmac returns to Gary Becker. He is one of the most influential economists from the end of the last century, severely criticized by scholars belonging to the second wave of feminism. There are two major lines of critique. The first one is formulated with reference to Beckers's assumptions about women's innate motivations which bind them to the domestic sphere (the family and the household), and the economic desirability of the division of labor within the family. The second one concerns his altruistic model (on which the traditional family presumably relies) of sharing common resources. Feminist economists consider this model susceptible of favoring tyrannical inter-gender relations by minimizing the competition and conflicts between spouses to the husband's advantage.

The following chapter aims to measure the 'Consequences of Intimacy and Violence in the Couple Relationships of Young Romanians on Their Future Life Plans'. Cristina Faludi rigorously identifies and conspicuously shows the short-term effects (the intentions) of usual practices related to intimacy and violence in the romantic relationship of young adults. Thus Faludi makes an important step towards understanding the sociology of inter-gender relations and the power of cultural stereotypes in perceiving and explaining personal experiences. The very interesting conclusions for the Romanian case could inspire pertinent research hypotheses about other countries. Faludi observes, for example, that young men are victims of harmful practices to a greater extent than young women; in order to explain such an unexpected situation, the author proposes the following hypothetical circumstances for further investigation: women's tendency to under-declare these type of practices, men's tendency to exaggerate the violence they endure, and women's sexual emancipation and the subsequent changes within the pattern of courtship. Another surprising situation is that, although a low level of intimacy in the couple and a high level of violence constitute strong predictors for separation from the romantic partner within the following three years, a low level of intimacy in the couple is also significantly associated with the intention among young women to marry and give birth to a child with the current partner within the next three years; a possible explanation could reside in the women's attempt to secure the given partnership by marriage and reproduction.

Reproduction represents a central issue within gender studies and it has also generated a tremendous number of polemics among scholars of bioethics, private law and political science. Therefore, a special chapter is dedicated by Andrada Nimu and Andreea Zamfira to it: 'Is My Reproductive Body Rightfully Mine? About Abortion and Individual Choice in Post-communist Romania'. The authors start by exploring different conceptions about the human body and the definitions of personhood. These are conceptual tools extremely useful in analysing, comparing and interpreting the opposite theoretical approaches to abortion, in understanding the controversies about women's reproductive rights versus the rights of the unborn. The chapter continues by tracing the history of abortion legislation and women's reproductive rights in Romania, and by presenting the evolution of different abortion-related discourses after the dismantling of the Communist dictatorship. The chapter also includes the authors' observations about Romanian women's concepts of abortion, today; these observations are based on research conducted on an online platform.

The fourth part of the volume scrutinizes the *Social, Political and Institutional Constraints on Women*, relying on five examples.

The thirteenth chapter focuses on the case study of women's (under)representation in a particular scientific domain: 'The Influence of Academic Self-concept on the Study Program Choice of Computer Scientists'. Analyzing the effect of intrinsic, extrinsic and social motives behind the selection of degree programs in computer science in Germany, the authors Silvia Förtsch and Ute Schmid overshadow pre-established arguments (such as the difference in performance) frequently used in explaining the gender gap. Their quantitative research clearly shows, for example, that, despite women's underestimation of personal abilities or women's lesser confidence with respect to their academic self-concept, their overall academic performances are in fact better than the ones achieved by men. Nevertheless, as it results from longitudinal data, the academic self-concept and motivational factors are strong enough to scale down the influence of academic performances upon choosing a degree program in computer science. Although the research sample is narrow and cannot provide a firm basis for generalizations, Förtsch's and Schmid's findings help us better understand the self-concepts leading to the persistence of gender differences.

The fourteenth chapter keeps the same general thematic approach, but this time the country under scrutiny is Italy: 'Women in Academic Medicine: The "Leaking" Process in Italy'. The authors Rita Biancheri and Silvia

Cervia remark upon another intriguing case of gender inequity but, unlike Förtsch and Schmid, who are particularly concerned with the issue of choosing a study program, they shift our attention to female careers. More exactly, to female careers in Medical Faculties. Despite the continuous feminization of the medical profession and of academic careers in Medicine, starting in the 60s, a significant number of facts indicate the still on-going process of gendering: the female-male gap in the retention of professors promoted from a lower to a higher academic position, and the high level of vertical segregation in the Departments of Medicine, for example. In order to illustrate a successful academic career path in Medicine, the authors present some female professors' profiles based on a set of interviews they have conducted with female Full and Associate Professors.

Analysing 'Female Labor Market Participation in Serbia', Natalija Perišić and Jelena Tanasijević witness generalized gender-based barriers for women in the labor market. The authors demonstrate that 'national market segmentation can be observed in each of the four dimensions' considered by them: segmentation between the primary and secondary labor market sectors, segmentation between the primary independent and the primary subordinate segments, racial segregation, and gender segregation. One can definitely call this approach on gender 'intersectional' because it is also sensitive to other factors likely to influence the experiences engendered by gender and the nature of the feminine and masculine categories. In their chapters, Förtsch and Schmid, and Biancheri and Cervia, also strive to identify intersectionalities with gender that could explain the particular situation in Germany and Italy. That is why these three final and other similar chapters may substantially generate positive changes in situations characterized by the persistence of a wide range of inhibiting stereotypes, traditionalism in organizing economic life, and so on.

And speaking about traditionalism, last but not least, the chapter 'Socio-cultural Factors Structuring Women's Access to Land and Natural Resources in Northwest Cameroon' by Ngambouk Vitalis Pemunta contains overwhelming evidence of gender-based inequities and inequalities generated by old socio-cultural norms. As our author highlights, African post-colonial societies constitute eloquent examples of overlapping sets of laws, regulations, customs and perceptions sustaining male domination and female subordination. Institutionalized, the patriarchal pattern of domination based on criteria like gender, class and ethnicity apprehend all aspects of women's and, of course, of men's life: marriage, property ownership, and social relationships, etc. One of the most visible effects observed by Pemunta is women's exclusion and the risk of becoming victims of gender-based violence and of serious pandemic diseases (HIV/AIDS, for instance).

The introduction to this collective academic undertaking is about studying the interplay between identities, codes, stereotypes and politics governing the various constructions and deconstructions of gender in Western and non-Western societies (Germany, Italy, Serbia, Romania, Cameroon, Indonesia, Vietnam, etc.). We, the editors, think that it is the right moment to invite the readers to discover the realm of gender studies contained in this volume and to reflect together with our authors upon the transformative potentialities of (the largely pervasive today) globalization and interculturality. One does not have to necessarily separate the enthusiastic and skeptical stances regarding this matter. Many times, realities are multifaceted, even contradictory. For example, as summarized by Bloom, Gilad and Freedman (2017: pp. 391-392):

'… in general, societies that undergo economic globalization tend to have greater exposure to other cultures; but this is not universally the case. Many countries remain culturally insular despite their relatively high flows of trade and foreign investment … under these conditions economic globalization is unlikely to translate into improvement in women's status.'

This introduction would not be complete if we did not acknowledge the precious help offered by our colleagues Elena Stoican and Cristina Ștefănescu for correcting the English spelling of the manuscript. We also want to thank Octavian Safta for his great effort of typesetting the entire manuscript according to our Publisher's guidelines. We want to warmly thank them for their exemplary collaboration, and their sincere and cordial support.

Bibliography

Adkins, Lisa & Beverley Skeags (eds.) (2004) *Feminism after Bourdieu*, Oxford: Blackwell Publishing.
Ariès, Philippe (1973) *L'enfant et la vie familiale sous l'ancien régime*, Paris: Editions du Seuil.
Bachelard, Gaston (2002) *The Formation of the Scientific Mind. A Contribution to a Psychoanalysis of Objective Knowledge*, translated from French by Marry McAllister, Manchester: Clinamen Press Ltd.
Badinter, Elisabeth (2006) *Dead and Feminsim*, translated from French by Julia Borossa, Oxford: Polity Press.
Beauvoir, Simone de (1949) *Le deuxième sexe: Les faits et les myths* (Tome I), *L'expérience vécue* (Tome II), Paris: Gallimard.
Bloom, Pazit Ben-Nun, Sharon Gilad & Michael Freedman (2017) 'Does exposure to other cultures affect the impact of economic globalization on gender equality', *International Political Science Review*, 38(3): 378-395.
Bordo, Susan (1993) *Unbearable Weight, Feminism, Western Culture and the Body*, Berkeley, CA: University of California Press.

Bourdieu, Pierre (1998) *La domination masculine*, version numérique, Paris: Editions du Seuil.

Bozon, Michel (2002) *Sociologie de la sexualité*, Paris: Nathan.

Delphy, Christine (1998) *L'ennemi principal* (Vol. 1 – *Économie politique du patriarcat*), Paris: Syllepse.

Duby, Georges (1996) *Féodalité*, Paris: Editions Gallimard.

Durkheim, Emile ([1897] 2008) *La prohibition de l'inceste et ses origines*, foreword by Robert Neuburger, Paris: Payot et Rovages.

Durkheim, Emile ([1950] 1990) *Leçons de sociologie*, Paris: Presses Universitaires de France.

Durkheim, Emile ([1913] 1975) 'L'évolution de la communauté de biens conjugale', *Année sociologique*, 12, reproduced in 'Mariage, droit et usages matrimoniaux', *Textes 3. Fonctions sociales et institutions*, foreword by Robert Neuburger, Paris: Les Éditions de Minuit, pp. 106-130.

Durkheim, Emile ([1901] 1975) 'Origines des problèmes des femmes', *Année sociologique*, 4, reproduced in 'La condition de la femme', *Textes 3. Fonctions sociales et institutions*, foreword by Robert Neuburger, Paris: Les Éditions de Minuit, pp. 131-153.

Durkheim, Emile (1938) *L'évolution pédagogique en France*, Paris: Alcan.

Durkheim, Emile ([1897] 1930) *Le suicide. Etude de sociologie*, Paris: Félix Alcan.

Federici, Silvia (2014) *Caliban et la sorcière. Femmes, corps et accumulation primitive*, translated from English, revized and completed by Julien Guazzini, Marseille, Genève, Paris: Entremonde.

Foucault, Michel (1976) *Histoire de la Sexualité*, Vol. I. *La volonté de savoir*, Paris: Gallimard.

Gallot, Fanny (2015) *En découdre. Comment les ouvrières ont révolutionné le travail et la société*, Paris: La Découverte.

Goffman, Erving (1977) 'La ritualisation de la féminité', *Actes de la Recherche en Sciences Sociales*, 14: 34-50.

Goody, Jack (1985) *L'évolution de la famille et du mariage en Europe*, Foreword by Georges Duby, Paris: Armand Colin.

Grimaud, Charles Abbé (1924) *L'épouse attrait du foyer*, Paris: P.Téqui.

Heritier, Francoise (2007) *Masculin-Féminin*, Vol. I. *La pensée de la différence*, Vol. II. *Dissoudre la hiérarchie*, Paris: Odile Jacob.

Laqueur, Thomas (1990) *Making Sex: Body and Gender from the Greeks to Freud*, Cambridge, Massachusetts and London: Harvard University Press.

Lenoir, Rémi (2003) *Généalogie de la morale familiale*, Paris: Editions du Seuil.

Lenoir, Rémi (1985) 'L'effondrement des bases sociales du familialisme', *Actes de la recherche en sciences sociales*, 57-58: 69-88.

Le Roy Ladurie, Emmanuel (1969) *Les paysans du Languedoc*, Paris: Flammarion.

Mauger, Gérard & Claude Poliak (2000) 'Lectures: masculin/féminin', *Regards sociologiques*, 19: 115-140.

Mennesson, Christine (1995) 'La construction de l'identité féminine dans les sports collectifs', *Regards sociologiques*, 9-10: 81-89.

Michaud, Jean (1960) *Les Etats généraux et le 14 juillet 1789*, Paris: Editions sociales.

Money, John (1995) *Gendermaps: Social Constructionism, Feminism, and Sexosophical History*, New York: Continuum.

Money, John (1986) *Lovemaps: Clinical Concepts of Sexual/Erotic Health and Pathology, Paraphilia, and Gender Transposition in Childhood, Adolescence, and Maturity*, New York: Irvington.

Montlibert, Christian de (2007) 'La presse économique et ses journalistes', in Christian de Montlibert, *Les agents de l'économie. Patrons, banquiers, journalistes, consultants, élus. Rivaux et complices*, Paris: Les Editions Raisons d'Agir.

Montlibert, Christian de (2002) 'Transformations politiques du système scolaire et stratégies d'appropriation', *Regards sociologiques*, 23: 113-123.

Montlibert, Christian de (2001) 'L'emprise de la féminisation sur le savoir sociologique', *Regards sociologiques*, 22: 41-48.

Muel-Dreyfus, Francine (1996) *Vichy et l'éternel féminin*, Paris: Editions du Seuil.

Oakley, Ann (2005) *The Ann Oakley reader: Gender, women and social science*, Bristol: Policy Press University of Bristol.

Riddle, M. John (1997) *Eve's Herbs. A History of Contraception and Abortion in the West*, Cambridge: Cambridge University Press.

Scott, Joan W. (1990) 'L'ouvrière, mot impie, sordide... ', *Le discours de l économie politique française sur les ouvrières. (1840-1860) – Actes de la Recherche en Sciences Sociales*, 83: 2-15.

Soulages, Jean-Claude (2007) *Les rhétoriques télévisuelles. Le formattage du regard*, De Bruxelles: De Boeck.

Stoller, J. Robert (1985) *Presentations of Gender*, New Haven and London: Yale University Press.

Testart, Alain (2014) *L'amazone et la cuisinière. Anthropologie de la division sexuelle du travail*, Paris: Gallimard.

PART ONE

SEXUAL BODIES AND GENDER IDENTITIES AROUND THE WORLD

CHAPTER I

Speaking to the Spirits: Thinking Comparatively about Women in Asian Indigenous Beliefs

Barbara Watson ANDAYA

1. Introduction

This chapter was inspired by a call from the religious studies scholar, Mary Keller, who has advocated new approaches to human bodies that are 'possessed' by ancestors, deities or spirits. She has argued for greater emphasis on the empowerment of the possessed individual rather than attributing their altered state to compensation for social marginalization or perceived inferiority. Her focus on empowerment is significant, since a universal feature of spirit possession is the predominance of women, especially older women (Endres & Lauser, 2011a: p. 10; Keller 2002: pp. 2-3). Indeed, in his pioneering study published more than forty years ago, I. M Lewis identified women 'past the menopause' as constituting a 'high proportion of shamans' (Lewis 1971: p. 85). While Lewis believed such women were responding to feelings of social or psychological deprivation, Keller argues that 'possessed' women in traditional belief systems occupy a respected status in the community as 'instrumental agencies'. Far more than passive channels of communication or simple agents, they are actively connected to the supernatural forces that possess their bodies and that speak through them (Keller 2002: pp. 9-10). Keller also reminds us that definitions of mediumship – the intermediary state that bridges the conscious self and the possessed body – are problematic, since there is an overlap with mysticism and trance. From a range of possibilities I have chosen to follow Peter Claus, who worked among the tribal Tulu of southern India. Like him, I see mediumship among acknowledged practitioners as 'the legitimate, expected possession of a specialist by a spirit deity, usually for the purpose of soliciting the aid of the supernatural for human problems' (Claus 1979: p. 29).

In discussing the position of women in societies where possession is 'a significant and uniquely powerful phenomenon' (Keller 2002: p. 8), I begin by referencing two studies that help explain my line of approach. The first is Carolyn Brewer's iconoclastic analysis of the changes brought to women's ritual status following the introduction of Christianity to the Philippines in the sixteenth century. She challenges the historicity of the well-known *Burning of the Idols,* painted by the nationalist artist Fernando Amorsolo in 1949, which depicts an indigenous priestess, young and nubile, offering up 'pagan' images to the fire as a symbol of her acceptance of Christian teachings. By contrast, as Brewer points out, Spanish sources repeatedly refer to these ritual specialists as 'old' (Brewer 2004: p. 110). My second reference comes from an article by Erin Cline, a specialist on China. She too noted the prevalence of older women among spirit mediums, but additionally drew attention to the lack of comparative research, commenting that although there are several studies of spirit mediums among overseas Chinese in Southeast Asia, there is little research on this group in contemporary China (Cline 2010: p. 520).

In conjunction with the expanding literature on spirit mediumship in Asian societies (Laycock 2015; Endres & Lauser, 2011a; Dawson 2010), these comments have encouraged me to think further about a topic in which I have been interested for some time – the role of older women in indigenous Asian belief systems, especially in regard to communication with supernatural deities (Andaya 2006: pp. 210-212). In contrast to the world religions, which allocated the preeminent ritual role to men, locally grounded religions across Asia (and indeed, in Africa and the Americas) typically provided a space for women, especially for those regarded as senior. As I have argued elsewhere, in Southeast Asia (and I suspect, in much of the non-European world), the presence of post-menopausal women as intermediaries between humans and powerful spirits was due to the 'male-like' status they assumed, since they no longer embodied the mysterious forces of reproduction that could endanger male virility and obstruct channels of communication with the supernatural (Andaya 2005: p. 113; Buckley & Gottlieb, 1988: pp. 6-8). Such attitudes explain why many Chinese communities favor men, although Emily Cline has drawn our attention to women as mediums in contemporary southern China. Yet possessed females could be themselves be imperilled by the ambiguities that infused the release of blood, and a male Chinese medium in Penang (Malaysia) remarked that any woman who went into trace while menstruating could be endangered because the 'god' would leave her polluting body (Kitiarsa 2012: p. 50; DeBernardi 2006: p. 259).

From a basic assumption that spirit possession should be taken seriously as a demonstration of female power in the religious domain, I place Southeast Asia in a comparative context, viewing 'older women' in Asian societies as instrumental agencies who connected their fellow humans with the spirit world. Although the advance of world religions and official views of spirit veneration as 'backward' have undermined this role, I argue that in regional terms Southeast Asia has retained many of the older traditions, and that female spirit mediums can still become people of importance in their community.

2. Spirit Mediumship: The Ambivalent Female

At the outset I recognize that in the Asian context my privileging of older women in regard to spirit possession requires some qualification, since we do at times encounter the idea of youth and virginity as a 'pure' state, necessary for communication with the gods. This is probably most evident in Japanese Shinto beliefs, where young women known as *miko* presided over Shinto ceremonies, received divination from the gods, and through ecstatic trance acted as mediums to a range of deities (*kami*) (Groner 2007). Given the focus of this chapter, however, the most important factor is their changing status. Prior to the Kamakura period (1185-1333), the *miko* were important figures, associated with the ruling class and with great shrines, such as Ise, and were often consulted on matters of state policy. At the village level they also operated as the means by which ordinary people could receive messages from local shrine deities and contact the spirit world to find the causes of disease (Kuly 2003: pp. 198-200). Yet as a more patriarchal and militaristic government evolved in Japan, the ritual function of the *miko* declined, and they became 'wandering shrine maidens' associated with an indigent lifestyle and even prostitution (Ruch 1990). The process was accentuated from the late nineteenth century, when the Meiji government in their determination to become 'modern', actively discouraged spirit mediums. Today a *miko* who dances or sells amulets and predictions at Shinto shrines is probably a university or high school student 'collecting a modest wage in this part-time position' (Kuly 2003: p. 201).

Yet although the *miko* certainly exemplify a widespread Asian view of virginity as a pure state, young women were also viewed as potentially capable of exercising dangerous powers in their relations with men. In China the so-called 'fox spirit' could easily metamorphose into a beautiful female who could both enchant and destroy her male victims (Kang 2013). A similar trope is found in reports from seventeenth-century Philippines, where the most dangerous manifestation of femaleness was in the spirits (*asuang*) who could take the form of a seductive young woman and lure men to their death (Rafael 1993: p. 189). One is reminded of certain Shan groups in contemporary northern Thailand, who, while believing that both men and women can become witches, feel that an attractive younger woman is especially likely to be involved with black magic or even take the form of a jealous witch spirit like those termed *phi mia noi*, literally 'the spirit of a concubine' (Tanabe 1991: pp. 197, fn. 25).

These comments lead towards a second area of qualification. Though middle-aged and elderly women are less likely to be accused of seducing young men, any association with spirit communication and the ability to tap supernatural powers could have negative consequences. Historians of Christian Europe have produced a huge body of literature that explores the disturbing slippage by which many 'wise women' who would once have been regarded as seers were accused of intercourse with the Devil and of using satanic powers for malevolent purposes (Levack 2013). Any discussion of the feminization of witchcraft in Asia would be best conducted with an eye to such studies, as well as those in Melanesia and Africa, which have demonstrated that accusations of 'black magic' increase during periods of community stress, being commonly directed towards women who are older, widowed, poor, physically handicapped, strangers, or otherwise marginalized. While Russia may be an exception (Kivelson 2014: p. 83), in late medieval and early modern Europe the, whose bodies were considered especially prone to possession by malign forces.

Despite the lack of extensive historical research, we can certainly find similarities in Asia. It is difficult, however, to track the evolution of such attitudes, since sources relating to alleged witchcraft at the community and state level are much more limited in Asia than in Europe. The documentation is best in China, but it is still possible for historians to reach different historical interpretations. Brett Hinsch, for instance, contends that as early as the second century BCE witchcraft had emerged as a 'new preoccupation' to become the most serious and feared crime under Han law. While men could also be accused of sorcery, it was generally believed that women had a particular ability to access 'black magic'. The execution and burning of witches was carried out in public, a grim warning of the fate that could await even members of the imperial family (Hinsch 2011: pp. 94-95, 111). On the other hand, ter Haar notes that although elderly women were often stigmatized as practicing harmful magic, witch-hunts as a social phenomenon were relatively rare in China. He attributes this to a relatively weak state reach and the lack of other groups or institutions interested in exploiting rumours of witchcraft for their own purposes (Ter Haar 2012; Ter Haar 2006: pp. 12, 30, 70).

Scholars of South Asia have approached the topic of witchcraft largely through the discipline of anthropology, and although early texts condemn occult practices, chronologically-framed discussions of possession are limited. Yet traditional Indian texts detail a number of ways in which 'witches' (known by many different names) can be identified, and it does appear that over time they became more linked to femaleness (Saletore 1981). Tantric practices that encouraged possession by divinities were often denounced as witchcraft, and in the early nineteenth century in western India more than a thousand women were killed as witches, far exceeding the victims of *sati*. In a disquieting persistence of such ideas, acts against 'witches' are still found in India's rural villages and tribal areas, especially after an epidemic or a failed harvest (Chaudhiri 2014: p. 24; Mullick 2003; Skaria 1997: p. 110).

Against this background it is worth noting that nearly a century ago, a Jesuit missionary working among the Munda tribal peoples of India linked witchcraft accusations to the infiltration of mainstream religious beliefs. He argued that persecution of alleged witches was a result of Hindu influences, introduced via Munda groups who had become more 'Hinduized'. A more recent study repeats this argument, but adds that this change also reflects the economic transition from a relatively gender egalitarian hunting-gathering society to more sedentary agriculture with an accompanying trend towards patriarchy (Mullick 2003: pp. 124-129).

The development among the Munda represents a specific case study, but an overview of the literature suggests that the effects of religious and economic changes on women's ritual status in Asia more generally display basic similarities. In Taiwan, for instance, the advance of Han Chinese influence saw spirit medium roles, formerly the preserve of women, arrogated by men (Brown 2004: p. 113). As noted above, evidence relating to witchcraft in mainland China is open to different interpretations, but the rise of the state appears to have encouraged witch-hunting campaigns because (as in Europe) people condemned as wizards and witches were viewed as threats to the official authority (Hinsch 2011: p. 94 ff; Siegel 2006: p. 18). In eighteenth-century Okinawa the promotion of Confucian ethics as the basis for administration and the accompanying condemnation of 'vulgar practices' led to an ineffective campaign against the female spirit mediums known as *yuta* (distinguished from the *noro*, the state-sanctioned clan priestesses). Here, says one authority, we can see a growing divide between an increasingly Confucianized government and a peasantry who remained 'steadfast to its traditional religious beliefs and practices' (Smits 1999: pp. 114-118).

To some degree one can discern a comparable pattern in Southeast Asia. Although complementary gender relations are considered a regional hallmark, the spread of the world religions tended to widen the differences between men and women. For instance, the idea of 'heaven' as a place of reward after death and 'hell' as a place of punishment was rarely if ever a part of indigenous cosmologies, but was highly developed in the religious ideas that reached Southeast Asia from India (Goh 2015). Those found guilty of casting evil spells (often stereotyped as elderly women) are doomed to punishment in one of the deeper hells. A graphic example is found among the paintings that decorate Bali's 'law court', the eighteenth-century Kertha Gosa pavilion, where a woman is shown with her tongue cut to ribbons, a punishment for practicing 'black magic' (Pucci 1992: pp. 79, 80, 110). It has been suggested that a cultural amalgamation with the Hindu deity Durga also accentuated the bloodthirsty aspects of Bali's powerful demon queen, Rangda, who is associated with the 'witch' Calun Arung (Emigh 1996: p. 81). In the Philippines Carolyn Brewer has argued that Christianity promoted a conceptualization and a vocabulary that created a specific and negative category whereby ritual specialists, the *babaylan* became *bruha* (Spanish 'witches') (Brewer 2004: pp. 86-89). Official condemnation thus encouraged beliefs that evil was not free-floating but was located in the body of certain individuals. In twentieth century Thailand a well-known scholar remembered that in the area where he grew up there were many spirits, *krasyy*, that took the form of old women and were believed to go out at night seeking food, which consisted of raw meat and excrement and new-born babies (Rajadhon & Gedney, 1961: p. 119). State edicts often supported community attitudes, and in Buddhist Burma a law dating to 1785 refers to the immersion of an individual in water to discover if they are guilty of witchcraft (Tun 1986: p. 102). Around the same period the Italian missionary Vicentius Sangermano (1758-1819) remarked that 'it is impossible to persuade the Burmese that there is no such thing in nature as witches and that they are not extremely malicious and hurtful'. In one type of trial by ordeal:

'… a suspected woman is placed upon a little bier, supported at each end by a boat, and a vessel full of ordure is emptied upon her. The boats are then slowly drawn from each other, till the woman falls into the water. If she sinks, she is dragged out by a rope of green herbs tied round her middle and is declared innocent; but if she swims she is convicted as a witch and generally sent to some place where the air is unwholesome.'

(Jardine 1984: pp. 149-150)

The tendency to associate the arts of 'black magic' with femaleness appears especially pronounced in communities subject to Christian influence. Indeed, although the status of male shamans was often higher than that of females, missionaries almost invariably identified 'witches' as women. As Carolyn Brewer has shown so dramatically in the Philippines, Spanish missionaries were particularly prone to see spirit propitiation in terms of witchcraft and Devil-alliance, and to condemn 'sorceresses' as the cause of infant death and miscarriage (Brewer 2000). The powers such women could tap were thought to present the Christian mission with its most serious challenge. A priest working in Vietnam in the late eighteenth century thus recounted how a young Christian woman tried to free herself from a spell that had caused her to be obsessed with a non-Christian man. She went to 'a heathen woman, a sorcerer' who gave her small pieces of paper on which red characters, evidently the name of a powerful spirit, were written. Following instructions, she swallowed the paper but rather than being freed from supernatural manipulation, she became permanently possessed (Forest 1998: Vol. III: p. 253).

While Islam never developed the same form of demonology as Christianity, and never targeted women specifically, the Qur'an does present Allah as a refuge from sorcerers who perform magic through tying knots (presumably divination) and through their control over *jinns*. Islamic commentators were unambiguous in their condemnation of all kinds of activities – devising love potions, providing talismans, predicting the future, and so on – which were seen as efforts to appropriate God's power (Durrant & Bailey, 2012: p. 108). Yet though historical sources provide little evidence of witch-hunts in Islamic societies, women were often targeted for punishment, especially when the community was faced with some unexplained catastrophe, such as an epidemic. In 1895 a future governor, of British Malaya, Frank Swettenham (1850-1946), claimed that 'plenty of people' could attest to the drowning of 'ancient Malay dames' accused of casting spells. The effects of economic depression in rural areas or the intrusion of modernization may explain other references that link hostile magic to spirits in the form of elderly women (Swettenham 1984: pp. 198-199).

Nonetheless, we must be careful in assuming that the world religions introduced unfamiliar concepts to Animist societies, Hans Schärer, who carried out fieldwork amongst the Dayak of Borneo before the Second World War, reported that 'formerly' the torture and murder of *hantuen* or witches was common (Schärer 1963: pp. 20-21, 50-59). There is little evidence, however, that women were singled out as targets. The Austronesian word *suangi* is usually translated as 'wizard' or 'witch', and in contemporary Indonesia is generally glossed as female. In premodern times, however, the German botanist George Rumphius (1627-1702) remarked that this term also referred to 'wild, uninhabited, dangerous places, rocks, and islands', and even rough-looking fruits or plants. Since men could also be *suangi*, it clearly was not gender specific (Rumpf 1999: p. 401; Slaats & Portier, 1993: p. 140). In his authoritative study of early Filipino society, William Scott contrasted sixteenth-century Spanish beliefs that mortals (mostly women) could develop demonic characteristics with indigenous conceptions that misfortune or calamity was the work of malicious spirits in human form. Much feared, these counterfeit humans were normally killed, but the relevant point is that they could as well be male as female (Scott 1994: p. 81; Andaya & Ishii, 1992: p. 510).

In this regard Southeast Asia may represent an exception to the general pattern that links malevolent magic to older females. On the Indonesian island of Flores, for example, Gregory Forth commented that the community he studied, the Nage, did not seem to regard witches as being mostly women (Forth 1993: pp. 119 fn. 2). Even in Bali, where the figure of the widow-witch Rangda exemplifies a relatively elaborated belief in witches (*leyak*), it is acknowledged that people of both sexes may have an aptitude for witchcraft (Covarrubias 1937: p. 344). Furthermore, as Conrad William Watson and Roy Ellen (1993: p. 3) have emphasized, witchcraft has never been considered a major social problem in Southeast Asia. Southeast Asia thus slides into a more general Asian context where the identification and persecution of 'witches' never reached the proportions that historians have tracked in early modern European, colonial America, Africa or even Melanesia. It may therefore be disturbing to see that some sea-going people in Indonesia, now more subject to the influence of world religions than in the past, are inclined to see submerged and dangerous reefs as inhabited by elderly female beings who are compared to 'Satan', or to believe that female river spirits, personified as 'Mrs. Mange' or 'Mrs. Thornback' are capable of inflicting anyone who annoys them with skin diseases and dysentery (Pannell 2007: p. 81).

3. A More Positive Picture

Having acknowledged that young women may also be ritually prominent, and that there are ambiguities attached to the 'wise woman' figure, I would now like to turn to a more positive picture, using Southeast Asia as a platform by which to approach broader questions. I am particularly interested in the cultural recognition of older women as a potential conduit to the spirit world, and their 'instrumental agency' in the transmission of messages from the supernatural. I argue that the absence of the forces of reproduction that blurred the femaleness of a post-menopausal body was combined with other factors that enhanced the social status of senior women, who were commonly regarded as repositories of community knowledge. In contemporary Bali, for example, when music accompanies the priestly chanting in Bali, it is the older women who indicate to the female singers which *kidung* (sung poems) should be performed (Susilo 1998: pp. 17-18). Historians, too, repeatedly encounter senior females in an instructional role. When an eighteenth-century Englishman entertained by the court of Banjarmasin (east Borneo) noted that an old woman 'whom I supposed to be their teacher' was in charge of the royal music and dancing, he was describing a situation found over much of the region (Beeckman 1973: pp. 77-79). In the same vein, a nineteenth-century missionary in Sulawesi remarked that the individuals most knowledgeable in the pre-Islamic literature of the region were not the 'gurus' (teachers), men who knew a little Arabic and Koranic texts, but royal women and female courtiers (Brink 1943: p. 184).

The bank of knowledge and experience possessed by older women also had critical applications in the lives of ordinary people, and they were widely respected as healers. According to an account from Melaka (west coast

Malay Peninsula) in the early seventeenth century, the 'doctors' were mostly 'dayas' (i.e., a wet-nurse or foster mother).

'… female physicians who are excellent herbalists, having studied in the schools of Java Major. They use plants and herbs in the form of plasters and potions to relieve illness – cloves, nutmeg, cinnamon, ginger, etc. They can distinguish illnesses by the appearance of the patient, breathing, etc.'

(Godinho de Eredia 1997: p. 48)

It is not surprising, therefore, to find that an ailing ruler in seventeenth-century Palembang (southeast Sumatra) asked the Dutch administration in Batavia to help him locate two female 'doctors' whom he believed would cure his illness (Andaya 2006: p. 126). In the Christian Philippines the prominence of female healers in contemporary times is anchored in the belief that spiritual potency is vital to the restoration of health. In this regard, it is commonly thought, women have greater powers than men in terms of persuasion and the ability to command supernatural forces (Lahiri 2005: pp. 23-44; Cannell 1999: pp. 272 n, 18).

A lifetime of experience also equipped women to take a prominent position in the ceremonies associated with major life cycles, most notably birth, and in Southeast Asia one is struck by the high status of the midwife. By contrast, in the Hinduized areas of contemporary northern India and Bangladesh childbirth pollution is deemed to be even greater than that resulting from menstruation, sexual intercourse, defecation or death, and the midwife or *dai* is regarded as a 'low status menial necessary for removing defilement' (Rozario 1998: p. 149). The situation was rather different in China and Japan, where capable and experienced midwives, especially in the urban areas, received not only social recognition but could also be well recompensed for their skills. Nonetheless, recent studies have shown how the practice of midwifery came to be dominated by male doctors who drew their knowledge from written, 'scientific' manuals and supported neo-Confucianist rhetoric, which included midwives in the 'nine categories' of despised professional women. Furthermore, even though Chinese female doctors and midwives continued to thrive, one can still note a tendency to link them with the death of children either through infanticide or abortion (Leung 1999: pp. 103, 123).

The pattern in Southeast Asian societies is quite different. To a greater extent than in China and Japan it seems that supervision of labor and childbirth continued to be in the hands of older women, whose familiarity with plants and other ingredients used in potions thought to contain magical powers explains their prominence as healers and midwives. For instance, one can point to the standing of the midwife (*bidan*) in Malay culture. Their presence at any birth was essential, not only in ensuring a safe delivery but because of the role they played in the rituals necessary to ensure that the baby was healthy and the mother regained her strength. An intriguing manuscript compiled in 1779 by a mosque official in Melaka lays out the ceremonies normally performed to guarantee the protection of a royal child. When his consort is seven months pregnant, the ruler summons four 'famous' mid-wives who are responsible for 'rocking the womb' (*mandi melenggang perut*, thought to give definition to the life forming inside the mother's womb) (Sudjiman 1983: pp. 69-61). Attention was focused on the umbilical cord and the placenta, since a skilled midwife could 'read' the umbilical wrinkles and predict an individual's future life (Laderman 1993: pp. 141-142, fn. 74; McKinley 1981: pp. 371-375). Practices in Timor provide a particularly striking example of the midwife's role, for here the midwife fastens a pouch containing the afterbirth to the central pillar of the house and ritually drops the soiled birth cloth on to the ancestral altar to affirm connections to preceding generations (Hicks 1984: p. 31).

Because of their longevity, their knowledge of tradition and customs and their status as mothers and grandmothers, older women in many Asian societies were also seen as naturally gifted mediators. In Southeast Asia, as in China, they are often depicted as intermediaries who set matters right when their menfolk fail to fulfil their social or family responsibilities (Kinney 2014: p. xxix). While this was probably most common in brokering marriage agreements, female liaison was also frequently used to reach compromises between contending parties, whether in commercial dealings or inter-state relations. Those of high birth were especially effective as negotiators because they commanded respect as maternal figures and because refusal of a mother's plea was culturally difficult. The capacity of senior Vietnamese women to resolve dynastic crises is mirrored repeatedly in indigenous sources from other areas. A fragmentary text from sixteenth-century Cambodia similarly mentions several instances where the women of the Khmer royal family, especially the Queen Grandmother, were instrumental in finding solutions to a political impasse. A striking instance occurred in Lan Xang (in modern Laos) in 1758, when the mother of two rival princes undertook a fast to the death to force them to come to some agreement (Andaya 2002: pp. 26-27; Stuart-Fox 1998: p. 111). So accepted was this practice that even Europeans at times used senior women to make contact with leaders of native forces, and in 1622 an elderly female convert in the southern Philippines assisted Spanish missionaries to make contact with Lumud groups (Paredes 2013: p. 72). Indeed, the recruitment of senior women as negotiators was sufficiently widespread for the Dutch East India officials to issue a warning that in 'serious and important affairs' company employees should never use women as intermediaries (Jacobs 2000: p. 65).

4. Older Women as Spirit Mediums

In focusing on the religious influence of Asian women in indigenous belief systems, I have presented a largely positive picture, especially in Southeast Asia. Here there are several possible reasons for the favorable attitudes towards older women and the general lack of negative stereotypes. In the first place, because Southeast Asia was until modern times a region of low population, any individual gained status by sheer longevity. An elderly woman's position would also have been enhanced because in societies where female celibacy was almost unknown and where child-bearing was the expected lot of all females she would have confronted the very real possibility of a premature death every time she became pregnant. Death during or after labor would have meant reincarnation as a restless, dissatisfied and voracious spirit, and the very triumph over such threats meant that a woman's status rose with every successful birth. In Timor, for instance, a mother was traditionally dressed in a head hunter's costume in post-birth rituals, with the sarong, headdress and neck pendants of a successful warrior (Barnes 1992: p. 41). Because a woman literally risked her life to bear children, it is understandable that a heavy emotional weight was invested in motherhood, and the *imaginaire* associated with maternal figures carried with it almost unassailable ideas of unselfishness and unstinting kindness (Andaya 2002).

In turn, as I have noted, age has been consistently recognized as carrying greater experience, greater knowledge, and greater skills. Within royal households, for example, older women were usually placed in charge of training younger ones, especially in activities like dance, which often played a sacral role (Brink 1943: p. 184). Outside the courts, ordinary women may not have been literate, but they had many other skills, such as weaving, which everywhere was a female task (in contrast to India). However, only those with many years of experience could master the most complex and ritually important designs. The Iban of Borneo considered weaving to be 'the warpath of women', and the creative ability of an older woman was celebrated by the tattoos on her hand, a public display of her achievements (Gavin 1996: pp. 70, 92). Among many other Southeast Asian examples, one could cite the Baduy of west Java, where the cloth of pure white used to wrap the dead is woven exclusively by older women (Andaya 2006: p. 221; Bakels 1993: pp. 321, 351). Similarly, knowledge of the ingredients and proportions necessary to produce certain kinds of dyes were almost always the preserve of mature females; in one village in Java elderly women traditionally functioned as ritual guardians of the indigo vat, the 'womb' of cloth (Heringa 1985: pp. 162-163). The same principles apply in relation to the propitiation of supernatural forces; accordingly, in Burma an older woman who acted as the leader of the work gangs who transplanted and harvested rice made the offering to the *nat* or spirit of the padi field (Nas 1966: p. 126). Early sources from the Philippines make frequent reference to indigenous priestesses, the *babaylan*, but they were not by any means exceptional. Toraja women from central Sulawesi (Indonesia), for example, filled the priestly office of *burake*, presided over great feasts, supervised the ritual dancing that preceded a battle or some raiding expedition, blessed the rice before planting and officiated at important life events such as birth and death (Nooy-Palm 1979: p. 285).

The status of older women as storehouses of traditional knowledge certainly contributed to their prominence as mediating conduits to the spirits in much of Asia, but biological factors created key boundaries as qualifications. The mysterious processes that ended a woman's reproductive years and made her more 'male-like' thus opened up a much larger social and ritual space than was available to younger women, while the assumption that they were no longer involved in sexual relationships established a tacit connection with the abstinence commonly required to channel ritual energies. In the larger Asian context India appears to be an exception, since Hindu women remained under their husband's authority and widows were condemned to a lifetime of mourning, with their personal influence significantly reduced. Nonetheless, local studies have shown that in India too there is a high incidence of spirit possession among older women, through whom the goddess can reach her devotees. A trance session recorded with a spirit medium in northern India indicated that virtually all those who come to consult the goddess through this 'respected mother' (*mātājī*) seek reassurance regarding illness, anxieties about the future, or misfortune (Erndl 2000; Schoembucher 1993: pp. 239-267). In East Asia the *yuta* of Okinawa and the *mudang* of Korea provide evidence of older practices once more widespread. Even in daily life the entry to this sexually neutral zone where perceptions of a dangerous fertility no longer applied opened up new doors for women of advancing age; in the hill tribes of Assam, for instance, pottery was traditionally made by widows and old women who had never married (Parry 1932: p. 128).

The ambiguity of the 'woman who is not woman' would have resonated deeply in Southeast Asian societies that regarded the crocodile who slid between land and sea, the legendary garuda, half-human and half-bird, or the male-female hermaphrodite with particular awe. While transgendered men have historically been prominent as spirit mediums in Southeast Asia, a similar ambivalence infuses the image of the older woman, whose female body, no longer bearing the signs of fertility, positions her at the margins of femaleness. 'In Thai spirit possession', said the respected historian Prince Damrong (1862-1943), 'the medium must be a middle-aged woman' (Kitiarsa 2012: p. 131) and in a much less researched area of Borneo one authority likewise noted that the spirit mediums (*balian*) were virtually all 'middle-aged or elderly women' (Winzeler 1993: p. xxviii). As an emblematic grandmother figure, the *nenek kabayan* of Indonesian literature mediates between two worlds, standing guard at entryways to the underworld, maintaining watch while heavenly nymphs bathe, or ruling over her kingdom below the sea (Peltier 1999: p. 15; Mulyadi 1983: pp. 32, 171). Although it is common to translate *nenek kebayan* as 'witch' with all its accompanying negative connotations, one scholar has reminded us that the original meaning is more like 'an old nanny', and very different from the witch of western folklore (Hakim 2000: p. 134). Demographers have also warned against the use of literary allusions as evidence for the realities of aging, but there is a remarkable interplay between the *nenek kebayan* metaphor and the widespread perception that older women had a special ability to act as channels to the spirits, a belief that allowed them to maintain their ritual role in birth, marriages and funerals even as religious authority was increasingly arrogated by men. For example, an old Javanese poem (dated to sometime between the tenth and fifteenth centuries) while describing a royal marriage, tells us that 'a nun, who was an experienced teacher', directed the ritual intended to pacify chthonic spirits before any important life-cycle event (Worsley et al., 2013: pp. 291, 574).

The shift in gender perceptions as a woman passed her child-bearing years not only opened the door to participation in activities otherwise threatened by the powerful forces of fertility, but could contribute to the notion that she had access to formidable and unseen powers. In pre-Chinese Taiwan (where indigenous cultures were very similar to the Philippines) Dutch East India Company officials described female shamans who were credited with the ability to control natural events like the strength of the wind and the coming of rain (Shepherd 1993: pp. 63-64). The Spanish in the Philippines reported that *aniteros* or 'priestesses' were often charged with rituals usually delegated to men, such as ceremonial blood-letting; Antonio Pigafetta (1491-1535), who chronicled Ferdinand Magellan's arrival in the Visayas in 1521, noted that 'only old women' could kill the pig offered in sacrifice. 'They have frequent Conversations with the Devil ... and ... sacrifice a Hog to him' (Blair & Robertson, 1903-1909, Vol. V: pp. 13, 33, 167-171). When investigating 'idolatry' and indigenous beliefs in the Philippine town of Bolinao, Spanish friars discovered that the transmission of Animist esoteric knowledge was entirely the domain of older women (Brewer 2004: pp. 83, 143-157). Similarly, an English description of Java in the early eighteenth century remarked that the 'pagans' (i.e., non-Muslims) usually chose older women who were proficient in 'witchcraft' to be their 'priestesses' (Corfield & Morson, 2001: pp. 422-423). Skilled communicators were also able to determine the outcome of an illness. As one Spanish observer in the Philippines put it in 1582, 'The priestess chants her songs and invokes the demon, who appears to her all glistening in gold.

When she enters trance, she declares whether the sick person is to recover or not' (Blair & Robertson, 1903-1909, Vol. V: p. 133). In this empowered state women were similarly able to convey messages from beyond the grave. In seventeenth-century Vietnam, the old and 'decrepit' sister of a deceased a governor was reportedly possessed by 'the devil', enabling her to 'skip as nimbly as if she had been a young girl' while proclaiming 'several extravagances' about 'the state and place her brother's soul was in' (Dror & Taylor, 2008: p. 153). Such comments hold true as we move into modern times. In Bali, for instance, elderly women used the medium of a trance-induced dance, the solemn *mendet,* to commune with the gods, while in the Bonerate Islands south of Sulawesi the fate of boats that did not return from fishing expeditions can only be divined through the trance/dance rituals of elderly women (Broch 1968: pp. 262-282; Covarrubias 1937: p. 273).

This historical heritage raises the question of spirit mediumship in a modernizing and globalizing world. Across Asia the modern state the state and institutionalized religion have been allies in the effort to displace or restrain popular religious practices that are at variance with the officially-espoused vision of modernity and rationality. Yet such efforts have faltered because 'no civic order promoted by any state has proven capable of meeting all the fundamental existential problems that people encounter' (Keyes, Kendall & Hardacre, 1994: pp. 6-7). Indeed, to a greater extent than elsewhere in Asia, research on Southeast Asia points to the resurgence of spirit mediumship despite a modern and increasingly urban environment. Some areas have gained a particular reputation for their ritual communities. For example, in northern Thailand, where senior women act as lineage elders in matrilineal ancestor cults and in propitiation ceremonies for the household spirits or in rituals held at planting and harvest, one researcher in the 1980s reported that 84 percent of the mediums he studied were female (Bertrand 2004: pp. 154-156; Tanabe 1991: p. 191; Wijeyewardene 1986: p. 146). In Vietnam too, mediumship is said to be 'heavily gendered' because of the prevalence of women in the religious sphere and the revival of spirit possession since the advent of a more open economic policies known as *Doi Moi* (Renovation) in 1986 (Phuong 2007; Malarney 2002: p. 98; Irvine 1984: p. 315).

It is also possible to appreciate the role spirit mediums can play in a changing social environment, especially in the proliferating urban centres where the juxtaposition of dire poverty and new wealth has widened the class gap. On the one hand, spirit mediums can provide some solace to those at the bottom of the economic ladder. In Malaysia the closure of many plantations has led to a drift of poor and uneducated Tamil Malaysians to the cities, and in working class communities spirit mediums are gaining in popularity. High status Indians can also regard such individuals as powerful, even if they do not seek their assistance (Willford 2005: pp. 51-52). On the other hand, it has been noted that in Thailand those looking for advice are very frequently educated and middle class, and mediums themselves gain national profiles through appearances as media personalities (Endres & Lauser, 2011b: p. 132; Morris 2000: p. 183).

In meeting the expectations of different audiences, rituals associated with spirit possession have themselves changed, especially when there is some overlap with mainstream religious norms. For instance, Rosalind Morris has shown that in northern Thailand the frenetic female dancing typical of spirit sessions in the late nineteenth century is rarely found in more decorous modern performances, where mediums may be possessed by past kings noted for their Buddhist devotion (Morris 2000: pp. 179-181). Rather than presenting themselves as an alternative to established religion, spirit mediums will position themselves as allies and devout believers, imbued with moral concerns; a Thai medium thus visits Buddhist temples frequently, a Malay woman used her earnings to go to Mecca, while her Christian counterpart in the Philippines (where mystical communication has been absorbed within many of the cults that flourish at the margins of Catholicism) always calls on 'God the Father' (Kitiarsa 2012: p. 138; Tanabe 2000: p. 309; Cannell 1999: p. 91). Further, the contributions of grateful followers, now in cash, can yield an income that makes spirit mediumship into a viable professional occupation, where 'consulting hours' can be advertized and prices listed. Although older females still predominate, a sign of this rising profitability is the greater number of male and transgendered mediums (Dawson 2014: p. 45; Brac de la Perrière 2011). In the 1960s in Burma it was estimated that less than four per cent of spirit mediums were male, often transgendered. However, an increasing number of spirit mediums are now transgendered gay men (Ho 2009: p. 274).

Spirit mediums are themselves responding to changing expectations and expectations of greater professionalism; in the 1990s in Jakarta, for example, Chinese Indonesian women attended spirit-writing training sessions with certificates that paralleled those of men in order to better communicate with their cult goddess (Dean & Zheng, 2009: p. 241). In the northern Thai city of Chiang Mai, spirit mediumship is a 'profession of inspiration' where individuals are 'called' as practitioners. The professionalization of members of urban-based ritual communities distinguishes them from rural cults, where mediums are usually from the same family and acquire their training as apprentices (Morris 2000: p. 111; Tanabe 2000: p. 309). Nor are today's spirit mediums necessarily confined in terms of their audience. Advances in global communication and mobility have enabled some to move transnationally, like the Vietnamese who operate in diaspora communities in the United States, Italy, France, and Australia and since 1986 are able to freely revisit Vietnam (Fjelstad & Nguyen, 2006). Despite the sceptical attitudes induced by the flows of modernity that permeate a rapidly changing world, there is no convincing evidence that spirit possession will inevitably disappear. Because human beings the world over will always experience times when access to supernatural forces seems to answer the personal problems encountered in daily life, there is every reason to believe that the need for 'instrumental agency' will continue.

5. Conclusion

I have presented a cautious argument that Asia provides a laboratory in which it is possible to examine the changing status of older women as state authority advanced, the influence of world religions increased, and as sedentary lifestyle and urbanization expanded. In many societies, including Southeast Asia, older women whose bodies were possessed by spirits were empowered through their ability to connect with the supernatural world. This stemmed from their seniority, their location in a sexually neutral zone, from their social position as mothers and mediators, their prominence as healers and midwives, and above all from their liminal position between male and female. When these features are combined, we can appreciate why their skills in communing with the supernatural were accepted and respected. Such abilities, however, were easily seen as vulnerable to perversion, so that a woman acting as a spirit medium could find herself blamed when misfortune struck either individuals or the community generally.

This discussion raises wider questions about the women as practitioners in Asia's contemporary religious life when female spirit mediums occupy a marginalized status, like the modern day *yogini* in India (Hausner 2013: pp. 32-44; McDaniel 2013: pp. 133-147). As we have noted, secularization has certainly made inroads, but possessed women still maintain an Asian presence. In remote areas of northern Japan, faint shadows of the past can still be found in the *itako*, blind women recruited as young girls and rigorously trained in a way that recalls the mediums of past times (Blacker 2004). Though traditionally regarded as 'mean people', the *mansin* of Korea are found in many villages, where they are actively consulted by female clients (Kendall 1985). In China female spirit mediums may attract a following because they may have a specific advantage in addressing women's concerns, and in Okinawa older women still act as *yuta*, who communicate with the spirits through shamanistic practices (Cline 2010).

It is in Southeast Asia, however, where female spirit mediums appear to be thriving, especially in the more accommodating and eclectic religious environments of Vietnam and the Theravada Buddhist states (Bernstein 1993). Research in the Islamic environments of Indonesia and Malaya is more limited (although in 2014 a Malay *bomoh* with his 'magic carpet' was called in to search for the missing flight MH 370), but once we move to the peripheries the role of women as intermediaries with the supernatural continues to surface (Peletz 1996: p. 164). Though Muslim and Christian proselytization has roundly opposed spirit veneration, women in search of ritual standing may still find meaning in the 'more durable traditions of shamanism' (Winzeler 1993: p. xxviii). Given these region-wide traditions, a historical and comparative base must provide the foundation for any explanation of the continuing role of older women in Southeast Asia as communicators with the spirits. It should then be possible to explore more fully the shifting and often ambiguous position of senior women, to establish shared similarities while identifying the singularities of local situations, and to show how these older connections reverberate with the present.

Bibliography

Andaya, Barbara W. (2006) 'Localising the Universal: Women, Motherhood and the Appeal of Early Theravada Buddhism', *Journal of Southeast Asian Studies*, 33(1): pp. 1-30.

Andaya, Barbara W. (2006) *The Flaming Womb: Repositioning Women in Early Modern Southeast Asia*, Honolulu: University of Hawai'i Press.

Andaya, Barbara W. (2005) 'Old Age: Widows, Midwives and the Question of "Witchcraft" in Early Modern Southeast Asia', *Asia-Pacific Forum*, 28: 104-147.

Andaya, Barbara W. & Yoneo Ishii (1992) 'Religious Developments in Southeast Asia, c.1500-1800', in Nicholas Tarling (ed.) *The Cambridge History of Southeast Asia*, Sydney: University of Cambridge Press, pp. 508-571.

Bakels, Jet (1993) 'The Symbolism of Baduy Adat Clothing on the Efficacy of Colours, Patterns and Plants', in Marie-Louise Nabholz-Kartaschoff, Ruth Barnes & David J. Stuart-Fox (eds.) *Weaving Patterns of Life*, Basel: Museum of Ethnography Basel, pp. 347-367.

Barnes, Robert (1992) 'Women as Head Hunters: The Making and Meaning of Textiles in a Southeast Asian Context', in Ruth Barnes & Joanne B. Eicher (eds.) *Dress and Gender: Making and Meaning in Cultural Contexts*, London, Oxford, New York, New Delhi, Sydney: Bloomsbury Publishing.

Beeckman, Daniel ([1718] 1973) *A Voyage to and from the Isle of Borneo*, London: Dawsons.

Bernstein, Jay H. (1993) 'The Shaman's Destiny: Symptoms, Affliction, and the Re-interpretation of Illness among the Taman', in Robert L. Winzeler (ed.) *The Seen, and the Unseen: Shamanism, Mediumship and Possession in Borneo*, Williamsburg, VA: Borneo Research Council Monograph Series, Vol. 2, pp. 171-206.

Bertrand, Didier (2004) 'A Medium Possession Practice and its Relationship to Cambodia Buddhism: The Grū Pāramī', in John Marston & Elizabeth Guthrie (eds.) *History, Buddhism and New Religious Movements in Cambodia*, Honolulu: University of Hawai'i Press, pp. 150-169.

Blacker, Carmen (2004) *The Catalpa Bow: Shamanistic Practices in Japan*, London, New York: Routledge.

Blair, Emma & James A. Robertson (1903-1909) *The Philippine Islands 1493-1898*, 54 Volumes, Cleveland: Arthur H. Clark.

Brac de la Perrière, Benedicte (2011) 'Being a Spirit Medium in Contemporary Burma', in Kirsten W. Endres & Andrea Lauser (eds.) *Engaging the Spirit World: Popular Beliefs and Practices in Modern Southeast Asia*, London and New York: Berghahn Books, pp. 163-183

Brewer, Caroline (2004) *Shamanism, Catholicism and Gender Relations in Colonial Philippines, 1521-1685*, Burlington, VT: Ashgate.

Brewer, Caroline (2000) 'From Animist "Priestess" to Catholic Priest: The Re/gendering of Religious Roles in the Philippines, 1521-1685', in Barbara W. Andaya (ed.) *Other Pasts: Women, Gender and History in Early Modern Southeast Asia*, Honolulu: Center for Southeast Asian Studies, pp. 69-85.

Brink, Herman van den (1943) *Dr. Benjamin Frederick Matthes. Zijn Leven en Arbied in Dienst van het Nederlandsch Bijbelgenootschap*, Amsterdam: Nederlandsch Bijbelgenootschap.

Broch, Harold B. (1968) 'Crazy Women are Performing in Sombali'. A Possession Trance Ritual on Bonerate, Indonesia', *Ethos*, 13(3): 262-282.

Brown, Melissa J. (2004) *Is Taiwan Chinese? The Impact of Culture, Power, and Migration on Changing Identities*, Berkeley: University of California Press.

Buckley, Thomas & Anna Gottlieb (1988) 'A Critical Appraisal of Theories of Menstrual Symbolism', in Thomas Buckley & Anna Gottlieb (eds.) *Blood Magic. The Anthropology of Menstruation*, Berkeley: University of California Press, pp. 1-55.

Cannell, Fenella (1999) *Power and Intimacy in the Christian Philippines*, Cambridge: Cambridge University Press.

Claus, Peter J. (1979) 'Spirit Possession and Spirit Mediumship from the Perspective of Tulu Oral Tradition', *Culture, Medicine and Psychiatry*, (3)1: 29-52.

Cline, Erin M. (2010) 'Female Spirit Mediums and Religious Authority in Contemporary South eastern China', *Modern China*, 36(5): 520-55.

Corfield, Justin & Ian Morson (eds.) (2001) *British Sea-Captain Alexander Hamilton's A New Account of the East Indies (17th-18th Century)*, Lewiston, New York: Edwin Mellon Press.

Covarrubias, Miguel (1937) *Island of Bali*, New York: Alfred A. Knopf.

Dawson, Andrew (2010) *Summoning the Spirits: Possessions and Invocation in Contemporary Religion*, London: I. B. Taurus.

Dean, Kenneth & Zhenman Zheng (2009) *Ritual Alliances of the Putian Plain*, Volume 1, *Historical Introduction to the Return to the Gods*, Leiden: Brill.

DeBernardi, Jean (2006) *The Way that Lives in the Heart: Chinese Popular Religion and Spirit Mediums in Penang*, Malaysia, Stanford, CA: Stanford University Press.

Dror, Olga & Keith W. Taylor (2006) *Views of Seventeenth-Century Vietnam. Christoforo Borri on Cochinchina and Samuel Baron on Tonkin*, Ithaca: Cornell Southeast Asia Program.

Durrant, Jonathan B. & Michael D. Bailey (eds.) (2012) *Historical Dictionary of Witchcraft*, Second Edition, Plymouth UK: Scarecrow Press.

Emigh, John (1996) *Masked Performance: The Play of Self and Other in Ritual and Theatre*, Philadelphia: University of Pennsylvania Press.

Endres, Kirsten W. & Andrea Lauser (2011a) 'Introduction: Multivocal Arenas of Modern Enchantment in Southeast Asia', in Kirsten W. Endres & Andrea Lauser (eds.) *Engaging the Spirit World: Popular Beliefs and Practices in Modern Southeast Asia*, London and New York: Berghahn Books, pp. 1-19.

Endres, Kirsten W. & Andrea Lauser (2011b) 'Contests of Commemoration: Virgin War Martyrs, State Memorials and the Invocation of the Spirit World in Contemporary Vietnam', in Kirsten W. Endres & Andrea Lauser (eds.) *Engaging the Spirit World: Popular Beliefs and Practices in Modern Southeast Asia*, London and New York: Berghahn Books, pp. 144-62.

Erndl, Kathleen M. (2000) 'A Trance Session with Mātājī', in Gordon D. White (ed.) *Tantra in Practice*, Princeton, NJ: Princeton University Press, pp. 97-118.

Fjelstad, Karen & Thi Hien Nguyen (ed.) (2006) *Possessed by the Spirits: Mediumship in Contemporary Vietnamese Communities*, Ithaca, NY: Cornell University Southeast Asia Program.

Forest, Alain (1998) *Les Missionnaires français au Tonkin et au Siam XVIIe-XIIIe Siècles: Analyse comparée d'un relatif succès et d'un total échec*, Paris: L'Harmattan.

Forth, Gregory (1993) 'Social and Symbolic Aspects of the Witch among the Nage of Eastern Indonesia', in Conrad William Watson & Roy Ellen (eds.) *Understanding Witchcraft and Sorcery in Southeast Asia*, Honolulu: University of Hawai'i Press, pp. 99-122.

Gavin, Traude (1996) *The Women's Warpath. Iban Ritual Fabrics from Borneo*, Los Angeles: UCLA Fowler Museum of Cultural History.

Godinho de Eredia, Manuel (1997, reprint) 'Eredia's Description of Malacca, Meridional India and Cathay', translated by John Vivian Mills, Kuala Lumpur: *Malaysian Branch of the Royal Asiatic Society*, 14.

Goh, Geok Yian (2015) 'Southeast Asian Images of Hell: Transmission and Adaptation', *Bulletin de l'École Française d'Extrême-Orient*, 101: 91-116.

Groemer, Gerald (2007) 'Female Shamans in Eastern Japan during the Edo Period', *Asian Folklore Studies*, 66(2): 27-53.

Hakim, Abdul bin Haji Mohd. Yassin (ed.) (2000) *Traditional Literature of ASEAN*, Brunei: Secretary General of ASEAN.

Hausner, Sondra L. (2013) 'The Category of the Yoginī as a Gendered Practitioner', in Istvan Keul (ed.) *'Yoginī' in South Asia: Interdisciplinary Approaches*, London: Routledge, pp. 32-44.

Heringa, Rens (1985) 'Kain Tuban. Een Oude Javanese Indigo Traditie', in Loan Oei (ed.) *Indigo. Leven in een Kleur*, Amsterdam: Stichting Indigo, Fibula-van Dishoeck.

Hicks, David (1984) *A Maternal Religion: the Role of Women in Tetum Myth and Ritual*, De Kalb: Northern Illinois University, Center for Southeast Asian Studies.

Hinsch, Brent (2011) *Women in Early Imperial China*, Lanham, MD: Rowman & Littlefield.

Ho, Tamara C. (2009) 'Transgender, Transgression, and Translation: A Cartographer of *Nat Kadaws*: Notes on Gender and Sexuality with the Spirit Cult of Burma', *Discourse*, 31(2): 273-317.

Irvine, Walter (1984) 'Decline of Village Spirit Cults and Growth of Urban Spirit Mediumship: the Persistence of Spirit Beliefs, the Position of Women and Modernization', *Mankind*, 14(4): 315-324.

Jacobs, Els M. (2000) *Koopman in Azië: De handel van de Verenigde Oost-Indische Compagnie tijdens de 18de eeuw*, Zutphen: Walburg Press.

Jardine, John (ed.) ([1893] 1984) *The Burmese Empire a Hundred Years Ago as Described by Father Sangermano*, Delhi: B.R. Publishing.

Johnson, Andrew A. (2014) *Ghosts of the New City: Spirits, Urbanity and the Ruins of Progress in Chiang Mai*, Honolulu: University of Hawai'i Press.

Kang, Xiaofei (2013) *The Cult of the Fox: Power, Gender and Popular Religion in Late Imperial China*, New York: Columbia University Press.

Keeler, Ward (2016) 'Shifting Transversals: Trans Women's Move from Spirit Mediumship to Beauty Work in Mandalay', *Ethnos*, 81(5): 792-820.

Keller, Mary (2002) *The Hammer and the Flute: Women, Power and Spirit Possession*, Baltimore and London: The Johns Hopkins Press.

Kendall, Laurel (1985) *Shamans, Housewives and Other Restless Spirits: Women in Korean Ritual Life*, Honolulu: University of Hawai'i Press.

Keyes, Charles, Laurel Kendall & Helen Hardacre (1994) 'Introduction: Contested Visions of Community in East and Southeast Asia', in Charles Keyes, Laurel Kendall & Helen Hardacre (eds.) *Asian Visions of Authority: Religion and the Modern States of East and Southeast Asia*, Honolulu: University of Hawai'i Press, pp. 1-18.

Kinney, Anne B. (2014) *Exemplary Women of Early China: The Lien Zhuan of Liu Zang*, New York: Columbia University Press.

Kitiarsa, Pattana (2011) *Mediums, Monks, & Amulets: Thai Popular Buddhism Today*, Chiang Mai, Thailand: Silkworm Books.

Kivelson, Valerie (2014) *Desperate Magic: The Moral Economy of Witchcraft in Seventeenth-Century Russia*, Ithaca and London: Cornell University Press.

Kuly, Lisa (2003) 'Locating Transcendence in Japanese Minzoku Geinô: Yamabushi and Miko Kagura', *Erudit*, 25(1): 191-208.

Laderman, Carol (1993) *Taming the Wind of Desire: Psychology, Medicine, and Aesthetics in Malay Shamanistic Performance*, Berkeley and London: University of California Press.

Lahiri, Smita (2005) 'The Priestess and the Politician: Enunciating Filipino Cultural Nationalism through Mt. Banahaw', in Andrew C. Willford & Kenneth M. George (eds.) *Spirited Politics: Religion and Public Life in Contemporary Southeast Asia*, Ithaca, NY: Cornell University Southeast Asia Program, pp. 23-44.

Laycock, Joseph P. (ed.) (2015) *Spirit Possession around the World: Possession, Communion, and Demon Expulsion across Cultures*, Santa Barbara, Ca. ABC-CLIO.

Leung, Angela K.C. (1999) *Women Practicing Medicine in Premodern China*, in Harriet T. Zurndorfer (ed.) *Chinese Women in the Imperial Past: New Perspectives*, Leiden and Boston: Brill, pp. 101-34.

Levack, Brian P. (ed.) (2013) *The Oxford Handbook of Witchcraft in Early Modern Europe and Colonial America*, Oxford: Oxford University Press.
Malarney, Shawn K. (2002) *Culture, Ritual and Revolution in Vietnam*, London: Routledge Curzon.
McDaniel, June (2013) 'Yoginīs in Bengali Religious Traditions: Tribal, Tantric and Bhakti Influences', in Istvan Keul (ed.) *'Yoginī' in South Asia: Interdisciplinary Approaches*, London: Routledge, pp. 133-48.
McKinley, Robert (1981) 'Cain and Abel on the Malay Peninsula', in Keith M. Marshall (ed.) *Siblingship in Oceania: Studies in the Meaning of Kin Relations*, Lanham and London: Association for Social Anthropology in Oceania, *Monograph*, 8: 335-418.
Morris, Rosalind C. (2000) *In the Place of Origins: Modernity and Its Mediums in Northern Thailand*, Durham and London: Duke University Press.
Mullick, Samar B. (2003) 'Gender Relations and Witches among the Indigenous Communities of Jharkhand', in Govind Kelkar, Dev Nathan & Pierre Walter (eds.) *Gender Relations in Forest Societies in Asia: Patriarchy at Odds*, New Delhi: Sage Publications, pp. 97-144.
Mulyadi, Sri R. Wulan (1983) *Hikayat Indraputra: A Malay Romance*, Dordrecht: Foris Publications.
Nash, June C. (1966) 'Living with Nats: An Analysis of Animism in Burman Village Social Relations', in Manning Nash et al. (eds.) *Anthropological Studies in Theravada Buddhism, Cultural Report*, 13: 117-136, New Haven: Yale University Southeast Asia Studies.
Nooy-Palm, Hetty (1979) *The Sa'dan Toraja: A Study of Their Social Life and Religion*, The Hague: Nijhoff.
Pannell, Sandra (2007) 'Of Gods and Monsters: Indigenous Sea Cosmologies, Promiscuous Geographies and the Depths of Local Sovereignty', in Peter Boomgaard (ed.) *A World of Water: Rain, Rivers and Seas in Southeast Asian Histories*, Leiden: KITLV Press, pp. 71-102.
Paredes, Oona (2013) *A Mountain of Difference: The Lumud in Early Colonial Mindanao*, Ithaca, NY: Cornell University Southeast Asia Program.
Parry, Nevill Edward (1932) *The Lakhers*, London: Macmillan.
Peletz, Michael (1996) *Reason and Passion: Representations of Gender in a Malay Society*, Berkeley, CA: University of California Press.
Peltier, Anatole-Roger (1999) *The White Nightjar: A Lao Tale*, Chiang Mai: École Française d'Extrême Orient.
Phuong, Pham Quynh (2007) 'Empowerment and Innovation among Saint Tran's Female Mediums', in Philip Taylor (ed.) *Modernity and Re-Enchantment: Religion in Post Revolutionary Vietnam*, Singapore: ISEAS, pp. 221-249.
Pucci, Idanna (1992) *Bhima Swarga, the Balinese Journey of the Soul*, Boston: Little, Brown and Co.
Rafael, Vicente L. (1993) *Contracting Colonialism: Translation and Christian Conversion in Tagalog Society under Early Spanish Rule*, Durham and London: Duke University Press.
Rajadhon, Phya Anuman & William J. Gedney (1961) *Life and Ritual in Old Siam: Three Studies of Thai Life and Customs*, translated by Gedney J. William, New Haven: HRAF Press.

Rozario, Santi (1998) 'The Dai and the Doctor: Discourse on Women's Reproductive Health in Rural Bangladesh', in Kalpana Ram & Margaret Jolly (eds.) *Maternities and Modernities: Colonial and Postcolonial Experiences in Asia and the Pacific*, Cambridge: Cambridge University Press, pp. 144-176.

Ruch, Barbara (1990) 'The Other Side of Culture in Medieval Japan', in Kozo Yamamura (ed.) *The Cambridge History of Japan*, Cambridge: Cambridge University Press, Vol. 4, pp. 500-543.

Rumpf, Eberhard Georg (1999) *The Ambonese Curiosity Cabinet*, translated from Dutch, edited, annotated and with an introduction by Eric Montaque Beekman, New Haven: Yale University Press.

Saletore, Rajaram N. (1981) *Indian Witchcraft: A Study in Indian Occultism*, New Delhi: Abhinav Publications.

Schärer, Hans (1963) *Ngaju Religion: The Conception of God among a South Borneo People*, The Hague: Martinus Nijhoff.

Schoembucher, Elisabeth (1993) 'Gods, Ghosts and Demons: Possession in South Asia', in Heidrun Brüchner, Lothar Lutze & Aditya Malik (eds.) *Flags of Fame: Studies in South Asian Folk Culture*, New Delhi: Manohar, pp. 239-267.

Scott, William (1994) *Barangay: Sixteenth Century Philippine Culture and Society*, Quezon City: Ateneo de Manila University Press.

Shepherd, John R. (1993) *Statecraft and Political Economy on the Taiwan Frontier 1600-1800*, Stanford: Stanford University Press.

Siegel, James T. (2006) *Naming the Witch*, Stanford: Stanford University Press.

Skaria, Ajay (1997) 'Women, Witchcraft and Gratuitous Violence in Colonial Western India', *Past and Present*, 155(1): 109-141.

Slaats, Herman & Karen Portier (1993) 'Sorcery and the Law in Modern Indonesia', in Conrad William Watson & Roy Ellen (eds.) *Understanding Witchcraft and Sorcery in Southeast Asia*, Honolulu: University of Hawai'i Press Honolulu, University of Hawai'i Press, pp. 135-148.

Smits, Gregory (1999) *Visions of Ryukyu: Identity and Ideology in Early-Modern Thought and Politics*, Honolulu: University of Hawai'i Press.

Stuart-Fox, Martin (1998) *The Lao Kingdom of Lān Xāng: Rise and Decline*, Bangkok: White Lotus Press.

Sudjiman, Panuti H. (1983) *Adat Raja-Raja Melayu*, Jakarta: University of Indonesia Press.

Susilo, Emiko (1998) *Gamelan Wanita: A Study of Women's Gamelan in Bali* (MA Dissertation), University of Hawai'i.

Swettenham, Frank ([1895] 1984) *Malay Sketches,* Singapore: Graham Brash.

Tanabe, Shigehuru (2000) 'Autochthony and the Inthakim Cult of Chiang Mai', in Andrew Turton (ed.) *Civility and Savagery: Social Identity in Tai States*, Richmond, Surrey: Curzon, pp. 294-318.

Tanabe, Shigehuru (1991) 'Spirits, Power and the Discourse of Female Gender', in Manas Chitrakasem & Andrew Turton (eds.) *Thai Constructions of Knowledge*, London: School of Oriental and African Studies, pp. 183-212.

Tayanin, Damrong (1994) *Being Kammu: My Village, My Life*, Ithaca, N.Y.: Southeast Asia Program, Cornell University.

Ter Haar, Barend (2012) *Where are China's witches?* Online. Available https://chinaleiden.weblog.leidenuniv.nl/2012/11/27/china-seminar-05-december-2012-barend-ter-haar-where-are-chinas-witches/ (accessed October 16, 2016).

Ter Haar, Barend (2006) *Telling Stories: Witchcraft and Scapegoating in Chinese History*, Leiden: Brill.

Tun, Than (1986) *Royal Orders of Burma, A.D. 1598-1885. IV A.D. 1782-1787*, Kyoto: Center for Southeast Asian Studies, University of Kyoto.

Wijeyewardene, Gehan (1986) *Place and Emotion in Northern Thai Ritual Behavior*, Bangkok: Pandora.

Willford, Andrew C. (2005) 'The Modernist Vision from Below: Malaysian Hinduism and "The Way of Prayers"', in Andrew C. Willford & Kenneth M. George (eds.) *Spirited Politics: Religion and Public Life in Contemporary Southeast Asia*, Ithaca, NY: Cornell University Southeast Asia Program, pp. 45-68.

Winzeler, Robert L. (1993) 'Introduction', in Winzeler, Robert L. (ed.) *The Seen, and the Unseen: Shamanism, Mediumship and Possession in Borneo*, Williamsburg, VA: Borneo Research Council.

Worsley, Peter, Suryohundoyo Supomo, Thomas Hunter & Margaret Fletcher (eds.) (2013) *Mpu Monaguna's Sumanasāntaka: An Old Javanese Epic Poem, Its Indian Source and Balinese Illustrations*, Leiden: Brill.

CHAPTER II

The *Bissu*: Study of a Third Gender in Indonesia

Leonard Y. ANDAYA

1. Gender Ideology

While work on the 'third gender' in Southeast Asia is still in its infancy, it is drawing inspiration from the volume and sophistication of contemporary Western writing, itself an outgrowth of the increasing politicization of the gay movement. In its efforts to affirm a social space in Western society, gay scholarship has built upon the insights developed by the women's movement that challenges conventional notions of sexual bodies and gender identity. New research has revealed that from antiquity to the eighteenth century medical theory and popular culture emphasized the existence of one sex: a male body and mind inscribed on an incomplete and subordinate female body. But by the Renaissance period of the sixteenth century in Europe, the idea of a two-sex model was beginning to gain in popularity. By the early eighteenth century the paradigm of two genders founded on the two biological sexes was becoming dominant, and by the nineteenth century, 'scientific evidence' was used to support this particular cultural construction of gender ideology (Lacqueur 1990; Herdt 1994: pp. 23, 26; Trumbach 1994: p. 111).

The nineteenth-century Darwinian revolution introduced the idea that the differences between male and female were innate and due to such factors as morphology, brain size, tool use and the evolution of speech. The rise of the science of sexology in this period reinforced the idea that male and female were innate categories in all forms of life. From this view of 'sexual dimorphism', it was argued that throughout history there had always existed a two-sex, two-gendered system, the former determined biologically and the latter by culture. Heterosexuality was seen as the highest evolutionary form, and the female aspect was portrayed in a complementary but subordinate position to the male. With heterosexuality declared the 'norm' all other forms of behavior became a deviation (Herdt 1994: p. 28).

The principal determinant of sex categories was based on the observed differences in sexual organs between what the society called 'male' and 'female'. Each sex was then associated with particular cultural role expectations that determined masculine and feminine gender. Much of the concern of gay activists is Western society's determination to force conformity to this two sex/gender models. Not only has this caused unnecessary suffering among those who could not fulfill one of the two roles that society expected of them; it also branded them as 'freaks' and therefore subject to discrimination and abuse (Grosz 1991: pp. 34-36). Recent studies of the human body, however, have challenged the Western model and revealed the clear political and cultural agendas in the construction of ideas of sex and gender. Elizabeth Grosz rejects the simplistic sexual dimorphism which is a residual belief from the nineteenth century, and points to medical studies that describe a continuum of sexual bodies. While these bodies are located mainly at the male and female poles, between them are others that exhibit varying mixtures of male and female physical attributes (Meigs 1990: pp. 99-112). With the two-sex paradigm no longer able to shelter behind 'scientific' biological evidence, the concomitant two-gender arrangement is also now under closer scrutiny.

Studies of non-Western societies have provided much of the evidence to argue for a more flexible view of gender construction. For example, Meigs has noted that while the Hua of the eastern highlands of Papua New Guinea determine male and female gender based on genital differences, there are situations in which these criteria do not apply. One striking manner of distinguishing the genders is through possession of menstrual blood, vaginal secretions, parturitional fluids, and semen. Because such substances can be transferred, there is a crossover in classification. Children, premenopausal women, postmenopausal women who have had two or less children, and old men are said to be *figapa* ('like a woman'); on the other hand, postmenopausal women who have borne three or more children are believed to be defeminized and belong to the category *kakora* ('like a man'). In each of these cases, the absence of particular fluids associated with each category allows the individual to cross genders (Meigs 1990: pp. 99-112). Herdt argues that in Melanesian society semen is equivalent to mother's milk; both are critical fluids that contribute to physical strength, puberty, and biological reproduction, i.e., to adulthood. Ritual homosexuality becomes a means by which men can inseminate boys so that they obtain this 'scarce resource' and thereby become initiated into malehood (Herdt 1984: pp. xiv, 12, 21, 26, 40-41, 67). And in Oman, according to Wikan, it is the sexual act that determines gender (Wikan 1977: pp. 304-319). The Kodi in west Sumba (Indonesia) regard male and female as abstract categories referring to ways of acting. Male agency is active, mobile, transformative, in the sense of being able to effect change; by contrast, female is stable, unmoving, and substantive, providing the continuing bases for links through unchanging substance. Each individual contains both male and female souls that are attached to the human head (Hoskins 1990: pp. 303, 305).

With medical and cultural evidence extending the scope of sexual and gender classifications, it is now possible to conceptualize two, three, or more sexes and genders (Bolin 1994: pp. 447-486; Morris 1994: pp. 15-43). New studies on the 'third' sex and gender are beginning to make useful contributions to the debate on sexed bodies and gender ideas[1]. Traditional 'third gender' groups are being redefined in line with the new attitudes influenced by the gay movement, as is occurring in Thailand today (Jackson 1997: pp. 181-183). But the gay movement and the new direction of third sex/gender studies are a postmodern phenomenon engaging in the ongoing philosophical debate on individualism and human agency. There are, nevertheless, 'third' sex/gender groups who do not regard their position in this light but as a necessary part of the wholeness of society. One such group is the *bissu* of South Sulawesi, Indonesia. In my discussion of the *bissu* as a 'third gender', I am using 'third' to indicate another space, not between a society's dominant paradigm of male/female sex, masculine/feminine gender, but outside it. Beginning with their cosmogonic myths and throughout history these special individuals were located by nature and function outside societal norms, yet they remained crucial to the functioning of the system.

2. Cosmogony, Sacred Beings, and the Third Gender

The direct link between sacred powers and a 'third' sex/gender is well established in many cultures, including several in Southeast Asia[2]. The most detailed descriptions come from the Malay-Indonesian archipelago. In 1901 Adriani and Kruyt noted among the Bare'eToraja of central Sulawesi (Indonesia) a small group known as the *bayasa*. They were male priests characterized by being effeminate, uninterested in sex, and never participating in warfare. Their penis size, it was rumored, was only half a finger long. Using a special language, they could summon spirits (*wurake*) to conduct them heavenward in order to recover the soulstuff (*tanoana*) which had fled an individual, causing her to fall ill (Adriani & Kruyt, 1912, vol. 1: pp. 362, 364-365; vol. 3: p. 38). The *bayasa* clearly occupied a third space among the Bare'eToraja in both sex and gender, which is the community's way of explaining their 'suprahuman' abilities.

For the Kodi in Sumba certain individuals assume a gender-ambiguous role in which the male performs as a female, though the reverse is rarely the case. The RatoNale or 'Seaworm Priest' is considered to be powerful because he has crossed sexual boundaries and united male and female values in himself. By controlling two opposing energies, the priest applies this power for the regeneration of the rice crop, rain in the coming year, and other rites

---

1   The contributions in Herdt (ed.) (1994) provide excellent examples.
2   An important early article on this topic: van der Kroef 1956, pp. 394-418.

of renewal. During these rituals, the male priest practices confinement, immobility, and a body posture associated with women. His activities are in keeping with the belief that the highest-ranking deities are 'double-gendered', i.e., possessing two genders, and addressed as both mother and father. The double-gendered deity known as Mother Binder of the Forelock/Father Smelter of the Crown combines the female weaver and the male metalworker to create the individual soul. The ability of the chief priest to cross genders and therefore to draw from both the female and male sources of energy is regarded as the reason for his potency (Hoskins 1993: p. 147; Hoskins 1990: pp. 277, 281, 287, 303, 305).

Among the Ngaju Dayak of Kalimantan, Indonesia, individuals known as *balian* and *basir* are believed to represent the deity. According to nineteenth-century observers, the *balian* (meaning 'someone who becomes another') were women and the *basir* (meaning 'barren, unfruitful') were men who dressed in women's clothes, but wore no headcloth. They were respected and even protected by the laws of the community, but people also said they would be ashamed if their daughters or sons or relatives became *balian* or *basir*. The *basir* were said to be recruited from 'hermaphrodites' and impotent men, though the (male) observers offered no explanation as to what was meant by 'hermaphrodite' or even 'impotent'. *Balian* were sometimes well-born women, but they were mainly selected from the slave class. Because *basir* and *balian* acted as mediators between the community and the spirit world, as well as between the two mythical groups (Watersnake people and Hornbill people) into which the Ngaju were divided, they belonged to neither moiety but to the entire community. In the special language used in religious chants, they were termed *tambonharueibungai* ('the Watersnakes which form a unity with the Hornbill'). The Watersnake deity was associated with the Underworld, and the Hornbill deity with the Upperworld, and the *balian* and *basir* thus ritually represented both the supreme godhead and the united dualities of the community. As sacred intermediaries, they were both especially valued as sexual partners during re-enactments of the sacred events associated with primeval creation. Dayak women, while 'known for their modesty and retiring character', thus encouraged their sons to have sexual intercourse with a *balian*, who were 'more honored than the priests'[3].

From this material it seems that the *balian* and *basir* were characterized by sexual and gender ambiguity, a condition recognized by many societies as signs of the sacred. They engaged in sexual orgies as part of the 'chaos' preceding creation, thereby gaining access to the prodigious powers associated with this primeval period. Devotees were assured potency and fertility by worshipping the deity through sexual acts with the *balian* or *basir*. While some *balian* and *basir* maintained celibacy, others moved between

---

3   An 1846 account by Hupe, cited in Schärer 1963: pp. 53-58.

ritual and secular prostitution, creating attitudes of ambivalence toward them among the general population. By the end of the nineteenth century it appears that the *balian* and *basir* were regarded with awe and respect in their sacred position, but with a certain contempt in their mundane existence, where they had come to occupy a third sex or third gender role (Murray 1992: pp. 257-258; Schärer 1963: pp. 58-59).

For the Iban in Borneo, the *manang* ranked next to the village chief in importance. Of the *manang*, it was the male *manangbali* who was regarded with the greatest respect. He wore female clothing in obedience to sacred commands conveyed through dreams, but it was necessary that he be 'sexually disabled' before doing so[4]. He was then treated like a woman and performed female tasks. His standing derived from his ability to cure illness, his role as a peacemaker, and his willingness to place his wealth at the disposal of his followers (Roth 1896, v. 1: pp. 270-271). Among the Iban in the Sibu district, the *manangbali* may not fulfill the male idea of success in adventure and farming, but he is still respected for his skill in matters of sickness and disease, a role associated with women (Sutlive 1992: pp. 281-282)[5]. Here a distinction is made between an Iban, as an ordinary member of the society, and a *manang*, indicating that they are two different types of beings (Roth 1896 v.1: pp. 280-281).

Among the Iban, as with the NgajuDayak, sexual and gender ambiguity was (and is) associated with sacred beings. Any connection between the *manangbali* and the male is removed by his acting and dressing in conformity with society's prescription of femaleness. Sacredness is also underscored by the *manangbali*'s efficacy as a healer, a skill shared by other third gender priests/priestesses. Healing power is linked to the gods, and priests/priestesses access these primeval energies through the periodic ritual enactment of creation. By reproducing the act of creation, the priest/priestess is able to remove any imperfections which have caused human beings suffering or pain. In this sense, a 'third gender' is assumed by these sacred practitioners because they perform functions not associated with established male and female gender roles.

The sources are sketchy, but there is some evidence that courtiers known as sida-sida may once have exercised a priestly function in Malay kingdoms. However, the common translation of sida-sida as 'eunuchs', (Wilkinson 1893: p. 418) may not be appropriate since the Malay court text, the Sejarah Melayu, refers to a certain court official named Tun Indera Segara, who is

---

4   Roth does not explain how an individual was 'sexually disabled'. See Roth 1896, v. 1: p. 270.

5   For graphic examples of the 'female' role of the *manangbali* in Iban rituals like those associated with paddy planting and headhunting, see Masing, James Jemut (1997) *The Coming of the Gods: An Iban Invocatory Chant* (Timang Gawai Amat) *of the Baleh River Region, Sarawak*, Canberra: Department of Anthropology, Research School of Pacific Studies, pp. 217-227, 401-404.

said to be a descendant of a sida-sida[6]. Another definition is given by Teuku Iskandar, who says that it refers to 'a court official (perhaps a type of priest [pendeta])' (Iskandar 1970: p. 1103). In defining this word, Iskandar, an Acehnese speaker, may have been influenced by the Acehnese meaning of the term. In Acehnese the word sida is derived from the Sanskrit siddha, meaning 'the learned one' or 'scholar' which becomes in Acehnese 'an initiate, aide to a religious teacher'. But when the word is doubled, sida-sida, it assumes the meaning of 'a court official' and 'eunuch'. The use of the term sida-sida for eunuchs in Aceh appears to be supported by a late sixteenth-century description of a pavilion built specifically for the eunuchs and called 'Ida-Sida' [sic] (Dos Santos Alves 1990: p. 111, fn 84). Although the functions of the sida-sida are not explicitly described, in one ceremony they are said to have appeared from 'within' (daridalam), which could have only meant the inner chambers of the court, where the royal women were housed (Samad 1979: p. 75). The link between the sida-sida and court women is also implied in the eighteenth-century Misa Melayu from Perak, which groups the *sida-sida,* the *bentara,* and the *dayang-dayang* ('court maidens') together (Raja Chulan 1968: p. 90). Based on these few intriguing statements, and on what is known about other courts in Southeast Asia, one could suggest that the *sida-sida* may have been a pre-Islamic priestly class whom outside observers assumed to be eunuchs because of their androgynous behavior and because apparently similar figures were found in Islamic courts in India and the Middle East. Like eunuchs, the *sida-sida* were found in the inner chambers, perhaps to guard the palace women, but more likely because they were entrusted with the sacred regalia and the preservation of the ruler's spiritual powers.

In mainland Southeast Asia a Mon origin myth collected in contemporary Thailand begins with the four elements. After a period of creative process, the element Earth gives birth to a Female Being. She, in turn, takes clay and creates a number of animals into two forms, male and female. From the element Fire comes the Male Being. In time the Male and Female Beings meet, and they decide to create from clay and the four elements three sexual natures: male, female, and neuter. From the male and female beings come children, but the love of the female for the male arouses the jealousy of the neuter. Being sexless and unloved, the neuter kills the male. The neuter is unloved but is depicted as occupying equal place with the other two sexes (Guillon 1991: pp. 22-23)[7]. The same trinity returns in other scenes of creation and regeneration, evident in the language which has male,

---

6   The sentence reads: 'Ada punakanTun Indera Segara itulah asal sida-sida...' (Winstedt 1938). Stuart Robson, in a personal communication, has suggested that it could refer to the fact that Tun Indera Segara may have come from a family which provided *sida-sida.*

7   A version from Lan Na in northern Thailand repeats the same myth, probably dating from the period when northern Thailand was part of the Mon Dvaravati civilization.

female, and neuter elements (Morris 1994: p. 20). But the inclusion of the third sex in the origin myths does not in itself provide a sacred exclusive role to the neuter, or the third sex/gender as in insular Southeast Asia. The difference may lie in the fact that the Mons belong to an Austroasiatic language and culture group, and the island societies to an Austronesian heritage.

Outside Southeast Asia a well-known example of third sex/gender and its relation to the sacred is the *hijra* of northern India, who are classified as *sannyasi,* or 'other worldly people', alongside ascetics and religious mendicants. One *hijra* explained: 'We are neither man nor woman and have been separated from God, so that God grants our special prayers in every place to us only' (Nanda 1990: p. 11). Though the *hijra* are impotent men, and some even castrated, they are believed to have the powers to confer fertility. They are therefore often invited to celebrate a marriage or the birth of a son. It is their culturally accepted role as ascetics, as neither man nor woman, which has institutionalized the *hijra* in northern Indian society. The fact that many also engage in homosexual prostitution for economic reasons does not undermine the respect for the *hijra*'s ritual function (Nanda 1990: pp. 3-4, 10-11).

The *hijra* find legitimacy in their identification with a number of androgynous Hindu deities in the myths, the most popular of whom is Ardhanarisvara, the Siva who is half man and half woman. Visnu and his avatar Krisna are sometimes also depicted as androgynous, and they, like many of the Hindu deities, move in and out of sexes. In the Tantric form of Hinduism the Supreme Being is described as complete, containing both male and female sexual organs (Nanda 1990: pp. 20-21). But the most striking example of the idea of the sacred whole comes from the androgynous merging of Siva and his spouse or *sakti*, Parvati (O'Flaherty 1980: p. 317).

A study of the *hijra* in India exemplifies some of the points made above about third gender roles in other societies. The *hijra* are allocated a place in the society alongside other-worldly individuals, and the extensive and rich repertoire of Hindu and Hindu Tantric literature provides a strong underpinning for their existence. Yet a distinction is made between the sacred and secular roles of the *hijra*. Their sacred role demands certain functions, such as the involvement in sexual activity in fertility rituals. But it is when sacred functions are transferred to the secular sphere – when, for example, fertility ritual is transformed to ordinary prostitution – that *hijra*, and other similar third sex and third gender groups in the societies discussed above, become objects of ridicule and scorn in the community. There is space for a third gender as a highly respected and feared sacred being; but this space is constricted and undesirable in the secular world, where the *hijra* function as ordinary beings.

70

Further examples could be cited of 'third gender' roles in other non-Western societies. Each one provides information regarding groups which were once crucial to the well-being of their societies but which in the modern world are becoming increasingly marginalized[8]. Although these descriptions may have come from cultures widely separated in time and place, they reveal certain shared features. The third sex/gender group is regarded as being neither male nor female nor a composite of both. It is their ambiguous status that locates them beyond society's more conventional sexual and gender dualism, and provides the signifier associated with the primal creative force. By accessing this source of sacred power through a ritual replay of creation, such groups can restore and reconstruct the defects and failings of humanity. Their healing power and links with the sacred assure them a revered status in their ritual role but not their human one. In all the myths the third sex/gender is allocated a sacred space, but as clearly evident in the Mon creation myth, it nevertheless remains 'unloved'.

Many of the features associated with the third sex/gender in the societies discussed above are also found among the *bissu* of South Sulawesi. Nonetheless, their significance can only be properly assessed in the historical and social context of Bugis society.

3. *Bissu*, Arajang, and White Blood

Shelly Errington suggests that in island Southeast Asia the study of gender requires an understanding of the local system of power and prestige, and how gender is mapped onto these ideas (Errington 1989: p. 58). In her own study of the Luwu Bugis in South Sulawesi, Errington describes that society as fitting the model of an 'exemplary state'. The center is represented by the ruler and his family, the possessors of 'white blood'[9], the supernatural 'bodily' fluid which determines power and prestige in the realm. As one moves away from the center toward the periphery, the quantum of white blood, along with power and prestige, diminishes. The Bugis create elaborate genealogies in order to assure that marriages are beneficial in preserving and even adding to the quantity of white blood in the family.

---

8   Those most frequently mentioned in the literature are the native American *berdache*, the *xanith* of Oman, and the *mahu* in Polynesia. On the *berdache*, see Roscoe 1991; Williams 1986; Whitehead 1981: pp. 80-115. On the *xanith*, see Wikan (1977). On the *mahu* in Tahiti, see Besnier 1994: pp. 285-328; Levy 1973.

9   On white blood, see Errington 1989: p. 51. The Bugis term is *toma'daratakku'* or 'those possessing white blood'. *Takku'* is a type of tree which has a milky sap in its branches, hence the reference to 'white blood'.

Crucial in this role are the royal women, who are regarded as the prime repositories of the flow of this precious sacred fluid. In accordance with the 'exemplary center' model, the petty nobility in the periphery are as assiduous (and often more so) than those in the center in maintaining their genealogies and protecting their claims to white blood. Their women, hence their family status, are fiercely guarded, contributing to the notorious reputation of the Bugis for quickly resorting to violence in defense of their womenfolk. Throughout history noble women have been forbidden to marry commoners, a prohibition that was given sacred sanction by the tale of La Bulisa' recounted in the *I La Galigo*. Because I La Bulisa' flouted this injunction, he was punished by supernatural forces which caused his death through the bloating of his stomach (Pelras 1996: p. 86)[10].

A vital component in the maintenance of white blood hierarchy is the *bissu*. To understand the important role they play in Bugis society, one needs to examine the sacred traditions which are attached to this group. The *bissu*, along with the regalia (*arajang*), are believed to have descended from the Upperworld to accompany the first white-blooded rulers to the earth. Among the more traditional Bugis royalty and nobility, the *bissu* are an essential part of the sacred beings and objects maintained in special dwellings to concentrate power. Preserving the progeny of these first rulers, those still possessing this sacred fluid, becomes then the primary concern of the *bissu*. The *bissu*'s position in society is reaffirmed in rituals, in Bugis manuscripts or *lontara'*[11] in the sacred Bugis epic known as the *I La Galigo*[12], and in certain *bissu* texts written in a special 'language of the gods' (Hamonic 1987). Because the rituals were public, and many of the lontara' and the epic cycle were recited on special occasions, the contents were well-known in the community. Preserving the white-blooded rulers and assuring the well-being

---

10 The concept of *busung* can be traced to Proto-Austronesian, and the word itself appears to have survived in South Sulawesi societies. See Blust 1981 v. 2: pp. 292-300. According to one source, I La Bulisa' was the slave of Guru riSelleng, a principal god in the underworld. Assuming the form of a crocodile, he stole a piece of clothing from his master and then ascended into Java pretending to be a divine personage (*totompo'*) (Hamonic 1980: p. 69). For a discussion of the position of women in Makassar genealogies, see Cummings 1999: p. 128ff.

11 The term comes from an early practice of writing on narrow strips of lontar palm leaves, which are then joined and rolled to form 'books'. Much of the early lontara' would have been sacred texts, including oaths and treaties.

12 Pelras believes that the epic was the work of *bissu*. To this day they continue to be the main preservers and scholars of episodes from the *I La Galigo*, considered one of the oldest written epics in Southeast Asia. Although the *I La Galigo* cycle has numerous episodes and differing versions, it displays a remarkable stylistic and linguistic unity. It is believed that the basic framework, the principal episodes, and the main characters and their relationships formed the core from which later poets added episodes in the epic style and language (Pelras 1996: pp. 32-34, 56-57; Kern 1954).

of society were regarded as tasks especially suited to the *bissu*, whose origins were intimately linked with the gods at the very beginning of time.

In ancient Bugis creation myths the creator is an androgynous deity who gives birth to a male sun and a female moon. A quarrel occurs between the two, and they will not cohabit. While both are capable of self-impregnation, the sun cannot reproduce and it is the moon who gives birth to the stars, certain metals (gold, iron), and to the first generation of 'monstrous' plants, animals, and other creatures. Some Bugis believe that the crocodiles and other reptiles are representations of these monstrous ancestors. Among the forty deities created was the deity of the tree, regarded as the initiator of the *bissu*[13]. A reconciliation between the sun and the moon occurs soon after the latter's various creations appear. This leads to a division of power and a union of the two, from which come the gods who are celebrated in the *I La Galigo*. The Bugis cosmogonic myth counts the *bissu* among the 'monstrous' creations, which are all replete with sacred powers.

The *bissu* origin is linked to the androgynous character of the female moon deity. Androgyny is an ancient universal formula for expressing wholeness, the co-existence of opposites, and perfection within one being, rather than the idea of sexual completeness and autarchy (Eliade 1975: p. 174)[14]. Because of her alienation from the male sun, the female moon conceived from within herself. The ensuing offspring, among whom were the *bissu*, albinos, dwarfs, negroids, and other asexual beings, were considered to be powerful because they originated from the most sacred unity before the separation which brought about the second creative process. They are associated with a period of 'chaos' that is highly charged with the spiritual potency of the undifferentiated godhead. The splitting of this primordial unity produces a second creation based on the complementarity of male and female principles. In contrast to the first, when both the sun and the moon become impregnated but are unable to conceive (sun) or conceive sterile offspring (moon) (Hamonic 1977: pp. 43, 46), the second creation exemplifies fertility and reproduction between the male and female beings. It is this latter period that provides the context for the origin episodes in the *I La Galigo*, where *bissu* officiate at royal marriage and birth rituals to assure the perpetuation of the sacred white blood of the ruling house.

---

13 Large trees are today still highly venerated, especially those with more than forty branches. It is no coincidence that forty *bissu* are required in the most significant ceremonies. The association of the *bissu* with plants is affirmed in the creation myth and provides a popular explanation for the efficacious links between the two in the *bissu* role as medicine men and as selectors of certain types of woods for the construction of ships and houses (Hamonic 1987: pp. 156-158, 223).

14 Benedict Anderson has made the same point in regard to Javanese kingship, where the masculine and feminine are combined in one, but 'sharply juxtaposed' and held in a 'tense, electric balance' (Anderson 1972: p. 14).

During certain ceremonies the *bissu* demonstrate in dress and behavior the merging of both the male and female principles, and the replacement of profane with sacred space and time. In their ritual role the *bissu* assume a symbolic androgynous state that re-establishes primordial conditions. In this period of 'chaos', the prodigious power released is harnessed by the *bissu* in order to remake an imperfect creation (i.e., restore the health or soul of a sick person or crops), to produce a new creation (i.e., at the initiation of a priest/priestess, the birth of a child, or during the growth of a new crop), or to be placed at the disposal of the rulers of white blood. Performed by the *bissu*, such rituals are indispensable in ensuring the well-being and prosperity of the ruler and the community. They also highlight the importance of the *bissu*, whose presence affirms the continuing links with the gods.[15]

Regarded as 'different' and outside normal society, the *bissu* are respected and feared when they perform their sacred roles. They use a separate language, a 'language of the gods', while reciting or writing down their sacred texts. Their status in Bugis society is legitimized through the myths and legends that link them with the ancient gods and the rulers of South Sulawesi. Until the mid-twentieth century, *bissu* were found in every royal court serving as advisors and as keepers of the regalia. Although they did not belong to the *toma'daratakku'* ('those possessing white-blood', i.e., the noble or royal line), the *bissu* could also trace their origin to the deities. Their links to the heavens are reaffirmed in epics such as the *I La Galigo* and in the writings by *bissu* in praise of their royal patrons.

In the *I La Galigo* there are three categories of *bissu*. The first consists of *bissu* born of the gods who belong to the purest nobility and are associated with the courts. The second group is composed of *bissu* who possess land and palaces. *Bissu* from these two groups bear the titles of *Datu Bissu* (Lord *Bissu*) and *Bissu Lolo* (The Younger [Lord] *Bissu*) and do not seem to have any religious function. Some of the *bissu* attached to the courts are mentioned as nursemaids to the princes[16]. The third type of *bissu* bears the title of *Puang* (Lord) or *Puang Matoa* (Elder Lord). They move in completely different circles from the court-oriented and landowning *bissu*, and only congregate to perform important religious ceremonies (Hamonic 1987: pp. 29-39).

According to these categories of *bissu*, there were those who, like the godrulers, were nobility of white blood; others had a purely religious role. Significantly, there have been princesses in the Makassar kingdom of Gowa, an ethnic group closely related to the Bugis, who incorporated the word '*bissu*' into their titles. But there is no historical evidence of a *bissu* ever

---

15 Mircea Eliade has developed these ideas in a number of his publications (1975, 1965). See Beane & Doty, 1976: pp. 212-213, 218.

16 Being a nursemaid in South Sulawesi society was a highly honored post because milk relations were valued as much as ties of blood. A milk mother is as close to the child in later years as his/her own blood mother (Andaya 1981: pp. 57, 315, fn. 12).

74

exercising political leadership in any of the South Sulawesi kingdoms. As spiritual advisors to rulers, or as ritual practitioners calling upon gods to save or protect the land belonging to the white-blooded rulers, their influence was usually indirect. Because their religious role receives so much attention in the *I La Galigo*, the *bissu* tend to regard this epic work as a ritual manual. From specific episodes in the *I La Galigo* it may also be possible for the historian to deduce their spiritual function in former times.

Throughout the *I La Galigo*, reference is made to the sacrifice of *bissu* and other 'monstrous' beings, such as dwarfs, albinos, and negroids (*oro*), all of whom are offspring of the moon in the initial creation (Hamonic 1987: p. 158). In one fragment from the *I La Galigo*, the *bissu* are summoned to do battle with one another so that their spilt blood will release the souls (*bannapati*) from the Upperworld and enable Datu Sénngeng to give birth. The blood sacrifice proves efficacious, and Sawérigading is born, followed by his twin sister, Wé Tenriabeng. Those *bissu* who were sacrificed to ease Datu Sénngeng's suffering regain their lives after the birth. In a subsequent episode Sawérigading summons the *bissu* once again to shed their blood so that Wé Cudai can give birth. When the child is born, it is dressed as a *bissu* but lies motionless. The *bissu* fetch their musical instruments and perform a dance which enables the child to gain movement. She then undergoes the proper initiation and becomes a *bissu* (Koolhof 1992: pp. 26-27, 36-37)[17]. The power of ritual performance and music is again emphasized when Batara Lattu and Datu Sénngeng order the *bissu* to dance before Sawérgading to prevent his marrying his sister (Koolhof 1992: pp. 33, 37).

The special relationship of the *bissu* and the godrulers is underscored in another episode. One day the king of the gods, Topatotoe ('He who determines fate'), decides to send his son, Batara Guru, to descend and govern the earth. On earth Batara Guru meets Wé Nyilitimo', the princess sent from the Lowerworld, and they wed and rule the earth together (Matthes 1943: p. 487). After a time the godrulers return to the Upperworld, leaving the earth with no rulers and no order. For a period of seven (some say seventy-seven) generations, there is disorder on the earth, when 'people become like fish eating one another (*sianré-anrébalé taué*)'[18]. No longer able

---

17 The shedding of blood to create life and activate or provide motion to the *bissu* princess represents an ancient theme with resonances in many societies. One striking parallel comes from the Nahua in Mexico. In the second series of creation in Nahua cosmogony, the fifth sun fulfills the requirement for light but is unable to traverse across the skies. Only through the sacrifice of the divine blood of the gods, and in later years the blood of human beings, can the sun continue its journey and hence establish the sequence of seasons and the flow of time (Florescano 1994: pp. 8-17).

18 In ancient Indian literature it is known as the concept of *matsyanyaya*, or the 'logic of the fish'. In the Cycle of Ages humans will degenerate and lose their sense of natural duty. There will be no longer any rulers, and a society without a king cannot be viable. It is in this period that the 'logic of the fish' will prevail (Lingat 1973: p. 207).

to tolerate these conditions, humans appeal to the gods to restore the godrulers on earth so that peace and harmony can again prevail. The gods finally relent and send a second set of godrulers to earth: some are sent from the Upperworld (the *tomanurung* = 's/he who descended') and some from the Lowerworld (*totompo* = 's/he who ascended'). They are usually found standing on a flat stone in an open field accompanied by *bissu* and sacred objects, which become the regalia. Members of the community greet them and ask them to rule. They agree, and these godrulers of the 'white blood' become the founders of the royal houses of the various kingdoms. The sacred objects become the regalia (*arajang*), and the *bissu* the priestly guardians of both these new rulers and the *arajang*. The white-blooded rulers, the *arajang*, and the *bissu* – all of whom originated from the world of the gods – continue to maintain their intimate and supportive relationship and their unique sacred place in the human community[19].

4. The *Bissu* in History

Given the early modern European repugnance towards lesbians ('tommies', 'Sapphists') and homosexual males ('mollies', 'Sodomites') (Meer 1994: 137-186; Trumbach 1994: 111-136), there is little likelihood that the Portuguese in the sixteenth century or officials of the Dutch East India Company (VOC) in the seventeenth and eighteenth centuries would have been drawn to examine the *bissu* in South Sulawesi. It is also unfortunate that scant evidence is available from indigenous documents, such as the *bissu* texts or the Bugis chronicles. I have therefore used more detailed studies of the *bissu* in the nineteenth and twentieth centuries in conjunction with older European and indigenous sources in order to reconstruct the historical role of the *bissu* in Bugis society during the early modern period. Through an examination of the *bissu* in South Sulawesi society, I have also attempted to contribute to the ongoing discussion of how cultures create a space for genders other than those of 'male' and 'female'.

One of the earliest historical accounts of the *bissu* comes from a Portuguese observer, Antonio de Paiva, who visited Siang on the west coast of South Sulawesi in 1545. He speaks of the *bissu* as 'priests of the king', who wore their hair long, dressed like women, and adopted the voice, the gestures and the customs of women. They married and had sex only with other men because it was believed that contact with a woman in thought or

---

19   For a brief account of the early traditions regarding the establishment of royalty in South
      Sulawesi, see Andaya 1981: pp. 10-13.

76

deed would lead to the destruction of their religion. Any *bissu* accused of contravening this rule was sentenced to death by fire (Jacobs 1966: p. 251).

I am aware of no other evidence relating to the *bissu* until the second half of the seventeenth century. Between 1666 and 1669 all South Sulawesi was engulfed in a war, with the VOC and its Bugis allies led by Arung Palakka ranged on one side, and the Makassar kingdom of Gowa and its Makassar and Bugis allies on the other. In this struggle there was no neutral ground and every state, whether large or small, was fighting for its very survival[20]. Under these circumstances, the courts mobilized all forces at their command, both sacred and profane. In the Makassar court of Gowa, the Malay poet Encik Amin wrote a panegyric to the stalwart Makassar warriors who proved more than equal to the forces of the enemy (Skinner 1963). Among the Bugis courts, the *bissu* were apparently employed to call upon the gods to favor their white-blooded rulers. One Bugis manuscript written by *bissu*, for example, tells the story of Arung Palakka's heavenly origins. It is not simply an entertaining legend but a form of oral magic which reactivates the beginning of time in order to endow the favored ruler with powers of that primeval period.

In this tale of sacred time a direct relationship is drawn between *bissu* intervention and the success of Arung Palakka, a descendant of the white-blooded rulers who himself ruled in Bone from 1672-1696. The story begins unambiguously with the statement that it is about 'Puatta Torisompae' ('Our Lord who is given Obeisance', an epithet which was applied to Arung Palakka). But the crucial actor in the story is Anurungeng Telinoé, who is a *bissu terru*[21]. By falling into a state of trance, the *bissu* is able to see considerable activity in the Upperworld. Preparations are being made by the great lords to send the Datu Pammusu' ('The Warrior Lord') to earth to govern Bone and restore the soul[22] of the Happy Land. Anurungeng Telinoé's soul then ascends via the rainbow to the Upperworld to the very summit of the heavens. He requests from the Creator, Topabarrebarreédé, the seed, 'the Valuable Invincible Essence', which would become the Pillar of War, the Restorer of the Happy Land. The Creator is sitting at his Palace of Shining Mirrors and agrees to grant the request. To assist this Pillar of War, the *bissu* prepares weapons with which to neutralize the enemy, and gathers supernatural plants which exist in the highest heavens and are used to make

---

20   For an account of that war and its implications for South Sulawesi, see Andaya 1981.

21   'Anurungeng' is a special title held by *bissu* who are able to intervene on behalf of humankind, and a '*bissu terru*' is a *bissu* able to foresee the future.

22   'Restore the soul' is a reference to the Bugis-Makassar belief that when one is caused shame (*mappakasiri'*), one is as if dead. Only through the removal of this shame (*siri'*) can the soul be restored (Zainal Abidin 1983: pp. 32-33; Andaya 1981: pp. 15-17).

special potions. The seed is then introduced into the womb of Datu Sénngeng who descends to earth by means of the rainbow[23].

The format used in the tale is that of the *I La Galigo*, and so the listeners would have immediately understood the episode as occurring in sacred time, during the time of Creation when there was still a link between the world of the gods and the world of humans. In this well-known episode the change in the identity of the seed, from the *I La Galigo*'s Sawérigading to the seventeenth-century Arung Palakka, would not have been jarring to the listeners. The *bissu*, as creatures of the moon associated with the very earliest of creations, were believed to be capable of returning to this sacred time to 're-create' or 'create' for the benefit of society. That Arung Palakka was the focus of this *bissu* ritual creation suggests that it was produced in the seventeenth century in order to arouse the Bugis for battle. A similar response was elicited from Malay warriors in Melaka facing battle with the Portuguese, when they are read the *Hikayat Muhammad Hanafiah* to challenge them to emulate the bravery of the hero of that story (Brown 1953: p. 168). Through the telling of such tales the *bissu* confirm their intermediary role between the human community and the world of the gods, and reaffirm their crucial function in assuring the survival of those of white blood.

With the involvement of the whole of South Sulawesi in the wars during the second half of the seventeenth century, the *bissu*'s role became even more prominent. In addition to writing and reciting tales to invoke the power of the gods and inspiring the people, they were also employed in one case as the first line of defense. When faced with an invasion by the army of the powerful state of Bone, the much weaker Lamatti forces called upon the assistance of the *bissu*. The Puang Matoa ('Elder Lord', i.e., the head of the *bissu*) in Lamatti, a very old woman (*makkunrai ridi'*) dressed in red, was borne on a palanquin to confront the Bone troops. She was accompanied by around a hundred female *bissu* (*coré-coré*) waving swords (*alameng*) and weaver's wooden shuttles (*walida*) while chanting their sacred spells (*memmang*). As they approached, the Bone troops fired on them but no one was injured. The *bissu* continued their march, this time to the east, and again no one was struck by any of the enemy's missiles. Having accomplished their task, the *bissu* then retired[24.]

In this account the Puang Matoa is female, as is her *bissu* following. They carry the *bissu* instruments of the *alameng* and the *walida*, which are the sacred male and female symbols used in ceremonies to ward off evil

---

23 NBG (NederlandsBijbelgenootschap Collection), Hs. 183 (in Bugis script), University of Leiden Library, Eastern Manuscripts Division, fols. 1-14.

24 Andaya 1981: p. 86, quoting from *Lontara'na H.A. Sumangerukka*, fols. 33-34, owned by H. A. Pancaitana, ex-Datu Pattojo; *Lontara'na Wajo'*, owned by Prof. Mr. Andi Zainal Abidin, No. 273, fol. 309; and *Lontara'na Sukku'na Tana Wajo'*, owned by Andi Makkaraka, compiled by La Sangaji Puanna La Sangaji Puanna La Sénngeng, Arung Bettempola (eighteenth century), no folio, Section 23.

spirits (Matthes 1943: p. 502). The participation of the female *bissu* in Lamatti is in keeping with the depiction of *bissu* in the *I La Galigo*, where they are almost all prominent women[25]. There is some ambiguity in a few cases, where a *bissu* may possess a female personal name and be given a male title, or a female title may be used to refer to a *bissu* with a male personal name[26]. Within the epic many royal women become *bissu*, and one of the heroes even expresses a wish that his unborn child be a daughter so that she can join the *bissu* ranks. When the child is born, it is a daughter fully dressed in *bissu* clothing but inert. It requires intercession by the *bissu* and their sacred instruments before the child can be infused with the spirit and initiated to full *bissu*dom (Koolhof 1992: pp. 36-37).

In contrast to the prominence of female *bissu* both in the *I La Galigo* and in the account of Lamatti, the descriptions by Paiva in the sixteenth century and James Brooke in the nineteenth only mention male *bissu*. According to Brooke, who visited the Bugis kingdom of Wajo' in 1840, certain men dressed as women performed female tasks. He described a practice whereby a male child who exhibited effeminate tendencies would be presented to the ruler by his parents. These youths, according to Brooke, often exercised great influence over their lords (Mundy 1848, v. 1: pp. 82-83). He made no reference to female *bissu*.

The first detailed study of the *bissu* was made by B.F. Matthes, a renowned Dutch missionary scholar of the nineteenth century. He observed that the male *bissu* were considered impotent and therefore had access to the princesses of the court. Because of this belief any sexual contact between the *bissu* and the princesses was punishable by drowning, a fate usually reserved for those convicted of incest[27]. Matthes further commented that the women *bissu* performed all types of domestic (hence female) chores in the courts, though this was viewed simply as 'passing the time'. Their true function lay in performing ceremonies dealing with rites of passage of the royal progeny. In this role the *bissu* called upon the spirits or deities (*réwata*) to descend to earth and enter their bodies as well as the special altar (*lamming réwata*). Only when they were possessed by the spirits did they become true *bissu*. It was during these occasions that the *bissu* danced, sang, and performed their cures. They practiced their skills not only in the courts but among influential

---

25   Kern's *Catalogus* mentions some eighty *bissu* names from the *I La Galigo*. Only three were male, all of whom came from one area, Mallimongeng (Kern 1954: p. 68). Anderson reminds us that the *bedaya* in Central Java were a special group usually composed of women who were responsible for guarding the regalia and performing sacred court dances (Anderson 1972: 14, fn. 29).

26   For example, Wé Tenridio', a female name, is sometimes referred to as Batara (m) *Bissu* and sometimes Batari (f) *Bissu*. La Oddang Riwu', a male name, is associated with the rice goddess, Sangiang Seri (Hamonic 1987: p. 35).

27   In 1545 the Portuguese Antonio de Paiva reported that the punishment for sexual intercourse between a woman and a *bissu* was death by fire (Jacobs 1966: p. 251).

non-royal Bugis, Makassarese, and Chinese. They also officiated at ceremonies sponsored by individuals fulfilling vows. There was usually a procession led by the Puang Matoa, followed immediately by female *bissu* carrying a betelbox and a cuspidor, and a large number of dancing and singing *bissu*. The ceremonies culminated with the sacrifice of a buffalo, regarded as a symbol of the moon, the creator deity of the *bissu* (Hamonic 1987: p. 157; Matthes 1943: pp. 498, 511, 515).

The situation of the *bissu* today has been studied most intensively by the French scholar, Gilbert Hamonic. In vocabulary and in the social arena he noted little difference between the *bissu* (known among themselves by the *bissu* language term of *saladéwi* = 'false women') and a homosexual (*calabai'* = 'false women') or lesbian (*calalai'* = 'false men'). The status of the *bissu*, however, was far higher because of their unique spiritual role in the community. It is believed that the gods mark the *bissu* sexually from birth as a sign that they are destined to become *bissu*. Something of the nature of this sexual malformation is conveyed in the concept of *koro*, a pathological fear among Bugis males of the retraction of the penis into the groin. The Bugis in Bone attribute the sign of '*bissu*-ness' to the very first *bissu* who was born with an umbilical cord in the shape of a sacred naga serpent which could not be severed from the body (Hamonic 1977: pp. 39, 41, 42, 46).

Once a child is chosen by the gods, he is raised among women but tutored by a *bissu*. He is taught the *bissu* language or 'language of the gods' (*basa déwata)*, the sacred *bissu* texts (which he must commit to memory), *bissu* dances and chants, preparation of offerings, and the precise steps in rituals. From the stage of being a '*bissu mamata*', i.e., an unripe *bissu*, he progresses until he becomes a '*bissu tanré*' (high *bissu*). In that final stage he must undergo the *ma'rebba* (to fall, die) ceremony, in which the soul leaves the initiate's body and wanders in the other world for one, two or three days, during which time the *bissu* maintain a constant vigil of singing and dancing. At a given moment, the Puang Matoa, or leader of the *bissu*, provides a sign to indicate the return of the soul to the body and the creation of a new *bissu*. The initiate thus becomes a *bissu nasolo' ridéwata* ('*bissu* blessed or acknowledged by the gods'). During the Dutch period the ceremony was banned and Indonesian authorities continue to regard it with disapproval today, although it is conducted clandestinely on very special occasions (Hamonic 1977: pp. 42, 46).

When Hamonic was in South Sulawesi in the mid-1970s, he was told that a child of noble blood 'marked by the gods' could be present at all the major *bissu* ceremonies. That person was nevertheless placed somewhat apart from the *bissu*, though he was respected and honored with the title of *kunéng lolo* ('young kunéng'). Hamonic was told that the *kunéng lolo* were not permitted to become true *bissu* because this role was reserved for commoners Hamonic 1977: p. 42). But this is contrary to the *I La Galigo*, knowledge of which is regarded among the *bissu* as essential, and which they acquire during their apprenticeship. In the *I La Galigo* many of the *bissu* are of noble or royal stock with female names. The fact that Matthes defines *kunéng* as 'a female *bissu* title' (Matthes 1874: p. 22) suggests that the *bissu* in the *I La Galigo* were either sexually female bodies or sexually male bodies provided with female names. The mixing of male and female characteristics in a *bissu* is considered essential for the proper fulfillment of their ritual role.

Hamonic draws an ingenious relationship between Bugis royal marriages and the *bissu*. He records the myth of the male sun and the female moon at the beginning of time, who were both capable of impregnation. The sun, however, could not reproduce, while the moon gave birth to stars, who proved to be infertile. It was therefore left to human beings to introduce fertile reproduction in the world. When those of white blood came to earth, they were to fulfill this function of fertility with the assistance of the *bissu*. The royal wedding is the greatest manifestation of this fertility ritual and the prominence played by the *bissu*. In the *bissu* language, the same written characters can be transcribed as *matelo* ('to die') or *mattelo* ('to make love') (Hamonic 1977: pp. 43-44, 46). In keeping with the practice of word-play in *bissu* literary works, *matelo/mattelo* expresses the double meaning of death/love leading to new life/creation.

5. Conclusions: *Bissu* and Third Gender

Because of the paucity of material on the *bissu* in the early modern period, one can only suggest the type of functions they might have once performed. From descriptions in the *I La Galigo*, it appears that in an earlier period the *bissu* were counted among the nobility of the land and regarded as religious practitioners. By early modern times (c. 1400 – c. 1800) the association of *bissu* with nobility and royalty is only retained in the names of individuals mentioned in the chronicles. In these texts the principal function of the *bissu* is primarily if not wholly religious, and involves not only officiating at rituals but also creating verbal/written magic to enhance the spiritual powers of the white-bloods. So respected and feared is the power of the *bissu* that they are also employed to repel all threats, whether human or supernatural, which may endanger the white-blooded rulers.

These particular functions do not seem to have waned in the nineteenth century, but a change in social and political circumstances forced certain modifications of the *bissu*'s role in society. Although the royal courts were still the primary locus of *bissu* activity, the rise in the wealth of non-white blooded individuals, including Chinese, provided another source of support for the *bissu*'s spiritual prowess. Both men and women *bissu* are mentioned, though it appears that the female *bissu* perform tasks clearly defined as female activities.

Twentieth-century studies of the *bissu* are far more comprehensive. They indicate that the strength of Islamic fundamentalism and the pervasive influence of modernity have undermined the status of the *bissu*. Soon after the creation of the independent Republic of Indonesia in 1950, a decision was made to eliminate the remaining sovereign kingdoms (with a few exceptions) within its borders. This act deprived the *bissu* of their royal patrons and their principal *raison d'être*. With the center of power now lying outside Sulawesi, and with the intrusion of national and international media, new medical advances, and universal primary education, the *bissu*'s principal sources of legitimacy – their rituals and their sacred texts – have now become irrelevant. The *bissu* are still summoned to perform at weddings of prominent officials or members from high nobility, or to officiate at particular ceremonies soliciting divine intervention in order to end droughts, ward off epidemics, etc. But the occasions for such ceremonies are becoming less and less frequent.

A true *bissu* is one who has been tutored by a *bissu* and undergone special initiation rites. With the *bissu*'s function in modern society practically disappearing, few are being recruited to continue this tradition. Many of the Bugis are beginning to equate the *calabai'* ('false women') and *calalai'* ('false men') with the *bissu*, a misconception which is reinforced by the necessity of using *calabai'* and *calalai'* to act as *bissu* in important ceremonies requiring forty *bissu*. The *calabai'* and *calalai'* perform sexual and societal roles associated with the other sex, and while some of the *calabai'* are *bissu*, not all *bissu* are *calabai'*. Some *bissu* have wives and children and lead a life of a male when not in a *bissu* role. It is believed that *bissu* have both a male and a female spirit spouse who were responsible for calling them to this once highly revered position[28].

The presence of the *bissu* as an institution in South Sulawesi has made the society accustomed to the idea of individuals who do not fit the ordinary categories of male and female. As long as the *bissu* perform their sacred role, they are accepted and revered. But when they revert to a mundane existence, they are expected to behave according to society's ideas of male and female roles. Unfortunately, detailed evidence about the *bissu* is almost solely about male *bissu*, to whom the following observations are of necessity confined. Some marry and have families and assume a male role; others assume a female role by marrying males or having sexual relations with males; while a third group continues to eschew any sexual contact with others, living in the

---

28   The call from the spirits is manifested in a physical way through catalepsy or mutism. This
     state can only be overcome through special ritual cures, which precede a full initiation
     ceremony to make the individual a full-fledged *bissu* (Pelras 1996: pp. 82-84, 165-167).

regalia house as guardians of the *arajang*[29], and conducting their lives almost exclusively in the *bissu* sphere.

The first case is acceptable because the individual maintains the mainstream idea of division of gender roles between males and females. In the second case, there is less acceptance or toleration because the anatomical sex is seen to be in conflict with sexual preference and gender roles. Nevertheless, this group is judged by another standard when assuming the *bissu* role. In the third case, there is greater acceptance of the role of the *bissu* in ritual and increasingly in cultural tourism. Any opposition arises from those who believe that the *bissu* are a thing of the past and should be eliminated along with all 'feudal' remnants. Despite hostility from many Muslims, among the Bugis population there is still a residue of reverence for these special individuals with their ancient links to the ancestral gods. In short, the community accepts the existence of male, female, and *bissu* roles, but is less tolerant of the intermediary gender positions of male female or female male[30].

It has been demonstrated that ideas of dimorphism in sex and gender roles were a social construction of Western scholars in the nineteenth century. So influential have been their writings that any other sex or gender permutations were regarded as 'deviant', and hence anti-social. This formulation of sex and gender roles went largely unchallenged despite substantial evidence of androgyny in classical literature and in the Christian tradition (Bullogh 1976: pp. 113, 117). 'Androgyny' was even described by philosophers, poets, and theologians as a 'state of exalted being, the ideal completion of humanity in a condition of transcendence' (Garber 1995: p. 207). However, there was no group which existed within European society which exemplified this androgyny; androgynous beings remained amorphous creatures of myth and fable.

In a number of non-Western societies, on the other hand, stories of androgynous deities remained part of the living tradition, and there were groups of individuals who exemplified in their symbolic and in some cases in their daily lives the combining of the male and female elements. One would have expected that the presence of these groups, such as the *manang bali* among the Iban in Borneo or the *bissu* in South Sulawesi, would have facilitated the acceptance of a 'third' sex and gender category. In the case of Iban and Bugis societies, however, no other sex or gender category except for

---

29   The regalia of the kingdom is supposed to have come with the godrulers from the Upper- or Lowerworld. There is therefore an affinity among the regalia, the royal household, and the *bissu* since they all originate from the world of the gods.

30   The *berdache, hijra* and the *xanith* are biological males, but dress, behave, work, and are treated as women. In this sense they are 'male women'. In some African and native American societies there is a gender status called 'manly-hearted women', biological females who work, marry, and parent as men and have a social position as 'female men' (Lorber 1994: p. 17).

male and female was created in the human community. All creation, except the gods and their sacred priests/priestesses, was conceived as being either masculine or feminine. Even in the case of the Kodi in Sumba, where ordinary individuals are said to contain both male and female 'souls' attached to different parts of the head, only male and female gender play any role. A few individuals may cross gender roles because it is seen as a potent means of concentrating power for important periods in the life of a society (Hoskins 1990: p. 275), but the boundaries crossed are only between the male and the female.

Based on a close reading of the sources on the *bissu* in South Sulawesi, the evidence suggests that Bugis society acknowledged a division between male and female sexuality that was then posited in terms of gender dualism. There was, however, a sacred and ritual 'third' category of gender represented by the *bissu*. This 'third' gender role was appropriate and hence respected in the sacred realm during *bissu* ceremonies, but highly inappropriate and condemnatory if practiced in everyday life. As with the Kodi in Sumba, male and female were the only categories in Bugis society, and it was the complementary interaction between the two which assured the proper functioning of the community. The *bissu*, on the other hand, originated from another world and were associated with the gods. In keeping with their sacred position, it was proper in South Sulawesi that they should be classified not as mortal Bugis but as a unique third category of being.

Acknowledgments

This research was previously published: Leonard Y. Andaya (2000) 'The Bissu: Study of a Third Gender in Indonesia', in Barbara W. Andaya (ed.) *Other Pasts. Women, Gender and History in Early Modern Southeast Asia*, Honolulu: University of Hawai'i at Manoa, Center for Southeast Asian Studies, pp. 27-46.

Bibliography

Adriani, Nicolaus & Christian A. Kruyt (1912) *De Bare'e-Sprekende Toradja's van Midden – Celebes*, Batavia: Landsdrukkerij.
Ahmad, Abdul Samad (ed.) (1979) *Sulalatus Salatin-Sejarah Melayu*, Kuala Lumpur: Dewan Bahasa dan Pustaka.
Andaya, Leonard Y. (1981) *The Heritage of Arung Palakka: A History of South Sulawesi (Celebes) in the Seventeenth Century*, The Hague: Martinus Nijhoff.

Anderson, R.O'G. Benedict (1972) 'The Idea of Power in Javanese Culture', in Claire Holt (ed.) *Culture and Politics in Indonesia*, Ithaca: Cornell University Press.

Atkinson, Jane Monnig & Shelly Errington (eds.) (1990) *Power and Difference: Gender in Island Southeast Asia*, Stanford: Stanford University Press.

Beane, Wendell C. & William G. Doty (eds.) (1976) *Myths, Rites, Symbols: An Eliade Reader*, New York: Harper Colophon Books.

Besnier, Nico (1994) 'Polynesian Gender Liminality through Time and Space', in Gilbert Herdt (ed.) *Third Sex, Third Gender*, New York: Zone Books.

Blust, Robert (1981) 'Linguistic Evidence for Some Early Austronesian Taboos', *American Anthropologist*, 83(2): 285-319.

Bolin, Anne (1994) 'Transcending and Transgendering: Male-to-Female Transexuals, Dichotomy and Diversity', in Gilbert Herdt (ed.) *Third Sex, Third Gender*, New York: Zone Books.

Brown, Charles Cuthbert (1952) 'The Malay Annals', *Journal of the Malayan Branch of the Royal Asiatic Society*, 25(2-3): 5-276.

Bullogh, Vern L. (1976) *Sexual Variance in Society and History*, New York: John Wiley and Sons.

Cummings, William (1999) *History-Making, Making History: Writing the Past in Early Modern Makassar*, Ph.D. Dissertation in History, Honolulu: University of Hawai'i.

Djajadiningrat, Hoesein (1934) *Atjehsch-Nederlandsch Woordenboek*, Batavia: Landsdrukkerij.

Dos Santos Alves, Jorge (1990) 'Une Ville inquiète et un Sultan barricadé: Aceh vers 1588 d'après le Roteiro das Cousas do Achem de l'Evêque de Malaka', *Archipel*, 39: 93-112.

Eliade, Mircea (1975) *Myths, Dreams and Mysteries*, New York: Harper Books.

Eliade, Mircea (1965) *Mephistopheles and the Androgyne: Studies in Religious Myth and Symbolism*, New York: Sheed and Ward.

Errington, Shelly (1990) 'Recasting Sex, Gender, and Power: A Theoretical and Regional Overview', in Jane Atkinson & Shelly Errington (eds.): *Power and Difference*, Stanford: Stanford University Press.

Erringon, Shelly (1989) *Meaning and Power in a Southeast Asian Realm*, Princeton: Princeton University Press.

Florescano, Enrique (1994) *Memory, Myth, and Time in Mexico: From the Aztecs to Independence*, Austin: University of Texas.

Garber, Marjorie (1995) *VICE VERSA: Bisexuality and the Eroticism of Everyday Life*, New York and London: Simon Schuster.

Grosz, Elizabeth (1991) 'Freaks', *Social Semiotics*, 1(2): 22-38.

Guillon, Emmanuel (1991) 'The Ultimate Origin of the World, or the *Mula Muh*, and Other Mon Beliefs', *Journal of the Siam Society*, 79(1): 22-30.

Hamonic, Gilbert (1977) 'Les "fausses-femmes" du pays Bugis (Célèbes-Sud)', *Objets et Mondes*, 17(1): 39-46.

Hamonic, Gilbert (1987) *Le langage des dieux: cultes et ouvoir pré-Islamiques en pays Bugis Cékèbes-Sud, Indonésie*, Paris: Editions du Centre National de la Recherche Scientifique.

Hamonic, Gilbert (1980) '*Mallawolo*, Chants bugis pour la sacralisation des anciens princes de Célèbes-Sud. Textes et traductions', *Archipel*, 19(1): 39-46.

Herdt, Gilbert (ed.) (1994) *Third Sex, Third Gender: Beyond Sexual Dimorphism in Culture and History*, New York: Zone Books.

Herdt, Gilbert (ed.) (1984) *Ritualized Homosexuality in Melanesia*, Berkeley: University of California Press.

Hoskins, Janet (1990) 'Doubling Deities, Descent, and Personhood', in Jane Monnig Atkinson & Shelly Errington (eds.) *Power and Difference*, Stanford: Stanford University Press.

Hoskins, Janet (1993) *Play of Time: Kodi Perspectives on Calendars, History, and Exchange*, Berkeley: University of California Press.

Iskandar, Teuku (1970) *Kamus Dewan*, Kuala Lumpur: Dewan Bahasa dan Pustaka.

Ito, Takeshi (1984) 'The World of the *Adat Aceh: A Historical Study of the Sultanate of Aceh'*, Dissertation, Melbourne: Australian National University.

Jackson, Peter A. (1997) 'Kathoey><Gay><Man: The Historical Emergence of Gay Male Identity in Thailand', in Lenore Manderson & Margaret Jolly (eds.) *Sites of Desire, Economies of Pleasure: Sexualities in Asia and the Pacific*, Chicago: University of Chicago Press.

Jacobs, Hubert (1966) 'The First Locally Demonstrable Christianity in Celebes, 1544', *Studia*, 17: 231-305.

Kern, Rudolf Arnold (1954) *Catalogus van de Boeginese, tot de I La Galigo-cyclus behorende Handschriften*, Makassar: Matthestichting.

Koolhof, Sirtjo (1992) *Dutanna Sawérigading: een scène uit de I La Galigo*, Eindscriptie Valgroep Talen en Culturen van Zuiduoost Azië en Oceanië, Rijksuniversiteit te Leiden.

Kroef, J.M. van der (1956) *Indonesia and the Modern World*, Part II, Bandung: Masa Baru,

Laqueur, Thomas (1990) *Making Sex: Body and Gender from the Greeks to Freud*, Cambridge, MA: Harvard University Press.

Levy, Robert (1973) *Tahitians: Mind and Experience in the Society Islands*, Chicago: University of Chicago Press.

Lingat, Robert (1973) *The Classical Law of India*, translated from French by John Duncan Martin Derrett, Berkeley: University of California Press.

Lorber, Judith (1994) *Paradox of Gender*, New Haven and London: Yale University Press.

Masing, James Jemut (1997) *The Coming of the Gods: An Iban Invocatory Chant (*Timang Gawai Amat) *of the Baleh River Region, Sarawak*, Canberra: Department of Anthropology, Research School of Pacific Studies, Australian National University.

Matthes, Benjamin Frederic (1874) *Boegineesch-Hollandsch Woordenboek-en verkaring van een tot opheldering bijgevoegden ethnographischen atlas*, The Hague: Martinus Nijhoff.

Matthes, Benjamin Frederic (1872) 'Over de Bissoe's of heidensche priesters en priesteressen der Boeginezen', in Ds. H. van den Brink, *Dr Benjamin Frederik Matthes. Zijn Leven en Arbeid in dienst van het Nederlandsch Bijbelgenootschap*, Amsterdam: Nederlandsch Bijbelgenootschap.

Meer, Theo van der (1994) 'Sodomy and the Pursuit of a Third Sex in the Early Modern Period', in Gilbert Herdt (ed.) *Third Sex, Third Gender*, New York: Zone Books.

Meigs, Anna (1990) 'Multiple Gender Ideologies and Statuses', in Peggy Reeves Sanday & Ruth Gallagher Goodenough (eds.) *Beyond the Second Sex*, Philadelphia: University of Pennsylvania Press.

Morris, C. Rosalind (1994) 'Three Sexes and Four Sexualities: Redressing the Discourses on Gender and Sexuality in Contemporary Thailand', *Positions*, 2(1): 15-43.

Mundy, Rodney (1848) *Narrative of Events in Borneo and Celebes, Down to the Occupation of Labuan: from the Journals of James Brooke, Esq. Rajah of Sarawak, and Governor of Labuan. Together With a Narrative of the Operations of H.M.S. Iris*, London: John Murray, second edition.

Murray, Stephen O. (1992) 'Profession-defined Homosexuality: Introduction', in Stephen O. Murray (ed.) *Oceanic Homosexualities*, New York: Garland.

Nanda, Serena (1990) *Neither Man nor Woman: The Hijras of India*, Belmont: Wadsworth Publishing Co.

O'Flaherty, Wendy (1980) *Women, Androgynes, and Other Mythical Beasts*, Chicago: University of Chicago Press.

Pelras, Christian (1996) *The Bugis*, Oxford: Blackwell.

Raja, Chulan Ibni Hamid (1968 [1919]) *Misa Melayu/oleh Raja Chulan*, Kuala Lumpur: Pustaka Antara.

Roscoe, Will (1991) *The Zuni Man-Woman*, Albuquerque: University of New Mexico Press.

Roth, Henry Ling (1896) *The Natives of Sarawak and British North Borneo*, London: Truslove and Hanson.

Schärer, Hans (1963) *Ngaju Religion: The Conception of God among a South Borneo People*, The Hague: Martinus Nijhoff.

Skinner, Cyril (1963) (ed.) *Sja'ir Perang Mengkasar* (The Rhymed Chronicle of the Makassar War), The Hague: Martinus Nijhoff.

Sutlive, H. Vinson Jr. (1992) 'The Iban Manang in the Sibu District of the Third Division of Sarawak: An Alternative Route to Normality', in Stephen O. Murray (ed.) *Oceanic Homosexualities*, New York: Garland.

Trumbach, Randolph (1994) 'London Sapphists: From Three Sexes to Four Genders in the Making of Modern Culture', in Gilbert Herdt (ed.) *Third Sex, Third Gender*, New York: Zone Books.

Whitehead, Harriet (1981) 'The Bow and the Burden Strap: A New Look at Institutionalized Homosexuality in Native North America', in B. Sherry Ortner & Harriet Whitehead (eds.) *Sexual* Meanings: *The Cultural Construction of Gender and Sexuality*, Cambridge: Cambridge University Press.

Wikam, Unni (1977) 'Man becomes Woman: Transsexualism in Oman as a Key to Gender Roles', *Man*, 12(2): 304-319.

Wilkinson, Richard James (1959) *A Malay-English Dictionary*, London: Macmillan.

Williams, L. Walter (1986) *The Spirit and the Flesh: Sexual Diversity in American Indian Culture*, Boston: Beacon Press.

Winstedt, Richard Olaf (1938) 'The Malay Annals of Sejarah Malayu', *Journal of the Malayan Branch of the Royal Asiatic Society*, 16(3): 1-226.

Zainal Abidin, bin Farid (1983) *Persepsi Orang Bugis, Makasar tentang Hukum, Negara dan Dunia Luar*, Bandung: Penerbit Alumni.

CHAPTER III

How Globalization and the Neoliberal Turn Are Shaping Gender Relations in Hanoi

Sarah MURRU

1. Introduction

Without any doubt, a good way to grasp gender relations in Vietnam today is by analyzing the meaning assigned to the couple. Looking at the meaning the Vietnamese State has gradually given to couples informs us about its vaster plan for governing society. This is particularly the case since its economic renovation of 1986, called *Doi Moi*, which was designed to open the country to the international market-based economy and the circulation of capital. Thus, the heterosexual couple has for long been a useful tool in implementing policies. However, the shift in civilians' consumer practices – encouraged by the State – has unexpectedly weakened this figure and led to an increase in divorces and single mothers choosing to raise their children alone. In this chapter, I shall focus on the effects of the Vietnamese State's opening to globalization, with a turn to neoliberalism, on gender relations in general, on the Vietnamese couple in particular, and on the subsequent phenomenon of the increase of 'Single Moms'.

My findings are derived from two field trips in the province of Hanoi, in 2014 and 2015, to understand Single Moms' motivations to depart from the traditional institution of the family and grasp their resistances in this context[1]. In the spirit of feminist methodologies of research, the aim was to develop a study grounded in their experience of subordination and reflecting their multiple identities as women, mothers, and outcasts of Vietnamese society. Using mixed methods – interviews, participant observation, focus groups, documents – my findings are the result of encounters with various married women, members of NGOs working on gender issues, government organizations in charge of gender and the family, and the exchange with 43 Single Moms (both urban and rural).

The term 'Single Moms' is the one used by these women to define themselves and refers to mothers who are raising their child/children without living with the father – whether this situation is due to a divorce, an

---

1   For a detailed account and analysis of Single Mom's resistance in Hanoi, see my Ph.D. dissertation (Murru 2016).

unwanted pregnancy out of wedlock, or a desired and deliberate choice to get pregnant and raise the child alone[2]. As it will be highlighted, these women all have in common a will to get out of multiple subordinations that are ascribed to them when inside a marriage and its larger ties to the extended family – a situation that the country's new social organization has made possible.

To fully understand these changes and how they inform us on wider gender relations in today's Vietnamese society, I shall first present how the Vietnamese couple has historically been at the center of the State's preoccupation. This will give way to an outline of *Doi Moi*'s influence on gender, on the Vietnamese couple – with the evolution of sexual behaviors of men and women – and on the advent of the figure of the Single Mom.

2. The Vietnamese Couple, a Useful Tool

The couple in Vietnam is to be understood as a functional entity, dependent on the larger family kin. Tradition holds that when a couple gets married, it moves into the husband's parents' house. Therefore, couples have long been useful to families, who relied on marriage's unification to form alliances with other valued families – for prestige, political influence, or economic prosperity.

In this configuration, the members of a couple have very different roles. Families rely greatly on men, because the duty of guarantying the proper care and worship of ancestors belongs to them. Indeed:

'... [a] child was in debt to his parents for giving him life, housing, clothing, and food. Although this debt could never be repaid (for a child benefited not only from what parents provided, but also from the accumulation of merit by one's ancestors), it was his moral obligation to observe filial piety by taking care of his parents in their old age, worshiping them when they were dead, looking after their graves, and producing a son to carry on the ancestral line.' (Phinney, 2003, p. 185)

Therefore, great pressure lies on women to give birth to a son and ensure the continuity of the lineage. Boys are thus usually favored and prioritized in terms of access to education (especially higher education), and other expenses.

On the other hand, girls are raised to become proper wives. A popular saying depicts daughters as 'ducks' that will 'fly away' from the nest to join

---

2   Harriet Phinney (2008) studied the specific case of older women 'asking for a child'. This implied they were considered too old to marry but dearly desired to have a child. Therefore, many of them went on to ask a man to impregnate them "no strings attached", guarantying secrecy of the progenitor. For further information on this specific kind of Single Mom, see Phinney (2003).

another family. Therefore, girls are perceived as costing money, since they will one day leave and participate in the economy of another family. A boy, conversely, will bring a daughter-in-law when he marries, granting him an added economic value (Bélanger 2000, Hirshman & Vu, 1996). As a couple marries, their income serves the expenses of the extended household with whom they live. The parents can then 'retire' and take care of their grandchildren while the new parents are at work. Furthermore, tradition holds that, once married, a girl takes on the household work load so her mother-in-law can rest (since she used to be in charge before the arrival of the daughter-in-law). The relationship between these two women has traditionally been marked by submission and deference, as the mother-in-law, previously subordinated, now has a sense of power over her daughter-in-law (Werner 2009).

Apart from being a strategic element in family alliances, the Vietnamese couple has also been useful to the State in order to govern its population in the proper direction. There has, indeed, been a tradition of influencing the formation of couples to fit larger political interests. On this matter, Harriet Phinney (2008b; 2003) carried out amazing work analyzing the evolution of the discourse of love throughout key times in Vietnamese history, further highlighting the instrumentalization of such discourse. She shows how the notion of love at one time was a sentiment, influenced by Confucian values, that was not necessary to engage in marriage and that was said to grow with time and through mutual servitude. Later, the notion of romantic love inherited by the French culture was introduced during the Colonization. The colonial administration was looking for ways to depart from the Confucian model, which was viewed as feudal and reactionary. To do so, it had to diminish the power/weight of the traditional family, considered to be a pillar embodying Confucian values. Thus, worshiping romantic love, through poetry and other forms of art, had the effect of drastically changing the motives behind the formation of couples and the nature of the choice to marry. Later, during the Revolution to free the country from colonialism, the discourse shifted to focus on love of the country in order to encourage commitment and devotion in fighting for the nation. Young civilians were encouraged to postpone love and marriage for the greater purpose of serving the country. With the advent of the socialist State, love then becomes an object to be governed, as the State needed the families' commitment to its project and participation in the land reform, collectivization of labor, and abandonment of private property. Then begins the State's regulation of the formation of couples through laws on marriage and the family[3].

These laws promote a free and progressive marital system. The underlying objective is to make the individual responsible to the State, not to

---

3   See the 1959 *Law on Marriage and the Family* and the subsequent reforms in 1986, and 2000.

90

the family or extended kin. Therefore, in the first Law on Marriage and the Family of 1959, equality between men and women was inscribed. Furthermore, women were encouraged to work outside the household because the State needed the participation of the biggest number of citizens to rebuild the country after war.

The formation of couples has thus been at the center of the State's preoccupation to guarantee the success of its various projects. This becomes even more so with the advent of *Doi Moi*, as will be further emphasized in the next section.

3. *Doi Moi*'s Influence…

In 1986, recognizing the failure of its planned economic policies and aspiring to become competitive on the international scene, the Socialist Republic of Vietnam took a major turn in its economic policy, opening up to the global market economy. This transformation is called *Doi Moi*, which means 'renovation' and signifies the new plan for a 'socialist market economy' (An & De Tréglodé, 2008). This entailed the abandonment of central planning and collectivization of land – returning land ownership to individual peasant households –, and an opening to the private sector. Furthermore, under strict pressure to follow the International Monetary Fund's 'structural adjustment' program, most of the State factories were downsized and closed to promote private enterprise.

Doi Moi has had the effect of widening employment opportunities. Other social effects appeared. Hanoi resident's standards of living doubled since 1986. There was a parallel increase in private leisure services and consumer items, such as motorized vehicles, smart phones, foreign films, and an opening in the access to the internet, literature and international media. Consequently, this also strengthened social stratification with the creation of a highly visible urban moneyed class (Bélanger et al., 2012). The country was transformed on many levels. In big cities, Western style stores and malls opened. In Hanoi, you can find modern coffee shops nearly at every corner. Where modesty used to be a respected value, one is now defined by his wealth and possessions. Finally, *Doi Moi* drastically marked the younger generation born after 1986, which has only known this modern lifestyle. This has created huge generational gaps with older generations who lived through wars and communism.

3.1 ... on gender

With the establishment of the Socialist Party and Government, strong efforts were made to develop a body of laws and institutions promoting gender equality. Based on statistics, the international community has congratulated the country's records of low maternal mortality, and high adult female literacy and participation in the labor force. Moreover, the State created institutions in charge of gender issues, such as the Vietnamese Women's Union (VWU), 'one of the oldest and largest national organizations of women in the world' (Schuler et al., 2007: p. 384), and the Institute for Family and Gender Studies (IFGS), formerly the Center for Women Studies. However, many studies highlight that there is a real gap between the egalitarian legal base and the reality of persistent gender inequalities in the Vietnamese society. Authorities and the institutions that depend on them, like the VWU, are in part responsible for this, as they paradoxically still hold onto and promote conservative views about gender roles.

Indeed, since the State's project highly depended on motherhood, it developed an essentialist definition of what it means to be a woman, linking it to her 'natural destiny' of becoming a mother. This essentializing discourse can be found everywhere, in the body of the law, as well as in the communications of institutions devoted to women and the scientific studies they conduct (Drummond 2006; Werner 2004; Barry 1996). As a matter of fact, in the 1986 Law on Marriage and the Family, Chapter I, Article 3, it is stipulated that: '[t]he state and society shall protect the mothers as well as their children, and shall assist the mothers in fulfilling their *noble tasks of motherhood*' (Nguyen 1993, emphasis added). Furthermore, in the revision of the law of 2000, Chapter 6, Article 2 maintains that: '[t]he State, society and the family shall be responsible for protecting women and children rights, and assist mothers in *fulfilling well their lofty motherhood functions*' (Nguyen et al., 2002: p. 28, emphasis added). Therefore, women are given special social and legal status through childbearing, as a commentary on the 1986 Law further develops:

'The issue of reproducing oneself and [humankind] through the means of bearing children gives women an elevated position as mother in the family and society. Bearing children in order to reproduce for the family simultaneously reproduces the existence of the race, the nation, develops society and the population. This matter requires that we must protect mothers and create excellent conditions so that each mother is able to fully realize the function of bearing children and of raising their children. Children are simultaneously children of mothers and fathers, as they are the country's young generation. ... We must protect children, improving the wholesome development of their constitution, intelligence, ethics and morals in order that they become the next generation to continue the work of the previous generation. ... Therefore, there is a need to put forward in the Law on Marriage and the Family principles protecting mothers and children.'

(Nguyen 1993: pp. 31-32)

The State and its institutions thus defined 'female nature' in terms of the ability to give birth. Their femaleness is thus located in their bodies (Rofel 1999: p. 246). The VWU is a great governmental agent in this process as it has the duty to:

'... educate mothers to realize their great responsibilities in the ideological and cultural revolution and in the formation of future generations, show them how to bring up children according to scientific methods, and encourage them to set good examples to their children in the family and society.'

(Vietnam Women's Union and Center for Women's Studies 1989: p. 175).

The VWU claims motherhood as Vietnamese women's principal defining characteristic. In this perspective, reproduction is no longer a private matter, but becomes a public matter of State concern: '[o]nce she reproduces she becomes a topic of concern, of anxiety; she becomes someone to be educated' (Phinney 2003: p. 252).

Alongside the VWU, the IFGS was established in 1985 to conduct research on emerging issues in the fields of family and gender in Vietnam. The main objective was to provide the Government with scientific data to help in its legislation and policy-making process. The IFGS is thus a reliable consultant of the Vietnamese State. Further studies on motherhood also stress the importance of 'socializing' girls so they will become good wives and mothers. This education toward motherhood promotes many beliefs and sayings about woman nature: 'women who have had children are thought to be more beautiful, complete, and feminine than childless women. (...) Biological children, particularly sons, give women power, status, and prestige' (Bélanger 2004: p. 108).

This continues to strongly tie women to the sphere of the household. Furthermore, women are considered as the guardians of a family's harmony and are therefore expected to be deferent, loyal servants who will be able to safeguard peaceful relations among family members. When things go wrong, the wife is blamed for lacking the skills to maintain harmony (Nguyen 2015). There is thus a 'gender norm that makes many women feel they cannot fulfill their responsibilities as a mother or a socially acceptable person if they do something to disrupt the image of the happy family' (Vu et al., 2014: p. 638).

In the end, a woman's value in today's Vietnamese society still highly depends on her ability to be a mother; whether it means to give birth to a boy to ensure family lineage, or to raise proper Vietnamese citizens to serve the State's projects. Women are expected to be subordinate and obedient in many ways. We thus observe a type of syncretism between the socialist "progressive" model that has imprinted the legislation, and the persistence of traditional Confucian values that influence the implementation of these measures (Werner & Bélanger, 2002).

3.2 ... *on couples*

After a decade of collectivization, the State had to instill among its citizens the desire to consume. Therefore, it turned once again to the couple, which was viewed as a potential consumer unit that would serve the political-economic goal of integration into the market economy. To educate its citizens about consumer practices, the State built a huge campaign on family planning: the 'Happy Family' Campaign (HFC). Launched in the late 80s, it is a culminating effort by the Vietnamese State to immerse itself in private and family matters in order to govern them towards its own objectives. Therefore, as the decades went by, and the State's projects evolved, so did its redefining of the couple, family, love, and motherhood (Barbieri & Bélanger, 2009). In the late 1980s, the State created a new organization that was designed to focus specifically on population and family planning: The National Committee for Population and Family Planning. Its main mission was to promote the idea of a 'Happy Family' through large scale propaganda (Murru 2017). The HFC thus entails 'an intensified focus on the population as the means for producing a modern Vietnamese citizenry' (Phinney 2005: p. 219).

Therefore, throughout the cities, family planning billboards and posters flourished, depicting the 'Happy Family' composed of a father, mother, boy and girl, all well-dressed. Indeed, 'the 'Happy Family' was orderly and had an adequate income, stable conjugal relations, and two children whose parents were educating them properly' (Phinney 2003: pp. 125-126). On some of the billboards, the slogan read 'stable population, wealthy country, happy family' (Phinney 2005: p. 220). Family planning communication linked family size with family finances, happiness, prosperity, and national wealth (Gammeltoft 2001). Thus, *Doi Moi* policies reinforced dependence on the family, where motherhood is central, in three ways:

'First, they make individuals dependent on the marital unit for survival in the new marked economy, which renders economic stability the benchmark of a successful marriage. ... Second, they encourage a gendered division of marital labor, which reinforces patriarchal norms that promote male homosociability. ... the underlying criteria for the Vietnamese happy family policy is determined by the success of the marital project itself, a project ... described in terms of social reproduction and economic stability, not individual or couple satisfaction.'

(Phinney 2008a: p. 654)

What the State did not plan was that this incitement to achieve a respectable social status and consumer abilities would have effects on men and women's consumption of sexual relations as well, further weakening the solidity of the couple the State relied on.

3.2.1 Enjoying new capitalist goods: sexuality and women as merchandise

As I was dialoguing with Single Moms and married women in Hanoi, a recurring subject concerned men indulging in 'social evils'. Generally, the issue they faced was with a (ex)husband spending all his money and time after work on drinking, gambling, and the company of other women. Women talked about this as being 'a new trend' - implying this has not always been the case (Rydstrøm 2006).

Generally speaking, men and women are depicted as having different sexual needs. For men, sexuality is understood as a means by which they demonstrate virility. On the contrary, women are said to demonstrate love and devotion to their husbands by engaging in sexual intercourse. Line Gammeltoft (1999: p. 181) observes that:

'… it is widely recognized that men like 'something different' (*cua la*) and that men – in contrast to women – cannot control their sexual urges when they are away from their wives … While women are said to be able to live without it easily, sex is usually considered to be a necessity for men.'

As it is also depicted in a popular proverb, comparing men to sticks and women to sand: 'Men go from place to place poking holes in the sand, leaving a trace behind them but forgetting where they have been' (Werner & Bélanger, 2002: p. 22).

Even though society's view of love evolved, as outlined above, and couples gradually advocated for free love between men and women, infidelity in marriage, nevertheless, used to be very severely condemned (Hong 1998). The fact that it is now generally 'accepted' for men to have an active sexual life outside of his conjugal house is new. Men and women did, of course, engage in extramarital sexual relations prior to *Doi Moi*. But what has fundamentally changed is an increase in opportunities to do so. Further analyzing women's concerns, I discovered that it was the result of a larger plan to commercialize sexual practices.

As Lisa Drummond (2000: p. 9) emphasizes:

'*Doi Moi* has made possible and encouraged the commercialization of leisure space and the commodification of leisure itself. Leisure is now consumption, direct or indirect, where previously conspicuous or even moderate consumption of leisure was frowned upon and discouraged.'

If spaces where a couple could meet were formerly rare, private spaces to be alone and where anonymity is assured are now widespread – be it in night clubs, dance halls, karaoke's or cafes, but also in barbershops, hairdressers, or massage parlors. If one wishes, and has the means to pay for it, a couple can be escorted to a private room upstairs or behind the front desk to enjoy intimacy (Duong 2001; Hong 1998).

Thus, *Doi Moi* has had the effect of changing sex into a consumable good. Women, in this configuration, are a merchandize to be purchased. Sex has become a pleasure available for anyone with the sufficient income to afford for it (Huong 2010). As it was highlighted by one of my interviewees, the compulsion to regularly replace the old with the new is attached to consumerism:

'I don't believe in Vietnamese men, they don't respect the marriage and the wife. For them, having an affair is just like hanging around, it's not serious. In general, they want to have new things [implied here is women], they are always looking for new things, when they get used to something, they feel poor so they want to have new things.'

(Hong, 30.01.2015)

Together with the information collected during my fieldwork, many recent studies also attest to an increase in extra-marital sexual relations and the general image of it as being a casual pleasure like any other leisure (Jacka 2010; Ghuman et al., 2006; Rydstrøm 2006; Gammeltoft 2002; Duong 2001). However, as Harriet Phinney demonstrated in a study on the proliferation of HIV/AIDS in the country, this has to be understood within the shifting economical context of Vietnam:

'We must do so by recognizing that men's extramarital relations are not simply the product of individual decision making or moral failings. They are a gendered part of social organization and, in the case of Vietnam, the unintended effect of state policies … First, the global market economy has led to the commercialization and sexualization of men's leisure in Hanoi. Compared with past generations, men today are more likely to spend their leisure time and disposable income at establishments that use women to attract customers. Second, the market economy has produced a new male identity that links consumption to sexual activity. Third, Hanoians have more time and money than they did before *Doi Moi*, which enables them to consume the goods marketed to them.'

(Phinney 2008a: pp. 650-653)

Furthermore, if before the 1980s, people's preoccupations were mainly turned towards surviving in a difficult economic context and assuring enough food was set on the table, now various factors unite to change the meaning of sexuality. Phinney (2008a: p. 652) mentions that:

'*Doi Moi* has instigated an iterative process among a global market economy that produces men's desire for women outside the home (and supplies these women), facilitates a notion of masculinity tied to commercialized and sexualized leisure (ensuring the demand for sex workers), and generates the means to purchase these sexual *commodities*.'

In addition, these sexual services, compared to other social goods, are considered cheap and thus affordable by a large part of the society.

This phenomenon has also been encouraged by the business sector that has set a new frame for contracting deals. With the purpose of encouraging and facilitating economic transactions, it has become a tradition to celebrate contracts by going out for food and drinks and treating clients with the services of sex workers. As a result, a lot of the consumption of sexual relations today happens in the context of socialization between groups of men. This has sometimes had the effect of pressuring a sense of virility among a group, such that if a man refuses to participate in sexual pleasures offered to him, he is viewed as weak and shameful by others (Phinney 2008a; Hong 1998). Why does this consumption of leisure only concern men? It is because of the strong roles as educators and guardians of the family harmony that are conferred on women, keeping them in the household outside of work and diminishing their free time and opportunities to engage in other activities.

The aim here is not to demonize the image of the Vietnamese man, since this trend was mentioned by unhappy married women and Single Moms. However, it points to an aspect of the "modern Vietnamese masculinity", where status and virility are measured in one's capacity to earn money and spend it on social goods, sexuality being one of them.

3.2.2 Women's sexuality and abortion

Female virginity before marriage and women's sexual fidelity to their husbands represent strong Confucian values that have guided morality for ages. A failure to respect this used to be severely punished. Indeed, as summarized by Bélanger & Hong (1999: p. 80):

'… [before] socialism, an unmarried pregnant woman had her nape shaved and smeared with lime and was publicly insulted. Some were even killed, and others committed suicide. The repercussions were also important for the women's family. In some villages, her parents had to pay a fine and her father could be denied his right to attend meetings in the village communal house.'

Today, as for many aspects in Vietnam's society, things have changed (Leshkowich 2012). Female virginity before marriage is still considered a strong value, but it is not as strictly observed. The view society holds about female sexuality is still imprinted with traditional considerations. Generally understood, married women are rarely portrayed as desiring or even enjoying sex, but are instead viewed as passive victims to male desires. They engage in it mainly for the purpose of having children (Jacka 2010; Ghuman et al., 2006; Hong 1998). Young women, on the other hand, are said to engage in sexual intercourse, mainly to show their boyfriend that he is truly loved. As Bélanger & Hong (1999: pp. 75-76) outline in their study:

'… a desire to express personal feelings of love and commitment motivated first sexual intercourse for them. Many of them had had sexual relations with subsequent boyfriends as well, further suggesting that not all women wait for marriage plans to have premarital sexual relations. … For these women, having sex was not only because of closeness but also a way to strengthen the existing bond. By having sexual relations, they felt their boyfriends would love them more, would feel more committed to them, and would be more likely to marry them.'

Thus, we can see that women's sexual behavior has shifted as well, but for different reasons than men. Throughout my research, I have not found any study or account that reported women engaging in sexual relations to satisfy their own needs or by pleasure. However, this also remains a strong taboo, which probably makes it difficult to account for in research.

Alongside this opening towards premarital sex, is the shifting behavior of young girls towards consumer goods as well. As it was explained to me by one of my informants:

'For younger girls, I think it's worse because they only care about money, house, and material things. They don't really care about themselves. They even say that love and the romantic things belong to the old people. Now if you love a girl, you have to give her an iphone, ipad, things like that.'

(Ha, 26.01.2015)

It seems that sex has become, among other things, a means for young girls to get access to consumer goods they cannot afford or, in some cases, to simply earn money in order to afford a modern lifestyle. In particular, this is depicted about students who do not earn a salary to satisfy their cravings for modern goods and services:

'Some of my friends that have other girls outside, almost all are students because they want the material, they are still young and don't have the money. And also, the parents don't allow them to have money or a boyfriend. So they don't really know about love and they don't really care about it. It's very easy for a man of my age [34] to buy sex from a student. I have a friend, he even has four students. He showed me their pictures on his phone. He says that to have a woman of my age is very hard because they need a lot of money, because they already have some, so they need more. But a student, she has nothing, so she is happy with small things.'

(Ha, 26.01.2015)

In addition, it seems that married women are not immune to having extra-conjugal relations as well. Apart from one study mentioning it (Vu 2010), I have not found any other written account of it. However, throughout my discussions with married women, some talked about 'their friend' or 'their colleague' who was married but also had a boyfriend. Although it is uncertain if they were using this 'other' person to talk about themselves or not, it nevertheless shows that, while remaining very taboo, it is something occurring and talked about in Vietnamese society today.

Nonetheless, due to very poor sex education, these new sexual behaviors among young Vietnamese women have a huge impact on the increase of abortions. Abortion is legal since 1954. But since the 1990s, Vietnam has maintained one of the highest rates of abortions among developing/emerging countries (Huong 2010; Bélanger & Hong, 1999; Bélanger 1997). Although they do not wish to get pregnant, studies have highlighted that few women engaging in sexual relations use contraceptive methods – or they use them incorrectly or inconsistently. Generally, there is a belief that contraceptives are for married couples who do not wish to have more children than they already do (Nguyen et al., 2002; Bélanger & Hong, 1999).

In addition, abortion services in Vietnam are widely available and affordable (especially in big cities). Bélanger and Hong's study has highlighted that, even in medical centers, communication on contraception and sex education is very poor. They were surprised to find out that, throughout their informants, 25% had had several abortions, meaning that their knowledge on how to avoid pregnancy had not improved, and they continued to have unprotected sexual relations. In their opinion, it is because abortion offers a lot of privacy (women do not need authorizations and little information is required of them – it is easy to lie). In comparison, the act of buying contraceptives at a pharmacy is visible and breaks the secrecy of one's active sexual life. Abortion has become, in the mind of some young women, a means of contraception. Therefore, it does not really matter if they get pregnant because they can always get an abortion (Gallo & Nghia, 2007; Bélanger & Hong, 1999; Johansson et al., 1998).

In the end, *Doi Moi* and the propaganda exercised by the State to create a consumer society on its territory have had unpredicted effects on sexual behaviors, further weakening 'the couple' that the State so dearly relied on. One unintended effect, which is analyzed in the next section, is the increase of Single Moms.

3.3 ... on the increase of Single Moms

In this context of evolving dynamics between men and women, influenced by a changing Vietnamese society encouraging consumption, another actor is increasingly taking space in this society: The Single Mom. Women are increasingly questioning and rejecting their appointed place inside the family structure for many reasons (Murru 2016).

First, with changes in society come huge generational gaps. Nowadays, girls are brought up with more freedom and social liberties. What is most expected from them is that they obtain great results throughout their education and maintain proper behavior. Since education takes up more time than before and is considered the priority, daughters devote less time than they used to on household chores like cleaning and cooking (Ngan Binh 2004).

However, mothers-in-law expect their daughters-in-law to conform to a traditional familial organization. That is to say, since roles in the family are assigned by age and gender, having her son get married and bring in a daughter-in-law, usually means that the mother-in-law will now be able to relax and enjoy the fact that the daughter-in-law will take over looking after the household – her younger age implying she must serve her older mother-in-law (Drummond 2006; Knodel et al., 2004). When the couple has children, the mother-in-law then takes care of them (especially if the wife has a job outside of the house). But it is the daughter-in-law's responsibility to attend to the household chores, whether or not this wife has a full-time employment. These include everything from cooking and cleaning, to buying food, doing laundry, and managing the household budget. In addition, it also includes taking care of her in-laws in whatever service they might need (and possibly her husband's brother or sister still living with them) (Werner 2004).

Therefore, when young girls enter marriage nowadays, they are faced with a radically different lifestyle than the one they had been used to while living with their parents. Some girls have never had to cook and thus do not master the basic skills that are expected of them. This can cause the mother-in-law to complain and criticize her harshly (Bélanger & Pendakis, 2010; Werner & Bélanger, 2002; Barry 1996). Some women I spoke with mentioned that a severe conflict arose when they asked to hire a maid, as the mother-in-law judged that it was the daughter-in-law's responsibility to take care of these matters and was shocked that this option was even considered. Generally, throughout my encounters, conflict with the mother-in-law appeared to be one of the major problems for previously married Single Moms, as well as for those who had never married, stating that this was a complicated configuration and duty they did not wish to participate in, or were happy they never had to.

Second, another difference in behavior observed before and after marriage is between the members of the couple. On the one hand, girls try to show off their best features to attract the best suitable mate. They pay strong attention to having perfect looks, a perfect behavior, and showing that they have obtained a great education. The characteristics of a desirable spouse are: 'sibling order; family social and economic situation; level of education; type of employment; personal demeanor, skills, talents and general character; parental permission; and (…) beauty' (Phinney 2003: p. 60). On the other hand, boys need to demonstrate their high interest in the girl to convince her and her family that he is the best candidate for her. This is done by demonstrating romanticism and paying for outings and gifts.

However, it seems that all of these efforts diminish or disappear once the couple gets married. The husband does not feel obliged to win the heart of his girlfriend and her family anymore, and does not pay attention to his wife's needs as much. The wife is said to be so busy with children and taking care of the extended family that she does not take care of her looks as much in order to please her husband (Nguyen 1998, 2009). As one of my informants stated:

'In Vietnam, we always say that love is something very good but marriage destroys the love. When you are in love, you show off. Women have to be good and have a high price.

The men need to do many things to "get the woman". So the women have to be very beautiful, very clever, very perfect to show the man they are of value. That's why men in love always try very hard to buy the girl [laughing], the man is the buyer. But after marriage, he shows the real him. Almost all Vietnamese women don't have a really good time after marriage.'

(Ha, 26.01.2015)

With the fact that, in today's Vietnamese society, most women have a full-time job outside the house, getting married means they get a double load of work, which limits their opportunities to have any other activities (Nguyen 2009; 1998). For many women, 'marriage, regardless of the fact she loved her husband and had wanted to marry, had reduced her mobility in life, took her away from her friends' (Phinney 2003: p. 79).

Third, men's behavior which was described in the previous section strongly impacts women's unhappiness and conflict in marriage. In a context where extra-marital relationships are increasing, and have become common, women are expected to relinquish fighting against their husband's mischiefs for the sake of protecting family image (Vu 2008). Conflict is never well perceived. 'Normally, men are the pillars of the house. You know, in Vietnamese house the pillar is very necessary to hold the building. But right now the men in the house are acting like a bonsai' (Le, 09.02.2015). This ambivalent situation, where women are constrained to duties they were not used to perform, dealing with generational conflicts with the in-laws, and a husband's behavior they despise, yet are not allowed the space to protest or voice discontent, is encouraging more and more women to divorce.

Indeed, divorce has been increasing gradually, mainly under the impulse of women (Phinney 2003). Motivations to divorce are usually to be found in family conflict, but also due to a high rate of domestic violence (Larsson 2014; Rydstrøm 2003b). However, along with the fact that divorce is highly discouraged in society and by family members, it is also a very long and tedious process. For example, before the paperwork for divorce will even begin, the procedure involves a process of 'reconciliation' where a couple must meet three times with a 'reconciliation committee'. The procedure to file for a divorce is therefore, in and of itself, designed to discourage it. Studies indeed show that many preliminary demands for divorce do not come to conclusion (Vu et al., 2014). Nevertheless, despite these obstacles, divorce rates are increasing, which signals that there is a high and determined demand for terminating marriage unions in Vietnamese society today, however difficult the process might be.

In the end, my study demonstrated that Single Moms are creating a deconstruction of the dominant discourse on motherhood, gender, and happiness. Even if being a Single Mom is harshly stigmatized and criticized, the reality of the quality of life these women experience surpasses their marginalization. Women testified to having more free time and liberty to

101

decide how they wanted to use it. Being relieved from the duties imposed on a wife and being able to enjoy a bigger part of their income (since they do not have to share or use it for the needs of the extended family), they have more free time and more money to enjoy various leisure activities or social goods they could not previously afford. All of them testified to a great sense of freedom and liberty attached to their condition as Single Moms: *I can make it on my own!* Moreover:

'... [their] initiative to find happiness for themselves is one step towards changing the traditional psychology of women's inferiority complex, their passivity, and their tendency to hide secret feelings and aspirations to a point of taking the initiative to affirm their right to happiness ... From a place of accepting, being shy, timid, and bashful, or maintaining one's virginity and faithfulness... to a place where they display boldness to dare to destroy inferior feelings, to dare to preserve individual happiness.'

(Nguyen 1996: p. 131)

What is even more surprising is that they are increasingly empowering themselves as a community. They have created a great number of Facebook pages and forums on the internet to exchange about their situation and to give advice to each other[4]. This has led to creating 'Single Moms offline events' where they meet face to face and develop friendships. One Single Mom I met created a small business of vocational training. She helped other Single Moms lacking qualifications to learn how to sew and furthermore to get a job. The success of her plan allowed her to open other shelters to welcome Single Moms and their child/children when they temporarily had no place to stay.

In the end, this is an unwanted consequence of the State's plan to develop consumer units. Because men and women have been encouraged to work and increase their purchasing power, women usually have the economic means to support their children alone. This, in turn, as it has been demonstrated, has had the effect of weakening marital unions and discouraging single women to get into this configuration. Therefore, "the couple", that the State and the traditional family so dearly relied on, is becoming less and less relevant in Vietnamese society today.

---

4   This, of course, is mainly the case for urban women having access to the internet. Rural women, on the other side, rarely have access to the internet. However, some groups of rural Single Moms still managed to attract NGOs and expose them to their marginalized situation. For a detailed account of how a group of Single Moms developed into a self-sufficient cooperative (after receiving help and support of an NGO), see my Ph.D. dissertation, Murru (2016).

4. Conclusions

With the opening of the country towards globalization and its neoliberal economic turn, Vietnam's society has been marked by huge transformations. Some of these changes were the effects of a planned campaign orchestrated by the State to encourage families to consume, others were unintended boomerang effects of a shifting individualistic society encouraging a sense of personal wellness. We are thus left, on many levels, with a sort of schizophrenic Vietnamese State. It promotes capitalist economic behaviors while maintaining an authoritarian communist political organization. It enforces a progressive gender agenda while strongly holding onto conservative values.

This chapter was aimed at highlighting these discrepancies and their impact on gender relations. It has been emphasized that the 'couple' has long been the strategic tool used by the State and the institution of the family to fulfill their larger goals of governance and prosperity. However, the advent of *Doi Moi* has given couples more autonomy and incentives outside of family life. The enticement to consume new capitalist goods and services has also rubbed off on sexual behaviors of men and women. It has been shown that the company of sex workers has become an affordable leisure, and extra marital relations have also become a mainstream fun activity outside the home. On the other hand, the essentialist norms of motherhood and multiple subordinations that are ascribed to women inside the traditional family have strengthened inequalities between men and women. In this context, and because women are also attracted to a different, modern, and autonomous lifestyle, they are increasingly departing (or simply refusing) this configuration.

How the State will further address these changes is uncertain. Nevertheless, these findings demonstrate that the country is experiencing an unplanned shift in gender relations with the advent of an increasingly empowered female youth. Single Moms are changing the narrative about family configurations, about the place of women in that sphere and, more generally, about the "appropriate path" a woman should follow in life. Among the next generation of citizens, there will also be an increasing number of children that will have lived with separated parents – or simply with their mother – who will probably have internalized alternative discourses on the family. In the end, it is undeniable that the monitored opening towards globalization by the Vietnamese State has had the effect of drastically transforming gender relations in the country.

Acknowledgments

This chapter is derived from a section of my Ph.D. dissertation: Sarah Murru (2016) *Single Moms in Vietnam: An Approach in Resistance Studies*, Université Libre de Bruxelles. This study was made possible thanks to generous funding from the Belgian National Fund for Research – Fonds National de la Recherche Scientifique (FRS-FNRS). In addition, I would like to warmly thank Firouzeh Nahavandi and Roselie Kroeker for their reviews of my work, Dr. Caroline Kroeker Falconi for a very precise proofreading, as well as the editors of this volume for their recommended revisions.

Bibliography

An, Yann Bao & Benoît De Tréglodé, (2008) 'Moi et Mutations du Politique', in Stéphane Dorvet & Benoît De Tréglodé (eds.) *Viêt Nam Contemporain*, Paris: Les Indes Savantes, pp. 119-151.

Barbieri, Magali & Danièle Bélanger (2009) *Reconfiguring Families in Contemporary Vietnam*, Stanford: Stanford University Press.

Barry, Kathleen (1996) 'Introduction', in Kathleen Barry (ed.) *Vietnam's Women in Transition*, London: Macmillan Press Ltd, pp. 1-18.

Bélanger, Danièle, Lisa B.W. Drummond & Van Nguyen-Marshall (2012) 'Introduction: Who Are the Urban Middle Class in Vietnam?', in Van Nguyen-Marshall et al. (eds.) *The Reinvention of Distinction: Modernity and the Middle Class in Urban Vietnam*, Singapore: Asian Research Institute, pp. 1-20.

Bélanger, Danièle & Katherine Pendakis (2010) 'Vietnamese Daughters in Transition: Factory Work and Family Relations', *The Asia-Pacific Journal: Japan Focus*.

Bélanger, Danièle (2004) 'Single and Childless Women of Vietnam: Contesting and Negotiating Female Identity?', in Lisa Drummond & Helle Rydstrøm (eds.) *Gender Practices in Contemporary Vietnam*, Singapore: Singapore University Press, pp. 96-116.

Bélanger, Danièle (2000) 'Regional Differences in Household Composition and Family Formation Patterns in Vietnam', *Journal of Comparative Family Studies*, 31(2): 171-189.

Bélanger, Danièle & Khuat Thu Hong (1999) 'Single Women's Experiences of Sexual Relationships and Abortion in Hanoi, Vietnam', *Reproductive Health Matters*, 7: 72-82.

Bélanger, Danièle (1997) 'Modes de Cohabitation et Liens Intergénérationnels au Vietnam', *Cahier Québécois de Démographie*, 26(2): 215-245.

Drummond, Lisa (2006) 'Gender in Post-DoiMoi Vietnam: Women, Desire, and Change', *Gender, Place and Culture: A Journal of Feminist Geography*, 13(3): 247-250.

Drummond, Lisa (2000) 'Street Scenes: Practices of Public and Private Space in Urban Vietnam', *Urban Studies*, 37(12): 2377-2391.

Duong, Le Bac (2001) *Sexuality Research in Vietnam: A Review of Literature*, Hanoi: Ford Foundation.

Gallo, F. Maria & C. Nguyen Nghia (2007) 'Real Life Is Different: A qualitative Study of Why Women Delay Abortion until the Second Trimester in Vietnam', *Social Science and Medicine*, 64(9): 1812-1822.

Gammeltoft, Tine (2002) 'The Irony of Sexual Agency: Premarital Sex in Urban Northern Viet Nam', in Jane S. Werner & Danièle Bélanger (eds.) *Gender, Household, State: DoiMoi in Viet Nam*, Ithaca: Southeast Asia Program Publications, pp. 111-128.

Gammeltoft, Tine (2001) 'Faithful, Heroic, Resourceful: Changing Images of Women in Vietnam', in John Kleinen (ed.) *Vietnamese Society in Transition: The Daily Politics of Reform and Change*, Amsterdam: Het Spinhuis, pp. 265-280.

Gammeltoft, Tine (1999) *Women's Bodies, Women's Worries: Health and Family Planning in a Vietnamese Rural Community*, Surrey: Nias and Curzon Press.

Ghuman, Sharon, Manh Loi Vu, Tuan Huy Vu & John Knodel (2006) 'Continuity and Change in Premarital Sex in Vietnam', *International Family Planning Perspectives*, 32(4): 166-174.

Hirshman, Charles & Manh Loi Vu (1996) 'Family and Household Structure in Vietnam: Some Glimpses from a Recent Survey', *Pacific Affairs*, 69(2): 229-249.

Huong, Bui Thu (2010) 'Let's Talk About Sex, Baby: Sexual Communication in Marriage in Contemporary Vietnam', *Culture, Health, and Sexuality: An International Journal for Research, Intervention and Care*, 12(1): S19-S29.

Huong, Pham Quynh (2010) 'Parent Children Communication towards Sexual Relationship of Youths in Hanoi', *Vietnam Journal of Family and Gender Studies*, 5: 52-70.

Jacka, Tamara (2010) 'Gender, the Family, Sexuality, and Governance: Vietnam and China', *Critical Asian Studies*, 42(2): 311-322.

Johansson, Annika, Thu Nga Nguyen, Huy Tran Quang, Du Dat Doan & Kristina Holmgren (1998) 'Husband's Involvement in Abortion in Vietnam', *Studies in Family Planning*, 29: 400-413.

Hong, Khuat Thu (1998) 'Study on Sexuality in Vietnam: The Known and the Unknown Issues', *Population Council South and East Asia Regional Working Paper* No. 11, Hanoi.

Knodel, John, Loie Manh Vu, Rukmalie Jayakody, Huy Tuan Vu (2004) 'Gender Roles in the Family: Change and Stability in Vietnam', *Population Studies Center*, 4:1-25.

Larsson, Viveca (2014) *A Suffering Heart: On the Health of Women Living with Violence in Vietnam*, Dissertation, Umea University.

Leshkowich, Ann M. (2012) 'Finances, Family, Fashion, Fitness, and… Freedom? The Changing Lives of Urban Middle-Class Vietnamese Women', in Van Nguyen-Marshall et al. (eds.) *The Reinvention of Distinction: Modernity and the Middle Class in Urban Vietnam*, Singapore: Asian Research Institute, pp. 95-114.

Murru, Sarah (2017) 'La Résistance des Mères Célibataires au Vietnam; ou l'Echec d'un Modèle d'Education à la Maternité', *Education et Sociétés*, 39(1): 69-83.

Murru, Sarah (2016) *Single Moms in Vietnam: An Approach in Resistance Studies*, Ph.D. Dissertation, Université Libre de Bruxelles.

Ngan Binh, Ngo Thi (2004) 'The Confucian Four Feminine Virtues (tu duc): The Old Versus the New – Ke thua Versus Phat huy', in Lisa Drummond & Helle

Rydstrøm (eds.) *Gender Practices in Contemporary Vietnam*, Singapore: Singapore University Press, pp. 26-46.

Nguyen, Huu Minh (2009) *Vietnamese Marriage Patterns in the Red River Delta: Tradition and Change*, Hanoi: Social Sciences Publishing House.

Nguyen, Minh Thang, Thu Huong Vu & Marie-Eve Blanc (2002) 'Sexual Behavior Related to HIV/AIDS: Commercial Sex and Condom Use in Hanoi, Vietnam', *Asia-Pacific Population Journal*, 17(3): 41-52.

Nguyen, The Giai (1993) *The Law on Marriage and the Family: Answer to 120 Questions*, Hanoi: Nha Xuat Ban Chinh Tri Quoc Gia.

Nguyen, Thi Khoa (1996) 'The Real State of Forestry Workers' and Peasants' Families in the Area of Paper-Making in North Vietnam', in Kathleen Barry (ed.) *Vietnam's Women in Transition*, London: Macmillan Press Ltd, pp. 226-236.

Nguyen, Thi Khoa (1993) 'The Single Mother', *Vietnamese Studies*, 3: 44-60.

Nguyen, Thi Quynh Trang (2015) 'The influence of Traditional Beliefs on Vietnamese College Lecturers' Perception of Face', *Journal of Education for Teaching*, 41(2): 203-214.

Phinney, Harriet (2008a) 'Rice Is Essential but Tiresome; You Should Get Some Noodles: DoiMoi and the Political Economy of Men's Extramarital Sexual Relations and Marital HIV Risk in Hanoi, Vietnam', *Farming Heath Matters*, 98(4): 650-660.

Phinney, Harriet (2008b) 'Objects of Affection: Vietnamese Discourses on Love and Emancipation', *Positions: East Asia Cultures Critique*, 16(2): 329-358.

Phinney, Harriet (2005) 'Asking for a Child: The Refashioning of Reproductive Space in Post-War Northern Vietnam', *The Asia Pacific Journal of Anthropology*, 6(3): 215-230.

Phinney, Harriet (2003) *Asking for the Essential Child: Revolutionary Transformations in Reproductive Space in Northern Viet Nam*, Dissertation, University of Washington.

Rydstrøm, Helle (2006) 'Sexual Desires and "Social Evils": Young Women in Rural Vietnam', *Gender, Place and Culture: A Journal of Feminist Geography*, 13: 283-301.

Rydstrøm, Helle (2003a) *Embodying Morality: Growing up in Rural Northern Vietnam*, Honolulu: University of Hawaii Press.

Rydstrøm, Helle (2003b) 'Encountering "Hot" Anger. Domestic Violence in Contemporary Vietnam', *Violence Against Women* 9(3): 676-697.

Schuler, Sidney R. et al. (2007) 'Constructions of Gender in Vietnam: In Pursuit of the 'Three Criteria'', *Culture, Health, and Sexuality: An International Journal for Research Intervetion and Care*, 8(5): 383-394.

Vu, Ha Song et al. (2014) 'Divorce in the Context of Domestic Violence Against Women in Vietnam', *Culture, Health and Sexuality: An International Journal for Research Intervention and Care*, 16(6): 634-647.

Vu Ha, Song (2008) 'The Harmony of Family and the Silence of Women: Sexual Attitudes and Practices among Rural Married Women in Northern Viet Nam', *Culture, Health & Sexuality*, 10(1): S163-S176.

Vu, Hong Phong (2010) 'Reviewing Vietnamese Masculinities', *Vietnam Journal of Family And Gender Studies*, 5(1): 64-78.

Vietnam Women's Union and the Center for Women's Studies (1989) *Vietnamese Women in the Eighties*, Hanoi: Vietnam Women's Union.

Werner, Jane S. (2009) *Gender, Household and State in Post-Revolutionary Vietnam*, London: Routledge.

Werner, Jane S. (2004) 'Managing Womanhoods in the Family: Gendered Subjectivities and the State in the Red River Delta in Vietnam', in Lisa Drummond & Helle Rydstrøm (eds.) *Gender Practices in Contemporary Vietnam*, Singapore: Singapore University Press, pp. 26-46.

Werner, Jane S. & Danièle Bélanger (2002) 'Introduction: Gender and Viet Nam Studies', in Jane S. Werner & Danièle Bélanger (eds.) *Gender, Household, State: DoiMoi in Viet Nam*, Ithaca: Southeast Asia Program Publications, pp. 13-28.

CHAPTER IV

Gender and Asexuality in Academic Sources

Petra FILIPOVÁ

1. Asexuality as a Sexual Orientation?

The study of asexuality in general, and as a sexual orientation in particular, is a relatively new one. Despite the increase in the amount of research done on the subject in the past decade, researchers have still merely scratched the surface of the issue. This chapter strives to point out some gender-related issues concerning the available research on the topic of asexuality from the mid-nineteenth century up until the most recent work on the subject, in order to establish the sexually saturated background against which the modern study of sexuality (and asexuality) is set, and to explore how gender ties in with the debates on a newly emerging sexual orientation.

According to the concise overview of the history of sexology provided by The Kinsey Institute, physicians and philosophers of the ancient world already took interest in the subject, making observations about sexual behavior and ethics as well as providing the first insights into the inner workings of sexual responses (Haeberle 2014). The eighteenth and nineteenth centuries saw the rise in the frequency and intensity of discourse about sex, be it medical discourse, psychiatric discourse and attempts to unveil the origins of mental illness in sexual behavior, or legal practice and criminalization of various sexual acts (Foucault 1978: p. 30). The medicalization and criminalization of sexuality is present in various documents and studies from the nineteenth century: one worth mentioning in the context of the study of asexuality is a widely known reference book called *Psychopathia Sexualis* (1886) by a German psychiatrist, Richard von Krafft-Ebing. In this volume, Krafft-Ebing describes dozens of cases while explaining his categorization of sexual dysfunctions, and among them, an anomaly he calls *anaesthesia sexualis,* explained as 'an absence of sexual instinct' (p. 36) or 'an absence of sexual feeling' (p. 42). In Krafft-Ebing's work, *anaesthesia sexualis* is treated as an illness, not as a possibility of a sexual orientation, and he attributes this condition to various causes, such as: 'cerebral disturbances, states of psychical degeneration, and even anatomical signs of degeneration … organic and functional, psychical and somatic, central and peripheral [causes]' (pp. 42-47). However, in the full definition there are traces of the current understanding of asexuality. Described as a state in which 'all organic impulses arising in the sexual organs, as well as all concepts, and visual, auditory, and olfactory sense-impressions, fail to excite the individual sexually' (pp. 36-37), *anaesthesia sexualis* is not merely treated as an inability of physical arousal made possible by the organic impulses, but takes into consideration the possibility of concepts, i.e., fantasies or thoughts, as well as the role of human senses in sexual excitation. Krafft-Ebing mentions seven individual cases of patients reporting absence of sexual feeling (six male, one female). Out of those seven, several patients were found mentally challenged, of low intelligence or with symptoms pointing towards other mental illnesses. Other cases mention emotional distance or coldness. Three of the accounts explicitly state that the patient was completely healthy except for the lack of sexual feelings: a man in his early thirties who 'has never experienced libido' and reported an interest in getting married, even though he 'felt that he was incapable of the sexual act' (p. 43); another young man who 'never felt libido [and] had a distaste for women and a loathing of coitus' (p. 43); and a 35-year-old woman, the only female patient out of the seven mentioned: 'fifteen years married … [she] never had any erotic excitement in sexual intercourse with her husband. She was not averse to coitus, and sometimes seemed to experience pleasure in it, but she never had a wish for repetition' (p. 43). While these early mentions of people without any sexual feelings or instinct cannot be taken as first scientific mentions of asexuality as a sexual orientation, considering they were mentioned in chapters on sexual dysfunctions, they are nonetheless important to understand the historical reach of the idea that all human beings are naturally sexual – and in clarifying that asexuality has not been historically absent from people's lives. An interesting point can also be made towards the demographics of patients mentioned in Krafft-Ebing's work: only one of those cases describes a female patient, which could be attributed to the perceived lower importance of a woman's sexual pleasure, allowing for the possibility that other women would not have stepped forward or described their lack of sexual feelings to a physician, considering the state as something that was usual for most of the women in the world.

One of the key names in the establishment of asexuality as an orientation is undoubtedly Alfred Kinsey. In the famous 'Kinsey Reports' (1953; 1948), he popularized the concept previously introduced by European researchers: that of human sexual orientation as a scale rather than simply two extremes. Known as the Kinsey Scale, human sexual orientation is measured from 0 to 6, where 0 means *exclusively heterosexual* and 6 *exclusively homosexual*, taking into consideration an individual's past and present behavior and attractions. A separate category named X was introduced in Kinsey's tables and charts to represent individuals with 'no socio-sexual response' (Kinsey et al., 1948: p. 658), where *socio-sexual* is determined to mean sexual behavior including at least one other person of any sex. Kinsey's definition of the X category is further clarified in the second Report, together with a brief summary of the statistical findings on this group: according to Kinsey's research, 'after early adolescence there are very few males in this classification ... but a goodly number of females belong in this category in every age group ...' (Kinsey et al., 1953: p. 472). This finding lends credence to the speculations made about Krafft-Ebing's work – that women were predisposed not to talk about their lack of sexual attraction or desire, and that it is possible such a feeling was considered standard for women. The prevalence reported by Kinsey for the X group was 3 to 4% of the unmarried men in the study, 14-19% of the unmarried women, 1-3% of the married women aged between 20 and 35, and 5-8% of the previously married women (Van Houdenhove et al., 2014: p. 177; Kinsey et al., 1953; Kinsey et al., 1948). These numbers point towards the conclusion that there are more asexual women than there are asexual men, a concept perpetuated and largely considered true even nowadays, despite the lack of reliable and world-wide research to prove the absolute validity of this notion. In view of the time period of Kinsey's studies, it is possible to speculate that women in the middle of the twentieth century were still not accustomed to thinking and/or talking about their sexuality, which could have resulted in elevated numbers of the X category regarding women. Knowledge about the ways women could achieve pleasure was not readily available in ways it has been since the rise of Internet with its freely accessible resources, and in this, women could have been merely dissatisfied with their sexual lives, as well as misinformed about their own capabilities of achieving orgasm, to the point that they might have reported a lack of interest in sex as such.

Another important point to be made is about the politicization of asexuality as a tool of subverting the status quo of the society's approach to sexuality. Several decades after 'Kinsey Reports', Myra T. Johnson published 'Asexual and Autoerotic Women: Two Invisible Groups' (1977), which could technically be called 'the earliest article to dedicate itself fully to the exploration of asexual experiences' (Owen 2014: p. 119) in general, and of female asexuality in particular. In this paper, Johnson used letters written by potentially asexual women to editors of women's magazines to point out and discuss the omission of asexual and autoerotic females from the texts in the publications of those years. Johnson provided a definition for these individuals as 'men and women who ... chose not to engage in sexual activity' (1977: p. 99). According to Van Houdenhove et al. (2014: p. 176), Johnson was also the first to use the term *asexual* to describe people, her article being published several years before Storms' 'Theories'. She also provided a definition for these individuals as 'men and women who, despite their physical or emotional condition, sexual history and relational status or ideological orientation, chose not to engage in sexual activity' (Johnson 1977: p. 99). She makes several interesting points in her article, well above the usual discussion of asexuality at that time: as she noted, when the word *asexual* was used then, 'its meaning [was] usually left vague, with its definition ranging from "unexpressed" sexuality to "absence of sexual desire" due to "loss of the sex glands" or to psychiatric disorder' (1977: p. 96). Johnson mentions several problems that asexuals have or might have experienced throughout history, e.g., asexual men using the Vietnam War as an escape from the society that expected both men and women to 'move in couples' (1977: p. 97), or historical views of female sexuality as something that should be restricted to the point of asexuality, possibly being considered a religious duty, which later transformed into something which needed to be cured (1977: p. 98). From the perspective of gender, it is interesting to note the expectations for men and women to 'move in couples' (1977: p. 97) – this particular phrase suggests that the time period was rife with heteronormative expectations placed both on men and women. It would be possible to speculate on how equally these societal pressures were distributed among genders, i.e., whether or not asexual women faced more pressure to get married, or at least enter a romantic relationship, than asexual men. Unfortunately, no such data are available from the time period in which asexuality was still a largely unknown subject. In addition, Johnson also makes it clear that she does not endorse the radical feminist view of the institution of heterosexual sex as an act of male domination and female passivity. The author considers also that this radicalization of asexuality might result both in shaming the women who still want to have sex with men and in presenting the asexual woman as 'a political symbol – her identity still lost in the slogans, and her reality going unnoticed' (Johnson 1977: p. 104). The difference between an asexual and an autoerotic (or autosexual) woman in Johnson's writing is addressed as well: 'the asexual woman ... has no sexual desires at all [while] the autoerotic woman ... recognizes such desires but prefers to satisfy them alone' (1977: p. 99), which does not strictly correlate with the current most typically used view of asexuality, but it is nonetheless an important acknowledgment of the existence of asexuality in the time when this was not a well-known subject matter. The importance of Johnson's article therefore lies in her astute observations as well as in her description of asexual women as invisible, 'abandoned by the sexual revolution and the feminist movement', their existence ignored, denied, and having their asexuality dismissed as caused by 'religious, neurotic, or political reasons' (Van Houdenhove et al., 2014: p. 177). Interestingly, while Johnson points out the invisibility of asexual women, she does not discuss asexual men and the potential difficulties of negotiating asexuality and masculinity together.

Positioning a sexual orientation against a whole system or regime perceived as unjust is something known especially in connection with some radical feminist groups who employed the idea of political lesbianism, e.g., in the pamphlet 'Political Lesbianism: The Case against Heterosexuality' (1979). The pamphlet suggested that all feminists should choose political lesbianism as a way of disrupting the male influence on their lives. Adrienne Rich expressed similar ideas, claiming that heterosexuality is enforced on women 'as means of assuring male right of physical, economic, and emotional access' (Rich 1996: p. 135). She pointed out also that women who are 'imprisoned in prescriptive ideas of the "normal" share the pain of blocked options, broken connections, lost access to self-definition freely and powerfully assumed' (p. 140). Interestingly enough, the pamphlet defines a political lesbian as 'a woman-identified woman who does not have sexual relations with men. It does not mean compulsory sexual activity with women' (Onlywomen Press Collective 1981: p. 5), which suggests that the same concept could have been termed political asexuality, since a woman desiring or participating in sexual contact with women would most likely be termed simply lesbian or bisexual. The letters of women reacting to this pamphlet suggest that the idea of political lesbianism was not met with approval: some of the answers even claim that it goes against feminism itself, against the proclamation that feminism supports women in any situation (Onlywomen Press Collective 1981: p. 13). Nowadays, a similar disagreement could emerge in the asexual community about the question of positioning asexuality strictly as a political notion working against the sexual order of the society. Asexuals in general (Decker 2014) seem to favor the idea that society should recognize non-sexual relationships as having the possibility of being equally important as sexual ones. However, the asexual community does not seem willing to stop defining asexuality as a natural sexual orientation in order to become a political scapegoat in the fight against hypersexualization in the media and in the society.

2. Asexuality in Diagnostics

The aforementioned hypersexualization of the society stems from reinforcing the idea of sex, or at least desire for sex, as natural behavior that should be present in a healthy individual's everyday life. In 1980, the American Psychiatric Association published the third revised edition of their *Diagnostic and Statistical Manual of Mental Disorders* (DSM-III), including Inhibited Sexual Desire Disorder, later renamed Hypoactive Sexual Desire Disorder (HSDD). DSM-III placed asexual individuals firmly into the space of mental disorders, even though APA removed homosexuality as such from the list of mental disorders seven years earlier. Almost thirty years later, the question of whether or not asexuality should be perceived as a disorder is still not closed, despite the recent changes made in the classification of sexual desire

112

disorders. The 2013 edition of the manual, DSM-5, does not dissuade previous concerns, such as the worry that the idea of an overlap between HSDD and asexuality might only place asexuality more firmly into the position of a disorder (Flore 2013). DMS-5 allows for the possibility that a person's lifelong lack of sexual attraction might be better explained by asexuality, in which case the diagnosis of a desire disorder is not made (Emens 2014: p. 312). However, the diagnosis (or non-diagnosis) is still rooted in the expectation of a lifelong and unchanging condition. The presence of clinically significant distress is still required for the diagnosis of HSDD, and several researchers point out some problems that might arise with this diagnosis. First of all, distress can be present based on various factors. Nurius pointed out the necessity of considering social expectations and social sanctions as early as 1983, questioning to what extent was the distress reported by a non-heterosexual person caused directly by sexual orientation itself, as opposed to distress being an indirect consequence of norm-breaking (Nurius 1983: pp. 132-133). While non-heterosexual, non-asexual people might experience distress as an indirect result of breaking the rules of heteronormative society, asexual individuals go against the societal norms seemingly focused on sex, and thus can experience distress as well (Yule et al., 2013: p. 137). Moreover, Chasin underlines the connection of distress and mental disorder in relation to sexual orientation as an issue previously connected with homosexuality as well. Well after the removal of homosexuality as such from the APA's diagnostic manual in 1973, the remaining category of ego-dystonic homosexuality, a state in which an individual experiences marked distress at their unwanted sexual orientation and expresses wishes to change it, allowed for the diagnosis of people 'who were lesbian or gay and distressed about their sexual orientation' (Chasin 2013: p. 412) as having a mental disorder. The APA dropped the use of ego-dystonic homosexuality only in 1987 (APA, 'Use of Diagnoses'). Chasin (2013: p. 412) links this category with the use of distress as a diagnostic criterion for HSDD:

'... [any] attempts to make a gay person straight are called either corrective or reparative therapy and widely regarded ... to be unethical. The days of 'ego-dystonic homosexuality' ... are behind us, and, as feminists, we would never stand to let them return. Corrective or reparative therapy enacted upon asexual people and a diagnosis for ego-dystonic asexuality should be no different.'

Despite DSM-5 allowing for the existence of asexuality, the decision on whether or not a person suffers from a sexual disorder instead of being asexual lies firmly in the hands of the clinician handling the case. The DSM-5 also creates gendered differences not only in the classification of desire disorders[1], but in the diagnostic criteria as well. The possibility of asexuality instead of the female sexual interest/arousal disorder and male hypoactive sexual desire disorder respectively is described as follows:

'If a lifelong lack of sexual desire is better explained by one's self identification as "asexual", then a diagnosis of female sexual interest/arousal disorder would not be made … If the man's low desire is explained by self-identification as an asexual, then a diagnosis of male hypoactive sexual desire disorder is not made.'

(DSM-5: pp. 434-443)

Especially in the case of female sexual interest/arousal disorder, the inclusion of the word 'better' leaves room for psychiatrists and psychologists to assess to what extent an explanation of asexuality is deemed more appropriate than treating the person as having a sexual disorder. That is not to say that the statement relating to male HSDD does not allow for a similar possibility in any case. But the formulation does seem to suggest a difference between a state that can be somewhat explained by self-identification as asexual in the case of men, and a state that can be seen as better explained by a sexual disorder in the case of women. However, the formulation also seems to employ a different scale of how little sexual desire is required for men and women to be allowed to explain their state as asexuality: while the definition for women employs 'a lifelong lack of sexual desire' (DSM-5: pp. 434-443), the one for men includes neither the lifelong criterion nor the requirement for a complete lack of desire, instead talking about 'low desire' (DSM-5: pp. 434-443). This could suggest that women are asked to validate their asexuality through the argument of a lifelong and unchanging state, as well as a complete lack of desire, successfully erasing the possibility of female demisexuality[2] or gray-asexuality[3]. Another conclusion to draw from these differences in wording could be that low desire in men is viewed as similarly clinically significant as a complete lack of desire in women, perpetuating the stereotype that 'to "be a man" is to be sexual, have sex, and overtly perform one's (hetero)sexuality' (Przybylo 2014: p. 233).

---

1   The previously gender-non-specific HSDD is divided into two separate categories for men and women: female hypoactive desire dysfunction and female arousal dysfunction were merged into a female sexual interest/arousal disorder, while the male category retained the former name of HSDD as a male hypoactive sexual desire disorder.

2   People who do not experience sexual attraction unless they form a strong emotional connection with someone.

3   People identified as gray-asexual, also known as gray-A, can include, but are not limited to those: who do not normally experience sexual attraction, but do experience it sometimes; who experience sexual attraction, but a low sex drive; who experience sexual attraction and drive, but not strongly enough to want to act on them; people who can enjoy and desire sex, but only under very limited and specific circumstances.

3. Empirical Discourse

The beginning of the empirical discourse regarding asexuality is attributed by many, if not all, current researchers to Anthony Bogaert and his 2004 article 'Asexuality: Prevalence and Associated Factors in a National Probability Sample'. As the title suggests, the study was based on the national probability sample, including more than 18,000 British citizens, out of which roughly 1% (57 men, 138 women) responded in agreement with the statement 'I have never felt sexually attracted to anyone at all' (Bogaert 2004: p. 279). Aside from the number of asexuals in the population, Bogaert looked at the possible predicting factors of asexuality: these included demographics (age, marital status, education, social class, race/ethnicity), sexual experience (age of the first sexual experience of any kind, total number of sexual partners, frequency of sexual activity over the last 7 days), health (self-perceived state of health, presence of long-term illness, medical condition, or permanent disability), physical development (onset of menarche, weight, height), and religiosity (existence of religious affiliation, frequency of attendance at religious services) (Bogaert 2004: pp. 281-282). The results indicated that asexual people had fewer sexual partners, a later onset (and lower frequency) of sexual activity, and less sexual experience with partners, which, according to Bogaert, 'provides some validation of the concept of asexuality' (2004: p. 282). Furthermore, asexual people were somewhat older than sexual people, more women than men reported being asexual, and more than 40% have experienced a long-term cohabiting or marital relationship. Asexuals were more likely to come from lower socioeconomic conditions and achieve lower education than sexual individuals. Poorer health, shorter height and lower weight also seemed to be more likely in asexual individuals, as well as higher religiosity with regard to attending services (2004: p. 282). Bogaert's proposals sparked the interest of other researchers in the subject of asexuality – however, his findings that there are more asexual women than men have not been conclusively proven. In 2010, Poston and Baumle published 'Patterns of Asexuality in the United States' using data from the 2002 National Survey of Family Growth (NSFG), which had questionnaires distributed among people aged 15 to 44. Attempting to elaborate on the prevalence and demographic of asexuality as reported in the United States, since Bogaert's data had been obtained from a British sample, the authors admitted that the questions posed in the NSFG could be problematic in relation to asexuality. The first set of questions, apart from the problematic classification of 'sex' as only vaginal between a man and a woman, 'oral or anal' in cases of two men and 'sexual contact' in case of women, assessed only the behavior and/or past experience of the participants. With regard to sexual identity, the questions failed to provide an adequate option of no sexual attraction or no sexual desire:

'Do you think of yourself as heterosexual, homosexual, bisexual or something else?; Are you … only attracted to the opposite sex; Mostly attracted to the opposite sex; Equally attracted to the opposite sex and the same sex; Mostly attracted to the same sex; Only attracted to the same sex; Not sure.'

(Poston & Baumle, 2010: pp. 517-518)

Furthermore, these surveys failed to take into account possible non-binary gender identities of participants: while in 2002, terms such as 'agender' or 'gender-fluid' were not too widely known, there might have been participants who could have had trouble answering questions asked through the lens of a strict view of gender as binary. Participants were determined to be asexual by the authors based on the expected 'asexual response' to all three abovementioned questions[4] (Poston & Baumle, 2010: p. 518). This approach most likely excluded many participants from (and unnecessarily included others in) the category of 'asexual': asexuals who have had sex, non-asexual people who have not had sex, asexual people who chose to identify as hetero- , homo- or bisexual due to low visibility of the label 'asexual' and its non-inclusion in the survey, etc. The data collected through this survey show that:

'Almost 5% of the females and more than 6% of the males report that they have never had sex in their lifetimes … almost 1% each of both the females (0.8%) and the males (0.7%) are "not sure" about their sexual attraction … the weighted percentage … of females and males giving the 'something else' response to the question on sexual orientation are 3.8% and 3.9%, respectively. Of all the respondents giving an "asexual" response to any one of the three questions, only 0.6% of the females and 0.9% of the males gave the asexual response on all three dimensions.'

(Poston & Baumle, 2010: pp. 519-520)

While the results of this examination of the NSFG questionnaires provide a number close to Bogaert's estimation of 1% of the population, it is difficult to draw any solid conclusions based solely on the prevalence of expected answers when the same conclusions could easily be ascribed to several other groups of people. In Poston and Baumle's study, the numbers of women and men giving the 'asexual response' to these questions were roughly the same, indicating that the distribution of asexuality throughout the population might not be as strictly leaning towards women as previous researchers have suggested. However, due to the highly subjective method of determining asexuality and the vague and imprecise questions asked of the participants, it would be ill-advised to consider Poston and Baumle's findings as the key to

---

4   Participants answered 'no' to the questions about whether or not they ever had sex, chose 'something else' as their sexual orientation, and answered 'not sure' to the question about sexual attraction.

the asexual demographics. A survey conducted in 2014 by a website focused on asexuality found that out of 10,880 self-identified asexual respondents, roughly 62% identified as 'Woman/female', 12% as 'Man/male', and 26% as 'Other' (The Ace Community Census 2014: p. 6). While these findings support the assumption that there might be more asexual women than men, it is also important to note that this survey has been conducted via a website focused on asexuality, indicating that the respondents were asexuals already aware of their asexual orientation, with enough information and terminology to discuss their identities. However, the general population also comprises a significant portion of people without Internet access or without the knowledge and resources necessary to clearly adopt an asexual identity, or to find the particular website conducting the survey. Furthermore, as suggested by Ela Przybylo's article which is discussed in detail below, claiming an asexual identity even privately might prove more difficult for men who have been raised in a community strictly adhering to the stereotypical rules of masculinity, in which sexuality has played a significant role in the construction of one's identity as male. In addition, this survey has shown that more than a quarter of self-identified asexual people in the survey have claimed an identity outside of the gender binary: this factor would be necessary to include in any future considerations of research on asexuality in general.

An interesting finding was made by Brotto and Yule in their 2011 article 'Physiological and Subjective Sexual Arousal in Self-Identified Asexual Women'. A study of physiological responses of asexual women to sexual stimuli was based on the premise that:

'Whereas men show patterns of genital arousal that correspond to their stated sexual orientation ... lesbian and heterosexual women showed the same degree of increase in vaginal pulse amplitude VPA..., regardless of their stated sexual orientation and irrespective of the stimuli shown – whether heterosexual, homosexual, or non-human primate.'

(Brotto & Yule, 2011: p. 701)

It was hypothesized that while viewing an erotic film, asexual women would thus show the same levels of genital arousal as heterosexual, homosexual, or bisexual women, but that levels of reported subjective arousal would be lower, which was supported by the findings, leading to the conclusion that 'asexuality is not a sexual dysfunction – or perhaps, more precisely, it is not a disorder of sexual arousal' (Brotto & Yule, 2011: p. 707). While significant for the study of asexuality in general, this research also highlighted the differences in the physical responses to sexual stimuli in men and women, and thus the necessity of revising the way we think about sexual arousal and sexual responses based on these differences.

Feminist scholars are beginning to notice and take interest in the subject of asexuality as well, as best demonstrated by Routledge's 2014 collection of essays titled *Asexualities: Queer and Feminist Perspectives,* edited by Karli J. Cerankowski and Megan Milks. As they explain in the introduction, the title of the collection comes from the way they perceive this project as both queer, in that it is:

'… making sense of the social marginalization and pathologization of bodies based on the preference to not have sex, along with exploring new possibilities in intimacy, desire and kinship structures' and feminist one 'in its attention to structures of power and oppression, specifically around gender, as well as sexual object choice.'

(Cerankowski & Milks, 2014: p. 3)

However, the essays in this collection focus on the experiences of both female and male asexuality. Grossman and Przybylo explain in their respective articles how masculinity is automatically connected to the sexual and how men, both as characters in fiction and as people living in everyday world, have trouble reconciling their asexuality with the traditional ideas of masculinity performed as heteronormative sexuality. Ela Przybylo's article, 'Masculine Doubt and Sexual Wonder: Asexually-Identified Men Talk about Their (A)sexualities', explores 'the discourses that make asexuality more or less implausible and uninhabitable for men' (Przybylo 2014: p. 225). Through interviews with three asexually identified men, Przybylo shows how these men have trouble reconciling their asexuality with the traditional ideas of masculinity performed as heteronormative sexuality. While two of the interviewed asexuals identified explicitly as male, the third interviewee seemed more vague about his gender, stating that he is of masculine gender, but that he does not feel strong connection to his masculinity: 'I don't look at the "M" of my license and feel … upset about it or anything but I could do without it … I don't feel overly feminine either, just, you know, whatever' (Przybylo 2014: p. 226). In this, it already becomes apparent that some asexual men might have trouble identifying with a masculine identity, possibly on the basis of not being included in the male bonding rituals or male identity affirmation based on performing sexuality. Przybylo claims that the men she has interviewed were all 'highly aware of the pressures that exist for men to have sex, to be sexual, and to exaggeratedly mobilize their sexuality to bond with other men and to fit in' (2014: p. 227). Przybylo also explains the concept of sexual imperative, which, according to her, works on four planes: privileging sex above any other activities, conflating sexuality with the self, coding sex as healthy and good without any regard for context, and emphasizing that sex is the 'glue' to any romantic relationship (2014: p. 228). All of these four planes can be explored when talking about asexuality in general and asexuality in the media in particular: one of the interviewees also hints that looking at television programs shows how characters of a mature age who have never been married are portrayed as 'some sort of a loser type' (2014: p. 229), which underlines the importance of examining how asexuality might be represented or discussed in popular media. The importance of sexuality for a masculine identity becomes apparent from the responses of another interviewee, who describes his adolescence as 'playing along' with the way his friends started to organize their activities around the sexual, e.g., looking at porn magazines or discussing sex. The interviewee himself recalls not having any interest in the topic, attempting to understand himself through the concept of being gay or being a late bloomer: furthermore, the man also states that he feels he has 'lost out socially because … a lot of social activities seem to be … centered around sex' (2014: p. 229). This difficulty in socializing with other men might contribute to the difficulty in reconciling a masculine and an asexual identity. Another problem is pointed out by an interviewee who claims that the culture pressures men to 'perform sexually, like that's the essence of manlihood' (2014: p. 230). While asexual men might recognize the societal and cultural pressure to be sexual as a construct, due to their own unwillingness to participate in such activities, the ever-present burden of having to perform sexually is already ingrained in their minds from early age. Even in romantic relationships, sex is often perceived as inevitable and unavoidable: an interviewee who was married for several years speaks about having sex mostly to please his wife while understanding it as something he had to do in order to maintain their marriage: 'I wanted these other things in a relationship other than sex that are more important to me but after a while I felt like sex is the most important thing' (2014: p. 231). Przybylo then mentions the male sexual drive discourse, which presumes that 'men have a physiological and biological drive or libido that requires that they regularly engage in sex' (2014: p. 231). Sex is positioned as a biological necessity of survival, an indispensable part of what it means to be male (and masculine) in the modern society, representing another obstacle asexual men have to overcome in order to reconcile their asexuality and their masculinity. Przybylo's article highlights the importance of considering asexuality not only from the perspective of women, but also from the viewpoint of men as well.

In another article from Cerankowski and Milks' book, Labuski poses a question about whether or not asexuality could also be measured based on behavior, talking about women with chronic genital pain who are unable and/or unwilling to perform what constitutes the normative idea of sex: penetrative vaginal intercourse. Labuski also reveals that quite a few of these women have stated that they only sought the treatment for their chronic genital pain because of their partner, that they would not have started with the treatment if it were only for themselves, which could hint at a possible overlap with asexuality among these women. Studying how these women cope with their inability to engage in penetrative vaginal intercourse also reveals how other kinds of intimacy, sexual and non-sexual, can be equally meaningful and can help people build their relationships in a different way.

Chasin's article 'Making Sense in and of the Asexual Community: Navigating Relationships and Identities in a Context of Resistance' (2014) points out another important aspect of the relationship between gender and sexual orientation necessary to consider while talking about asexuality. According to Chasin, being read as non-heterosexual, or more precisely, gay or lesbian, is primarily a concern of interpreting gender presentation of an individual by others, not a matter of sexual orientation *per se*; thus, homophobia is rooted not only in fear of or dislike for sexual minorities, but also in great part in the social policing of gender (Chasin 2014: p. 4). Heteronormative gender structures exclude and point out people who fail to perform gender in a socially accepted way, e.g., by failing to perform or display heterosexual desire and/or attraction. Asexual people can thus also be affected by homophobia 'because they are especially likely to not participate in aspects of heteronormative gender related to the economy of sexual desire (e.g., conventional heterosexual flirting, dating, and/or sexual behaviors; dressing to be *hetero* 'sexy')' (p. 5). Furthermore, asexual people are vulnerable to homophobia and transphobia because they might be read by others as gender non-conforming, regardless of their gender identity; in addition, Chasin also points out that while 23% of the respondents in the asexual survey mentioned above selected neither 'male' nor 'female' option as their gender, a half of these people answered that they were also not transgender, and a quarter of the 23% responded that they were 'unsure' about their gender identity (p. 6). This could potentially be the result of the uncertain status of non-binary identities such as agender or gender-fluid within the label of transgender, but also an indicator of the connection between gender identity or gender presentation and sexual orientation.

Sexuality appears to be an important factor in gender expression, as seen previously on the examples provided in Przybylo's article about asexual men, where one of the respondents claimed that it appears as if performing sexuality was 'the essence of manlihood' (Przybylo 2014: p. 230). For this reason, it is crucial to closely examine asexuality and asexual people from the perspective of gender in future research, in order to further explore whether, and how, gender is influenced by sexual orientation and vice versa.

4. Final Remarks

As we have seen in this revision of the specialized literature, asexuality has moved from the field of the mythical and unbelievable into the area of issues worth debating from various viewpoints. All of the examples above illustrate how studying asexual experience can prove a valuable asset to various topics within the field of gender studies. Hypersexualization and heteronormativization of the society which prescribes behavior and self-expression is based on the assumption that every person is sexual. From the earliest works of sexology, sexual desire, attraction and behavior has been naturalized and prescribed as a universal human experience. Discussing the minority which showed no signs of sexual attraction or behavior has stood at the periphery of academic study of sexuality until very recently; when such a discussion is included it is often aimed at medicalizing signs of asexuality as pathological or indicative of underlying mental or physical issues. Past approach to sexuality and gender expression has likely prevented the full exploration of asexuality in the past, and taking into consideration factors such as the position of women during the rise of sexology as a discipline throughout the twentieth century allows for discussions on the possible historical causes for some of the conclusions found in the research of the time. Gender stereotyping often generates a negative impact on both men and women, and poses difficulties for the construction of a person's self as well as gender and/or sexual identity. Furthermore, recent discussion and research on marginalized, non-binary gender identities create an opportunity to explore in greater detail how gender and sexuality interact. Examining a community of people who do not experience sexual attraction to any gender and of which roughly a quarter does not claim a gender identity from within the gender binary could provide great insight into the inner workings of gender and sexuality.

Bibliography

Bogaert, Anthony (2004) 'Asexuality: Prevalence and Associated Factors in a National Probability Sample', *The Journal of Sex Research*, 41(3): 279-287.

Brotto, Lori A. & Morag Yule (2011) 'Physiological and Subjective Sexual Arousal in Self-Identified Asexual Women', *Archive of Sexual Behavior,* 40: 699-712.

Cerankowski, Karli J. & Megan Milks (eds.) (2014) *Asexualities: Feminist and Queer Perspectives*, Abingdon: Routledge.

Chasin, DeLuzio CJ. (2014): 'Making Sense in and of the Asexual Community: Navigating Relationships and Identities in a Context of Resistance', *Journal of Community & Applied Social Psychology*, 25(2): 95-191.

Chasin, DeLuzio CJ. (2013) 'Reconsidering Asexuality and Its Radical Potential', *Feminist Studies*, 39(2): 405-426.

Decker, S. Julie (2014) *The Invisible Orientation: An Introduction to Asexuality*, New York: Skyhorse Publishing.

Diagnostic and Statistical Manual of Mental Disorders, Fifth Edition, Washington D.C.: American Psychiatric Association Publishing.

Emens, Elizabeth (2014) 'Compulsory Sexuality', *Stanford Law Review*, 66(303): 303-386.

Flore, Jacinthe (2013) 'HSDD and Asexuality: A Question of Instruments', *Psychology & Sexuality*, 4(2): 152-166.

Foucault, Michel (1978) *The History of Sexuality*, translated from French by Robert Hurley, New York: Random House, Inc.

Haeberle, Erwin J. (2014) *The Birth of Sexology*, Bloomington, IN: The Kinsey Institute for Research in Sex, Gender, and Reproduction, Inc.

Johnson, Myra (1977) 'Asexual and Autoerotic Women: two Invisible Groups', in Harvey L. Gorchros & John S. Gochros (eds.) *The Sexually Oppressed*, New-York: Associated Press, pp. 96-109.

Kinsey, Alfred, Wardell Pomeroy, Clyde Martin & Paul Gebhard (1948) *Sexual Behavior in the Human Male*, Philadelphia: Saunders.

Kinsey, Alfred, Wardell Pomeroy, Clyde Martin & Paul Gebhard (1953) *Sexual Behavior in the Human Female*, Bloomington, IN: Indiana University Press.

Krafft-Ebing, Richard von (1894): *Psychopathia Sexualis* (7th ed), translated from German by Charles Gilbert Chaddock, Philadelphia: The F. A. Davis. Company Publishers.

Nurius, Paula (1983) 'Mental Health Implications of Sexual Orientation', *The Journal of Sex Research*, 19(2): 119-136.

Onlywomen Press Collective (eds.) (1981) *Love Your Enemy? The Debate between Heterosexual Feminism and Political Lesbianism*, London: Onlywomen Press Collective, Ltd.

Owen, Ianna H. (2014) 'On the Racialization of Asexuality', in Karli J. Cerankowski & Megan Milks (eds.) *Asexualities: Feminist and Queer Perspectives*, New York: Routledge, pp. 119-135.

Poston, Dudley L. Jr. & Amanda K. Baumle (2010) 'Patterns of Asexuality in the United States', *Demographic Research*, 23(18): 509-530.

Przybylo, Ela (2014) 'Masculine Doubt and Sexual Wonder: Asexually-Identified Men Talk About Their (A)sexualites', in Karli J. Cerankowski & Megan Milks (eds.) *Asexualities: Feminist and Queer Perspectives*, New York: Routledge, pp. 225-248.

Rich, Adrienne (1996) 'Compulsory Heterosexuality and Lesbian Existence', in Stevi Jackson & Sue Scott (eds.) *Feminism & Sexuality a Reader*, New York: Columbia University Press, pp. 130-141.

The Ace Community Census (2014) *Preliminary Findings from the 2014 AVEN Community Census The Asexual Census. Asexual Visibility and Education Network.*
Online. Available https://asexualcensus.wordpress.com/2014/11/02/preliminary-findings-from-the-2014-aven-community-census/.

Van Houdenhove, Ellen, Luk Gijs, Guy T'Sjoen & Paul Enzlin (2014) 'Asexuality: Few Facts, Many Questions', *Journal of Sex & Marital Therapy*, 40(3): 175-192.

Yule, Morag A., Lori A. Brotto & Boris B. Gorzalka (2013) 'Mental Health and Interpersonal Functioning in Self-Identified Asexual Men and Women', *Psychology & Sexuality*, 4(2): 136-151.

PART TWO

CODES WITHIN WOMEN'S AUTO- AND HETERO-REPRESENTATIONS

CHAPTER V

Communist Dictatorship vs. Romanian Women Poets' Discourse of Resistance in the 70s and 80s

Daniela MOLDOVEANU

1. Dismantled Personal Identity

In an epoch when speaking one's mind out loud meant, with very few exceptions, compromising, denouncing or burying oneself, an acquaintance, a friend or a relative, the Romanian female poets of the two generations under scrutiny turn the confessional poetry paradigm they adopted naturally, out of a need of self-acknowledgment, into a weapon to be used both against the shooter and the target, i.e., the Communist regime. They sketch the picture of inner turmoil and outer communist-orchestrated fragmentation with more metaphysical outrage than the male poets of their generation, because they choose to engage in the poetry crusade wearing Munch's 'Scream' as the colors of their literary creed and skin, regardless of the consequences. Furthermore, their verses seem to ask for suppression by instruments of censorship as some kind of recognition of their efficacy; consequently, they end up receiving a lot of attention from the members of the secret police.

The so-called 'Beatles' of Romanian poetry, the 'young and furious' poets who set the trend with their poetry anthology entitled *Air with Diamonds* (Mircea Cărtărescu, Traian T. Coşovei, Florin Iaru and Ion Stratan) take refuge in postmodernism as if it were the only 'highway to heaven', the consubstantial connection with the West being, as they felt at the time, instituted and preserved by this stringent seclusion in textual replicas of freedom. They write and speak the language of freedom and their rebellion ignores limitations, their revolt and irony reside in the obstinacy of not taking restrictions into consideration.

Women poets, in contrast, never feel free; this is an ineluctable trace of their condition and they accept and embrace it, and so Romanian poetesses of the 70s and 80s, like Ileana Mălăncioiu, Mariana Marin and Marta Petreu, write from and about the intrinsic void and (self-)imposed limitations; they search for truth and redemption in the tense areas of their conscience. According to Lacan's philosophical vision in *Séminaire sur l'Éthique*, emptiness or a certain lack determines the artist to create *ex nihilo* around this gap: 'Il y a identité entre le façonnement du signifiant et cette introduction dans le reel d'une béance, d'un trou'[1] (Lacan in André 2010: p. 79).These poetesses place at the centre of their verses the inability to change, through poetry alone, a state of affairs which no one can speak of directly and freely, but which cannot be neglected either. Therefore they adopt a more direct style of description and re-writing of femininity, aware of its ever-growing importance and force. The ability to influence mindsets and social identities by resizing private identity makes Romanian feminine confessional poetry a paradigm that will finally have a defining subversive role in changing totalitarian policy.

It is a war on two fronts: just as they overcame the prejudices of male domination, the confessional poetesses above-mentioned eliminate the ascendancy of coercive thinking over the human being, which is why their poetry is so important in the context of the Communist regime. The ethical and heretical Ileana Mălăncioiu and Mariana Marin, the intimist-visceral Marta Petreu, displaying the iconoclastic nature of corporality, of language as a mark of the body eviscerated and recomposed toward the anathemization of conformism of any kind, represent the complex facets of the feminine confessional approach through confronting its own limits. In this respect, Claudia Rankine (2001: pp. 134-135) observed that 'The construction of self, then, becomes a process in motion determined by indeterminacy through a strategy of fragmentation'; thus, there will be frequent talk about 'fragmentation coherence'. They create their scriptural world to perceive it and live it simultaneously, as in a dream, which, not infrequently, even if it seems a capacity, may as well become a curse which highlights their self-destructive background, their convulsive identity.

Assuming the first-person singular discourse and discovering the personal voice are the Romanian confessional poets' strategies for placing the self in a position of superiority in relation to itself, for, says Raphael Molho (in Mihăieş 2005: p. 90): 'The being that descends into the inner space is ... a being of transcendence. It freezes at the boundary between two worlds, equally competing ... and parallel ...'. The mirroring and exorcism of deep vulnerability, of flaws, fears and disorientation, turns into a valid attempt of the individual, of the female poets, in our case, to objectify themselves, and therefore to cancel themselves and reorder coherently according to the transcendence of immanence.

We thus identify the American confessional paradigm as the source of inspiration of Romanian female poetry written in the 70s and 80s, since the power of the new poetic language it proposes comes from deep within, gravitating around the forever-controversial textual authority: the individualized lyrical ego. The confessional paradigm gives birth, almost naturally, to its own critical approaches as it captures the reader, turning him

---

1 'There is identity between the shaping of the signifier and the insertion of a gap, a hole into reality' (my translation).

126

or her into an accomplice who gets to feel that the language of inner turmoil is the mother tongue. That is why, from the classic hermeneutic approach to the Ricoeurian 'hermeneutics of suspicion', Romanian confessional poetry lends itself both to 'a close reading' as well as to an 'extrinsic approach', given the historical and political context it stems from.

Romanian female confessional poetry of the 70s and 80s oscillates between two hypostases of the lyrical ego as defined by Alexandru Muşina (2004: pp. 135-154). The 'hyperemic ego' assigned by Gottfried Benn to expressionists is the one that facilitates contact with the 'world beyond' through the concreteness of sensation, of emotion toward a certain external ineluctable state of affairs, and records them without claiming their inoculation by metaphysical meanings. It's a bi-mundane perception where a field of reference and of biological limitation slips to another, i.e., the field of the desirable. The expression of self occurs here only by capturing the aimed-at magnetizing horizon, but it cannot be precisely articulated either. Thus, the feeling of physical and mental blockage in an alien world can be found everywhere in Mariana Marin's *Aripa secretă* (*The Secret Wing*) and *Atelierele* (*The Studios*), in Marta Petreu's *Loc psihic* (*The Psychic Place*) and in Ileana Mălăncioiu's *Urcarea muntelui* (*The Climbing of the Mountain*).

On the other hand, the 'individualized ego' heralds the postmodern poetic revolution, the re-consideration of human importance, the 'new anthropocentrism' (Muşina 2008: p. 32) when the human being becomes 'concrete, whole and irreducible'. The postmodern condition in poetry brings the individual to the fore; a person who cannot be reduced to another or to a social or symbolic function, an individual who has a tumultuous inner life, soul, crises of conscience and identity. This leads to poetry regaining superiority over prose in terms of psychological accuracy. Existence will be a continuous exploration of the world and body as fragment adrift, and the individual's effort to understand itself, to find meaning, hence the 'biographical poetry' of the individualized ego (see Mariana Marin and Marta Petreu via Sylvia Plath and Anne Sexton), or of the 'corporalized ego'.

The latter conjugates the verb 'to be' as feminine, inducing a particular psychism to it. The tensional entity so born justifies itself in the text through the ontological vocation of the conflict the 'language games' now come to reflect, finding it in full development. Lyotard (2003: pp. 24-25) puts the postmodern condition under the sign of *agony*, hence the fundamental dramatism and self-denial: '… to speak is to fight, in the meaning of to play, and language acts reside in a general agony'. And this is precisely what the Romanian women poets do regarding the Communist establishment.

Besides the implicit autobiographical pact Romanian confessional poetry proposes, there is an inborn dose of autofiction which naturally places 'phantasia' in the heart of 'mimesis' to show us, if there was still the need, that these two achieve a paradoxical symbiosis that determined and determines various theoretical speculation about the status of the lyrical and empirical ego, and of fictional and real ego in the text economy.

As emphasized above, the confessional side involves going inward into intimacy, into the dark corners of being in order to reveal and articulate them in semic coherence. The confessional poetesses' image of self is built from fragments selected from the relativity space *par excellence*. It is precisely this approach of entrusting secrets that brings the poet closer to the reader. Sometimes the confessional atmosphere gives the reader a refreshing feeling of power, conferring upon him/her a privileged status, along with 'responsibility'. The ego thus regains in poetry its 'civil' subjectivity and 'materializes' by assuming now the first-person-singular discourse. The artistic ego will wear the mask of the empirical ego. Assuming the discourse and discovering the personal voice are strategies for placing self in a position of superiority over itself. Also, the implicit readers of this type of poetry are the female poets who rediscover themselves through their lyrical ego, most often an unfaithful, mythicizing mirror.

Carol Muske (1977: p. 11) notices how this kind of poetry:

'... quickly became popular as a kind of verbal emergency, the post-trauma voice ... the enactment of the voice of extremity not simply as a literary convention, rather as a moral event.'

In addition, Adrienne Rich, together with Sylvia Plath and joined by Mariana Marin from her first volumes, consider the metaphor the primary language that turns the territory of reverie and dream or rebel imagination into the realm called 'home', which proposes a reality to match the intensity of inner experiences.

The 80s represent a turning point in Romanian poetry which announces, paradoxically, that if we take into consideration the restrictive ideologies of the moment, the young and untamed spirit of the century, it enables, even though out of time, a connection to the postmodernist paradigm, already established across the Ocean. Unfolding the political and social map of that period, charted by the communist doctrine, it seems hard to imagine how it was possible to adopt a libertine literary-artistic trend with chaotic tendencies and extremely permissive in its execution, and which emphasized 'poesis' to the detriment of the 'mimesis' most appreciated and supported by the 'proletkultists'[2]. For, as described by one of the top-line representatives of that period, Mircea Cărtărescu (1999: p. 150):

'The new poetry ... is "plugged to the real" ...The poems are long, random, overwhelmed by images. The reality is presented twisted by an unlimited subjectivity, characterized by the colloquial, the insignificant, and the sordid' (my translation).

---

2   Adepts of the Proletkult, an organization aimed at promoting a class-based cultural movement as expression of working-class (proletarian) identity and ideology.

As main sources of inspiration, alongside those classical ones such as romanticism or expressionism, agglutinated or parodied in various doses and dilutions, I mention here the poetry of the beatniks Allen Ginsberg and Lawrence Ferlinghetti; Frank O'Hara's personism; and the biographism of confessional poetry from Robert Lowell and John Berryman to Sylvia Plath, Anne Sexton and Adrienne Rich. The outcome is a mixtum compositum which singularizes the poets according to the way they choose to orchestrate the whole, combining all these influences in order to emphasize their originality.

If social leveling was customary back then, they looked for and found a way to annul it in literature, avoiding, as much as possible, the guillotine or the noose of censorship. The young poets were writing as if they were truly free or trying to free themselves. Thus, Cărtărescu (1999: p. 155) observes how:

'… the 80s literary generation succeeded … in creating a new sensitivity and a new poetry … it was an open and tolerant liberalism for a great number of existential and aesthetic experiences' (my translation).

The Procrustean bed begins to adjust itself according to the poetry written now: one can notice the colloquial tone, irony, self-irony versus metaphor, the playfulness, jocularities of style and prosody, intertextuality, parody, abdication of metaphysics, self-referentiality, recovering the relationship with the reader, the moral and civic revolt, transitivity, authenticity, directness, biographism, deconstruction, and more. It is a poetry, which, beside the fact that it readjusts the meaning of language on a psychological and social level, succeeds in changing mentalities and, consequently, destinies.

The need for literary renovation in those years corresponded to the desire for political, social and, last but not least, moral liberation, and thus any radical change symbolically implied a break-off from the past by the isolating present. In this respect, Gheorghe Crăciun (2002: p. 283) emphasizes:

'The poetry of the 80s is strongly connected to the socio-cultural context in which it was born and which represents its favorite field of exploration … What's important now … is reality as a place of all life's tensions and what it is also important … is the biographical ego of the one writing' (my translation).

And, not least significant, the reader's part, for which poetry has a performative value, begins to take shape.

The core of the new Romanian poetry was represented by the so called *Monday Literary Circle*, spiritually led by Nicolae Manolescu; but just as important were the representatives of the literary group *Echinox*. These literary-artistic nurseries infused a capitalistic-bohemian breeze into an atmosphere of general stuffiness, somehow purifying the air inside the infernal 'bolgias'3. These artists were called 'the terrible children', and not few times the communist party treated them as such – 'the young generation,' equivalent with an explosive 'state of mind' and invested with a large capital of trust and hope owing to their revolt. This eventually turned into a socio-political element, culminating in the1989 revolution.

Their strength was culture, the critical spirit, 'irony and self-irony' which Ţeposu (2006) considers the foundation of postmodern mentality, as well as 'the ludic discourse' considered by Manolescu as the grain of sand that developed 'the pearl' of rhetoric for most of the important poets of that period. Information was devoured with a hunger for freedom on every level. Thus, their poetical creed expressed in treatises and theoretical texts enjoyed an even larger and stronger diffusion than, by comparison, that of the new wave of the 2000s[4]. A rather strong and 'aggressive' wave provided dynamite for the 80s generation's desire to preserve the already-old guiding marks. Manolescu (2008: p. 1304) believes that: 'a new paradigm … is very probable. Postmodernism starts to belong to the past'. In other words, it 'classicizes', contrary to all its textual intentions and mechanisms.

In the eighth decade anthologies were published in order to give unity to the new poetical vision and to impose a 'generation' through spiritual and mental cohesiveness; for example: *Aer cu diamante/Air with Diamonds* (Mircea Cărtărescu, Traian T. Coşovei, Florin Iaru and Ion Stratan) and *Cinci/Five* (Bogdan Ghiu, Ion Bogdan Lefter, Mariana Marin, Romulus Bucur and Alexandru Muşina). However, the textual identity of the representatives of postmodernism (some of them 'heretics') can also be defined according to a parasitic sphere of influence (surrealism) or to those outside the paradigm itself (romanticism, expressionism, confessional poetry), and which individualize it from case to case.

The literary critic Ion Bogdan Lefter (2005: pp. 155-167) proposes a classification of the numerous poets, most of them part of the *Monday Literary Circle*, according to their rhetoric and favorite subjects: 'the prose-prone'[5], 'the conceptualizers'[6] and 'the proud moralists'[7]. This differentiation is notable mostly when fashionable poetry (represented by 'the prose-prone' poets) is separated from the other trends. The risk resides in the omission or the facile expulsion of some important figures; for example, the poetry of

---

3   The ditches of the eighth Circle of Hell in Dante's *Divine Comedy*.

4   The poets, prose writers, theorists and critics of the consolidation of the paradigm were, among others: Mircea Cărtărescu, Alexandru Muşina, Gheorghe Crăciun, Marin Mincu, Al. Cistelecan, Radu G. Ţeposu, Ion Bogdan Lefter, Nicolae Manolescu, and more.

5   Romulus Bucur, Mircea Cărtărescu, Dumitru Chioaru, Traian T. Coşovei, Denisa Comănescu, Magdalena Ghica, Florin Iaru, Alexandru Muşina, Liviu I. Stoiciu, etc.

6   Liviu Antonesei, Bogdan Ghiu, Ion Bogdan Lefter, Marta Petreu, Ion Stratan, Eugen Suciu, etc.

7   Nichita Danilov, Mariana Marin, Ioan Morar, Ion Mureşan, Petru Romoşan, Matei Vişniec, etc.

Mariana Marin, Ion Mureşan and Marta Petreu is considered by Cărtărescu (1999: p. 157) 'valuably spectacular but quite undeveloped as poetics'.

Lefter (2005: pp. 47-48) also involves the newer poetry of the young poets of the 80s in a dialogue with the old generation of Romanian poets, finding for each of them a tutelary spirit from which they claim the pattern of the poem, even unconsciously, in an ineludible intrusion of the influence. Thus, there are 'the Arghezians' who 'develop their poems "extensively"' (Mircea Cărtărescu, Alexandru Muşina, Magdalena Ghica, Liviu Stoiciu, Florin Iaru, Traian Coşovei), 'the Barbians' who 'follow an "intensive", abstract and concentrated pattern' (Marta Petreu, Ion Stratan, Bogdan Ghiu) and 'the Bacovians' who prefer 'the direct confrontation, in solitude, with the world and its large categories' (Mariana Marin, Ion Mureşan, Petru Romoşan).

At this point, it must be mentioned that the feminine reflection upon the self and the world, in a Bacovian style – the new femininity of a debtless or concession-free lucidity, and articulated, for example, by Mariana Marin and Marta Petreu, either hermetically-metaphorically, or lapidarily and in an excessively conceptualizing manner – will create a confessional poetry of verbal implosion. And, even if this confession does not represent a paradigm *per se* in our case, but only the branch of a genealogy of vision and inner experience, the more it particularizes the scene of postmodernism with themes and discourses of immanence which are inseparable from the instinct of truth and ethics, and the more important it becomes. All these occur in a time when humankind, besides a 'dictatorship for mind and heart' (as labeled by Mariana Marin), has literature as part of its own being along with the vital organs, and sees the only way for liberation – even when dragged from the self and perverted by small or big battles with corrosive history – as the exposure of whatever is most intimate and irrepressible.

Even if the new poetical turn rejects the advantages of modernity, it is important to identify the points of tension in which postmodernity meets with expressionism; for instance, with the most schizoid and convulsive elements as a means of reference to exteriority. It is then that all of these – transferred afterwards to the 'narrative ipseity'[8] (Sartre 2004), and psychologically guaranteed and ontologically resized by dilution in the spacious melting-pot of rhetoric and confessional poetic discourse – could establish, in fact, the text's ontology.

One expressionist super-theme is the nude exposure of feminine corporality; the image of the body as a metaphor for the emotional and mental stages of a woman seeking ways of liberation, and an emphasis which make use, in the subconscious, of the concept of truth as the prerogative of liberation from inhibitions, be they written or physical:

---

8   Identity.

'In an immense canvas work of the eminent artist Ferdinand Hodler … the abstract concept
of truth is allegorically represented by the image of a woman in the nude, whose light is
blinding the clothed masculine figures around her.'

(Bassie 2008: p. 38)

So here, as also depicted by Simone de Beauvoir (2008), we are dealing with
the woman who becomes a woman, declaring herself as such and, more
importantly, remaining an independent and conscious 'Subject', which no
longer slips into the masculine area of influence, playing the supporting part
of that vague 'Autre' which defines and completes virility rather than
defining itself. Now, the poetess emanates the light that uncovers the path to
self-conquered independence of body and mind.

On the other hand, Radu G. Țeposu (2006) makes his own classification
of contemporary poets: 'the jest and prosaic everyday life'[9]; 'the gnomic and
esoteric mannerists'[10]; 'the abstract and hermetical fantasticalness'[11]; 'the
crisis of interiority and the ironic and sarcastic pathos'[12]; 'the dramatic and
histrionic criticism'[13], and 'the refined sentimentalists'[14]. Being less
drastically elitist than Mircea Cărtărescu, Țeposu decants the sources of
postmodernism from a 'reversed romanticism' to an integrated expressionism. In this respect, Cistelecan (2006: p. 11) notes:

'Fundamentally, however, it is a "reversed romanticism" or an inhibited romanticism …
one that doesn't the new expressionism send to the margins, to provincialism. On the
contrary, it tries to make it compatible with postmodernism' (my translation).

Imagining postmodernism as a 'form of recovering "nihilism"'(Țeposu
2006), the author of the *Tragic and Grotesque History* sets into a consensual
dialogue the various influences of literary movements, which turns the new
poetical paradigm into a much more composite vision of the world. And this
vision –with ontological implications illustrated in the fiber of the discourse
on all levels, from semantics to semiotics, and, at the same time, less chaotic
and incoherent than it would seem at first sight – is based on 'irony'. It is a
structural irony which does not exclude nostalgia and melancholy, but ab-
sorbs them and purifies them of illusion, becoming aware of their own
spiritual emaciation which sets the foundation for reflexes against the
mentality of the age. In the poems of Mariana Marin or Marta Petreu these
two temperamental states (nostalgia and melancholy) are combined with a
sharp lucidity regarding the deconstruction of the self into elements of inner

---

9   In the works of Mircea Cărtărescu, Traian Coșovei, Liviu Ioan Stoiciu and Alexandru
Mușina.
10   Like Nichita Danilov, I. B. Lefter, Mariana Codruț.
11   Illustrated by Aurel Pantea, Ion Stratan, Ioan Moldovan.
12   Of Ion Mureșan, Mariana Marin, Marta Petru, Magdalena Ghica, Elena Ștefoi.
13   Represented by Petru Romoșan, Octavian Soviany, Mircea Petean.
14   The likes of Romulus Bucur, Dumitru Chioaru, etc.

stagnation, of inertia; thunderously denounced, only in order to be then dominated.

The state of demiurge remains the prerogative of the text that orders emotions and feelings; thus, deep interaction with reality will be managed and maintained through writing. Radu G. Țeposu (2006: p. 67) states that 'All the illusions of the postmodernists, if any, are textual in nature, related to technique, to development', and he confronts romantic irony, which is of an ontological nature, to the irony of postmodernism, whose function is more critical and rhetorical, designed to bring transcendence down into immanence or to make immanence the only valid measuring unit for reality, especially since: 'Reality has been replaced by the idea of real' (Ibid.: p. 58).

Apart from 'the idea of real' turned on all its textualist-ontological facets, 'the expression' of reality, its perception and internal reverberations have a decisive importance not only for the expressionists, but also for the representatives of the confessional literary trend of the eighties, who owe a lot to their precursors, the likes of Ileana Mălăncioiu or Angela Marinescu. Although this affinity remains mainly one of status, the thanatophoria[15] and erotophagy[16] in Marta Petreu and Mariana Marin's works approach a postmodern rhetoric and come from a world irretrievably decentered. Even if the great metaphysical themes are also found in their poetry, they are inevitably recalibrated. Weeping and anger build to an implosive syntax, and the 'autophagy' of Romanian women's poetry of the 80s comes not only to consume a particular vision inoculated with the germs of decomposition, its secret ploy is to destroy an entire social mechanism through personal dismantling.

After this digression, it is no wonder that critical discourse on women's poetry also undergoes changes and acquires important nuances. Nicolae Manolescu (2001) welcomed the debut of the young poetesses of the 80s, focusing on the lack of illusion in their poetry, which is cerebrally registered without any metaphorical restraints. He is surprised by the seriousness of these poetesses compared to the more playful style of masculine poetry, especially when playfulness does occur it has a deeply tragic side to it, and reiterates the scenario of ongoing mortification, along with sentimental and pathetic poses which are not by any means devoid of irony or self-irony.

Radu G. Țeposu (2006: p. 138) speaks of postmodern feminine poetry as soaked in sarcasm, as a kind of 'rebellion of the senses and of the instincts … shyness is abandoned in favor of direct confession, devoid of rhetorical tricks …', while Marin Mincu (2007) sees young 'textualist' poetesses as the heiresses of an 'blasphemous nihilism', because of the 'aggressive tone, the virility' of the discourse and the importance of conveying an ethical message.

---

15   Affinity toward death.
16   Devour the object of affection.

This inner necessity of finding the truth through poetry, positions such poets as Ileana Mălăncioiu, Mariana Marin and Marta Petreu as supporters of the 'expressionism' described by Charles Taylor (1989: pp. 370-390); the language of this trend of thought outlines the origins of a subjectivity seen as the 'expression' of an interiority which no longer remains isolated, but provokes itself to fulfill its latencies and potential and it does, at the moment of its articulation and externalization.

'... the voice of the nature within us ...This notion of depth is related ... to the understanding that we have of ourselves, as being expressive, as articulating an inner source'.

(Taylor 1989: pp. 370-390)

In the case of the above-mentioned poetesses, the written endeavor of confession keeps on constant alert the 'intrinsic intentionality' to extract and decant matter, and the existentialist substance of self-realization, beyond the prerogative of the lyrical ego.

At this point, it is important to emphasize the traces of originality that make the lyrical universe of each poetess discussed here a space for liberating confession as a personal mark, but also a strategy for the mental fight for freedom from a communist regime in full bloom. In mapping the arch-text of female poetry of the 70s and 80s, one identifies the design of personal(istic) identity, as shown, for example, in the works of Mariana Marin, Marta Petreu and Ileana Mălăncioiu.

The favorite themes of the 80s poets revolve around the constant attempts to search for personal identity, and also the definition of otherness that proves intrusive and corrosive in regard to their mental integrity. The mask and the duality – the appeal to the supporting character, which is actually the main character in the hierarchies of traumas that need verbalization – remain some of the most used and useful strategies of self-escape and self-cancellation.

2. Outraged Textual Identities

As a representative of Romanian women's poetry of the 80s, Mariana Marin builds battle arenas within nearly every poem in her collection The Studios, where personal and social identity are placed face to face (here, Adrienne Rich is an important source of inspiration) as antagonistic parts of the same contorted entity. Exteriority is defined by the communist regime, and interiority by that thanatophoria which can be found in all of Martha Petreu's poems, as well. At the same time, interiority also presupposes that the lyrical ego becomes one with the voice of the private identity, for only in this way can it articulate its tribulations. Writing remains an alternative life, the body of the repressed that heals by throwing itself into the world so that its scars can be 'read' and even opened and exsanguinated of the accumulated poison. Our poetess leads poetry to the limit of enlisted life as an important factor of dissidence and normality; that is why love, disease, death, and happiness are subsumed to the same irrepressible need for truth.

This is not poetry that demonstrates a thesis, but one that seeks its textual identity in conjunction with the needs of immanence, and of a conscience constantly tortured by the idea of not having been able to fulfill its vital project, which is actually poetry: a lucid mirror of the mind and soul of the poetess engulfed by the fear of demystification. Her imaginary world derives from the atmosphere of the concentration camps in the Second World War. Like Sylvia Plath, Mariana Marin, in addition to the elegiac vision that both poetesses cast like a net over the world, primarily rebels against her own self, writing her poetry in view of this, only in a less pathetic tone than that of the American poet. Metaphor is used to describe the ontological space where Marin feels safe, but which she will abandon along the way, when, one by one, the masks fall off. *The Dowry of Gold* of the poet will be exactly this lesson of courage; the freedom to make sacrifices for what one thinks can stand for salvation in the end: poetry.

Mariana Marin admirably manages to maintain an ethical and aesthetic continuity between the Self of indivisible ideals and the writhing Ego. This achievement prevails in the *Elegies* widespread in most volumes, which are a means of rendering the essence of poetry and, most important, the essence of it being impregnated with the chill of death and of the necessity of articulating truth as an identity of substance: '… personal identity is identity of substance … in consequence … is somehow more real or genuine than the identity of other things' (Noonan 2003: p. 63). For our confessional poetess, as for Butler and Reid, identity requires constancies inalienable by fluctuating external conditions, which were quite hard to achieve given the Communist regime.

Marin remains one of the most profoundly moral poets of her generation. This means that her sincerity about the inevitable cowardice of humankind under communism is of a merciless lucidity, and thus allows her to keep her identity of idealistic substance intact, meaning that she still believes in the destiny of the martyr of and for art. Her poetry causes mutations not only in her own conscience (which she is perfectly aware of; specifically that it requires great attention) but also in the public conscience, as emphasized both by Carmen Muşat (2009) and Radu Vancu (2009) in their articles. The latter compares the philosophy of the poet's verse to Kierkegaard's vision, according to which 'the aesthetic experience is valued only by its synthesis with ethics'.

Marin's *Elegies*, as with all her poems, prove to be negations of inner inertia to psychological and physical abuse caused by the communist regime: 'For years I have raised the evil in me,/hoping and hoping to survive the outer one' (*Elegy*). Although it involves splitting, the tearing up of the integrity of being and the unfettered jets of bile drowning her youthful effusions, the evil inside becomes equal in quality to the good outside. Private evil stifles by self-devouring the temptation to spill the cup of depression into the world, where it is likely to hurt concretely and gratuitously.

The Romanian poetess did not set herself boundaries in building textual alternatives to a universe flawed from the outside. Thus, we find that Marin is not in fact quite a textualist. She was actively involved in the fight against the regime, as witnessed by her poetry and her generation's colleagues. Florin Iaru reports, in a *Remember* article in the *Observator Cultural* magazine of 2003, that she became a dissident figure for whom the trigger and the mobilizing spark were the fact that the writer Paul Goma had taken a stand, as well as the trade union movements in Valea Jiului:

'From that moment Mariana Marin became a militant. She was the standard-bearer for serious uprisings of all artists of the eighties … for her it was that moment which decided her way of writing. That's all. A sort of poetic and feminine order in an increasingly disordered life' (my translation).

(Iaru 2003)

We see the personal identity of the writer beginning to impetuously conquer social identity and ipseity which, in turn, will influence her later plunge into reality. Here, the poem, sometimes too fragile, is taken by force, subject to the misinterpretation and annihilation of the original message:

'Should you break the poem's neck/ When you learn its writing's done out of you?/ Tormenting and pointless mutiny./ Do not be afraid:/ there is always someone/ (a sticky mouth)/ to whisper in your ear/ the truth of tomorrow/ and of history behind' (my translation).

(*Elegy II*)

Inner freedom of thought is constantly encroached on, and it must, in Big Brother's opinion, be confiscated and dealt with unreservedly.

The disintegration of personal identity in Mariana Marin's poems begins, as we shall find, with the corruption of community language. When the lyrical ego confesses that:

'… between me and you (it's said)/will always be a Europe or a Red Sea./The language in which I ponder the word death/is not the language in which you ponder the word love' (my translation).

(*Elegy XII*)

We understand how, from behind the Iron Curtain, feelings and moments universally accepted as being substantial, cannot tie to their natural signified. We have ahead a dark place of the irreparable break with the normality of a human being's freedom to feel; to feel oneself fully belonging to oneself, in death and love alike – which now strike one as being thanatophoric and erotophagous:

'I'm asking you to flee into the chasm given to us/ There, your freckles and your red hair/ will understand and will certainly love/ my breasts' language …/ between which death shall then spend the night' (my translation).

(Elegy XII)

The lack of hope gives birth to a dying language, touched by illness; it speaks the language of Death which is also the language of communist dictatorship, showing precisely why it is ineffective in establishing emotional interactions between those still alive in terms of consciousness integrity. The constant sensation of mind claustration is at the same time a curse and a means of self-preservation for the Romanian poetesses of the 70s and 80s, as Damasio (2002: p. 371) very well describes the phenomenon:

'Mais la conscience des patients atteints de "locked-in" demeure intacte. Ills sont par-faitement éveillés, alerts et conscients de leur activité mentale. Incapables, toutefois, de mouvoir …'[17].

The only salvation for Mariana Marin, and for her readers later, is the true image of her thoughts inserted into the poem; the lyrical ego fighting otherness, beyond the arena of the verse:

'I still wake up with my old unearthly language/ or stolen by a commando group/ banished to the outskirts of the alphabet …/ Isn't there any escape/ for our image/ enclosed in flesh and love inside the poem? …/ but how do we speak to Death/ when she approaches us, wrapped/ in cruel vowels among the living …' (my translation).

(Elegy IV)

She is deeply involved in the crusade against duplicity and treason at all levels, thus facing (inner) death with the courage of the apostles.

On the other hand, apart from a few poems that refer quite evidently to the communist regime, another representative of the Romanian poetry of the 80s, Marta Petreu, shows a preference for the egocentric exposé of intimacy analyzed in all its facets, to exhaustion. In her case, the visceral enlists the text along with theories of emotional corporality. Constantly provoking taboos, textual identity is built on the skeleton of a schizoid personality, and of conceptual language, sometimes brutal, with a hysterical voice that, thus, hides its own feminine fragility.

---

17   'But the consciousness of patients with "locked-in" remains intact. They are awake, alert and aware of their mental activity. Unable, however, to move…' (my translation).

Since her first volume, *Bring the Verbs*, Petreu proves she is aware of the importance of outlining her verbal portrait – that of the iconoclastic '*apocalyptic virgin*' – which later appears engaged in extensive, dialogue/monologue with Divinity. The verb becomes anathema, a means of evasion or influence, and takes over the driving force of the doomed universe.

Martha Petreu's imagination floods the world with écorchés[18] and visions of death, and at the same time, it indicates second degree states that are restrained, intellectualized, and which do not reveal the poet's pure emotion but represent the processing of this emotion in the brain-crucible of poetry. It aims to be both authentic and conceptualizing. Despair, depression, anger, cursing and physical suffering, obsession, gangrene, hysteria (Anne Sexton influences her themes), all these contribute to the reader's state of mind, and in *A Psychic Place* and the *Book of Anger*, Petreu proves to be a great master-orchestrator of inner self-centered, sarcastic and ironic decay.

As we will find out, the 'concept' is the ontological space in which Petreu isolates herself, seeking her own linguistic and semantic uniqueness in the Romanian women's poetry of her generation. Here, even love, which is always sought after, analyzed and classified, remains deeply conflicting and generates vast interrogations which arouse a lust to self-devour. Hiding the genuine face behind the mask as a dog buries bones reveals the daily disaster and the boldness of such defiance.

The same implosive rebelliousness is also found in several poems from Petreu's volume *Psychic Place*. Here, writers remain as white blood cells, defending the integrity and significance of most people's truth, except that, during this endeavor, the crusaders sometimes turn into offerings on the altar of their ideals:

'Writers are dying. Poets are dying. Oh …/ … They are now cannon flesh/ of a deaf war carried …/ they break ranks, writing. They bear/ on shoulders their uncorrupted brains, mortal brains …/ just as galaxies fade running towards red/ Under earth on earth libraries burn, their nerves burn/ shaking' (my translation).

(Homeland's Running towards Red)

Marta Petreu displays remarkable lucidity in describing the communist regime; she understands that times are awful, but not eternal: 'We live the fall. Not the end' (*Night Laboratory*). The poetess brings together concrete elements (the boot) and its opposite, spiritual matter (the brain) to render, in oxymoronic images, the cruel accuracy of oppression: 'Yes: I do possess the exact inventory/ of all crushing forms (look now/ my brain like a snail comforted by a boot' (*Winter Solstice*). She is aware that, beyond all shortcomings, the most terrifying thing is the regime's attempt at brainwashing, which is why she describes the process with appropriate irony

---

18   Visible muscular structures of anatomical figures without the skin.

138

and sarcasm: 'thoughts driven into a corner;/ My thinking species – ordinary cargo/ Only plant life brings benefits/ Soft dreamy skulls, tender water lily buds' (Water Lily Skulls in the Cemeteries of Innocents).

Accordingly, it is no wonder that Petreu sees in writing – and even in utopias that remain equal to themselves – an opportunity to escape and to develop: 'Speech about great expectations/ Remember the preludes: only here/ our verbal substance grows' (*Night Laboratory*). But the feeling of claustrophobia, of the inner blocks of poetesses immersed in the perfectly lucid awareness of helplessness, overwhelm both Marta Petreu and Mariana Marin, in their verses: 'Yes, that small writing/ Canvas of young dead' (*Elegy*).

It is the same in Ileana Mălăncioiu's poetry. A representative figure of the 70s, her death allegories carry their back-to-front message, denouncing, in eloquent *absentia*, elements that could not be directly mentioned during the Communist regime, and which everyone knows what or whom they are regarding: 'Someone saw to it we no longer really be/ Not even two together and it did/ And all is harder to endure'(*From Silence*); 'You know what I think of; what everyone/ Thinks of' (*The Great Hope*); 'One kind of fall/ One kind of deliverance/ We wait to drop on us from the clouds/ On a great day' (*Silence*). Metonymy and synecdoche weave deep layers of meaning in the poem, with absence and silence becoming so strident, that, as Serge André (2010: p. 80) notes: '… la satisfaction … pourrait viser le Non-Être plutôt que l'Être'[19].

The poems in Mălăncioiu's volume *The Climbing of the Mountain* are built on two antagonistic reference levels, overlapping in their simultaneity of lucid feeling, and invaded by symbols just to make the routine of terror bearable. Paradoxically, by this artifice of the amalgamation of spheres of reference, this routine appears to be even more attached to its concreteness, stressing the precision and perseverance with which generalized anxiety cripples the inner universe:

'The whole city was dead-full/ They were out on the main street …/ They seemed …/ Too many and there was no more room/ For those of us who are still alive …/ The fantastic delirium frightened us,/ For everyone had someone in the street/ And we wouldn't want them to be locked in the cemetery' (my translation).

(Nightmare)

The Climbing of the Mountain deliberately begins with the Nightmare poem– followed by two homonym poems strategically placed –which is emblematic of the state of affairs and of the spirit described throughout the book. Life now acquires oneiric meanings, its legitimacy thus being plunged into the abyss. It becomes equivalent to a bad dream, saving that it is impossible for the thanatic lyrical ego to wake up anywhere other than in the same delirium

---

19   '…the satisfaction … could aim at the Non-Being rather than the Being' (my translation).

('When I dream I wake up beyond/ And I'm sorry there is no sun anymore/ And I slowly pull the earth across my face/ And it hurts'), or in prison ('And forgotten in his dreamy world/ Awaiting spring in which he still has hope/ That we will come again out of the shade' – I Am a Human Who), or in the grave ('... from time to time/ Earth comes down on someone' – The Beginning of the End), the three becoming synonymous when a coming into the light no longer seems possible. As in the myth of Plato's cave, shadows are no longer distinguishable from the living; in fact, everything that lives, somehow, dies ('Do not be afraid of death anymore/ More than of the life you live'– Illusion).

The inevitable impression of eternity ('Oh God, how we all fear/ That this spring will come, too, for nothing,/ That summer and autumn will come/ Only what we dream of won't' – *The Great Hope*) that permeates Mălăncioiu's verse does not accentuate the depressive-passive side ('Any road leads still there/ Time of melancholy has passed' – *Song*), but the socially responsible and reactive side of the poet ('Something should raise the dead/ From the silence they were bound to' – *From Silence*). And that mobilizing spark surprisingly becomes the descent into the Inferno of the lyrical ego, generically embodying the individual, subject to communist doctrine through the extensive comparison between his will and soul, and the realm of the dead: 'All this endless string/ Of people buried standing/ So as to leave more room' (*Buried Standing*).

Derived from the social, the personal ordeal will change – 'dominated entirely by chance', as Georges Minois (1998: p. 361) states, referring to Camus's hell at whose limit:

'Being becomes … synonymous to hell. Being aware of the futility of existence, of the fact of being thrown into a world without purpose, destination, meaning, to be "alien" to others: this is what hell means. All we can do is to look at our own condition lucidly, from a defying position.'

This is in fact the subject of defiance in Ileana Mălăncioiu's poetry; she is constantly playing with the prospect of a genuine Hell, considered a desirable and more gentle alternative to Communism:

'I saw with eyes half open the Angel of Death,…/ I was more afraid than ever,/ I wanted more than ever to exist/ and there was my Guardian Angel/ Dressed as a policeman …/ When nervous it was walking before the gate/ And I woke up shouting terrified:/ Haven't you seen the Angel of Death?' (my translation).

(*Angel of Death*)

Mălăncioiu keeps her deeply expressionist roots, antagonizing – especially in *The Climbing of the Mountain*, through the purity of biblically inspired language – a 'wooden language' stiffness, the mark of inertia of the 'Mind of the Nation'. Between Emily Dickinson's poetry and that of Adrienne Rich, the poetry of Ileana Mălăncioiu has the depth of allegories of death and imagines ethereal but imposing characters, lost specters, angels, butterflies, symbols of the haunting of mind and soul, which transfers the clarity and strength of the after-life into the world of the concrete, which can, to a certain extent, be defeated. The ritual of the mask, of small rhetorical interrogations which overturn the existing mentality, makes 'the parable' an ontological safe space where Mălăncioiu hides her secret wing, comb and enchanted foal. Those totem-like objects will prove to provide salvation to the extent to which they are vested with thaumaturgic[20] properties and only if the lyrical ego can live the 'Beyond' as if it were 'Here'. The chronotope of the real world is characterized by the pain caused by loss; thus the lyrical ego always crosses the 'forbidden zone' toward the ideal self.

The only important concern in *The Climbing of the Mountain* remains that of the inner effects the infinite ascension-purgatory implants in the soul, and also in the history of a nation, reflected, not infrequently, in personal psychosis. The mystery of the Eucharist appears now charged with profane elements:

'I cannot complain of hunger, / My food comes from heaven/ But I fear for the god/ Who will feed on me .../ I'm too black, too sad/ My sacrifice may seem to him/ Even leaner than it is/ And worse and more bitter' (my translation).

(I Cannot Complain)

It pushes the subject, with a spirit affected by disease, on to a secondary stream of life: 'In another world, in another life, in another dream/ Something closer to chimaera/ Long pursued, or in my own death/ That will change atmosphere a little, anyway' (*In Many Ways It May Come*). The poetry redeems and in a way artistically compensates a posteriori for the wounds of lost generations that had fallen prey to the Communist gangrene. If we read it and value it from the present perspective, taking into consideration that the point of reference is and was the audacity to speak up in a world of mumblings, Ileana Mălăncioiu's discourse of resistance stands for another kind of fight, a more insidious one: the one that changed the mentality about the ethics of taking a stand, no matter the risks, the censorship amputations or the imminent dangers of the time.

3. Conclusions

In A Theory of the Secondary developed by Virgil Nemoianu (1997: p. 102):

---

20   Miraculous, magic.

'... the pathological reality becomes both the modeller and the modelled, new semic features arise, and the disease is integrated into a new circuit of symbolic meanings' (my translation).

Thus, what the pathological reality saves becomes equivalent to disintegration and reconstruction within a scenario of self-denial, which is the domain of the poetesses under scrutiny. The lyrical ego wears the mask of the universal and supreme victim; Death therefore comes as an alternative of objectification, of escaping to life from the posture of prey always hunted, in a continuous inner suppression. The construction of otherness is based on a process involving the sublimation of lack of freedom in the prospect of death, described in a sarcastic framework. This process aims at disclosing the truth rather than metamorphosing – Serge André (2010: p. 75) notes in this regard that: 'Pour Lacan, ce n'est pas le Beau qui est visé dans la sublimation, mais le Vrai, et le vrai n'est pas nécessairement beau à voir'[21].

Theorizing postmodernism, Brian McHale (2009: p. 58) notes that:

'... by placing himself at the forefront of his work ... the artist represented in the act of creation or destruction is himself inevitably a work of fiction. The real artist always occupies a higher ontological level than his imagined, fictional self, and therefore is twice superior to the fictional world ...'.

With regard to the Romanian confessional female poets, things are different – completely the opposite, actually: the 'fictional' artist is far more superior to the flesh and blood one in 'the absolute ontological boundary between life and death' (McHale 2009), where he/she comes to get rid of his/her 'real' body, thus leaving on paper a mythical character, which is, paradoxically, more impregnated by authenticity and ontological weight than the 'living' being which, in the hierarchy, is intended to be a secondary character.

The 'death of the author' makes reference to an inter-text of another subversive text which suddenly starts to write itself, enriched with a dramatic substance which guarantees the lack of any kind of restraint from the reader who is instantly mesmerized. 'The ontological void' the poems suffer from, becomes in this case, an overflow.

What turns Mariana Marin and Martha Petreu into postmodernist heretics (therefore no less postmodern through the immanent condition and status assumed in their time), is 'integrated experimentalism', with the ontological guarantee of the manner they choose, or are chosen, to write in, faithful to a constant need to appeal to metaphysics, be it more of a verbal artifice rather than the philosophical basis for integrating thought.

The textualism these neo-expressionist poetesses adopt acquires an aura of tragedy and rebelliousness, even to the annihilation of the self as part of the Communist establishment. The war that was started and carried out on

---

21 'For Lacan, the process of sublimation is not aimed at beauty, but at truth, and truth is not necessarily beautiful to see' (my translation).

paper or, on the contrary, the bohemianism and decadence, give birth to another *alter ego* that in turn gave rise to an alternative world, by means of 'ipseity' and the discourse of resistance. Therefore an identity 'split', personal annihilation or an exacerbation of the negative, encountered in the work of Romanian poetesses of the 70s and 80s, is the mark of an internalized and decisive battle. We witness how dictatorship is eluded through self-inflicted hatred; our poetesses choose to cross the line and rebel in their poetry – first against their own incapacity. In doing so, they manage to seed the grain of 'normality' that stands for an oasis of morality in the desert of immorality, i.e., the Communist regime.

Bibliography

André, Serge (2010) *Le symptôme et la création*, Editions Le Bord de l'Eau: Collection La Muette.

Bassie, Ashley (2008) *Expresionismul*, Oradea: Aquila.

Beauvoir, Simone de (2008) *La femme indépendante*, Paris: Gallimard.

Cărtărescu, Mircea (1999) *Postmodernismul românesc*, Bucharest: Humanitas.

Cistelecan, Alexandru (2004) *Al doilea top*, Braşov: Aula.

Cistelecan, Alexandru (2006) 'Postmodernismul bovaric' (Foreword), in Radu G. Ţeposu (2006) *Istoria tragică & grotescă a întunecatului deceniu literar nouă*, Bucharest: Cartea Românească.

Crăciun, Gheorghe (2002) *Aisbergul poeziei moderne*, Piteşti: Paralela 45.

Damasio, Antonio R. (2002) *Le Sentiment même de soi. Corps, émotions, conscience*, Paris: Éditions Odile Jacob.

Iaru, Florin (2003) 'In memoriam Mariana Marin', *Observator Cultural*, No. 164 (April).

Lefter, Ion Bogdan (2005) *Flashback 1985: Începuturile 'noii poezii'*, Piteşti: Paralela 45.

Lefter, Ion Bogdan (2005) *Puzzle cu 'noul val'. Addenda la falsul tratat de poezie Flashback 1985*, Piteşti: Paralela 45.

Lyotard, Jean-François (2003) *Condiţia postmodernă*, Cluj: Idea Design & Print.

Manolescu, Nicolae (2008) *Istoria critică a literaturii române. 5 secole de literatură*, Piteşti: Paralela 45.

Manolescu, Nicolae (1999) *Arca lui Noe. Eseu despre romanul românesc*, Bucharest: Gramar.

Marin, Mariana (2002) *Zestrea de aur*, Bucharest: Muzeul Literaturii Române Publishing House.

Marin, Mariana (1999) *Mutilarea artistului la tinereţe*, Bucharest: Muzeul Literaturii Române Publishing House.

Marin, Mariana (1991) *Atelierele*, Bucharest: Cartea Românească.

Marin, Mariana (1986) *Aripa secretă*, Bucharest: Cartea Românescă.

Marin, Mariana (1982) 'La întretăierea drumurilor comerciale', in Mariana Marin, Romulus Bucur, Bogdan Ghiu, Ion Bogdan Lefter & Alexandru Muşina, *Cinci*, Bucharest: Litera.

Mălăncioiu, Ileana (2010) *Sora mea de dincolo*, Bucharest: Litera Internaţional.

Mălăncioiu, Ileana (2007) *Urcarea muntelui*, Bucharest: Corint.

Mălăncioiu, Ileana (2003) *Recursul la memorie. Convorbiri cu Daniel-Cristea Enache*, Iaşi: Polirom.

Mălăncioiu, Ileana (1999) *Linia vieţii*, Iaşi: Polirom.

Mălăncioiu, Ileana (1992) *Urcarea muntelui*, Bucharest: Albatros./ (1985) Second edition, Bucharest: Litera.

McHale, Brian (2009) *Ficţiunea postmodernistă*, Iaşi: Polirom.

Mihăieş, Mircea (2005) *Cărţile crude. Jurnalul intim şi sinuciderea*, Iaşi: Polirom.

Mincu, Marin (2007) *O panoramă critică a poeziei româneşti din secolul al XX-lea*, Constanţa: Pontica.

Muske, Carol (1997) *Women and Poetry. Truth, Autobiography, and the Shape of the Self*, The University of Michigan Press Ann Arbor.

Muşat, Carmen (2009) 'Mariana Marin: identitatea etic-estetic. "Toate minciunile despre libertate"', *Observator Cultural. Supliment* (October), 236(494).

Muşina, Alexandru (2008) *Poezia: teze, ipoteze, explorări*, Braşov: Aula.

Muşina, Alexandru (2004) *Paradigma poeziei moderne*, Braşov: Aula.

Nemoianu, Virgil (1997) *O teorie a secundarului*, Bucharest: Univers.

Petreu, Marta (2011) *Apocalipsa după Marta*, Iaşi: Polirom.

Petreu, Marta (2001) *Falanga*, Cluj-Napoca: Biblioteca Apostrof.

Petreu, Marta (1997) *Cartea mâniei*, Bucharest: Albatros.

Petreu, Marta (1991) *Loc psihic*, Cluj-Napoca: Editura Dacia.

Petreu, Marta (1983) *Dimineaţa tinerelor doamne*, Bucharest: Cartea Românească.

Petreu, Marta (1981) *Aduceţi verbele*, Bucharest: Cartea Românească.

Rankine, Claudia (2001) 'The First Person in the Twenty-First Century', in Kate Sontag & David Graham (eds.) *After Confession. Poetry as Autobiography*, Saint Paul, Minnesota: Graywolf Press.

Ricoeur, Paul (1984) *Metafora vie*, translated from French by Irina Mavrodin, Bucharest: Univers.

Sartre, Jean-Paul (2004) *The Imaginary: A Phenomenological Psychology of the Imagination*, translated from French by Jonathan Webber, London and New York: Routledge.

Taylor, Charles (1989) *Sources of the Self: The Making of Modern Identity*, Cambridge Mass.: Harvard University Press.

Ţeposu, Radu G. (2006) *Istoria tragică & grotescă a întunecatului deceniu literar nouă*, Bucharest: Cartea Românească.

Vancu, Radu (2009) 'Mariana Marin: identitatea etic-estetic: "Poezie şi adevăr"', *Observator Cultural. Supliment* (October), 236(494): 1–7.

CHAPTER VI

Corporeality and Sexuality in Women's Autofictions: A Few Romanian Examples

Florina-Elena PÎRJOL

1. Autofiction – Writing the (Feminine) Self in Postmodern Times

A well known preconception, which, just like any 'literary' preconception, occurs mainly in the field of critical reception, says that literary genres of a personal nature, such as biographies or personal diaries (the genre of maximum 'honesty') are the area of expertise of women writers. According to the same preconception women's writing, with all its negative features, among which lyricism, excessive psychologizing, simplistic or, on the contrary, intricate phrasing, loose structure, etc. is bound to operate in the most comfortable and apparently the most accessible literary area: that is the 1st person narrative.

The autobiographical novel, on one hand, and diary writing and the epistolary genre, on the other hand, are well represented in history by women writers, but not exclusively as a token of the contemporary movement for women's emancipation, if we consider the success of Madame de Sévigné's letters. However, autobiography, as a classical literary genre, 'reserved to important figures of the day', as Serge Doubrovsky put it, remains a genre inaccessible to women writers, who are denied access to a public 'voice'.

Moreover, should Käte Hamburger's radical position be acceped 1st person narrative cannot even be included in the category of literary fiction: 'The phenomenology of 1st person narrative texts reveals that they belong to a non-fictional literary genre, although they are considered genres of epic fiction' (Hamburger 1993: p. 337). Therefore, against the background of the increasing tendency to mistake the fictional for the literary, the so-called 'feminine writing', a concept which makes more sense in politics than in literature should be excluded from the vast field of literature. Once the concepts of 'autobiography' and 'fiction' were redifined, when postmodern philosophers and historians rethought the notions of 'reality' and 'truth', autobiographical writing was no longer a convenient option even for women writers. In the meantime, they had acquired sound literary voices of their own coming out from under the authoritarian regime of the 1st person narrative.

The name Simone de Beauvoir is of great importance for the French cultural space as well as for the international one, not merely as a writer of high quality literature, but mainly as producer of an ideological discourse that gave visibility to women writers. Marguerite Duras and Nathalie Sarraute are two other important names without whom the female literary voices of the 90s that made the autofictional genre famous would not have had that much force. Since this is a genre born on French ground, in response to a 'local' literary tradition and ideology, I am going to limit my analysis to French literature and try to shape a family-like environment for women's autofictions.

Beginning with the 70s and especially during the 80s, two decades influenced by the experimentalism of the 'Nouveau Roman' and by theoretical marginalization of personal genres, women writers began to seek legitimation strategies for a type of literature that was clearly 'in danger', to use Tzvetan Todorov's famous phrase. It was then that Hélène Cixous and Annie Ernaux began to refuse to indicate the genre on the cover or on the title page, thus anticipating a genre that would be based precisely on this generic ambiguity. Annie Ernaux would take this attitude to the extreme, eventually parting with the permissive genre of autofiction ('I feel a complete stranger to autofiction', she says) and defining her literature as a written report, a 'self-socio-biography', 'something between literature, sociology and history' (Ernaux 1993: p. 221). When Christine Angot, who would later become the icon of French autofiction emerged on the literary market, the distinction between fiction and autobiography was no longer a topic of interest to anyone. Autobiography was dead, long live autofiction!

Based on a comprehensive analysis of women's writing in contemporary France, Philippe Gasparini identifies two distinct directions, corresponding to two main patterns of women's autofiction: *emotional writing* (in the tradition of the 70s), represented by Christine Angot, Virginie Despentes, Marie Darrieussecq, Marie Ndiaye, Catherine Cusset, Lorette Nobécourt, Chloé Delaume, Elisabeth Barillé, etc.; and *traditional rational writing* (along the lines of Simone de Beauvoir), represented by Claire Gallois A. Ernaux (after 1983, when she published *La place*), Camille Laurens, Paule Constant, Catherine Millet, Emily Tanimura, Pauline Flepp. Any attempt to find the same patterns in Romanian literature is risky, to say the least. *Emotional writing* is represented by Henriette Yvonne Stahl, Anişoara Odeanu, Cella Serghi, Alexandra Târziu, Ioana Baetica, whereas *rational writing* is represented by Hortensia Papadat-Bengescu, Jeni Acterian's, diaries, or by Alice Botez, Adina Kereneş, Dana Dumitriu, Adriana Bittel, Gabriela Adameşteanu Ştefania Mihalache, Dana Dumitriu, Corina Cristea, Maria Luiza Cristescu. A thorough analysis would be required to answer the question why mostly women are drawn to autofictional writing, why they resort to this highly hybrid and fragile literary solution, supported by what Genette called a lame crutch, 'one foot in fiction and the other in the 'truth'. Sociology, history and gender studies, are the first called upon to bring the appropriate arguments in this analysis, and only secondly literature.

Canadian writer Madeleine Ouellette-Michalska comes up with a feminist answer to the question above. She suggests that this generic ambiguity stems from women's lack of confidence, given that they are traditionally seen as lacking an identity of their own, and defining themselves through a husband figure or other male figures of their lives:

'... the fact that she has occupied this awkward and ambiguous place of an intermediary element between nature and culture for so long incited the woman to develop all these tricks of the un-said, of saying without giving the impression that she reveals something, of the half true, half false discourse. And autofiction is her chance.'

(Ouellette-Michalska 2007: p. 81)

The author thinks that, broadly speaking, the essence of the genre is precisely the search for identity: 'a sense of historical bereavement of identity seemed to lead to autofiction' (Ouellette-Michalska 2007: p. 82). With this statement, she comes close to the theories of Elizabeth Molkou and Régine Robin, who define autofiction as a contemporary genre emblematic for Hebrew identity and impossible to dissociate from the Holocaust experience[1].

The publication of Marguerite Duras's novel *L'Amant*, in 1984, a turning point in the history of women's literature, is essential because it was the first novel to describe explicitly a woman's body and female sexuality, without pen names, coded allusions, or euphemistic descriptions. As a result, the 90s and especially the 2000s witnessed an impressive wave of female writers, many of whom authors of autofiction. They turned impudence into editorial politics, choosing outrageous titles for their novels: *Baise-moi* (Virginie Despentes), *Putain* (Nelly Arcan), *Sept petits histoires de cul* (Anne Cécile), *Jouir* (Catherine Cusset).

There are of course favorite subject matters of women's autofiction, which almost turn the genre into a therapeutic method, an identity modeling technique, with trauma healing properties. The relationship with one's mother, or, less frequently, with one's father, maternity, or writing itself are favorite topics in women's autobiographies or autofictions. Such topics often invite, explain, or simply accompany a central theme, that of trauma or abused sensitivity. Trauma becomes the core and underlying motive of this type of confessional writing, where the reader is a voyeuristic spectator,

---

1   On this topic, see also: Elizabeth Molkou (2010) *Identités juives et autofiction. De la Shoah à la post-modernité*, Sarrebrück: Éditions Universitaires Européennes; Régine Robin (1997) *Le golem de l'écriture de l'autofiction au cybersoi*, Montréal: Éditions XYZ, coll. 'Théorie et littérature'.

unlike the reader of autobiographical writings, who is made to feel like a confidant. Writing, just like patients' accounts in psychoanalysis, manages to 'repair' a woman's identity disrupted by either an abortion (Annie Ernaux), or by parental rape (Christine Angot), death of a child (Camille Laurens), expatriate experience (Malika Mokeddem, Maryse Condé), etc. Almost devoid of epic features, this type of 'feminine' autofiction[2] derives its force from language rather than from the story, and thus gives precedence to *sjužet* over tale.

Another topic preferred by autofiction women writers is the human body, and especially the relationship between body and language (a central theme in theories about *écriture feminine*, elaborated by Luce Irigaray and Hélène Cixous). For Roland Barthes, 'language is a skin ... trembling of desire', is that surface which seduces, but is also seduced. Body and writing as 'places' of intimacy seem to obey the same impulses, to 'bear' the same effects, to equally show and hide. Essayist and novelist Gheorghe Crăciun (2002: p. 16) wrote repeatedly about this relationship:

'My point is that writing motivations are mostly of corporal nature. Inside the relationship between the writing self and the text, the body may seem a reminder, a surplus, a useless atavism. The somatographic pact which I have on my mind here saves the body from sacrifice, thus giving corporeality to the written world' (my translation).

Somehow foreign to the exhibitionist, noisy and (falsely) superficial self-exposure done in autofiction, this deep exploration of the body-writing relationship remains rarely outside a sexual context. There are very interesting cases in which the autofiction invents a corporal otherness, an animal body, for example (as in Marie Darrieussecq's novel *Truismes* or in *Le Boucher*, by Alina Reyes) in order to emphasize this complex relation between writing, self (voice) and body.

We find a substantial amount of examples with regard to exploration, exhibition and even exploitation of the body, in 1st person erotic narratives, written by prose women writers who thus achieved their notoriety. Often accused of pornography, vulgarity or violent language, Catherine Cusset, Catherine Millet, Alina Reyes, Virginie Despentes, Catherine Breillat, Nelly Arcan, etc. still have the merit to contrast the self-centered, obsessive, sick that witness personal trauma discourse with the inner trouble and anxiety. Thus, they introduce an affirmative discourse, celebrating desire as an attribute of femininity, the releasing of guilt, of shame, in an extreme form of libertinism reminding of the libertines of the eighteenth century. Philippe Lejeune even welcomes Catherine Millet's gesture to nonchalantly expose her sexual experiences as 'an original anthropological and courageous act' (Lejeune 2009: p. 49).

---

2   This type of writing style is widely adopted by men writers, as well, among whom: Serge Doubrovsky, Philippe Vilain, Philippe Forest, etc.

2. The Rise of Romanian Autofiction: Cecilia Ştefănescu and Claudia Golea

In Romanian literature, the feminine autofiction has adopted this rather explicit sexual direction, without reaching, however, the violence or indecency staged by the French women writers (for which the Romanian public, rather conservative, was not ready yet). The urgent quasi-psychoanalytic, angry and narcissistic writing performed by Angot has had no adherence to the Romanian writers of the young generation. However, the way of displaying one's own sexual experience under one's real name (Claudia Golea), without nominal statement ('I am a blonde from Transylvania', writes Ştefania Mihalache) or under various disguises, more or less transparent, has been better received. The nominal identification is often done out of lack of 'courage' (or interest) to use their own name, by additional hints that highlight what Vincent Colonna called the 'thematic profile of the authorial figure': identity, personality, universe. If we transform the nominal criteria into a mandatory prerequisite for the existence of the genre, we note that, in the Romanian autofiction field, hardly anyone is willing 'to pay with his/her own person', as Doubrovsky warned.

Without this radical nominal commitment, the Romanian autofiction would be a soft variant of the French one, encompassing – in general – all the mutations of the autobiographical prose, in the context of redefining some key concepts such as reality, truth, author and authority and the decentralization of the subject (in Lacan's theories). When the identity between narrator and author is not explicitly assumed (and generally is not), it is transferred to the 'periphery' of the text: for example, the cover of the second edition of Cecilia Ştefănescu's novel (Polirom Publishing House, 2005) contains a photo of the author (looking at herself in the mirror). This gesture undoubtedly calls for a referential reading or, in any case, makes ambiguous and undermines the 'usual' fictional reading applied to a text whose author, narrator and protagonist do not bear the same name. Moreover, the 'autobiographical reading' of almost all novels is a more and more common gesture among contemporary readers, overflowing with media truth-centered messages (reality TV shows, commercials): 'the idea of an autobiographical writing has already been installed in the consciousness of future readers; and over time an autobiographical reading of the novel has become the rule'. (Vercier & Lecarme, 1982: p. 105).

Cecilia Ştefănescu does not belong to the literary group called 'Fracturi' or even to the '2000 generation', but rather continues a prosaic merge already validated by critics and represented by Simona Popescu or Mircea Cărtărescu. Member of the literary circle 'Litere', coordinated by the leader of the 80s writers, Mircea Cărtărescu, she made her debut in the collective volume *Ferestre '98*, followed, in 2000, by another group project called *Tescani 40238*. She made her individual debut in 2002, with a novel called *Legături bolnăvicioase* (*Sick Love*), an obvious pastiche of the famous Laclos's epistolary novel. Relatively anonymous in the first years after the release, despite being promoted as a scandalous novel about lesbian relationships, the book came out in a revised edition in 2005, in the collection 'Ego. Proza' (Polirom Publishing House). Naturally, the book was immediately included in the so-called 'Polirom generation' (even if the author did not fit thematically or stylistically into this generation, and neither did another writer then famous, Cezar-Paul Badescu, for example). Still, she benefited from its image, still strong after the earlier PR campaign 'Vote for the young literature' from 2004.

In Romania, the concept of 'écriture feminine', which has massively circulated since the '70s, does not have the theoretical allonge or the literary manifestations experienced in the West. By making both language and literature political, feminist authors even talk of some feminine 'invariants' visible in writing:

'The language issue is closely related to female sexuality. Because it does not seem to me that language is universal or neutral on the difference between the sexes. Before language, interpreted and supported exclusively by men, I raise the problem of the specificity of women's language: a language appropriate to the body, the sex and the imaginary of women. '

(Irigaray 1985: p. 114)

It is true that sensitivity shapes the literary discourse in different ways, but that does not turn the discussion into a gender debate, because there are plenty of men writing as female writers (as feminine writing is commonly and abusively perceived) and enough female writers having a cerebral 'manly' writing. Thematically, however, women are distinguished by a growing concern for body, sexuality, identity, maternity, etc.

Critics considered Cecilia Ştefănescu's novel the obvious sign of a strong new feminine voice. In addition, noted that her strengths also came from the 'feminine' sensual and sensory writing, focused on the body, with many poetic elements reminding us of Simona Popescu and Mircea Cărtărescu. The 'sick' liaisons are those between the narrator, a bohemian literature student, continuously weaving her letters tornadoes, which then become the concatenated frames of all the stories in the book, and the world, which she weighs with the eyes of a would be woman. The 'sick liaisons' are also those between the narrator and her lover, Alex, between her and Renato, between her and the objects surrounding her, turning them into real props of a so called feminine atmosphere.

The text is like a mosaic, overcrowded stylistically, displaying excessive aestheticism. It also has a minimal plot, as all the ego-fictions published after

150

2000.The search of sexual identity (of feminine identity in general) is the pretext theme that unravels, behind countless textual skinnings, the main voice of this novel about 'love mixed with sex and shame'. More than a type of speculative autofiction, in which the author builds an imaginary paper-self from real autobiographical data, *Love Sick* is a novel about different stages of womanhood. One stage is that of the teenager Kiki, which brings the opportunity to disseminate a series of literary themes, which became clichés after Cărtărescu's novels: the double, the erotism of the uncertain sex, the schizoid disorder, the dream, the maze, etc.). Another stage is that of young 'Cecilia', the literature student with lost illusions (bookish, of course). Finally, the last stage is that of the writer-reader which we encounter at the end of the novel, where the by-stages novel (the *Bildungsroman*) begins, the autofiction - an eminently fragmented, disruptive, fluctuating literary genre - ends.

Beyond the abundant stylistics and the repeated regressions into the years of childhood, the main story turns out to be a relatively simple one. While hiding under the normality of some hetero-transient relations, the narrator loves Alex, a fellow student girl, with the 'despair of a hungry and scrawny tomcat'. She especially loves her sensory presence: 'her heavy musky scent', 'her choking taste of dry quince'. Their relationship is shaped by everyday domestic details, gestures, bombastic and bookish scenarios: they have dates in unusual places, they defiantly judge the world while hidden in promiscuous bars, they are defiant like all teenagers, building their own bohemian and quite eccentric way of living. The betrayals – accidentally consummated with Renato or the theologian (the names of the characters are always gender-ambiguous) – are verbalized in some very unnatural ways.

Obviously, the characters' age and readings constantly urge the shaping of an ideology of youth (as in Gombrowicz's novels, and the author even chooses a significant and supporting epigraph from *Ferdydurke*). However, the lack of some ironic counterpoints and the lofty, serious and pompous verbiage somehow break the naturalness of the story. All that remains is the brilliant stylistic interface that fascinates through a sort of sensuality which, paradoxically, does not rely on sexuality. There is this sensual 'feminine' language, womanized by the narrator herself, in which some words acquire untranslatable variants. 'Half-girl-half-woman', the ego-centered voice, around which all reality takes shape and color, often recreates the ingenuous, sensuous rhetoric in Simona Popescu's novel *Exuvii* (*Pupas*):

'No, there was neither sex between us nor fantasies finished in masturbation or orgasm, because the wires linking us only led to innocent kisses and the fear of our bodies scattered on the sheets under the horrible morning light' (my translation).'

(Ştefănescu 2002: p. 92)

The nominal identity is not present in the novel, it is only vaguely suggested by those details that make up the authorial thematic profile. Authenticity, which is important as a special 'effect' for the autofictional genre, is canceled by the flamboyant style, infused with too much lyricism. Still, there are several reasons that qualify Cecilia Ştefănescu's novel as autofiction. First, the taboo subject: lesbian relationships or the exploring of some sexual 'alternatives' perfectly fit the topic pattern of autofictions: shocking, challenging, difficult or impossible to solve in the 1st person narrative, just like the classic autobiography tries to do (that is why Genette calls them 'shameful autobiographies'). Then there is fragmentation, the breaks of the stream of consciousness, all that mixing of personal writings (diarist notes, love letters or oneiric passages) almost completely missing in action, which are also specific to the French contemporary genre. Sometimes the text translates the random associations of the unconscious mind (as in Serge Doubrovsky's novel) turning towards the automatic writing:

'... aborted children, packaging, graffiti, ruins, time, Swatch, rats, rhymes, fishermen, air, chewing gum, miniskirts, greed, bulimia, paddles, vomiting, unicorns, memory, broken sounds, wheels on the asphalt, crowds, gravel, blond, obedient girls, spread legs, god, riding on a cloud, seduction, perfume, circulation, menstruation, friendship, love, marital status, ring on a finger, chubby children, mother, they are not what they seem ...' (my translation).

(Ştefănescu 2002: p. 186)

As with so many French autofiction authors, sex becomes in Cecilia Ştefănescu's book a method of searching for identity. In Angot's novels or in Virginie Despentes's scandalous writings, sex heals trauma (by excessive exposure). Or, it cynically and even violently exposes the obsolescence and the ridicule of love in the era of 'hyper-consumption' (Gilles Lipovetsky). Compared to the French autofictions, in Cecilia Ştefănescu's Love Sick, sex punctuates the heroine's sexual 'ripening' and it is often taken into context with exploring the world. Although varied and unusual – from masturbation and lesbianism to the half- consumed incest with Sandu, the narrator's brother – the sexual experiences in the book do not have the aggressive vocalization and gratuity that are specific to autofiction. They are over-aestheticized. Without mocking literature and its internal laws, as members of 'Fracturi' group used to do, the author is less interested in the parade of excesses, and more interested in the aesthetic potential of sexuality. She thus proves to be part of a literary tradition which, though interrupted by communism, used to be very strong in interwar Romania.

In a game of perspectives and narrative registers which deepens more and more this novelistic *mixtum compositum*, a strange (love) story weaves between the narrator and the evil, nasty Kiki. A story about the way from the crisis of puberty, with all its humors (hypersensitivity, crises of bulimia, inclination to self-mutilation), towards the explosion of femininity. There are

152

also ambiguities, flirtation, inconsistencies, the gentle lies, and the transition from the asexual, rompish adolescent to woman. Although infused with an excessive and cloddish poetry, there are numerous pages of feminine introspection, self-analysis and often corporalized narcissistic obsessions. And all these elements remind us more of the interwar female writers than the loose-mouth writers of the 2000 generation. This hyper-confessional blast is well maintained by gender-specific marks: the 1st person narrative, the *captatio* formulas, some familiar forms of address such as: 'to be honest', 'you are going to laugh, I know it seems hard to believe', as well as the use of the story telling past tense. All these sincerity markers call for a naive reading in full 'era of suspicion', when all you need is to believe. It is true that Love Sick presents many consecrated characteristics of autofictional genre: an apparently autobiographical discourse, taboo topics, a minimal plot, an obvious identity focus. Still, the pompous sound of the phrases, as well as the highly-charged stylistics, contradict the essence of autofiction as a genre.

The most striking case of confusion of the author with the narrator, who is also character of her own (auto) fiction, is Claudia Golea. She has not aspired to the great literary canon and has preferred to remain in the modest, but more accessible cultural area of consumption. She is the daughter of a diplomat, an English-Japanese graduate, and she has spent a lot of time in countries like Japan, Thailand, France and Egypt. Some of these cosmopolitan experiences are pretenses (and contexts) of her deliberately scandalous fictions. Critically acclaimed at the time of her debut (in 1998, at Nemira Publishing House, with a novel called *Planet Tokyo*) as a very promising novelist, Claudia Golea regressed gradually in later novels, turning into a rather simplistic and disordered writing. Despite being built on monotonous themes and, often, on a faulty construction, her literature still has a certain charm. Her books have triggered debates in local literary 'milieux' about esthetic authority vs. commercial authority, the change of the readers' expectations and the authors' pragmatic orientation towards the audience's demand. Quickly assimilated to this new type of literature, autofiction, although she has nothing to do with it, Golea writes literature full of 'feminine' topics. But she does it in a totally different key: no trace of ideology or philosophy, lots of schematized epic and a delicious humor.

The heroine-narrator assumes her 'frivolity' with self-irony, which is not that obvious in other writers of the same period (with Ioana Bradea's notable exception). This particular type of self-irony sometimes makes the reading of Golea's novels more pleasant or, in any case, more amusing:

'At the stupid Writers' Union it has therefore been said that *Planet Tokyo* and *Tokyo by Night* are some horrible pornography pieces with no literary value. It's all for the better. If I had been accepted in the Writers' Union, it might have gone to my head and I would have probably thought that I was a writer. And this comprehension would have turned me into a bearded man without balls' (my translation). (Golea 2007: p. 7)

Her books have become major bestsellers because of the fluid writing, the rather simplistic but mostly well written dialogues, deliberately placed within the market range. Her writing is very much alike the commercial American movies, because, as essayist Bogdan Ghiu noted, the recent literature is socially formatted and evolves into screenwriting. Hard-core erotic scenes and local colour (together with the change of the Western cliché perception on Japan, with geishas and shoguns) – brought Claudia Golea public success. Her success is first confirmed by the reprinting her books (and by her 'reallocation' to a publishing house that has more visibility, Polirom Publishing House). Success is not a common thing for a young Romanian writer, on a market still dominated by translations. Amid the audience's changing needs and sensitivity, her books have filled a void, introducing missing link in contemporary Romanian literature. They have disseminated and sold the idea of literature as fun, as *entertainment*.

Having written a commercial type of autofiction, that has no equivalent in Romanian literature, Claudia Golea has become closer to the younger generation from *Fracturi*. One is the 'new pornography' or the democratization of sexuality through which the Romanian literature shyly synchronizes with Western consumerist policies allowing anyone to reveal his/ her own true fantasies without being judged or socially marginalized. Other autofictional 'symptoms' are 1st person narrative as a mark of authenticity, family and society conflict, poetry mixed with cynicism, themes that come from the Beat tradition. And again: the hunger for reality (with its excessive experiences), the alert, concise writing, deprived of stylistics, which often imitates the American tradition of 'white writing' – in a journalist way, with many and often tough verbs, short sentences with strong impact.

Her first novel, *Planet Tokyo* (winner of the Nemira debut prize in 1997) has brought into question another concept that Romanian literary market was less familiar with: the non-fictional novel. This kind of prose writing, belonging to the recent American tradition, appears to be akin to autofiction because it describes facts, with a certain distance (which is not common to the autobiography as a genre), by fictional means. The author sets the limit or the meaning of 'truth' when it comes to recounted facts (either inside or outside the text). Moreover, the author claims a purely referential reading, bluntly stating the non-fictional status of this first novel:

'*Planet Tokyo* is lived to the full. It is nonfiction, but it is my only nonfiction novel. I have actually lived as I do in the novel. I have loved as I do in the novel. I have started writing my book because of the schizophrenia crises from which I have soon recovered' (my translation).

(Golea 2005: p. 11)

Denying the fictional status of her book (inherent in any story-telling, in any textual 'recovery') and emphasizing its traumatic core, Claudia Golea makes the same statement of absolute sincerity as all the world-famous authors of autofictions: Serge Doubrovsky Christine Angot Camille Laurens, and especially Annie Ernaux. The last one states that 'the material of my books lies at the intersection of historical and individual experience, and for that I don't need fiction' (Ernaux 2000: p. 21). Written in 1st person, in a natural and humorous way, without much subtlety, but with a really good way of telling stories and building vivid characters, the novel was enthusiastically welcomed as 'an exotic nonfictional *psychothriller*, located on the border between mainstream and paraliterature' (Cernat 2000: p. 18). The plot, perhaps the first attempt to portray the local experiences of a 'gaijin' meeting the Far Eastern civilization and culture, is quite simple. In early 90s, the narrator Claudia goes on a study trip to France, where she meets a very educated and refined young Japanese man, Hiroshi, who initiates her in the mysteries of tantric lovemaking. With his help, she gets to study at the prestigious university Tokyo Daigaku (abbreviated Todai). After arriving to Japan, the shock of the first contact with a foreign culture quickly vanishes and Claudia finally begins her studies: theater, film, media, literature and history of Japan. At the same time, she gets to form an inside perspective on habits, manners, vices and fantasies displayed by the inhabitants of this strange planet. Looking for extreme experiences, she escapes from the comfortable bourgeois Japan into the underground part of the country, where she sinks into the promiscuity of some dubious entourages of punks and libertines, connected to the criminal yakuza gangs. Next comes a flurry of orgies, interrupted by trances provoked by alcohol and drugs.

The most shocking episode before returning home is the hospitalization of the female character in a famous psychiatric hospital with a diagnosis of schizophrenia. Just like Western autofiction authors - children of excess, pushing the (writing) experience beyond the limit, eager to shock, to drive their readers mad and to get them out of their daily comfort -, Claudia Golea prepares a true Molotov cocktail of shocking experiences. And she places them, for an extra spectacular touch, in some exotic setting. In the dark and unfamiliar. The same trash mixture of violence, trauma, sex, stylistic formulas, varying from neutral to excessive colors, is to be found in other autofictions written by Virginie Despentes, Clothilde Escalle or Chloé Delaume.

The trauma topic, which can be also found in Claudia Golea's novel, is relevant to the aesthetics of the autofictional genre, but also to the feminine writing, as seen in feminist theories. At Matsuzawa, a psychiatric establishment using quite medieval methods, the female protagonist (also called Claudia, just like the author), descends to another inferno, that of the insane. She is so strongly sedated that she can no longer distinguish between daytime and dreamlike reality. Everything around becomes a prison and the atmosphere strongly reminds of Ken Kesey's novel, *One Flew Over the Cuckoo's Nest*:

'I wondered if they would do the same to me: remove my eyes, my spinal cord and just about everything I had. Now that's torture! After that, I would no longer be myself: I would be an owl-man or a monkey-manor a something-else-man. But I didn't care anymore: I got tired of Religions, and Texts, and Infernos. I was even ready to get a Huntington chorea just to get rid of Hatred and Intolerance' (my translation).

(Golea 2000: p. 131)

The brutally honest, unsophisticated writing becomes an atoning response to an emotional or physical shock. A way to manage pain. Placing reality into the fictional mold of language, authors such as Régine Robin, Christine Angot, Geneviève Brisac, Chantal Chawaf, Danielle Sallenave, Hélène Duffau, Camille Laurens, Annie Ernaux, etc. have all reacted to their extreme life experiences: rape, incest, violence, madness, loss of a loved one, incurable diseases. Insanity and frequent visits to psychiatric hospital, although softened by the narrator's 'I-don't-give-a-toss' humour, are recurring in Claudia Golea's books. This shows that they are more than just spicy details of an amazing biography. They actually give coherence to her novels and turns writing into an effective healing method.

Although she does not fully obey the stylistic pattern of the genre (urgent writing, less epic, verbs in present tense, discourse centered on the obsessive self-affirmation, etc.), Claudia Golea's books are definitely autofictions. The reason is that they all exploit, within the limits of fiction, several actions undertaken by a narrative-autobiographical protagonist that has the same name as the author on the cover of the book. Naturally, all writers project their fantasies, thoughts, imagination, life experiences in their books. But inserting real biographical facts into a fiction plot is different to putting your own name in a book, which means taking on to the bitter end all the ethical and aesthetic consequences. Because the name proves the existence of a person-referent, of a real author, palpable, who becomes the narrator and character of his/her own novel. This mere voyeuristic curiosity, permanently disturbed by uncertainty – 'Is it true? Is it not true?' – changes the focus from an aesthetic interpretation (based on literary value) to a more convenient one. This is perfectly common, though, in (post)postmodern times. And this perverse curiosity is the key to the success of the autofiction as a genre. Vincent Colonna feels that the sincere signature, placed inside the secure frame of fiction, is a privilege that the author uses 'to make the craziest statements, to tell the most compromising things, if only for fun. [The writer] can take on his/her most antisocial passions and ideas, without being held responsible for it and without harming his/ her credibility' (Colonna 1989: p. 223). The statement is correct with respect to the freedom to express anything, anyway – and Christine Angot or Michel Houellbecq fully demonstrate it in their books. Even Claudia Golea does it in her books, but in an almost completely depoliticized manner. However, the same statement is false when referring to the absence of consequences of this freedom. The growing number of trials in which authors of autofiction are involved on charges of assault on individual freedom proves it.

Tokyo by Night, first published in 2000 (Nemira Publishing House), is a sequel of the erotic-Japanese series. And it is still the same 'retinal' literature, as Duchamp used to say about cinematographic literature. Notwithstanding the displayed nominal identity, the novel deviates from biographical facts (a gesture that should have normally indicated the writer's literary evolution), focusing on exoticism, sex and crime plot, otherwise fairly mediocre topics. From the first pages, the novel exposes a disastrous family relationship, another favorite theme of male and female autofiction writers, but again the trauma healing is postponed by cynical humor. Back in Romania, Claudia gets a welcome to remember:

'I barely arrived on the fourth floor and there I was confronted with my father who was gasping to a fault. We had always had an explosive family relationship1. He rushed at me to beat me, and so I gave him a punch. I must admit he was stronger: the lard excess! He firmly gripped my head into his huge hands and hit it several times against the fourth floor walls, so that both my head and the walls clanged the same, then straddled me downright. "Welcome to the empire of the clenched fist!", I said to myself. The unpleasant feeling, however, was not the pain of the blows, but the fact that his cock, swelled out of so much pleasure of hitting me over and over again, hang on the crown of my head and trickled down on my forehead' (my translation).'

(Golea 2004: p. 25)

3. Autofiction – a Feminine Genre?

The general addressability, the authenticity effects, created not only through discourse, but also by the insertion of real, verifiable historical details into a plot strongly marked as fictional, all these are ingredients of a new type of literature. Humor and self-irony, the sovereign contempt for norms, canon and writers' vanity – are also specific to a genre which has been 'indexed' as pornographic, consumerist and non-fictional literature etc. Obviously, Claudia Golea's adventures are not to be compared to the sophisticated 'language adventure' that Doubrovsky referred to. All it matters to her is the story. Neither the supporting metatext, nor the reflections on writing. She is a 'week-end writer', according to her own definition, interested in attracting audience through an easy reading, juggling with the rhetoric of sincerity in the same way as the reality TV shows usually do. Although her ego is not even nearly as exacerbated as Angot's, for example, Claudia Golea also relies, on the bizarre and the unusual, as many autofiction writers of the 2000 generation do. And unable to create an original language or a style to translate the 'secondary', the exceptional dimension is reduced to a mere story.

Having been living for two centuries 'in a pragmatic unconsciousness' autofiction – as a way to solve the problems posed by (all) ego-writings in full postmodern era – crystallized in France. And it did so 'thanks to the unexpected convergence of three distinct literary lineages: the ego-centered tradition, the formalistic vanguard and the identity confession – mainly Hebrew, feminist and gay' (Colonna 1989: p. 319). Assimilated to psychoanalysis and often cautioned by female authors, autofiction cannot be understood outside the cultural context which has articulated it in the form – hard to approximate, always changing – it has today: the revolution of morals, 'la prise de parole' around the crimes against humanity, May '68, the 'arrest' of the individual in front of the TV (as Baudrillard used to say), the shaping of the postmodern ideology, globalization, etc. Posterity will decide, however, whether this type of literature has been a key moment in world literature or just the provisional mouthpiece through which female writers, reduced to silence for so long, could finally write about themselves.

Bibliography

Crăciun, Gheorghe (2002) 'The Somatographic Pact', *Observator Cultural*, Year 16, No. 133 (September).

Cernat, Paul (2000) 'Pulp nonfiction', *Observator Cultural*, Year 14, No. 24 (August).

Colonna, Vincent (1989) *L'Autofiction. Essai sur la fictionnalisation de soi en littérature*, Ph.D. thesis, coordinated by Gérard Genette, Paris: EHESS.

Ernaux, Annie (2000) 'Une place à part', interview avec Annie Ernaux, propos recueillis par Jacques Pécheur, *Le Français dans le monde*, No. 310.

Ernaux, Annie (1993) 'Vers un je transpersonnel', in Serge Doubrovsky, Jacques Lecarme & Philippe Lejeune (eds.) *Autofictions et Cie, RITM Series/Cahiers de sémiotique textuelle,* No. 6, Nanterre: Paris Université Presse X.

Golea, Claudia (2007) *Flower-Power Tantra*, Bucharest: Pandora M Publishing House.

Golea, Claudia (2005) 'I am talented at pranks', interview with Iulia Alexa, *Psychologies*, Year 13, No. 13 (July).

Golea, Claudia (2004) *Tokyo by night*, Iaşi: Polirom Publishing House.

Hamburger, Käte (1993) *The Logic of Literature*, Bloomington and Indianapolis: Indiana University Press.

Irigaray, Luce (1985) *Parler n'est jamais neutre*, Paris: Éditions de Minuit.

Lejeune, Philippe (2009) *Ainsi parlait Philippe Lejeune*, entretien réalisé par Kamel Riahi, Tunis, coll. 'Travelling'.

Ouellette-Michalska, Madeleine (2007) *Autofiction et dévoilement de soi*, Montréal: Éditions XYZ.

Ştefănescu, Cecilia (2002) *Legături bolnăvicioase*, Piteşti: Paralela 45 Publishing House.

Vercier, Bruno & Jacques Lecarme (1982) *La littérature en France depuis 1968*, Paris: Éditions Bordas.

CHAPTER VII

Diffused Gender Codes and Transcultural Outcomes in Jhumpa Lahiri's *The Lowland*

Adriana Elena STOICAN

1. Introduction

Relying on a cultural studies approach to literature of migration, this chapter focuses on Jhumpa Lahiri's[1] first generation female protagonist (Gauri) from her novel *The Lowland*. The plot is initially placed in Kolkata, around the late 1940s, when two brothers (Subhash and Udayan) are born. In the late 1960s, their lives take different turns as Subhash applies for a Ph.D. in the United States, while Udayan becomes attracted by the Naxalbari movement. This leftist political manifestation was ignited by the West Bengal peasant uprising against the landlords' feudal ownership and taxation policies (Mustafi 2012: np). Brutally repressed by the police, the insurgency triggered a chain of violent confrontations between the guerrilla revolutionaries and the Indian state. Udayan illustrates the profile of the young Bengali intellectuals drawn by the revolution's 'ideological romanticism' (Gupta 2015: np). (He is eventually executed by the police, while his parents and wife witness the whole scene). While in America, Subhash maintains connection with his brother especially via letters. Thus, he is informed about Udayan's marriage to a girl named Gauri, despite their parents' disapproval. After his brother's death, Subhash temporarily returns to India, where he is moved by Gauri's seclusion in his parents' house. Finding out that she carries Udayan's child, Subhash proposes to Gauri, meaning to offer her a new life in America. Away from India, Gauri gives birth to a girl, Bela, but her marriage with Subhash does not work. Gauri chooses an academic career over motherhood, secretly leaving for California, where she gets a teaching position. The discussion traces the character's evolution as she crosses temporal, physical and cultural borders. Considering a body of theories regarding transcultural

---

1   Jhumpa Lahiri was born to Bengali immigrant parents in London in 1967 and she grew up in the USA. Her fictional and autobiographical creations revolve around themes related to transmigrant transplantation, cultural clashes/and dialogues between the American and Bengali cultural outlooks. Her first collection of short stories, *Interpreter of Maladies* (1999) won the 2000 Pulitzer Prize for Fiction. The rest of her creations include two novels (*The Namesake*, 2003 and *The Lowland*, 2013), one collection of short-stories (*Unaccustomed Earth*, 2008) and an autobiographical work (*In Other Words*, 2015).

processes and nomadic identities, the discussion sets out to interpret Gauri's radical choice of transformation along disruptive lines. By analyzing her obstinate cling to individualistic norms of identity, the chapter attempts to formulate hypotheses regarding possible connections between transcultural changes, nomadic travel, transdifference and female (dis)empowerment.

The present analysis takes into account the cultural studies premise that culture is expressed by means of symbolic forms linked with a specific social context, deeply embedded in their texture (Ganser 2009: p. 20). This chapter considers the literary text as a witness and a repository of cultural experiences in the context of South Asian women's relocation, assuming that there is a link between processes of cultural displacement and Lahiri's background of transplantation. Without arguing that *The Lowland* is representative for the cultural evolution of South Asian female migrants, I consider that it offers insightful visions regarding the contemporary rhythms of cultural change. More precisely, the analysis sets out to identify peculiar intersections of gender norms that generate reconfigurations of female subjectivity in the context of migration. My interpretation of Gauri attempts to retrieve a personal account of female cultural redefinition, relying on the potential of 'creative literature to fill in the gaps|' (White 1995: p. 10) inherent in the sociological conclusions about migration. This kind of investigation is meant to offer |more biographical approaches, with an emphasis placed on individuals and their understanding of the 'realities' of their situation (White 1995: p. 14). Following these considerations, the next section presents a series of theoretical notions that will be applied in the discussion of the primary corpus. This body of theories connects processes of migration with cultural dimensions of gender and the transgressive potential of transcultural change.

2. Theoretical Background

2.1 Transcultural outlooks on cultures

'Transculturality' has long been considered a key theoretical notion for the study of migrant writing, since it is related to contemporary phenomena of migration and globalization. The transcultural approach offers an adequate understanding of the individual need to negotiate a plurality of cultural models in a context of changing boundaries and rapid developments in technology, transportation and communication. Transculturality involves the transgression of spatial and temporal boundaries and a questioning of the clear binaries connoted by them (Alexander 2006: p. 141).

One of the implications of the transcultural paradigm is that cultures are incomplete sets of practices that need to interact and enrich themselves through cultural exchanges:

'A transcultural model begins from the assumption that an individual or a cultural identity is never complete in itself because of its relations in a field of differences.'

(Berry 1999: p. 134)

As individuals realize that their familiar cultural spheres do not cover the whole set of human aspirations, they are more inclined to accept the validity of other cultural worlds. In this way, the need to transcend the boundaries of their own cultures shapes a transcultural perspective that frees them from a limited range of options:

'Transculture builds new identities in the zone of fuzziness and interference and challenges the metaphysics of discreteness so characteristic of nations, races, professions, and other established cultural configurations …'

(Epstein 1999: p. 25)

Therefore, the idea of cultures as self-transcendent entities is an important principle of transculturality that accounts for the necessity to acknowledge the relevance of other cultural worlds.

At this point, the notion of transdifference advanced by Ganser may be correlated with transcultural processes of identity transformation, since both approaches challenge binary categorizations. By defining transdifference as 'the collision of differences', Ganser argues that it expresses the inherent irregularity of identity negotiation processes (2009: p. 24). Considering that it captures overlapping layers of multiple differences, transdifference points to 'cultural and textual phenomena, that are incomprehensible via binary models of difference' (Ganser 2009: p. 25). However, Ganser warns against a conflation of transdifference with synthesis or hybridization/transculturation, stressing that the former does not entail dissolution of differences into cultural fusions. Instead, transdifference refers to the coeval interplay of differences that may result in 'dissonance rather than harmony' (2009: p. 27). I consider that a parallel can be drawn between transculturality and transdifference, in the sense that both involve a transgressive dimension. More specifically, a transcultural outlook involves a transgressive step that carries individuals into the realm of difference. Therefore, in the case of migrant identities, the transcultural urge to cross physical boundaries marks their passage into unfamiliar cultural worlds, providing full access to multiple differences. Relying on the intersections between transculturality and transdifference, the present analysis sets out to establish whether Gauri's cultural metamorphosis results in a transcultural synthesis or a dissonant cumulation of different norms. At the same time, the argument will also interpret the nature of her change in relation to mobility as a coordinate that may (dis)empower women migrants.

2.2 Transgressive urges and transcultural changes

The inherent transcendence of transcultural processes may be interestingly coupled with transgressive mechanisms, as strategies of contesting established cultural norms in the context of migrant relocation. The very idea of transgression carries geographical connotations, given its literal meaning of 'crossing a boundary' (Cresswell 1996: p. 21). At the same time, resettlement entails a shift to an 'out of place' status that contains potential for resistance (Cresswell 1996: p. 21). The notion of transgression serves as a useful tool for examining Gauri's strategy of contesting conventional identity roles. The character's rebellious stance demonstrates the importance of transgression as a mechanism of revealing 'the historical and mutable nature of that which is usually considered "the way things are"' (Cresswell 1996: p. 26). At this point, the notion of 'transiency of identity' (Ganser 2009: p. 25) serves as a rich conceptual instrument that provides further clarification to the epistemological end of transgression. Coming from the Latin *transire* ('to go across', 'to pass'), the term couples the idea of spatial and temporal change in relation to the dynamics of identity. On the one hand, the concept encodes the continuous flow of identity change along a temporal axis, its state of constant becoming that defies the possibility of essentialist perspectives (Ganser 2009: p. 25). On the other hand, the notion also makes reference to processes of identity transformation triggered by individuals' mobility across 'shifting borders and territorialities' (Ganser 2009: p. 25). Thus, the double connotation of this term may allow for a fruitful interpretation of the labyrinthine nature of Gauri's physical transgression that pushes her beyond normative expectations. The following section presents theories regarding the possibility of women's empowerment as conditioned by their access to a regime of mobility.

2.3 Gender and mobility

An important coordinate of the present analysis is the relation between mobility, space and gender, with a focus on the transgressive potential of women's motion. Mobility research has been concerned with gender since the 1970s, resulting in studies on immigration, work, generational mobility, the relation between space, gender and mobility, etc. (Kronlid 2008: p. 18). The patriarchal outlook on gender relations involves a traditional binarism that associates women with the private sphere and men with the public domain (Ganser 2009: p. 68; Cattan 2008: p. 87; Creswell & Uteng, 2008: p.

2). According to Massey, this dual perspective has also been coded as a space/feminine vs. time/masculine opposition (2001: p. 6). In other words, female identity is associated with a static condition, 'the antithesis of mobility' (Fay 2008: p. 70), while men stand for dynamic temporality, history, progress, civilization, etc. (Massey 2001: p. 6). An association of women with the private sphere has also meant the limitation of their mobility as an important mechanism of subordination (Ganser 2009: p. 69). Consequently, women's access to a mobile condition entails the potential to dismantle patriarchal conventions by subverting normative gender discourses (Ganser 2009: p. 74), 'acquiring new subjectivity' (Creswell & Uteng, 2008: p. 2) and gaining 'social mobility and sexual freedom' (Kronlid 2008: p. 24).

Despite the freeing connotations of female mobility, theoreticians' caution against the risk of creating a new binarism that would render it suprior to a settled condition. Thus, one should consider that not all kinds of movement are inherently beneficial (Kronlid 2008: p. 27) and that we should not 'trade the myth of the sedentary lifestyle, border and frontier, territory and proximity, for the myth of mobility, flows and networks' (Cattan 2008: p. 86). Instead, one should take into account the 'layered' and 'elusive' nature of the concept of mobility, considering manners in which it can be positively and negatively coded either as 'progress', 'freedom', 'modernity' or 'restricted movement, vigilance and control' (Creswell & Uteng, 2008: p. 1). Acknowledging these nuanced interpretations of mobility, the analysis of the primary corpus aims to reveal the stratified range of valences illustrated by Gauri's nomadic condition.

2.4 Nomadic itineraries and female (dis)empowerment

Nomadism has been glorified as a new paradigm for thinking subjectivity with a focus on deterritorialization, movement and connectivity (O'Sullivan 2000). This approach promotes nomadology as an epistemological condition of mobility that enables the crumbling of conceptual foundations (Deleuze and Guattari, 1987: p. 25), 'promoting a logic of the AND' (1987: p. 25), illustrating 'all manner of "becomings"'(1987: p. 21). Nomadism is associated with a rhizomatic manifestation of travel that involves states of 'discontinuity, rupture and multiplicity' (1987: p. 16). Nomadic practices have been envisaged 'as acts of resistance against hegemonic control over space as well as over the subject and its socio-cultural location' (Ganser 2009: p. 169). Feminism has taken over the nomadic vocabulary, to highlight the movement's 'acute awareness of the nonfixity of boundaries' (Braidotti 1994: p. 36). More specifically, feminist critics uphold 'nomadic transgression' as a strategy of trespassing established borders in order to create new subjectivities (Ganser 2009: p. 173). In other words, the adoption of nomadic theory by feminism enables the production of 'rhizomatic constellations of multiple identities and affiliations, as a transgressive strategy that goes against fixity and limiting structures' (Ganser 2009: p. 173).

Despite the rich implications of conceptual nomadism, one has to apply it cautiously, paying attention to existent critiques. One of the main objections refers to the 'epistemic violence' (Ganser 2009: p. 175) involved in the Western appropriation of the term, that effaces the specificity of traditional nomadism (Ibid.: p. 174). Thus, several critical voices (Pratt 1998; Kaplan 1996; Wolff 1992) argue that Western feminists, such as Rosi Braidotti and Chantal Mouffe, have overused the nomadic metaphor, turning it into an idealized condition for mobile intellectuals (Ganser 2009: p. 175). While actual nomads (refugees, migrant workers) do not belong to this sophisticated picture, the Western nomadic intellectuals are defined 'predominantly by hybridity, transcultural global mobility and agency' (Ibid.: p. 175). Along similar lines, Sten Pultz Moslund signals that the valorization of movement, transformation, nomadism and fragmentation creates new dichotomies and privileges regimes of mobility over conditions of settlement (2010: p. 14). Considering the link between mobility, gender and nomadic transgression, this chapter aims to establish the author's position regarding nomadic displacement and female (dis)empowerment.

2.5 Western individualism, South Asian interdependence

In order to understand the mechanisms of transcultural transformation in the context of South-Asian American encounters, the present discussion relies on several studies regarding specific aspects of South Asian and American cultures. Harry C. Triandis' socio-psychological investigation establishes that some cultures (the USA and other English speaking countries) tend to focus on the individual as the basic unit of social perception, while others favour a more group-oriented approach to identity (e.g., Africa, Asia, Latin America) (1993: pp. 159-160). Along similar lines, Joan C. Miller concludes that Americans are more inclined to promote an independent view of the self, while the Hindu Indians privilege an interdependent dimension of identity (1994: p. 4). An important feature that derives from a communitarian tradition is the promotion of a model of female identity as a cluster of roles that entail the notion of dependence: 'The identity of Hindu women is not an independent notion, but a series of role relationships as daughter, daughter-in-law, wife, and mother' (Deka 1993: p. 124). According to the Hindu Brahmanical ideology, the primary duties of a *pativratâ,* a Hindu faithful wife, involve cooking, becoming a mother and cultivating her passion for her husband (Hermann 2011: p. 81). A persistent idea about Hindu women foregrounds their need to be guarded and protected by a male figure, since they are 'unfit for independence' (Bose 2010: pp. 66-67). Women are also considered incompatible with the attributes of public life and therefore confined to the home sphere (Fuller 1990: p. 288). Having presented the theoretical framework of this chapter, the argument will continue with the analysis of the primary corpus, highlighting the intersection between transdifference, transculturality and nomadism in the fabric of Gauri's identity.

3. *The Lowland:* Disruptive Metamorphoses

In her latest novel, Lahiri seems particularly attracted by the logic of transgression, as she creates characters that embrace a trespassing stance in order to shatter conventional roles. By proposing to Gauri, Subhash seems to break an ethical standard, as this union is haunted by Udayan's ghostly presence. By marrying without his parents' approval, Udayan crosses a line, as he places an individual option beyond the family's aspirations. Gauri herself operates perhaps the most abrupt transgression of social roles, when she decides to leave Bela in Subhash's care. Unable to become involved in stable relationships, Gauri eventually falls in love with a woman, stepping out of her heterosexual condition. In her turn, young Bela struggles to accept her mother's gesture by constantly running away, struggling to transcend her need for attachment. The result of Bela's trauma is her choice to become a single mother, determined to find solace in an itinerant life[2].

Lahiri's previous work portrays most of the first generation Indian women immigrants as guardians of traditions, but *The Lowland* completely changes this pattern. In creating Gauri, it seems that Jhumpa Lahiri has intended to push the mechanism of cultural transgression to its extremes. Gauri is a first generation voluntary immigrant, who strives to define herself in opposition with traditional Hindu values. Even prior to her departure, Gauri is presented as a non-conformist young woman, attracted to academic pursuits. I agree with Habib's remark that before her marriage to Udayan, Gauri's 'unconventional life' (2015: p. 41) kept her 'aloof from traditional social customs' (2015: p. 41). Her decision to marry Udayan represents a first unconventional step, expressing a voluntary choice and not a Hindu traditional arrangement. Gauri's acceptance of Subhash's proposal and her relocation to America signal further transgressions. Migration by marriage

---

2   Bela's nomadic itinerary is the focus of a different paper, in course of publication: (Nomadic Paths to Transcultural Becoming in Jhumpa Lahiri's *The Lowland* and *In Other Words*).

with her brother-in-law is valued as an opportunity for reinvention in a dimension devoid of pressures to conform:

'She'd sat among so many passengers, passive, awaiting their destinations. Most of them, like Gauri, waiting to be freed in an *atmosphere not their own* ... This was the place where she could put things behind her.'

(Lahiri 2013: p. 99, emphasis added)

Gauri's feelings on her way to America suggest that she regards transplantation as an opportunity for self-reinvention in a novel cultural dimension. Thus, the specific difference of the American setting seems to afford the distance necessary for self-reinvention beyond particular constraints.

3.1 Embracing academia, fearing motherhood

The first indicator of Gauri's reinvention along rebel lines is her intention to continue her academic plans. During her pregnancy, she anonymously attends classes at the philosophy department of the university where Subhash is hired. Gauri's unconventional stance is also suggested by her sudden decision to give up visual markes of ethnicity, such as traditional Indian clothing. Gauri's atypicality is also foregrounded by her desire to avoid female members of the Indian immigrant community: 'I have nothing in common with them, she said' (Lahiri 2013: p. 109). Her apathic-hostile attitude towards conservative immigrants reveals Gauri's quest for redefinition in centrifugal cultural terms.

Another aspect that illustrates Gauri's transgressive urge is represented by her reluctance to become totally engaged in the motherhood condition. After giving birth, Gauri feels overwhelmed by her new responsibilities and she lets Subhash handle most of her tasks. Moreover, Gauri is keen on continuing her studies, indirectly reminding Subhash of the promise he had made before they got married. Dividing her time between looking after Bela and going to philosophy classes, Gauri perceives motherhood as an obstacle to her professional ambitions:

'She was not only ashamed of her feelings but also frightened that the final task Udayan had left her with, the long task of raising Bela, was not bringing meaning to her life.'

(Lahiri 2013: p. 129)

Gauri feels imprisoned by the motherhood role, envying Subhash's working schedule that keeps him away from parental duties. As Bela reaches 6 years old, Bela develops a secret routine meant to provide free time and solitude. Every day she leaves her daughter companionless at home, while she enjoys the autonomy of solitary walks:

'So it began in the afternoons. Not every afternoon but often enough, too often. Disoriented by the sense of freedom, devouring the sensation as a beggar devours food.'

(Lahiri 2013: p. 138)

Gauri's thirst for freedom outside the family sphere illustrates her yearning for empowerment as a condition of detachment from maternal responsibilities.

Bela represents the undeniable and definitive link between Gauri and Udayan, a bond that transcends the reality of Udayan's death. Her presence is a constant reminder of Udayan's loss and of Gauri's indirect involvement in loss of human lives. (Upon Udayan's request, Gauri agreed to spy on a policeman and inform Udayan of his daily schedule. She was not aware that Udayan's fellows were planning the policeman's assasination and needed an approximation of his daily routine). Perhaps Gauri's inability to create and maintain a bond with her own child springs from her incapacity to forget her past and forgive herself. Gauri's dedication to an academic career may illustrate her need to block the pain and guilt of her Indian youth. Equipped with the awareness that she cannot be a proper mother, Gauri redirects her efforts to the world of research. Although she spends most of her time at home with Bela, they are actually separated by Gauri's seclusion in the spare bedroom, turned into her office: 'Hours would pass, the door not opening, her mother not emerging' (Lahiri 2013: p. 157). Although Bela seems satisfied to share the home space with her mother, she registers Gauri's maternal attitude towards her research:

'She spoke of it as she might speak of an infant, telling her father one night at dinner that she worried about the pages being blown out an open window, or being destroyed by a fire.'

(Lahiri 2013: p. 158)

This detail clearly implies that Gauri's academic interest represents a rechanneling of her unexpressed motherly care for Bela. The next section discusses Gauri's decision to leave her family and the process of her self-redefinition as she starts a new life on the West Coast.

3.2 Transcultural reinvention via relocation

Gauri's decision to move to California, in itself another transgression, reinforces the idea that she cannot dissociate Bela from her shared history with Udayan. Gauri's abandonment of her mother role may express her attempt to resolve her trauma by ceaseless withdrawal. The character appears as an embodiment of individualistic values, as she chooses to focus on her own struggle and overlook the pain of her family members. Her radical choice is the only way she can approach her inner conflict by adding more distance between herself and the source of her sorrow:

'She entered a new dimension, a place where a fresh life was given to her. The three hours on her watch that separated her from Bela and Subhash were like a *physical barrier*, as massive as the mountains she'd flown over to get here. She'd done it, the worst thing that she could think of doing.'

(Lahiri 2013: p. 180, emphasis added)

Gauri's resettlement on the West Coast continues her personal itinerary of uprooting in the name of sovereign becoming. The character is presented in a recurring evasion from contexts that invoke the tragic circumstances of her youth. Mobility as peregrination becomes a particular healing strategy by which Gauri attempts to subdue her guilt and sufferance. Gauri values the nomadic freedom to relocate as a possibility to renounce attachments and thus protect herself from further anguish. Her redefinition along strong individualistic lines is facilitated by her unrestricted access to a mobile condition. This suggests that Gauri upholds nomadic travel as the only strategy that enables her transgressive redefinition. Her capacity to renounce family bonds and traditional female roles illustrates her intention to resist hegemonic coordinates of identity by simultaneously crossing physical and cultural boundaries. Gauri's voluntary transplantation from India to America and her transition from the East to the West Coast make up a chain of nomadic transgressions that helps her fashion a new subjectivity. The character's metamorphosis highlights the 'transiency of identity', since it engulfs the effects of becoming generated by the flow of time and shaped by Gauri's transition to a novel environment.

Interestingly, Gauri develops an equivocal outlook regarding the possibility of forming enduring bonds. While a rooted existence threatens her sense of freedom, Gauri needs to anchor her fragmentary life, as implied by her need to form certain bonds. The result of this dilemma is the shaping of her fractured subjectivity, split by the need to feel attached and safely detached from life's circumstances. Consequently, Gauri is willing to experience a series of casual relationships, being careful not to let these affairs turn into something that 'might complicate her life' (Lahiri 2013: p. 184). At the same time, Gauri learns to uphold aloofness, as a paradoxical form of connection that celebrates what I would call ghettoized individualism. As self-punishment for having abandoned her family, Gauri refrains from establishing other significant bonds:

'Given what she'd done to Subhash and Bela, it felt wrong to seek the companionship of anyone else. Isolation offered its own form of companionship ... She had no wish to overcome it. Rather, it was something upon which she'd come to depend, with which she had entered by now into a relationship, more satisfying and enduring than the relationships she had experienced in either of her marriages.' (Lahiri 2013: p. 184)

Gauri's option for reclusiveness illustrates her preference for a cultural model that privileges self-centeredness and individual freedom. Persistent in her rebellious stance, Gauri continues to reject interdependent parameters of identity formation. Her dependence on independence suggests the emergence of a composite identity profile that blends the character's flight from rooted structures with her impulse to cling to durable configurations. The fact that Gauri's anchor is her own being suggests that she enters a zone of self-sufficiency that condemns her to perpetual segregation.

Despite Gauri's permanent sense of guilt, her successive oversteppings illustrate that her adherence to an individualist set of norms is stronger than her capacity for altruism. After breaking up with her female lover Lorna, Gauri realizes that this abrupt change replicates the pattern of her shifting between identity roles:

'It was not unlike the way her role had changed at so many other points in the past. From wife to widow, from sister-in-law to wife, from mother to childless woman. With the exception of losing Udayan, she had actively chosen to take these steps. She had married Subhash, she had abandoned Bela. She had generated alternative versions of herself, she had insisted at brutal cost on these conversions. Layering her life only to strip it bare, only to be alone in the end.'

(Lahiri 2013: p. 186)

Her reflections suggest that Gauri's unconventional outlook involves her strong leaning for self-definition along autonomous lines. Her repeated acts of displacement represent transgressive stances against the limitations imposed by physical and cultural boundaries. The character's quest for self-rule seems the most important value that guides her nomadic existence. Moreover, the fact she can control her trajectory of resettlement and transformation highlights Gauri's feeling empowered by her ability to switch places and identity roles. As the above quotation reveals, Gauri values the freedom to shape her life more than the consequences of her acts. This suggests that her cultural metamorphosis privileges the norm of an autonomous self to the point of sacrificing everything in the quest for this ideal.

We may argue that Gauri is the holder of a transcultural profile to the extent that she embodies the transcendent urge to cross borders of any kind. In portraying this character, Lahiri inserts few (dilluted) details regarding her cultural specificity. There are no references to Gauri's relationship with her Bengali inheritance as it happens with most of Lahiri's characters belonging to the first generation. The only clue regarding the direction of Gauri's intended metamorphosis is her longing for freedom, associated with the impulse to transcend coercive norms, irrespective of their provenance. Lahiri seems to imply that the force of transgression is the most important generator of transformation, the creative energy that yields new patterns of identity while destroying those that generate pressure. At the same time, Gauri's despondency despite her desired transcending attachments suggests that the effort to transcend loyalties of any kind does not yield a balanced fusion. At this point, I suggest that Gauri's cultural outlook can be regarded as an intersection between forces of transcultural transgression and dissonant effects of transdifference. More specifically, her violation of normative roles seems to generate a confusing plurality of irreconcilable tendencies. The character's struggle with her own fragmentation becomes more apparent as she suddenly decides to visit India.

3.3 Identity negotiation through transnational travel

Gauri's reconnection with Kolkata is the result of an impulsive decision, triggered by her unplanned encounter with Bela, the first one since Gauri's desertion. Shocked by her daughter's utter rejection, Gauri changes her plans of attending a conference in London, plunging into a more personal journey to India. Despite Gauri's adoption of Western identity models, her decision to visit India foregrounds her understanding that the past is an undeniable coordinate of herself. At the same time, Bela's firm repudiation is a voice of the past that refuses to acknowledge Gauri's relevance. Perhaps Gauri's temporary reintegration into the setting of her youth represents an attempt to retrace her younger self. However, her return to a highly transformed locale points to Gauri's inability to retrieve that of part of herself that she has been ignoring. Her feeling of non-existence (Lahiri 2013: p. 247) illustrates the perceived dissolution of her identity coordinates, her inability to make sense of her fragmented self, which supports the interpretation of Gauri's transdifference. Confronted with these feelings, Gauri contemplates suicide, realizing that this is the unstated goal of her travel back home: 'The purpose of her return was to take her leave' (Lahiri 2013: p. 249). Her intention to end her life suggests that her professional success has not erased the traumatic traces of her youth. To use Bran's words, 'immigration empowers her [Gauri] professionally, but not personally' (2014: p. 305). In full adulthood, Gauri's personal crisis is triggered by the 'emptiness, husk of existence' (Lahiri 2013: p. 249), the result of her unconventional choices. Gauri's identity crisis illustrates the ambivalent potential of mobility in relation with women's empowerment. On the one hand, Gauri's depression suggests that the freedom to redefine herself along autonomous lines has not generated the desired fulfillment. Moreover, I argue that her transgresive urge has resulted in a vacuum of identity roles that induces feelings of confusion and desperation. Seen from this angle, Gauri's mobility provides the necessary freedom for personal reinvention while opening a chaotic dimension devoid of grounded references. This contradictory aspect of Gauri's mobility reveals the ambivalent nature of movement in relation to the possibility of empowerment.

Gauri's arrival in Kolkata during the Durga Puja festival places her into an intricate web of mythic representations regarding womanhood, which effect Gauri's understanding of her diffused identity coordinates. As one facet of the Great Goddess (Devi), Durga embodies the divine female energy Shakti, the dynamic aspect of the Absolute (Zimmer 1990: p. 208) that fuels the manifest creation (Rodrigues 2003: p. 18). At the same time, under the name of Mahishamardini, Durga is the Slayer of the Demon, a fearful symbol of female destructive potential (Rodrigues 2003: p. 32). When Gauri arrives in Kolkata, the omniscient narrator foregrounds this martial aspect of Durga, her 'resplendent, formidable' posture with the demon at her feet (Lahiri 2013: p. 243). I think one can correlate this combative aspect of the Goddess with Gauri's own transgressive self-definition, stronlgy imbued with her cruelty to Subahsh and Bela. The Durga Puja is also an 'implicit reminder of Sita's fidelity' (Rodrigues 2003: p. 302). This element alludes to Ramayana, whose hero (Rama) invokes Devi to help him win the fight with Ravana, the kidnapper of his wife Sita. From one angle, Gauri's decision to leave Subhash may stand for an act of wifely devotion to Udayan, whose loving memory she preserves. At the same time, the same gesture results in mercilessness towards Subhash and Bela, marking the destruction of family bonds. As well as Devi, Gauri herself is a bundle of contradictory attributes, since her destructive actions also have a creative counterpart, inherent in her academic accomplishment. Gauri's academic career involves a 'measured contact' (Lahiri 2013: p. 181) with her students which she comes to hold dear. This element underscores the connection between Gauri's teaching attribution and her nourishing potential that has remained unfulfilled by the motherhood condition.

Gauri's brief relocation to India during the Durga Puja is a desperate attempt to comprehend her scattered identity coordinates. Her desolation when faced with an empty existence expresses her awareness of an identity gap, the ironical result of her nomadic distrust of attachments. Her intention to commit suicide may express Gauri's inability to cope with the void of female attributes that she has deliberately generated. (She is a mother unacknowledged by her child, she has divorced Subhash and she displays wifely fidelity in her devotion to Udayan). This perceived gap in her identity fabric is to be interpreted as an effect of Gauri's voluntary shift to 'a hyper-individualized life in America' (Bran 2014: p. 313). Perhaps her intention to commit suicide springs from her desire to reunite with her late husband and share 'the bond of not existing' (Lahiri 2014: p. 247).

However, the fact that Gauri gives up her suicidal plans illustrates that she eventually comes to terms with her own ambivalence. Her brief reconnection with the setting of her youth functions as a catalyst for self-exploration that generates self-acceptance. Her cruelty to Bela and Subhash, her enduring love for Udayan, her long-lasting guilt and her professional creativity paint an image of womanhood as an enigmatic amalgamation of contrasting peculiarities. Seen from this angle, she echoes another facet of Hindu mythical femininity, namely *mahamaya,* the Goddess' supreme mystery, its ineffable and impenetrable nature (Rodrigues 2003: p. 312). Framed by the mythical layer of the Durga Puja, Gauri appears as one possible manifestation of the Hindu female energy, whose choices seem to escape the constraints of moral judgments. However, this transcendence of ethics may be difficult to conceptualize for a Western reader whose mythic version of pure womanhood, the Virgin Mary stands in stark contrast with the 'horrific – beautiful India's mother' (Zimmer 1990: p. 215).

I interpret Gauri's apparent pacification as an acceptance of her fragmented female self that becomes possible as she relocates to India during the religious celebration of multifaceted femininity. By placing Gauri's self-understanding in the Hindu context, Lahiri's may imply that Gauri's attempt to overlook her cultural roots by plunging into a deterritorialized dimension is not a productive strategy. This controversial character ironically finds more suitable identity references in the Hindu mythical layer that seems to accommodate ideas of contradictory, fragmented female selves.

A transnational feminist analysis argues that Gauri's subversive and composite profile is an expression of her 'counter-cultural life' (Habib 2015: p. 21). As a general term, transnationalism refers to cross-border relationships, patterns of exchange, affiliations and social formations straddling nation-states. It also denotes: 'processes by which immigrants forge and sustain multi-stranded social relations that link together their societies of origin and settlement' (Basch et al., 2003: p. 7). Gauri's rhizomatic transgression of conventional cultural patterns is interpreted as both a celebration of a 'liberated self' (Habib 2015: p. 21) and an expression of the 'multiplicity of a woman's role' (Ibid.). I agree with Habib in that Gauri certainly deconstructs the idea of a homogeneous Third World woman, as she constantly renounces Hindu patriarchal values. However, I would complete Habib's claim with the remark that Gauri's subversive stance is paralleled by her partial reliance on Hindu myths that accommodate the possibility of a layered female self. This suggests an inherent paradox of Gauri's transnational feminist stance that deconstructs the monolithic image of the Third World Woman by selectively relying on Hindu traditional sources. In this sense, I interpret the character's transcultural profile as that stage of Gauri's identity negotiation meant to harmonize her unsettling transdifference. More specifically, this strategy illustrates her ability to eventually orchestrate her inner fragmentation while transcending the idea of fixed cultural belonging. Eventually, Gauri couples a vision of extreme individualism with the faceted coordinates of womanhood supplied by Hindu myths.

4. Conclusions

By creating a first generation female Bengali immigrant who willingly departs from traditional Hindu norms, Lahiri breaks her customary vision of Bengali wives as holders of conservative outlooks. I consider that this thematic change is meant to introduce the author's message regarding the importance of transgression as a mechanism that enables (female)identity redefinition along freeing dimensions. Bran considers that *The Lowland* is not primarily a novel about assimilation, cultural translation or hybridity (2014: p. 320). The critic argues that processes of cultural adaptation and change are subordinated to the most predominant themes of 'family secrets and unresolved past traumas' (Ibid.). However, I propose a slightly different interpretation, arguing that Lahiri's interest in family relations and tragedies represents a subtle manner of shifting the focus from the idea of cultural specific identities to a realm beyond fixed cultural allegiance. By creating characters engaged in different acts of transgression, Lahiri foregrounds the importance of border crossing at the expense of attachment to distinct cultural contexts. In a sense, *The Lowland* can be read as a novel about the relevance of transgression in a world of fluid cultural borders and uncertain cultural belonging. Interestingly however, transgression for its own sake does not appear to be glorified, but presented as a preliminary step that shapes an enlarged cultural outlook. This chapter has demonstrated that Gauri's strong impulse to cross conventional boundaries does not automatically generate her transformation along transcultural lines. I would argue that an intermediate stage of her metamorphosis is a perceived plurality of facets that illustrates the character's transdifference. Ironically, Gauri's layered profile, a result of her nomadic transgressions, does not yield a balanced outlook. Instead, her attempts at redefinition against Hindu patriarchal values results in a perceived vacuity of roles that triggers an identity crisis. Tasting the bitterness of her dissonant profile, Gauri turns to her Hindu roots, as symbolized by her sudden homecoming. However, her temporary visit to India should not be idealized as a complete acceptance of origins that affords Gauri's reconnection with traditional values. Instead, I argue that her trip to Kolkata confronts Gauri with a Hindu vision of female fragmentation that helps her makes sense of her own diffused identity frame. In a sense, her brief return to Kolkata may be considered the beginning of her transcultural journey, prepared by Gauri's transgressive crossings. Eventually, Gauri's rhizomatic travel seems to make room for an appeasement of her conflicts, as signaled by a possible reconciliation announced by Bela's pacifying letter that acknowledges Gauri as grandmother. At the same time, Gauri's transformation along her nomadic itinerary illustrates the nuanced relation between female mobility and the possibility of empowerment. While Gauri's accelerated relocation enables her escape from entrapping conventions, it eventually signals a lack of stable references that demands to be fulfilled. Her paradoxical entrapment in a detached condition devoid of conventional roles illustrates the limit of a vision that privileges uprootedness/nomadic becoming at the expense of rootedness/settled being. Gauri's tormenting dilemma suggests that Jhumpa Lahiri wishes to foreground the equal relevance of grounded/rooted references and fluid/nomadic/rhizomatic coordinates in the fabric of contemporary identities on the move.

Bibliography

Alexander, Vera (2006) 'Investigating the Motif of Crime as Transcultural Border Crossing: Cinnamon Gardens and the Sandglass', in Christine Matzke & Susanne Mühleisen (eds.) *Postcolonial Postmortems: Crime Fiction from a Transcultural Perspective*, Amsterdam: Rodopi, pp. 139–160.

Basch, Linda, Nina Glick Schiller & Christina Szanton Blanc (2003) *Nations Unbound – Transnational Projects – Postcolonial Predicaments and Deterritorialized Nation-States*, London and New York: Routledge.

Berry, Ellen E. (1999) 'Nomadic Desires and Transcultural Becomings', in Ellen E. Berry & Mikhail N. Epstein (eds.) *Transcultural Experiments Russian and American Models of Creative Communication*, New York: Palgrave Macmillan, pp. 121-140.

Bose, Mandakranta (2010) *Women in the Hindu Tradition. Rules, Roles and Exceptions*, London and New York: Routledge.

Braidotti, Rosi (1994) *Nomadic Subjects: Embodiment and Sexual Difference in Contemporary Feminist Theory*, New York: Columbia University Press.

Bran, Ramona A. (2014) *Immigration: 'A Lifelong Pregnancy?' An Analysis of Jhumpa Lahiri's Fiction*, Dissertation, Dortmund: Technischen Universitat Dortmund.

Cattan, Nadine (2008) 'Gendering Mobility: Insights into the Construction of Spatial Concepts', in Tanu P. Uteng & Tim Cresswell (eds.) *Gendered Mobilities*, Hampshire: Ashgate Publishing Ltd, pp. 83-97.

Creswell, Tim & Tanu P. Uteng (2008) 'Gendered Mobilities: Towards an Holistic Understanding', in Tanu P. Uteng & Tim Cresswell (eds.) *Gendered Mobilities*. Hampshire: Ashgate Publishing Ltd., pp. 1-12.

Cresswell, Tim (1996) *In Place, Out of Place, Geography, Ideology, and Transgression*, Minneapolis, London: University of Minnesota Press.

Deka, Nalini (1993) 'India', in Loeb L. Adler (ed.) *International Handbook on Gender Roles*, Westport, Connecticut, London: Greenwood Press.

Delleuze, Gilles & Felix Guattari (1987) *A Thousand Plateaus Capitalism and Schizophrenia*, translated from French by Brian Massumi, London, Minneapolis: University of Minnesota Press.

Epstein, Mikhail (1999) 'From Culturology to Transculture', in Ellen E. Berry & Mikhail N. Epstein (eds.) *Transcultural Experiments Russian and American Models of Creative Communication*, New York: Palgrave Macmillan, pp. 15-30.

Fay, Michaela (2008) 'Mobile Belonging: Exploring Transnational Feminist Theory and Online Connectivity', in Tanu P. Uteng & Tim Cresswell (eds.) *Gendered Mobilities*, Hampshire: Ashgate Publishing Ltd., pp. 65-81.

Fuller, Marcus B. (1900) *The Wrongs of Indian Womanhood*, New York, Chicago, Toronto: Flemming H. Revell Company.

Ganser, Alexandra (2009) *Roads of Her Own. Gendered Space and Mobility in American Women's Road Narratives, 1970-2000*, Amsterdam and New York: Rodopi.

Gupta, Saibal (2015) 'Naxalbari Revisited', *The Times of India*. Online. Available https://timesofindia.indiatimes.com/city/kolkata/Naxalbari-revisited/articleshow/47044695.cms (accessed August 2016).

Habib, Sarah (2015) *Transnational Feminism and Literature: A Study of Women's Realities in The Lowland, Burnt Shadows and The Good Muslim*, M.A. Thesis, Dhaka: Brac University.

Herman, Phyllis K. (2011) 'Sîtâ Rasoîs and Úâkta Pît.has: A Feminine Reclamation of Mythic and Epic Proportions', in Tracy Pintchman & Rita D. Sherma (eds.) *Woman and Goddess in Hinduism: reinterpretations and re-envisionings*, Palgrave: Macmillan, pp. 79-95.

Kaplan, Caren (1996) *Questions of Travel. Postmodern Discourses of Displacement*, Durham, NC and London: Duke University Press.

Kronlid, David (2008) 'Mobility as Capability', in Tanu P. Uteng & Tim Cresswell (eds.) *Gendered Mobilities*, Hampshire: Ashgate Publishing Ltd., pp. 15-33.

Lahiri, Jhumpa (2013) *The Lowland*, New York, Toronto: Alfred A. Knopf.

Massey, Doreen (2001) 'General Introduction', in Doreen Massey (ed.) *Space, Place and Gender*, Minneapolis: University of Minnesota Press, pp. 1-16.

Miller, Joan C. (1994) 'Cultural Diversity in the Morality of Caring: Individually Oriented versus Duty-Based Interpersonal Moral Codes', *Cross-Cultural Research*, 28(1): 3–39.

Moslund, Sten P. (2010) *Migration and Literature and Hybridity. The Different Speeds of Transcultural Changes*, Basingstoke: Palgrave Macmillan.

Mustafi, Mitra S. (2012) 'Naxalbari: The Cradle of India's Bloody Class War', *The New York Times*. Online. Available https://india.blogs.nytimes.com/category/uncategorized/page/195/ (accessed September 2015).

O'Sullivan, D. Simon (2000) 'Cultural Studies as Rhizome, Rhizomes in Cultural Studies', *Cultural Studies and Interdisciplinarity, Trinity and All Saints College*, Conference/Workshop Item, United Kingdom: University of Leeds.

Pratt, Geraldine (1998) 'Geographic Metaphors in Feminist Theory', in Susan H. Aiken (ed.) *Making Worlds: Gender, Metaphor, Materiality*, Tucson, AZ: University of Arizona Press.

Rodrigues, Hillary P. (2003) *Ritual Worship of the Great Goddess. The Liturgy of the Durga Puja With Interpretation*, Albany: State University of New York Press.

Stoican, Adriana E. (2017) *Transcultural Fusion through Nomadic Transgression in Jhumpa Lahiri's The Lowland and In Other Words* (unpublished).

White, Paul (1995) 'Geography, Literature and Migration', in John Connell, Russel King & Paul White (eds.) *Writing Across Worlds Literature and Migration*, London and New York: Routledge, pp. 1-19.

Wilkins, Joseph William (2005) *Hindu Mythology. Vedic and Purãnic*, Elibron Classics Replica Edition Published in 1882 by Calcutta, Thacker, Spink & Co.

Wolff, Janet (1992) 'On the Road Again: Metaphors of Travel in Cultural Criticism', *Cultural Studies*, 7(2): 224-239.

Triandis, Harry C. (1993) 'Collectivism and Individualism as Cultural Syndromes', *Cross-Cultural Research*, 3(4): 155–180.

Zimmer, Heinrich (1990) *Myths and Symbols in Indian Art and Civilization*, Delhi: Motilal Banarsidass.

CHAPTER VIII

The Politics of the Feminine Body: A Manifesto and Three TV Series

Viorella MANOLACHE

1. A Discussion Chapter. Introductory (Con)Text

The present study lies in/on the line (border) opened by a debate focused on the relationship between image (with extensions/mirroring in television and cinema), gender studies and critical perspective, reassessing and insisting upon the inventory of the female subject in relation to the object, upon the representation and the body, in order to correct that which, in a psychoanalytic pitch, is supported through a (firm) non-distinction of subject and object[1]. A supra-abundance of concepts fits to deconstruct woman's image and its relation to a transparent medium, overcharge the infusion of meaning contained either in 'womanliness' or in 'feminization', through a rapid re-positioning, redefined in relation to simulation, to spatial-subjective convulsions and the consolidation of a personal/particular identity[2].

---

1   The theme is discussed in Žižek's *Zăbovind în negativ. Kant, Hegel şi critica ideologiei* (*Tarrying with the Negative*). Bucharest: All Publishing House, 2001, pp. 56-57, with insistence upon the Lacanian passage 'the feminine not all'. If the identity of man consists, in the symbolic, in assuming full (complete) symbolic mandate, woman remains marked by division. Not at all coincidentally, the selection of the three TV series for the present study re-distributes the Lacanian reporting to a 'not-whole woman', through a politics of snippets, of re-composition, of exteriorization in relation to space, certifying the effect of finding the symbolic source of female identity inside dynamic antinomies.

2   The 'dedoxification' concept is explicitly defined and used by Linda Hutcheon in reference to a triple registry: Postmodernism 'dedoxifies' cultural depictions from their political residues (Hutcheon 1989: p. 3) and indicates that the world is not knowable unless calling upon networks of significant, socially established systems, and events that make up culture. The 'dedoxification' action approves the idea/theory that postmodernism is part of a cultural authority crisis. Thus, dedoxification equals a challenge posed by postmodernism for any mimetic assumptions with respect to representation (Hutcheon 1989: p. 30). If 'to dedoxify' means to problematize by self-definition in terms of denaturalized primary meanings and a disclosure of ideology behind cultural norms, 'dedoxification', as an artificial/constructed term, supposedly accepts the operation of extracting particular meaning from a generality of issued opinions. The concept needs to be accounted for only at the confluence of cultural marks issued by specific societies that operate with certain cultural forms. 'Revelation', 'clash', 'unveiling through denaturalization' of what ideology

Lynne Joyrich (1996) pushes forth such a discussion by amending the difficulties of defining the 'feminine viewing subject' category, interested, in fact, both in the position and placement of the feminine in this context. There are no representative cases/species for the overall status of the feminine in the area of the visual, Joyrich decrees, which imports an interest for the modality of organizing images in postmodernism. Bridging such differing findings with what we proposed as an innovative concept that of serialfication, as the reunion of two concepts (postmodernism and representation) able to offer an optimal formulation for placing the image, the narration and the finality (as ideology producer) inside an interconnecting relationship. Postmodern practice accepts the cultural and reinvests it with a mediation mission in/through representations, while approving the ambivalent politics of postmodernism; in the case of serialfication effects, on one hand, a lack of depth, expressivity, significance, mono-dimensionality, and on the other, a flux of poly-significant, ideological flooding, replications and multiplications (Manolache 2015).

Certainly, the television series category holds the attributes of an enabling environment for case studies, careful to note the true-false report of ideological releases, favoring a formulation at the expense of another, even when not giving up stereotypes, replicate images or rhetorical strategies. There are, according to Bonnie J. Dow (1996), a particular policy of the 'television text' and a deepening of the television gap between feminine representation and representations of women. Bonnie J. Dow fixes as a method of work the nodal focusing on criticism, text, audience and 'theory television criticism', concerned by the political implications of discursive practices, for the purpose of preserving, through feminism, a set of political and practical ideas anchored in a movement dedicated to women's progress and the transformations of patriarchies. The present study follows, up to a point, this 'methodological design', which it particularizes by bringing the female body to the fore, through considering the status of the feminine as a fragment (thus both subject and object) which entails an acceptance of the body as a good conductor, a medium of representation, but also a faithful translator of political, economic, social and cultural realities. The relevance of the selected methods is aimed at harnessing and exploring theories on the relationship of the feminine with body anthropology, with television/image and discourse theories, by punctually insisting upon a visual politics of the feminine body and a Poetic Manifesto with an interest in fracturism and re-assembly; in fact, the text relies on a particular repositioning in the open context of dedicated prospects of (in a postmodern manner) feminism. In this sense, the three TV series approached will be The Bridge (2013, USA. FX Productions, Shine America), Bron/Broen (2011, Sweden/Denmark.

---

manages as rightfully true are the clues (sometimes hard, sometimes soft) associated with the concept.

Filmlance International AB, Nimbus Film Productions, Sveriges Television, Film i Väst, Zweites Deutsches Fernsehen, Danmarks Radio, Film i Skåne, ZDF Enterprises, Norsk Rikskringkasting, Media Programme of the European Community, Nordisk Film TV-Fond) and *The Tunnel* (2013, UK/France. Canal +, Kudos Film and Television, Shine, Sky Atlantic).

Anticipating a future formalization (already becoming actual) of the general rules of creation, concerned about the latent geometry of the film, B. Oprițescu (1973) customizes the direction (the way forward by observing, delineating, validating, limiting, prioritizing, and exhausting codes) that can direct the encoding method of the physiological and can reaffirm the method of binary cutting 'of both each fragment and of the whole, somewhere in the middle' arguing that between them there is a zero (a place/moment that marks a break in action) that the image may be considered either in isolation, or in a combination between two of its points: total stop or movement. The report imprints values upon the context and the sense of the two fragments and comparing their values (Oprițescu 1973: p. 279). Replacing the discussion in the core of the present, Hilary Radner and Rebecca Stringer (2012) consider necessary to approach the process of initial 're-vision' in the sense of seeing a 'different difference' and showing interest for that multiplicity already separated from homogeneity. Following the scheme proposed by Radner and Stringer, essential points which require our attention are: the recognition, completion, fixation and review of that 'space for women' (a space set exactly in the middle) as the locus of new female subjectivities, through revaluating and assigning a new meaning to body ('The dissected body'/'The body as detritus'; 'Fractured recomposing of the feminine body'); a reassessment of male identity, considering it a 'category with difficulties', of apparently pre-established hierarchies unable to claim any monolithic structure (hence 'The Truth Terrorist: the masculine anatomist of fractured feminine bodies'); valorization of crime as maximum intensity in the series of ingredients of the tragic category (calamity-pathos-retribution-punishment – Jayamanne 1995).

1.1 The dissected body. The body as detritus

Starting from David Le Breton's *Anthropology of the Body and Modernity* (2002), a possible first observation for the present study would take into account the fact that, in its fracturing hypostasis, the body can be conceived as a suture of different parts entering a recomposing process – both a symbolically representational endeavor and a factual scattering/fragmentation of significances; in fact, a visual rendition of the autonomous fragment. Unsurprisingly, Marshall McLuhan warned about the fact that an image of fragmented man is an articulating force within the homogenous Western world, recomposing through its hybrid energy a meeting of existing models inside social order, by accepting an equation in which the hybrid is a meeting/recomposing zone for two means, seen as moments of truth/revelation from which a new form germinates (McLuhan & Zingrone, 2006). Admitted just as property and not as essence, as a complicit way of rationing the world's form with its substance, the body is decreed in a Bretonian (2002) key to be an indication of rupture, at the same time disassociation, dissection or fracturing.

This hypostasis extracts its (re)sources from a popular mediaeval sociality (the carnival seen as a spectacle of mixed-indistinct bodies, both collective elation and 'confusing crowd', temporary, transfigured, grotesque, seen as a distancing from modern individualism, a status which the body itself cannot reduce to just one subject) and from an anatomist perspective considering the dissected man (although ontologically whole) as a body already imponderable.

The two perspectives can be accepted as flexible articulations for a dual registry of the body: a depreciating mode, of distancing (alter)positioning, and another mode, which reclaims substance identity by verifying Breton's (2002) sentences which distinguish between 'having a body' and 'being one's own body'. In the sense in which the body does not refer (does not send to) anything except itself, fracture becomes the frontier separating/uniting the self and alterity, affirming a statute without the alternative of the 'body seen as change'.

Establishing a work hypothesis in the proof stating that fracturation paradoxically implies a re-unifying/re-welding effect, the theoretical frame of our present study will accept a certain appetence for postmodern imports, in the sense in which it will show an interest in reassembling the carnival perspective in its anatomically-visual sense, using a transcription of the feminine within the visual registry of TV series categories.

In this sense we will appeal to the tri-phased registry of the original *Bron/Broen* and its two follow-ups, *The Tunnel* and *The Bridge*, series illustrating the hypostasis of body/corpse from/on the border/bridge/tunnel, uniting two halves belonging to two different women, fragments which become a formula for diagnosing social, cultural, economic, attitudinal-psychological or political halves within two distinct spaces.

One has to mention from the start that the image of a fractured feminine body is placed (not accidental for a politics of feminism subsuming their discourse on/within reflections of marginality accepted inside a complex registry of marginalia – Ferguson, Gever, Minh-ha & West, 1990) on the edge of the border/tunnel/bridge, accepting immediate/near-the-center space as a blurred margin, with a double effect of rejection and reassembly.

The bridge/tunnel/border can be perceived as 'heterotopic' (Foucault 2009) constructs, cutting – neutering formulations for juxtaposing more than one space upon a single place, with double circulating systems – of opening and closing, their function depending upon the type of society/culture inside which they develop sustaining any space-time variations, both isolating and permissive at the same time, superposing the coordinates of known or imagined spaces upon the already –perceived ones.

One cannot avoid the alloy between media culture and representational politics, a 'dedoxification' triggered by postmodernism and seen as an acceptance/perception of feminism as both socio-political movement and plural component of the history of art, as poetics and politics, which, via L. Hutcheon (1989), seems to have (already) taken dominion over the fertile soil of comments focused upon the subject.

Harmonized with the subject, the present study's novelty elements reside in/from an examination of hypotheses stating that: the feminine body (although fractured) remains a productive conduit of spaces; feminine halves mediate a circulating reflex, alternating between the sides of separating space; and the reassembly of feminine parts, visually intermediate, cannot be separated from the mechanism of politics with direct stakes within representation and identity

2. Fractured Recomposing of the Feminine Body: A Manifesto and Three TV Series

In its double denomination as poetics and politics, the image of the feminine body can be analyzed by referencing the nodal points of the *Fracturist Manifesto*, in the sense of verifying the mode/modality by which these (the points on the agenda) can resist any fracturing articulation within the registry of offered TV series.

In a non-casual way the visual politics of the feminine body, the Manifesto (Crudu & Ianuş, 2006) announces a framing already associated to the total refusal of notions, concepts, denominations and tags, by re-launching through a semantic-void disassociation, a recomposing of notions such as real and individual.

If, in a poetic key, notions, concepts, objects are common, politics decrees that emitted reactions can only be strictly individual, with representational effects, with a needed mention for the fact that dual registries are reciprocally deductible, overtaking any individual access through objects, through the other categories or the generalities of common language: politics traces the contours of poetics as finite and final end-product of representation.

As a work method, we will trace eight poetical solutions offered by the *Fracturist Manifesto*, in order to verify their pertinence in the key of feminine body politics, with the help of the aforementioned three TV series we will analyze (*Bron/Broen*, *The Tunnel* and *The Bridge*) an alloy already articulated in: a completely-excessive description of the framing within which an object is manifested, through de-conceptualization and with an interest in describing differences; avoiding pre-established and unusual situations; non-verbal reconstructions; recomposing through language; blurring the borders between/in the object of reaction and the reaction itself; the absent object, re-suggested by frames and situations; almost as a confessional reactions; the imperative establishes that objects endure, reactions change; the precedence of authenticity (Crudu & Ianuş, 2006).

The three TV series uniformly start, with no major prime/original registry changes, with delivering, without any warning intro, the linking media image: bridge, tunnel and again bridge.

In *Bron/Broen*, a corpse reconstituted from two halves belonging to two different women is left on the Øresund bridge, which unites the Swedish town of Malmo and the Danish capital Copenhagen, exactly on the border line between the two countries: one half, a Swedish politician, the other half, a Danish prostitute.

If The *Tunnel* overtakes, without any modification, the social status of the feminine parts, placing them on the Channel *Tunnel* (Folkstone & Calais), on the English-French border (half of a French politician and half of a British prostitute), *The Bridge* banks upon a certain contextual difference: on the Bridge of the Americas, on the border between El Paso, Texas and Ciudad Juarez, Chihuahua, the feminine corpse reunites the superior part of judge Lorraine Gates and the inferior part of an immigrant Mexican prostitute, statistically reconfirming the too many crimes/missing persons within the region adjoining the border space.

A first observation would take into account the fact that the offered framing delivers all the stereotypes/confections of the fractured feminine body (apparent duality of contraries: politician or superior; prostitute or inferior), which maintain a theatrical recomposing of the feminine one (lights go on in the tunnel/on the bridge as on a stage), in the sense of exerting a plural identity/representation.

If we accept the border as point of contact/center/workbench, the fractured feminine body accepts an entrance (superior part) and an exit (inferior part) which, beyond the notes of a prefabricated visual blueprint, willingly exacerbate feminine extremities.

Almost paradoxically, and against pre-established directions, the fractured feminine body becomes a conductor of bringing together and organizing a team, as a welding alloy.

Martin Rohde and Saga Noren, Karl Roebuck and Elise Wassermann, Marco Ruiz and Sonya Cross are part of the ad-hoc, casually welded teams investigating the crime, deepening their opinionated representations (of opinions, reaction modes, work instruments/methods used) with every second, but also insisting upon the socially-maladaptive feminine heroine (a blond in all three series, obsessed by rules, devoid of empathy, excessively organized, with no friends, traumatized, with overcompensating sexual pulsions, etc. (see Sonya Cross and the unsolved case concerning her sister).The perspective is counterbalanced by the imperfectly masculine hero recovering after a vasectomy, with all his failures as a family man who fathered five children with three different women.

In the key of an in-solitary which has to be obtained at any cost, the feminine-masculine interaction (in the manner of police movies, detectives complicate their lives/get involved with each other in an easily-explained chemistry!) is extrapolated by the journalist's profile (in *The Bridge*, for example, Daniel Frye's professionally-friendly relationship with Adriana Mendez overemphasizes her sexual option by outside-the-norm recourse to traditions and designs of a traditional community).

Certainly all three TV series fully make use of the fractured feminine body (although as an in absentia object, it's permanently suggested by using close frames and continuity shots) the one mediating a certain circulatory reflex, on each side of a separating space. In fact, the reflexes of a politics with direct stakes in representation and identity are strongly reaffirmed, in the sense of a geographical remake maintaining the bilingualism (hard to perceive in *Bron/Broen*), international alliances and any difference/rapprochement between spaces already separated by a border line.

Edward W. Soja (2010) proposes the term 'unjust geographies' for the direct involvement of the human body in a file of debates consisting in issues about abortion, obesity, stem cells, the registry of sexual practices, but also of body parts transplant, both fragmentation and reassembly, considered external order handlings of individual behavior (Soja 2010: p. 31). In fact, the discussion opens and reviews blank spaces, marked by thick layers, governed not only by a specific administrative convenience but also by cultural domination and social control, the diffusions of power stamping and preserving, inside exogenous generated geographies, the hierarchizing breakdown as prime worlds, second worlds, or the third world. It is precisely in the context of such perspectives that border strategies with unjust spatialization divide and fragment widening cultures and contrasting combative states. Soja insists in this regard, with punctual relevance for the equation of the present study and the chosen case study, on a 'cruel and violent' example along the fluid boundary between the United States and Mexico (see The Bridge), referring to those long corridors of the drug cartels which 'criminal unite' corridors lacking control, underground highways or sewers, 'stops' (tunnel/bridge) reconfirming the maintenance of insidious geographies (Soja 2010: p. 42).

Hence the relevance of space as reshaping force of representation and politics, of intervention in the constructed body, a perspective which Foucault would assess to heterotopological mechanisms, as a way of seeing and interpreting spaces and their effects. Starting from Foucault, Soja sees an equation between strategic spatial awareness and seeking 'spatial justice', in the sense in which geographies are social products, the result of human actions, transformable for either good or bad (see in this both his motivations and politics, in 'The Truth Terrorist').

2.1. 'The Truth Terrorist': the masculine anatomist of fractured feminine bodies

If *Bron/Broen* and *The Tunnel* cannot be separated from an exposure of Europe's crisis, with direct stakes in exposing modern society mired in its own problems (the names of the main characters in *The Tunnel* sound German as an allusion to the European Union's 'engine') and trying to replace these problems within the context of a public agenda, *The Bridge* seems more concerned with border social tensions (people and drug smuggling, forbidden subterranean crossing, illegal immigration, corruption, etc.).

'The Truth Terrorist' (the anatomist-murderer of the fractured feminine bodies) is the one who maintains, under the sign of authenticity, the prime, well-tempered narrative (violent social criticism) but with reactions which will later justify confession (the crime is just a personal revenge/the murderer has his personal reasons).

The European version cannot abstain from using the profile of a blogger-terrorist whose obvious intention is the violent/fracturing exposure of common social problems on both sides of the border, and to demand their solving through an integrated device with/of inverse numberings.

The attribution of a name such as The Truth Terrorist seems to function only for the European visual version, in the sense in which David Tate from *The Bridge* detours the action/focus of the whole series with a forwarding of locally (particularizing dysfunctions) in the present case, less territorial eco-anarchist-terrorist ingredients, and more narrative-continued by the story of those 'Lost girls of Juarez'. In fact, the screenplay option seems to focus exclusively upon intensity in defragmenting spaces inside their own relationships.

Through the mass-media's voice (the journalist), The Terrorist publishes his agenda: inequality politics is targeted, as well as the immigration problem, disabled persons, the homeless, and child protection politics. Far from being a hero of the 'evil-super-mensch' variety, the criminal is just an anatomist imbued with a type of extreme social conscience, using the feminine body as an instrument of regulating/signaling a violent warning against homogeneity, difference and the idea of halving at any price. The anatomist-criminal exposes/desecrates, up to a point, what is hidden behind (in one of the halves) of the welfare state denomination, stating his motives as programmatically-ideological declarations: if the citizens slip into society's safety nets and believe they are apparently protected, there are still dark forces devoted to the concept of pushing the hop, skip and jump to its ultimate consequences, doubling the threat and extrapolating the fracture.

Avoiding the feminine body's victim status, one can state that the fractured hypostasis, operated, in a political key, by the masculine, rethinks exactly those spatial reconfigurations of power (in its dissipative-dissected sense) through the feminine (re-welding/publicly exposed feminine presence).

In the same analytical note, Moira Gatens (1991) decrees that the phenomenological experience of woman can only be funded upon the bodily, at a distance from the neutrality advocated by liberal theories; and that any 'politicization' of identity interactions cannot be separated (fractured) from the code of rights, dependencies and power, citizenship and nationality, legal politics of privacy, relational responsibilities, anarchism or a politics of inter-sectorial identity.

3. Concluding Notes upon the Visual Politics of the Feminine Body

Received within the alloy image and representation as part of postmodern culture, with all that the conservative sociological turn-over implies, and reflected within the affirmation of 'cultural forms of otherness' (here, 'otherness' in the sense of undermining stability/ sanctity of both canon and tradition), the imagining effect can be seen as a politics of attaching sense to an image.

According to Teresa De Lauretis (1984) the foreign politics-pictorial turn decrees that man becomes through the body, a place of image; or that the body is a medium for the image/media means bodies, and the internal politics, as a corporeal turn, invests the body with a sense of surface accepting traces of socio-cultural changes. In De Lauretis interpretation key[3],

---

3   We cannot avoid mentioning in this sense the representational career of the fragmented man delivered by Edgar Allan Poe (*The Man that Was Used* Up – *A Tale of the Late Bugaboo and Kickapoo*), of brigade general John A.B.C. Smith, who fought in the war against the Bugaboo and Kickapoo tribes, and who represents a 'pile of something

language is a social place guided by the imperative: 'all that is personal can only be political'!

Teresa De Lauretis' finding occurs, upon the background of the 1980s, as a node of 'self-representation of de-sealing policies' engaged in feminist theory, anticipating what Linda Hutcheon will theorize by 'dedoxification' as an ideological effect produced and maintained by concepts/discourses, dominant cinema featuring a political function in the service of cultural domination, but not limited to it[4].

Marked by the displacement effect and with a stake in forcing the query status of the main problem faced by cinema, that of relationships and the link between sexuality and politics, de Lauretis precisely considers that the point of view of the viewer splinters, disrupting the consistency of identification. Not at all incidentally for the present approach, the three case studies are variations on the same theme, but loaded with triple viewer identification: three different spaces, three distinct locations, three spatial temperaments, three reactions, each of which relies in turn on specific multipliers and complications of the plot, and on conflict resolution. De Lauretis believes that there are 'languages', practices of the discursive apparatus, which produce different meanings and semiotic modes and which maintain that ideological formula needed for building an ideological subject (see in this regard tensions 'in the couple' Martin Rohde and Saga Noren, Karl Roebuck and Elise Wassermann, Marco Ruiz and Sonya Cross).

---

extremely bizarre' reclaiming his 'piece by piece' reassembly. In the same note, Marshall McLuhan (2006) reviewed the way of assembling children's poetry characters (Humpty-Dumpty who falls from the wall, breaks and cannot be repaired). Teresa De Lauretis starts her analysis of feminist semiotics and cinema with the image of Humpty-Dumpty, equating feminist politics and the image of the character's fall.

4   With explicit reference to successful Romanian cinema (Policeman, adjective, here, Policewoman, noun), Adriana Babeți (Amazons. A Story. Iași: Polirom Publishing House, 2013) insists on a possible typology/building scheme for heroines/stars in movies and detective series. They all are part of the training system from specialized academies, have higher grades, often act together with a partner or a mentor, take risks, initiate investigations on their own, pushing and defying the limits of law and the established frameworks. If the method is reminiscent of the scheme referred to by Umberto Eco to narrative structures in Fleming (with interest in the opposition between character and value, points c) and d) as Bad-Woman; Woman-Bond and Love-Death, Perversion-Candor) Babeți establishes two essential elements to this approach. The first is considering periodization and context (if in the full tide of feminism II, the balance sheet of policier films with female characters was negative, against the backdrop of European and American police organization with their noninvolvement of women and, especially, blocking their operational/terrain actions, TV series of the moment overinflate woman-policeman stereotypes through an 'obvious diminution of the feminist message'; one can thus speak of the 'woman-cop' as a real protagonist, only at the end of the 70s). The second fixes as a landmark the Blue Steel film (1989), Megan Turner/Jamie Lee Curtis thus opening the series of authentic policewoman constructions, 'equal in rights and skills' with her partner, thus reaffirming the 'subject-object' tension with interest in favoring the female both as a noun and as a topic.

The pivotal image of female parts remains essential, an opening sequence which follows a whole approach; a concern coupled by de Lauretis with the need for a conceptual aspect mission, suitable to meet a dual interrogative register: 'what are the conditions of presence of the image in cinema and film?'; 'what are the conditions of the presence of cinema and film in imaging, in the production of a social imaginary?' (De Lauretis 1984: p. 38). Sliding between positive image – negative image (in the abovementioned series, action deepens this explicit dichotomy, by investing with a central role the positive/upper –negative/lower snippets) is, for de Lauretis, a risky and cruel operation. The implications occur against the backdrop of the direct viewer absorption (the image is read immediately and is a significant in it) and the impossibility of disassociating from a context of patriarchal ideologies whose values, social-subjective and aesthetic-affective effects retain dominance inside social fabrics and implications. Read through this lecture grid, female stars are a direct product of such patriarchal imports, or of some stereotypes of female (pathology of) 'slimming': Saga Norén may be received as a borderline character, totally conforming to social norms, incapable of socializing, insensitive, with references to a possible Asperger syndrome (unexplained, but easy to guess in the symptomatology of the characters), emotionally and sexually frustrated; Elise Wassermann follows the scheme of construction of the Saga Norén character, adding a dose of sarcasm, preserving the lack of empathy, but relying on random sex as a form of superficial relationships/formula; Sonya Cross transcends this border positioning, however, borrowing the mixture of evident characteristics while evidently remaining in a position of patriarchal dependency (Hank Wade, her boss and mentor, is actually a paternal image, a psychoanalyst who keeps her under control, managing her deviations)[5]. Moreover, all three stars are nothing more than the product (subject) of an unresolved trauma: the relationship between the feminine and its double (here with the sister, either Jennifer or the absolute double, the twin sister, or Lisa). Integrated to a theoretical perspective issued by Teresa De Lauretis, characters lack any potential for pleasure and satisfaction, their guarantee occurring precisely on the grounds of politics, through the continuous production of meanings, positioning and transparencies in the area of practices and speeches (De Lauretis 1984: p. 86). Hence the guiding role of the sworn assertion of fundamental feminism, stating that if everything personal is also political, and then the space between these components needs to be crossed by

---

5   Teresa De Lauretis removes the notion of experience from the sensory data register, from pure mental-psychological relating with objects and events or the acquisition of skills and competences (such as repeated exposure), relating it to a sense of strategy/subjective technique (De Lauretis 1984: 159). All things being equal, the concept of 'habit'/'habit change' becomes a key element in producing a new/other social subject, marked by a recomposing/unification of disjoined parts.

resorting to experience as central element, which carries with it the reflexes and parts of bias, sexuality, corporality and political practice.

Not surprisingly the trend of feminine/feminist representations in TV series cannot be separated from a certain hypodermic (Real 1996) communication politics, operating through a double effect of exaggeration or underestimating the receiver's reactions. The alloy can be subsumed to the postmodern predisposition towards administering a return to politics through investing reception and audiences with the attribute of 'dispositive' for alternative (negotiated or oppositional) lectures for different groups (either voluntarily or involuntarily) involved in the act of decrypting messages.

One must make the absolutely necessary mention that the act of generalization and comparison (both image and text) imprints upon the receiver any neglect and/or favoring one perspective to the detriment of another. In fact, power relations are reinstated and a certain ideology is perpetuated, extracting its signs from the triple faceted construct of representation, look, oppression/affirmation, and deferring to a possible soft solution within a rejection of relativism/reconnection to/in the political dimension of the feminist project (Frunză 2002).

Within the (still) productive grounds of feminist-feminine representational politics (Pollock 2013; Norris 1997; Miller 1995; Curran & Gurevitch, 1992) a certain questioning of the ways in which, inside an impossibility of interpretative force equation, feminist-political judgments can be either ignored or considered to be relative, with recourse to a 'semiotic-feminine empowerment' as a mode of alternative deciphering of the message/image. One has to take into account a formulation for the 'higher political feminist project', reflected in the positively – satisfying possibility of reception/interpretation.

Against a direction of relative particularities, a way of 'reading against the grain' can be articulated, overtaking postmodernism through a visual alternative of a politically efficient text, which would deliver a unified message of power and action, domination and résistance, obedience and subversion. A contextual 'materialism' can thus be anticipated, seen as a performativity contextual and inter-textual sign.

In a Lyotardian (1979) sense, performativity can be substituted for legitimacy in a postmodern world forced to cohabit, and in which progress is still conditioned by imagination and implemented through its discovery of new moves, inventively applied to changing the rules of the game, an optimization of the process of knowing and enhancing research to the detriment of its valuing/perpetuation.

In fact, any politics of the feminine body cannot be separated from Foucault's (2009) perspective of the common center/edge – order/body fracture registry, in the sense in which any difference between the center and the edge will not describe a trajectory of spatial extremities but will pass in a fracturing way through the individuals themselves, while establishing that, when placed upon the separating line of space, the body remains a good conductor for both interiority and exteriority, a means of sense self-reproduction, of social success/failure quantum valuation.

If the body's (own) margins have been blurred/fractured, their re-welding implies the space imbued with the alloy of normal, metaphorical, symbolic, textual belts, a reassembly certifying unlimited spaces in which fracture represents the new stake of power in its race to fill all places by using strategies separated from those oppositions already perpetuated by philosophical-political Western tradition (Mihali 2006).

In a possible conclusion we can state that the visual politics of the feminine body articulate a framing of sociologically-imported origin (as an interpretation type of structure which affixes the particular to a larger frame), with nodal-programmatic points which can be found within contextually-organizing indexes of action and politics, selection guidance and revaluing modes of representation.

The findings of the present study can be added to the academic perspective ('Feminist Perspectives on the Body', The Stanford Encyclopedia of Philosophy) with an insistence on dual perspectives, *Bodily Image and Bodily Imaginaries* (Weiss 1999), fit to arraign a particular (con)text to a position sensitive both in form but also in being placed as a location: both an identity experience and as representation. The fragment is not a neutral construct; the fracture and breakup/re-composing themselves become ways of reviewing spatial, social and political concepts, reiterating the fact that the feminine symbolic identity can be placed as a conductor node (both subject and object) of language, poetics and politics.

Bibliography

Crudu, Dumitru & Marius Ianuş (2006) 'Manifestul Fracturist', *Agonia*, 9 September. Online. Available http://www.poezie.ro/index.php/essay/202813/Manifestul_Frac turist (accessed May 2016).

Curran, James & Michael Gurevitch (eds.) (1992) *Mass Media and Society*, London, New York, Melbourne Auckland: Edward Arnold.

De Lauretis, Teresa (1984) *Alice Doesn't: Feminism, Semiotics, Cinema*, Bloomington: Indiana University Press.

Dow, J. Bonnie (1996) *Prime-Time Feminism: Television, Media Culture, and the Women's Movement*, Philadelphia: University of Pennsylvania.

Ferguson, Russell, Martha Gever, Trinh T. Minh-ha, Cornel West (eds.) (1990) *Out There. Marginalization and Contemporary Culture*, New York: The New Museum of Contemporary Art.

Foucault, Michel (2009) *Le corps. Les hétérotopies*, Paris: Nouvelle Éditions Lignes.

Frunză, Mihaela (2002) 'Imaginea femeii în mass-media şi film. Perspective feministe', *Caietele Echinox*, 3: 206-222.

Gatens, Moira (1991) *Feminism and Philosophy: Perspectives on Difference and Equality*, Bloomington and Indianapolis: Indiana University Press.

Hutcheon, Linda (1989) *The Politics of Postmodernism*, London & New York: Routledge.

Jayamanne, Laleen (ed.) (1995) *Kiss Me Deadly: Feminism and Cinema for the Moment*, Sydney: Power Publications.

Joyrich, Lynne (1996) *Re-viewing Reception: Television, Gender, and Postmodern Culture*, Bloomington and Indianapolis: Indiana University Press.

Le Breton, David (2002) *Antropologia corpului şi modernitatea*, Timişoara: Amarcord Publishing House.

Lennon, Kathleen (2014) 'Feminist Perspectives on the Body', in Edward N. Zalta (ed.) *The Stanford Encyclopedia of Philosophy* (Fall 2014 Edition). Online. Available http://plato.stanford.edu/archives/fall2014/entries/feminist-body/ (accessed April 2016).

Lyotard, Jean-François (1979) *La Condition postmoderne: Rapport sur le savoir*, Paris: Editions de Minuit.

Manolache, Viorella (2015) 'Second-Order Identity: Banshee and the (re)launching the Serialfication Concept', in Gheorghe Manolache (ed.) *Intercultural Exchanges in the Age of Globalization*, LAP, Lambert Academic Publishing, pp. 135-151.

McLuhan, Eric & Frank Zingrone (eds.) (2006) *The Essential McLuhan*, Second edition, Toronto: House of Anansi Press.

Mihali, Ciprian (2006) 'Margini, concepte, corpuri, locuri', *Artă + Societate* 24, Cluj: Idea.

Miller, Daniel (ed.) (1995) *Acknowledging Consumption. A Review of New Studies*, London and New York: Routledge.

Norris, Pippa (ed.) (1997) *Women, Media and Politics*, New York, Oxford: Oxford University Press.

Opriţescu, Nicolae (1973) 'Geometria latentă a filmului', *Secolul 20*, 11-12(154-155): 275-285.

Pollock, Griselda (ed.) (2013) *Visual Politics of Psychoanalysis: Art and the Image in Post-Traumatic Cultures*, London: I.B. Tauris.

Radner, Hilary & Rebecca Stringer (eds.) (2012) *Feminism at the Movies: Understanding Gender in Contemporary Popular Cinema*, New York: Routledge.

Real, Michael (1996) *Exploring Media Culture. A Guide*, London, New Delhi, Thousand Oaks: SAGE Publications.

Soja, W. Edward (2010) *Seeking Spatial Justice*, Minneapolis, London: University of Minnesota Press.

Weiss, Gail (1999) *Body Images: Embodiment as Intercorporeality*, New York and London: Routledge.

Visual Support

Reid, Elwood, Björn Stein & Meredith Stiehm (creators) (2013, July 13) *The Bridge* (Television series), USA: FX Productions, Shine America.
Rosenfeldt, Hans (producer) (2011, September 21) *Bron/Broen* (Television series), Sweden/Denmark: Filmlance International AB, Nimbus Film Productions, Sveriges Television (SVT), Film i Väst, Zweites Deutsches Fernsehen (ZDF), Danmarks Radio (DR), Film i Skåne, ZDF Enterprises, Norsk Rikskringkasting (NRK), Media Programme of the European Community (support), Nordisk Film- & TV-Fond (support). Fernsehen (ZDF).
Vincent, Thomas, Hettie MacDonald, Udayan Prasad, Philip Martin, Dominik Moll (directors) (2013) *The Tunnel* (Television series), UK/France: Canal+, Kudos Film and Television, Shine, Sky Atlantic.

GENDER STEREOTYPES, COUPLE/FAMILY CONFIGURATIONS AND REPRODUCTION

CHAPTER IX

Gender Stereotypes in Emmanuel Lévinas' Concept of Subject

Marzena ADAMIAK

'The simultaneity of the equivocation of this fragility and this weight of non-signifyingness [non-significance], heavier than the weight of the formless real, we shall term femininity. '

(Lévinas 1979: p. 257)

1. Introduction

In this chapter I would like to consider the category of femininity given by Emmanuel Lévinas, mostly in his work *Totality and Infinity. An Essay on Exteriority* (1979), and the role that he envisaged for femininity in his theory of human subjectivity (Chanter 2001; Charlier 1982).

According to Lévinas, philosophy needs to overcome the existing ontological model based on the subjective-objective viewpoint in the case of human relationships. The other human being (see also Lévinas 1987b), when treated as the object, becomes only an element of the surroundings, and that condemns the ego to isolation. However, the Other, as the subject, threatens to treat the ego in an objective manner. This viewpoint entangles the subject in an unending game – or even battle – with the Other, for ontological pre-eminence. In the social sphere, this schema is best represented by the Hegelian model of the relationship between master and slave. For Lévinas, it seemed necessary to go beyond this schema so that it would be possible to have a philosophical, and especially ethical, understanding of human relationships. That is why, with regard to the Other, there is an uncompromising asymmetry in the philosophy of Lévinas, which means that the Other, during an encounter, is absolutely other, and in relationship to the subject it maintains a privileged position, due to which transcendence is made possible.

Lévinas states that the subject is only able to go beyond itself when it opens itself up to the Other, when it sacrifices itself to the Other. However, in order to sacrifice something it is first necessary to have it, which is why it is so important for the subject to have a solid constitution. Only a separated subject, as Lévinas says, is sufficiently prepared for this meeting, since it has already reached the limits of its monadic development. Hence, an independent subject meets the Other in the flash of an epiphany and at this moment moves beyond its ontological state. The Other is totally different, It exceeds the perspective of the ego, It is outside of being, and this is why It makes transcendence possible.

In the context of such an elaborately described meeting of the subject and the Other, it should to be noticed that Lévinas makes subjectivity as masculine and at the same time he describes femininity as one of the figures of otherness. However, it turns out to be a specific type of otherness. Lévinas frequently states that femininity is an incomplete otherness, and not the kind that has enough power to question the egoism of the subject and to open the dimension of transcendence. Since only a separated subject can enter into an ethical relationship, the woman does not have that possibility. Thus a sacrifice, in her case, is neither a subjective choice, nor an act of responsibility, but rather her destiny. The task of the woman is to look after the development of the masculine subject, ensuring his safety at home and risk in erotic relations. Then, however, femininity discreetly steps aside.

That notion of the woman as absolute otherness – as presented by Lévinas – appeared, to my mind so peculiar as to bring into question the ethics of Lévinas, as they are based upon the very concept of the Other.

2. He: Heroic and 'Virile' Subjectivity

In his work *Time and the Other*, in which ideas about the Other were just beginning to take shape, Lévinas was already writing not only about femininity as total otherness, he also called the subject 'virile' and stated that it exercises the 'virile power' (1987b: p. 54). Then, in *Totality and Infinity* – one of his most significant works – he writes 'I, heroic and virile' (1979: p. 270). This act of assigning sexual categories was very innovative in the field of philosophy. The subject which is usually treated as neuter with Lévinas takes on sexual characteristics (see also Lévinas 1987a; Lévinas 1985).

However, in *Totality and Infinity* subjectivity is assigned to a single gender, the masculine, but in a hidden manner, under the concept of the Same (*Le Même*). The thematisation takes explicitly on only feminine. The Same, being virile, is characterized by independence, high-rationality and the courage of being. Its constitution contains not only the aspect of transcendental consciousness, but also includes elements derived from the philosophy of life. Enjoyment (*jouissance*) is a source of the happiness for the egotistical subject, and happiness is the source of all independence. It is the joy of use, the expression of life – vitality par excellence. The Same, who is enjoying in himself, is full of life. He enjoys his subjective power, which

196

allows him to harness the elements (*les éléments*) and conquer the world. The Same affirms life.

On the contrary, when describing femininity, Lévinas uses terms such as: delightful weakness, gentleness, light-heartedness, timidity, but also animality and ultra-materiality. The significance of a feminine being consists in conditioning, allowing for the Same, the man, to be shaped. As summarized by Lévinas (1990: pp. 32-33):

'This is spirit in all its masculine essence. It lives outdoors, exposed to the fiery sun which blinds and to the winds of the open sea which beat it and blow it down, in a world that offers it no inner refuge, in which it is disorientated, solitary and wandering, and even as such is already alienated by the products it had helped to create, which rise up untamed and hostile. [To] overcome an alienation which ultimately results from the very virility of the universal and all-conquering logos that stalks the very shadows that could have sheltered it, should be the ontological function of the feminine, the vocation of the one, who does not conquer … For the inevitable uprooting of thought, which dominates the world, to return to the peace and ease of being at home, the strange flow of gentleness must enter into the geometry of infinite and cold space. Its name is woman.'

This apotheosis of feminine tenderness and the restraint of existence, which denotes a praise of the lack of ambition for gaining power, aims at affirming the woman in her destiny, in her identity which cannot de facto be equated with the Same. On the other hand, thought, which dominates the world is ontologically masculine.

Lévinas's concept of masculine subjectivity presented in his theoretical work has been built upon phenomenological descriptions that attempt to reach the essence of sheer source phenomena of the vernacular experience, in this case the experience of the sex. However, they were indubitably inspired by Judaism and *Old Testament* texts. Lévinas, as he himself declared, was a thinker who tried to combine two pillars of Western European culture in his work – the *Bible* and the Greeks. In his essay *Judaism and the Feminine* Lévinas (1990: pp. 31-32) describes the role played by biblical women but we can find there as well the biblical intuition of a male subject:

'The house is woman, the Talmud tells us ... The last chapter of Proverbs, in which woman, without regard for beauty and grace, appears as the genius of the hearth and, precisely as such, makes the public life of man possible, can, if necessary, be read as a moral paradigm. But in Judaism the moral always has the weight of an ontological basis.'

The last sentence shows that we are dealing here with an ontology of femininity. An ontology that is based upon the requirements of feminine conduct established through religious custom. Let us emphasize again that Lévinas does not bring to life a figure of man in his theory. He does not do that because, as I will attempt to demonstrate, it is to masculinity that all the other presented phenomena are ascribed, from the Same to the highest otherness of God.

Which are the main features of feminine ontology proclaimed by Judaism? Most importantly a woman-being is not detached from man. She is a mother of a son, a wife to her husband, a daughter of her father. She is destined to build the warmth and comfort of home which provides a safe haven for all male public activities related to social life or the implementation of divine plans. Lévinas points to the fact that the role of women in biblical events is considerable, yet their activity remains hidden. In accordance with Jewish accounts, a woman is not a being created to be autonomous – she is destined for sacrifice.

According to Lévinas, it is motherhood that is the quintessential destiny of a woman, which is the manifestation of tenderness and the ability to make sacrifices. But, in Judaism motherhood does not generate personal strength of a woman that can build the uniqueness of her subjectivity. Motherhood is woven into a wide context of the salvation of mankind, it is surrendered to human destiny.

However, even that noble function cannot ensure a woman a direct participation in experiencing transcendence. This can be attributed to female ambivalence and an identification of femininity with Eros. Thus, a woman does not only constitute an abode for the masculine spirit but she is also a source of all collapse, as Lévinas (1990: pp. 37-38) outlines:

'Woman is complete immodesty, down to the nakedness of her little finger. She is the one who, par excellence, displays herself, the essentially turbulent, the essentially impure. Satan says, an extremist text, was created with her.'

By containing this devilish element, femininity may not be allowed to participate in the true work of salvation. Therefore, a character of man is introduced in the Rabbinic thought, the prophet Elijah who is both father and mother to mankind. Lévinas (1990: p. 38) mentions that:

'True life, joy, pardon and peace no longer belong to woman. Now there rises up, foreign to all compassion for itself, spirit in its essence, virile, superhuman, solitary. It recognizes itself in Elijah, the prophet without pardon, the prophet of anger and punishment, a suckling of crows, inhabiting deserts, without kindness, without happiness, without peace. … the figure in whom is stored up for the Jews all the tenderness of the earth, the hand which caresses and rocks his children, is no longer feminine. Neither wife nor sister nor mother guides it. It is Elijah, who did not experience death, the most severe of the prophets, precursor of the Messiah.'

In this way even that feminine domain which is never shared with a man, the motherhood, has been incorporated into the masculine world. The figure of a woman that appears in the *Totality and Infinity* bears the features of a biblical woman. The subject called the Same, on the other hand, represents the authority and severity of Elijah. Elijah also becomes a representation of the higher kind of otherness that leads to transcendence. It demotes the female relationship with otherness to the most elementary level that is polluted with the risk of being reduced to pleasure.

3. She: Weak and Delightful Otherness

The woman is presented in *Totality and Infinity* as a necessary figure to describe the phenomenon of dwelling and erotic love. Meanwhile, a relationship with the Other can occur on many different levels, but the rule that pervades Lévinas's texts is clear: the more eroticism – the less transcendence. But, an erotic relation serves as a certain prototype for meeting the appropriate Otherness. In many references to Judaism, Lévinas reserves this particular Otherness and transcendence for figures such as God, the prophet, the master and the son. Here, man finds numerous figures with which he can identify himself, because these are always male figures, which are never defined by their sexuality, by Eros, whereas the woman is assigned to her erotic function, or more generally speaking, to her carnality. By saying this I mean that femininity is not the second sex, nor is it the other sex, but it is simply a sex.

According to Lévinas (1979: p. 256), in the erotic relation with a masculine subjectivity a woman is characterized by the essential tenderness:

'The epiphany of the Beloved is but one with her regime of tenderness. The way of the tender consists in an extreme fragility, a vulnerability. It manifests itself at the limit of being and non-being, as a soft warmth where being dissipates into radiance, like the "pale blush" of the nymphs in the Afternoon of a Faun, which leaps in the air drowsy with thick slumbers, dis-individualizing and relieving itself of its own weight of being, already evanescence and swoon, flight into self in the very midst of its manifestation. And in this flight the other is other, foreign to the world too coarse and too offensive for him.'

This fragment brings into light several myths or beliefs which are worthwhile. The question whether tenderness in fact decides about the essence of femininity seems to be banal on account of being blatantly problematic, and yet this is what Lévinas thinks. Moreover, he is very quick to reduce tenderness to weakness. But in fact the juxtaposition of these notions does not have to be so obvious. Tenderness may be treated as a basis which stems from maturity and power of the subject, not its frailty and fragility. Here, the phenomenon tendre contains in itself the meaning of timidity (*timidité*). The Beloved is not the Loving. We are dealing here with the difference between the past and the present participle with all the consequences that arise from this distinction. The phenomenology of the Beloved is based upon this fundamental solution that the active subject is virile.

It is from this perspective that French feminist philosopher Luce Irigaray (1993; 1991; 1986; 1985) reads, interprets and provides criticism of Lévinas's ideas. She claims that femininity is not here understood in relation to itself but from a male perspective. This male perspective is built on male intentions and erotic desires as ethical determinants (Irigaray 1991: p. 178).

In *The Fecundity of the Caress* – a text dedicated to Lévinas's work, Irigaray demonstrates in the chapter The Phenomenology of Eros how Lévinas's description of caress makes use of the female category to support the becoming of a male subject.

According to Irigaray, frailty, passivity and being secondary in relation to the male subject is expressed precisely in the category of the Beloved (*l'Aimée*). A Beloved is someone who is loved, and therefore does not display subjective activity. She waives it and yields to the temptation of being seduced, forgoes its own desire in order to enhance the desire of the lover. She abandons the place of all responsibility, its own ethical space. For this reason Irigaray suggests that a woman that participates in an act of love should be named a woman lover (*l'amante*). A woman lover is conscious of her sexuality and striving to actively pursue it, while the frailty of the Beloved stems from being imprisoned in an erotic status quo. Lévinas's economy of love is based upon the thwarting of a woman as a subject that desires together with a man as a subject. The male subject that Lévinas writes about not only loses a female otherness but it does not perceive itself as other in relation to her. In any case, this is what Lévinas's asymmetry is about, making the other absolute, but, as Irigaray claims, Lévinas overlooked the other sex, while at the same time he wrote about it.

One more example that demonstrates an uncertain position of the woman as the Other: 'The caress aims at neither a person nor a thing' – and he expresses this by saying that woman is the 'not-yet-being' (Lévinas 1979: p. 259). Therefore, it does not concern the subject or the object, but a strange, undefined sphere in between: between a being and not-yet-a-being, a no man's land, as Lévinas writes. One could ask: how should the word man be exactly interpreted here? Is the land not taken by a human being or a man? It is a significant difference, and if we were to follow Lévinas's considerations, one may get the impression that these notions have been involuntarily linked. Yet the expression: not-yet-a-being does not suggest, as one might conjecture, approaching feminine otherness to the proper otherness, that is the transcendence, but aspiring to be a subject. Thus, it is an otherness which does not want to be an otherness! There is a fundamental difference between the otherness of a Woman and the otherness of Infinity. Thus, the specificity of femininity consists primarily in the fact that it constitutes an intermediary figure which, through a paradoxical juxtaposition of notions, is nearly omnipresent. Not-yet-a-being but aspiring to be one remains frozen in between subjectivity and proper otherness.

Moreover, the situation of not-yet-a-being is not, according to Lévinas, a dynamic situation in a sense of the possibility to transcend it. This incompleteness is an ontological status of the feminine being. It is therefore not about the sexual difference, nor is it even about hierarchy. It is femininity that in itself is the difference. Lévinas does not take into account situations where a man is the Other for a woman. By making otherness the essence of the woman, and her being, as a hard ontological principle without nothing that this is only a male perspective, he suggests that the woman is the other also for herself, ergo, she cannot be the subject for herself.

Simone de Beauvoir, a precursor of feminist philosophy, knew Lévinas's idea about the ontology of the woman as the absolute otherness. She made a reference to it in the preface to *The Second Sex* (2011: p. 6):

'This idea has been expressed in its most explicit form by E. Lévinas in his essay *Le temps et l'autre* (*Time and the Other*). He expresses it like this [A]lterity is accomplished in the feminine. The term is on the same level as, but in meaning opposed to, consciousness. I suppose Mr. Lévinas is not forgetting that woman also is consciousness for herself. But it is striking that he deliberately adopts a man's point of view, disregarding the reciprocity of the subject and the object. When he writes that woman is mystery, he assumes that she is mystery for man. So this apparently objective description is in fact an affirmation of masculine privilege.'

From Simone de Beauvoir's perspective the figure of woman proposed by Lévinas is an effect of the paradoxical essentialism. Essentialism, because it is the nature or the essence of femininity that is being discussed, and paradoxical, because otherness – as absolute – was not supposed to be captured. Eternal femininity and The Secrecy which are considered by Lévinas to be a basic feature of feminine otherness (Lévinas 1979: p. 258) for a feminist are only myths that sustain the cultural patriarchy – the rule of men over women. Therefore, Beauvoir posed a question which Lévinas failed to do: why does femininity appear this way? Is it because, as the philosopher would like it to be, it is ontology or phenomenology of feminine nature, or the phenomenological image of a certain social reality? Feminine otherness is problematic, as Beauvoir emphasises. Above all, one should ask what a woman is and to what degree the description of this phenomenon which is culturally fixed must coincide with the potential of a female human being.

4. 'The Empirical Countertruth'

The main argument usually used against this feminist interpretation of Levinas's figure of femininity is to point out its non-empirical nature. The Woman, as a phenomenon, is supposedly an abstract concept, separate from empirically existing women. This, however, gives rise to the following questions: what is the relationship between the concept of femininity and a real, concrete woman in the work of Lévinas?

Firstly, it could be stated that the separation from empirism is one of the founding ambiguities of phenomenology. Husserl's disapproval for empirism, especially towards one of its concrete manifestations –

psychologism, results from a well-recognized need, of a Cartesian pedigree, to lead philosophy (as fundament for all sciences) to ground the entirety of knowledge. However, how could one avoid an entanglement into empiricism? Where should we set the boundary between a body experienced as one's own, and its material fundament?

A good example for this consideration is found in *Totality and Infinity* in the description of femininity through the phenomenon of dwelling. Lévinas states that the forming, virile subject needs a safe place to rest and integrate – a home. This is where we meet femininity, which makes it a real home, allows the dwelling. In Lévinas's thinking (1979: p. 270) the home means an internal, subjective dimension of a bodily character; the home ensures safety and care for the Same, who has to face the Elements and work:

'[The home] is possessed because it already and henceforth is hospitable for its proprietor. This refers us to its essential interiority, and to the inhabitant that inhabits it before every inhabitant, the welcoming one par excellence, welcome in itself – the feminine being. Need one add that there is no question here of defying ridicule by maintaining the empirical truth or counter truth that every home in fact presupposes a woman? The feminine has been encountered in this analysis as one of the cardinal points of the horizon on which the inner life takes place – and the empirical absence of the human being of feminine sex in a dwelling nowise affects the dimension of femininity which remains open there, as the very welcome of the dwelling.'

Thus, according to Lévinas, the phenomenology of the woman presented here would constitute a description of a certain part of an individual human being, independent from its empirical sex. This particular part, categorized as femininity, is meant to be characterized by weakness, ultra-materiality, ambiguity, and other characteristics outlined by Lévinas, with irreducible otherness as a truly essence.

Lévinas is convinced that the reader finds it obvious that the presented descriptions of femininity are not directly related to existing women. But he fails to develop this notion further, which is a pity. It appears here that some form of a biological-cultural experience constitutes the basis for analysis, accepted by the philosopher without a critical reflection. This is why, despite certain reservations, an approach between a phenomenological description of femininity, and a woman tout court, cannot be avoided. It is enough to analyze the Lévinasian ontology of femininity, to note its social, historical and biological conditioning. The phenomenon collectively described as femininity would have to undergo a change of name, in order to relate to both sexes. Lévinas's ideas would seem less antiquated if masculinity and femininity, combined to form an androgynous human being, were not described in such a stereotypical and uncritical manner.

Despite being aware of Husserl's initial failure in relation to the category of the Other, Lévinas ultimately treated the phenomenon of femininity in an instrumental manner himself. Otherwise – if he perceived the woman as ontologically different, a separate subjectivity, finally as the Other – in accordance with his own assumption of absolute asymmetry, he would recognize the impossibility of thematisation. The experience of the Other is not available for experience of the subject, the otherness is absolute.

On the other hand, one could pose the following question – if, for Lévinas, the recognition of femininity, as essentially connected with home, is not tied to the social status of empirical women. In this case, on the basis of what experience does our author create such a description? If it is mainly on his personal experience, then the respective perspective – as Jacques Derrida (2005: p. 412) rightly pointed out – is inevitably masculine:

'*Totality and Infinity* pushes the respect for dissymmetry so far that it seems to us impossible, essentially impossible, that it could have been written by a woman. Its philosophical subject is man (vir). … Is not this principled impossibility for a book to have been written by a woman unique in the history of metaphysical writing? Lévinas acknowledges elsewhere that femininity is an ontological category. Should this remark be placed in relation to the essential virility of metaphysical language? But perhaps metaphysical desire is essentially virile, even in what is called woman.'

In response to the questions concerning the correlation between the phenomenon of femininity and empirical women (see also Critchley 1992), Lévinas tries to separate both perspectives. However, he is not very convincing in doing that as he ignores social issues and the fact that it is difficult to define the difference in meaning between sex and gender. In any case, it is not certain whether the phenomenological femininity presented by the philosopher even corresponds to the notion of gender as his concept of femininity relates to the act of procreation, which is obviously a biological fact that requires not only a phenomenological but specific sex differentiation. For this reason, regardless of Levinas's reservations, one cannot avoid the approximation of a phenomenological description of femininity to a woman tout court. It is enough to examine how Lévinas's ontology of femininity unfolds only to notice how it is conditioned socially, historically and biologically.

However, if, following Lévinas, we identify femininity with a docile, frail and passive not-yet-a-being, we will have to call strong, independent, and active women masculine. If male activity is to be the sole type of activity, a woman faces a limited choice that leads to nowhere. She may be feminine and yield by being such, forgo any actions, or she may be masculine and forego herself differently. Is there a way out of this deadlock? Above all both categories of masculinity and femininity need to be revised, and judged critically. Not only does Lévinas fail to do it, but he sanctions cultural stereotypes by granting them an ontological dimension. Lévinas does not reflect upon where all these features that characterize femininity come from and when he comes across them in his considerations he refers to them as the essence of femininity. He creates an ontology of femininity which is supposed to have nothing in common with real women. It is typical for his writings that there are no analogical reservations that masculine subjectivity has nothing to do with men. One could, ultimately, ask whether Lévinas's phenomenology of femininity reaches the essence of femininity? Or does it rather become compromised by elevating empirical observations to the rank of universal phenomena? Is phenomenon just a magic word, supposed to transform empiricism into phenomenology?

5. Closing Remarks

Summarizing, what exactly does Lévinas describe when he talks about gender? We read that femininity is weakness, docility, fearfulness, an incomprehensible secret, animality, carnality, Eros, Thanatos, and in the end – absolute otherness. Masculinity, on the other hand, is vitality, activity, work, enjoyment, freedom, egoism, atheism, and, above all, the subject. I agree with Simone de Beauvoir and Luce Irigaray that Lévinas's phenomenology conjures well known myths that culture has created in order to cope with feminine otherness.

Femininity becomes here a name to denote a set of phenomena which are experienced by humanity and which, for different reasons, must be excluded from the model of a being, which is referred to as masculine. The femininity here described appears to justify masculinity. The fragility and the vulnerability of the loved being require a loving being that is strong, protective and brave and has experience with the brutal and painful reality. Femininity requires masculinity, so it requires a subject. The Same, on the other hand needs the Other such formed not to transcend himself, but to find affirmation for himself. Thus, Him and Her are entangled in a game which bars them from transcendence. It is a game of masculinity and femininity.

But, the hardest thing to understand is Lévinas's intention for this very same masculine subject to open up to feminine otherness. It seems the philosopher longs metaphysically to increase femininity's importance and by placing femininity in the realm of otherness, he treats it as a manifestation of that longed-for Infinity. That does not work. The feminine Infinite is not the masculine Infinite. This is a very important difference. The woman comes to mind in a different way than God: 'The feminine will never take on the aspect of the Divine … The dimension of intimacy, not the dimension of loftiness, is opened up by the woman' (Lévinas 1990: p. 37). But it is the dimension of loftiness that is of importance.

Still-not-being, but nonetheless vying for being, the woman inhabits a grey area between subjectivity and otherness. And, I believe that the woman, defined in such a way, undermines all of Lévinas's ethical ideas. If ethics is based on meeting the Other, on openness and transcendence, and the woman may not participate either as the subject or as the correct form of the Other, then she must be excluded from what Lévinas calls the basic philosophy of humankind. So, maybe the mankind is the better word indeed. Thus, femininity plays its role in the maturation of the Same only to withdraw discreetly and not interfere with the ethical meeting of a man and God. The Same does not recognize the primordial creator in the feminine otherness regardless of all the metaphysics of birth. It is Elijah, and not a woman figure, that is the father and mother of Israel.

Bibliography

Beauvoir, Simone de (2011) *The Second Sex*, translated from French by Constance Borde & Sheila Malovany-Chevallier, New York: Vintage Books.

Chalier, Catherine (1982) *Figures du Féminin. Lecture d'Emmanuel Lévinas*, Paris: Les Éditions du Cerf.

Chanter, Tina (ed.) (2001) *Feminist Interpretations of Emmanuel Lévinas*, University Park: The Pennsylvania State University Press.

Critchley, Simon (1992) *The Ethics of Deconstruction. Derrida and Lévinas*, Oxford: Blackwell.

Derrida, Jacques (2005) 'Violence and Metaphysics: An Essay on the Thought of Emmanuel Lévinas', translated from French by Alan Bass, in Jacques Derrida, *Writing and Difference*, London & New York: Routlege, pp. 97-192.

Irigaray, Luce (1993) *An Ethics of Sexual Difference*, translated from French by Carolyn Burke & C. Gillian Gill, Ithaca: Cornell University Press.

Irigaray, Luce (1991) 'Questions to Emmanuel Lévinas', in Margaret Whitford (ed.) *The Irigaray Reader*, Oxford: Blackwell, pp. 133-139.

Irigaray, Luce (1986) 'The Fecundity of the Caress: A Reading of Lévinas, Totality and Infinity section IV, B, The Phenomenology of Eros', in Richard A. Cohen (ed.) *Face to Face with Lévinas*, Albany: State University of New York Press, pp. 231-256.

Irigaray, Luce (1985) *This Sex Which Is Not One*, translated from French by Catherine Porter & Carolyn Burke, Ithaca: Cornell University Press.

Lévinas, Emmanuel (1990) *Difficult Freedom, Essays on Judaism*, translated from French by Sean Hand, Baltimore: The Johns Hopkins University Press.

Lévinas, Emmanuel (1987a) 'Philosophy and the Idea of Infinity', translated from French by Alphonso Lingis, in Emmanuel Lévinas, *Collected Philosophical Papers*, Boston: Martinus Nijhoff Publishers, pp. 47-60.

Lévinas, Emmanuel (1987b) *Time and the Other & Additional Essays*, translated from French by Richard A. Cohen, Pittsburgh: Duquesne University Press.

Lévinas, Emmanuel (1985) *Ethics and Infinity: Conversations with Philippe Nemo*, translated from French by Richard A. Cohen, Pittsburgh, PA: Duquesne University Press.

Lévinas, Emmanuel (1979) *Totality and Infinity. An Essay on Exteriority*, translated from French by Alphonso Lingis, The Hague & Boston & London: Martinus Nijhoff Publishers & Duquesne University Press.

CHAPTER X

The Division of Labor within the Family and Altruism: A Feminist Critique of Becker's Models

Oana CRUSMAC

This chapter tries to analyze to what extent Becker's models from *A Treatise on the Family* comprise the male bias and whether they can be considered as a backlash against the feminist movements and the social changes they accompanied. The chapter will be focused only on two models that can be found in the *Treatise*, namely the household production model (Chapter 2) and the altruistic model (Chapter 8). My approach is based on Ferber's analysis of the male majority encountered in the economic field (Ferber 1995: p. 357), as well as on the criticism leveled by feminist economists such as Bergmann (2005; 1989), Folbre (2004; 1999), and Nelson (2005; 1996).

Feminist economists dismiss the neoclassical economic approach that draws a 'strict boundary between a world of altruism (the family) and a world of self-interest (the market)' (Badget & Folbre, 1999: p. 314). Feminists consider that the classical and neoclassical models are 'impregnated with male bias' because the number of women specializing in this field is considerably much lower than in any other domain (sociology, psychology, anthropology, mathematics, etc.) and also because the rational and autonomous individual (or the institution perceived as an individual) is described as similar to the self-image of economists (Nelson 1996: p. 22). Moreover, feminist economics puts carework in its center, which has been a challenge to mainstream economics for whom the 'autonomous, self-interested individual neither requires care nor has any inclination to provide it' (Nelson 2005: p. 4). This chapter will follow this aspect, and I will try to analyze from a feminist perspective two of the models proposed by Becker: the division of labor within the family and the altruistic model.

The structure of the chapter is as follows: in the first section I will present the narrow context in which *A Treatise on the Family* emerged. I will cover both the economic theories that rival with Becker's models as well as the general feminist criticism on his models and methods. In the second section I will present the social changes that occurred during that period: the second wave of feminism, the growing rate of female employment and the introduction of affirmative action for women. The third section will be focused on Becker's household production model and his specialization recommendations while the fourth section details the altruistic model. Both sections will also comprise the criticisms advocated by feminist economists.

The last section, the fifth, will conclude that Becker's models do not only embed traditional, male-biased conceptions on gender roles, but also recommend even more patriarchal measures in order to repeal the achieved developments that serve gender equality. As such, I will conclude that Becker's models represented a backlash against feminism, which he refused to take seriously. The methodological pursuit will consist of the text analysis of Becker's aforementioned models.

1. The Outline of the New Home Economics

According to Bittman, the manner in which members of the family dedicate their time to paid and household work can be presented from two perspectives: the sociological one and the economic one. Sociological work is mainly dominated by two theories: exchange theory which emphasizes the causal relationship between bargaining and the resources each member brings into the family (this theory is also employed by economists) and a theory that highlights the pervasive effects of socially constructed gender norms (Bittman et al., 2003: p. 187). Economists, on the other hand, have three different models of distribution within the family: Becker's altruistic model, cooperative bargaining models, and non-cooperative bargaining models (Pollak 1994: p. 148). Becker treated the family as a single decision making agent where its members pool their resources. For feminist economists, the family that behaves as a sole individual is, most likely, dictatorial (Ferber & Birnbaum, 1977: p. 22). This approach, where the family was considered a single decision making agent, emerged between 1950s and 1980s and was then followed by a different approach, namely the cooperative bargaining model, with which it competed. Bargaining models reject Becker's altruistic model and consider that the bargaining between men and women is symmetrical, where 'one's input into production and consumption decisions depends on one's alternatives to joint production' (Braunstein 2008: p. 964).

Gary Becker is considered one of the most important economists of the twentieth century. His work stands out as one of the first attempts to merge economic thinking to areas previously linked to sociology, such as family and gender relations. While his work has received numerous acclaims within the circle of economists (including the Nobel Prize in 1992) for depicting family in terms of utility maximization and rational behavior, he has been severely criticized by feminists. This feminist critique of Becker's work led to the shaping and strengthening of feminist economics.

As Ferber (2003: p. 9) notes, Becker is considered the founding father of the 'new home economics', although he was not the first to bring the household and the family in the field of economics. The first attempt at this new line of economic theorizing was made in 1934 by Margaret Reid who explicitly argued that 'the household is the locus of production as well as consumption' (Ferber 2003: p. 9). Reid viewed household work as productive labor and she contributed to an easing of the classification of household work: because we cannot directly see the monetized (or market) value of household work, it has sometimes been thought that it is not work *per se*, but leisure time. For Reid, the 'distinction is reflected in the so-called *third-person criterion*', where work is 'an activity that you would be willing to pay someone else to do this for you, or, more generally, for which market substitutes are available' (Reid in Folbre 2004: p. 22), whereas leisure cannot be externalized.

Becker's main contribution consists of extending the neoclassical economic theory to the realm of the family and the household. However, he left 'the methods and key assumptions largely unchanged', which has 'formalized and reinforced out-dated assumptions about male and female roles' (Nelson 1996: p. 133). Bergmann (1989: p. 43) notes that most economists consider 'the inferior market position as something women have freely chosen, as a normal and generally benign adaptation to "their responsibilities" for housework and child rearing'. These economists do not question how women came to choose housework instead of market labor or whether they have actually made a choice. Folbre is also against the neoclassical tendency to take preferences as a variable that does not change over time or across populations. She considers that this is a method employed, as it is easier to construct economic models on wishful thinking rather than identifying the actual preferences of a specific audience (Folbre 2004: p. 20). This has been intensely criticized by other feminist economists such as Bergmann (1989: p. 51) who rejects the economists' 'habit of dismissing case studies as "anecdotal evidence", having no value at all'. Bergmann opposed the economists' practice of supplanting empirical research with imagined scenarios (Olson 2007: p. 482). She argued that economists should employ methods similar to those of anthropologists and behavioral scientists (Olson 2007: p. 483).

The unpaid household work has gained an important role in the economic theories of the family along with Becker's theory, who notes that besides the constraints generated by income, families also face a time constraint (Becker 1993: p. 21). Becker builds his theory on the family starting from two fundamental assumptions of the economic approach: the maximizing behavior and the market equilibrium. Moreover, as emphasized by Pollak, biased or not, 'Becker's conclusions depend on the auxiliary theoretical assumptions which are not specific to the neoclassical economics and which lack empirical evidence' (Pollak 2002: p. 7). Pollak (2002: p. 10) notes that a third fundamental assumption of the economic field is missing, namely stable preferences, and that Becker partially approaches it in the form of 'altruistic preferences' as an auxiliary assumption. This new form of preferences is divided into two categories: interdependent or non-selfish preferences (the primary auxiliary assumption) and altruistic preferences (the secondary auxiliary assumption). Feminists have been critical with regard to the manner in which preferences are approached by the neoclassical theorists. Folbre (2004: p. 18), for example, stresses that neoclassical economists ignore the origins of individual preferences because this makes it 'difficult to question whether a voluntary exchange is *fair* or *unfair*'.

As it will be outlined below, feminists reject Becker's assumptions because: maximization is carried out by rational and autonomous individuals (the economic men) and women do not fall into this category; economic language preserves the dichotomy of masculine versus feminine traits (Nelson 1996: pp. 21-22); market equilibrium means governmental intervention; altruistic preferences are actually the dictator husband's preferences; interdependent preferences are, in fact, dependent preferences in the case of women (feminists consider that the neoclassical model on the family economics does not have any interdependent members, but only members dependent on the main earner of the family). In regards to the latter aspect, feminists also stress the fact that 'family work may sometimes be coerced rather than altruistic' (Badgett & Folbre, 1999: p. 314).

2. Social Changes: Feminism, Affirmative Action and Female Employment

We shall not omit, however, that Becker developed this new theoretical approach in 1981, in *A Treatise on the Family*, meaning after the peak of the second wave of feminism. The temporal overlap between the two should be observed in light of another opposition: while in the 60s and 70s feminists demanded changes in the private sphere based on the slogan 'the personal is political', Becker rejected the state's intervention in the structure and functions of the family or any kind of departure from the traditional view on the family. Moreover, the vocabulary chosen by Becker has often been criticized by feminists because it presents a favorable patriarchal system where active or benevolent agents were presented in a masculine form, whereas selfish and passive agents were presented in a feminine form (Nelson 1996: pp. 61- 62). Considering the above, can Becker be considered a backlasher of the feminist claims?

Firstly, we should note that feminism was one of the most important engines of change that developed during the twentieth century in the United States. The first wave of feminism, which lasted until the 1920s, was defined as 'equality feminism' and demanded and managed to obtain equal legal status for women and men in the public sphere: voting rights for women and access to employment (Miroiu 2004: pp. 56-58). The effects of these achievements have improved women's lives. Folbre (2004: pp. 30-31) notes that:

'Women's right to vote played an important part in the evolution of the welfare state. Many public policies, such as the provision of public education and subsidized childcare can be interpreted as efforts to socialize the costs of caring for dependents.'

The second feminist wave emerged after Simone de Beauvoir published *The Second Sex* in France, in 1949, and after Betty Friedan published *The Feminine Mystique* in 1963 in the United States. Both publications marked the transition 'from equality feminism to difference feminism' and emphasized the idea that 'biology is not destiny' (Miroiu 2004: p. 65). As such, the second wave of feminists switched the focus of their movement from the public to the private sphere. The core belief was that equality between men and women was not achieved as inequality persisted in the private realm, mostly in the family. Friedan's work unmasked the myth of the happy American housewife, revealing that in reality these women live an unfulfilling and bored life because they are limited only to child raising and house work (Miroiu 2004: p. 65). The second wave of feminism succeeded to facilitate access to contraceptive measures, introduced legal sanctions against rape and domestic violence and offered women access to jobs previously opened only to men (McRobbie 2009: p. 32). The latter achievement was managed through a change in public policy: the appearance of affirmative action for women.

Affirmative action emerged in the United States following the Executive Order 10925 issued by John F. Kennedy in 1961 which required that government contractors 'take affirmative action to ensure that applicants are employed, and employees are treated during employment, without regard to their race, creed, colour, or national origin' (OCED). In 1971, in an order issued by Nixon, affirmative action was expanded to include women in the target group. It also mentioned 'the objectives and their accomplishment in a given time' (Sowell 2004: p. 5).

Affirmative action has been defined as:

'… a public or private program designed to equalize the opportunities for employment or admission for historically disadvantaged groups by considering even those characteristics that have been used to deny them an equal treatment.'

(Duncan in Shaw 1988: p. 763)

The purpose of affirmative action is to remedy discrimination and to reconfigure the distribution of income and opportunities as it should have been if society were fair from a competitive point of view (America 1986: p. 77).

Affirmative action programs include, in addition to the corrective element mentioned above (remediation, reconfiguration, equalization), a compensatory component, both of which are disputed by critics. Opponents of affirmative action claim that although women and racial minorities deserve compensation, it is unjust that this compensation is made on the expense of white, innocent men. As such, affirmative action is seen as rather an 'institutionalized discrimination against white men than a program against discrimination' (Leonard 1989: p. 61).

We should also take into account the argument put to the forefront by Richard America: he considers that the rejection of affirmative action on the grounds of 'innocent payers' masks in fact another reason, namely that some individuals do not want to give up on present benefits that they obtained in an unjust manner: collectively received as a result of past discrimination that was made in their name (America 1986: pp. 73-74). Thus, taking into account the foregoing, we can say that this argument against affirmative action may be associated with a defence of the status quo.

As a result of both second wave feminism and affirmative action programs in the United States, female employment substantially increased while homemaking has continuously declined. The most notable acceleration of this trend occurred between 1960 and 1990. Thus, while in 1960 only 40.3% of women were employed (from the total of all women involved in productive labor, both paid and unpaid), in 1990, the percentage raised to 67.3%. Subsequently, the percentage of homemakers of all women involved in productive labor decreased from 56% in 1960 to 32.7% in 1990 (Folbre & Nelson, 2000: p. 126). If we compare the last figure with the percentage of 70.2% of women engaged in house work that was encountered in 1870, we can easily see why some theorists, such as Becker, have been prone to confute the deviation from the traditional family.

3. Becker's Household Production Model: Gender Norms and Segregated Specialization

In the model developed by Becker in *A Treatise on Family*, couples maximize the utility of their family through resource pooling: both incomes and household work (Pollak 2005: p. 3). Becker claims that if the joint income will be distributed between the partners at no cost, then it will provide an optimal Pareto equilibrium that maximizes the average earnings of the whole population (Willis 1987: p. 70). In the second chapter of *A Treatise on Family*, Becker develops the model on the division of labor within the family and the household, and he considers that resource pooling involves not only the efficient distribution of resources (hence the altruistic model which will be discussed below), but also their maximization.

The first part of the model on the division of labor considers that all family members are equal and that they have no intrinsic differences (Becker 1993: p. 32). Activating in any field (employment or household) involves a certain specialization and an accumulation of human capital. Becker claims that it is more efficient that the individual who specializes in paid work to invest in the human capital specific to this field (H1) and that the individual who specializes in household labor to invest in the human capital relating to the private sphere (H2) (Becker 1993: p. 34). The division of labor is not limited, therefore, only to differences in the allocation of time (where time allocation is deeply intertwined with the process of 'doing gender' – Folbre 2004: p. 21), but also implies a similar division in the allocation of specific investments in human capital. For Becker (1993: pp. 35-36), within less numerous families (his thesis focuses on the nuclear family) it is more efficient that members specialize exclusively in one area, this specialization being profitable for all members of the family.

A second part of the model regarding the division of labor within the family brings to the forefront the fact that investments in a certain human capital are determined by intrinsic differences between the sexes (Becker 1993: p. 37). Becker considers that women have a biological motivation to devote more time for raising children, which determines them to have a *comparative advantage* over men in the household. This is why he believes that an efficient family will allocate women's time mainly in the household and men's time mainly in the labor market (Becker 1993: pp. 37-38). For Bergmann (in Olson 2007: p. 488), men's market advantage 'is derived from employment discrimination and men's traditional refusal to assume their fair share of domestic responsibilities'. She notes that the comparative advantage does not explain why men choose to devote themselves to leisure activities within the household and do not get involved in raising children or in other household activities (Bergmann 2005: pp. 182-183). Moreover, it is hard to see how this sex-based specialization in household work is efficient for single-parent families, especially for single mothers or for LGBT families.

According to Becker, this separated specialization involves a dependency on others. He constructs his model based on the fact that, traditionally, women have relied on men to provide shelter, food and protection while men have relied on women for raising children and taking care of the household (Becker 1993: p. 43). Becker's proposal for the sex-based division of labor and its subsequent specialization is rejected by feminists who rightfully ask: 'if women "naturally" choose to specialize in care, why do societies develop coercive rules and practices that make it difficult for them to do otherwise?' (Badgett & Folbre, 1999: p. 317).

Moreover, according to Becker, this specialization would reduce or prevent abusive behaviors because family members are altruists (Becker 1993: p. 49, p. 53). But this assumption is inconsistent since the next chapters of the *Treatise* assign altruism to the (male) breadwinner and selfishness to children and wife.

In the supplement to Chapter 2 (1993 enlarged edition), Becker explores the efficiency causes of the exclusive specialization of the family members. He considers the increase in women's participation in the labor market and the growth of their incomes as the triggering factors of the reduction of family's utility determined by the decrease of fertility rates and by the increase of divorce rates (Becker 1993: pp. 55-56, p. 350): from 1950 to 1977 divorces had doubled, the birth rate had fell by one third, women's income had increased by 40%. Becker's position was contradicted by both feminists as well as economists' and sociologists' research. Thus, Echevarria & Moe (2000: p. 81) show that the reduced fertility that occurs at the same time with the increase of women's participation in the labor market is actually caused by different and opposite patterns of the two phenomena: historically, fertility trends follow a reverse U-pattern whereas the economic participation of women had a U-pattern, their participation decreased at the beginning of industrialization and (after equal education opportunities) then increased. Moreover, the two authors point out that women's education, not their income, is the main determinant of fertility: educated women have more knowledge about methods of contraception and have different life plans than traditional women. Becker (1993: p. 356) rejects this argument by assigning a minimal role to the contraceptive pill in regards to the decline of fertility. A second opinion which rejects the relationship between the decline of fertility and the increased economic participation of women is made by Easterlin (1987) who emphasizes the relationship between fertility and the desired standard of living of individuals, the latter being determined by the standards of living they experienced when they were growing. Thus, the generational cohorts born after the Second World War had more children because the U.S. economy was expanding, while their children had to deal with an increased competition on the labor market and with a less stable economy (Easterlin in Willis 1987: p. 71).

Although Becker argues above all that women's participation in the labor market leads to the increase of divorces, in Chapter 10 he claims that the main cause of this increase is the insufficient accumulation of information in the preliminary stage of the family, namely on the marriage market. The above argument starts from the premise that women are more motivated to leave the family when they obtain a greater utility outside the family. Although Becker maintains that the husband's increased income leads to fewer chances of divorce, research shows the opposite: the husband's income has no impact on the decision of divorce made by their wives, and women's increased income has no effect on the decision to divorce, but rather their experience on the labor market – that is, their chances of finding a source of income on the labor market, outside marriage (Huber & Spitze, 1980: pp. 82-83).

The lack of empirical support of the claim that fertility and divorce rates are determined by women's income is noticed by Ben-Porath, who notes that the two changes that occurred in the 1950s (the decline of fertility and the increase of divorces) have not been accompanied by a noticeable acceleration of women's wages (Ben-Porath 1982: p. 57). Ben-Porath suggests that these changes were rather strengthened by welfare programs, as well as by the emergence of the contraceptive pill and of the feminist movement. Becker recalls that women's movements[1] have encouraged the reduction of the time dedicated to child raising and the increase of women's participation in the labor market, as well as the self-expression through divorce, but he minimizes the importance of these movements, considering them rather the *effects*, not the causes, of the changing roles of women[2].

Becker rejects the idea that the differences between men's and women's income are determined by discrimination and he considers that men have a higher income because they have invested more in the human capital specific to the labor market, while women have focused on the household (Becker 1993: p. 63). The last part of this argument has been rejected by feminists who propose the opposite, namely equal opportunities in education and employment, whereas Becker supported women's exclusive specialization in the private sphere as he considered this would be more efficient for the whole family. As a response to Becker's position, Bergmann notes that rationality and discrimination are not mutually exclusive, on the contrary (Bergmann 1989: p. 45).

Moreover, Becker seems to support this discrimination because, in his opinion, women are less efficient as they have less energy, precisely because they are engaged in the household work (Becker 1993: p. 75) which they perform anyway[3]. He does not take into account that the economic participation of women might lead to a greater involvement of men within the household, but he assumes that they are more rested because they have more free time (Bergmann 2005: p. 54).

This explanation of the income differences (based on biology, tiredness and the lack of human capital invested in the labor market) has been rejected and criticized by feminist economists because this is a circular argument

---

1   Becker does not use anywhere in the *Treatise* the terms of feminism/feminist and he rather prefers to talk about 'women's movements'.

2   This cannot be sustained from a temporal point of view, the second wave of feminism appeared in the early 50s in France and in the early 60s in the U.S., meaning at the same time with the increasing of women's participation on the labor market.

3   Which, for Becker, is their task due to intrinsic biological reasons – so biology is an important determinant of income disparities.

(Nelson 2005: p. 2): women specialize in the household because they earn less on the labor market and they earn less because they are specialized in the household, thus the lower income of women become a self-fulfilling prophecy (Ferber & Birnbaum, 1977: p. 20, p. 25). On this aspect, Ben-Porath highlights that Becker does not make a clear argument on income differences: do biological reasons (reinforced by the rational economic account) explain gender roles and women's lower income, or do the latter determine gender roles and thus biology plays a minor role? (Ben-Porath 1982: p. 53). Bergmann considers that income differences are the result of the discrimination encountered at the employer's level (Bergmann 2005: p. 183), while other feminists argue that lower incomes are the result of the oppression encountered in the family.

Moreover, we find in the *Treatise* a position that supports perpetuating the difference between men's and women's income because this makes the choice of specializing exclusively in the household to be the most rational decision that women could make (Becker 1993: pp. 74-75). While this position is questionable from a feminist standpoint, the rationality invoked by Becker masks something else, namely the prevalence of a patriarchal culture accompanied by a lack of opportunities. On this issue, Sen (in Badgett & Folbre, 1999: p. 316) highlights that 'women often lack a concept of themselves as individuals with interests separate from those of their family members'. This, according to Tronto (in Badgett & Folbre, 1999: pp. 316-317), is determined by the fact that 'robbing individuals of opportunities to effectively pursue their own self-interest may encourage them to live through others, using caring as a substitute for more selfish gratification'.

Becker manages his argument so as to suggest that the separated specialization of spouses is also beneficial for children, but in fact the exclusion of women from the labor market is favorable to the altruistic husband – the exclusive specialization in different fields minimizes competition (a situation convenient to the husband) and conflicts (and hence there is no need for negotiation) between spouses (Ferber 2003: p. 11). Becker's argument according to which children have more benefits when the woman depends on the husband's income and dedicates herself exclusively to the household is contradicted by empirical evidence, such as The World Development Report from 1993 which shows that an increase in the wife's income has a greater positive impact on the children's wellbeing than in the case in which the husband's income increases (Echevarria & Moe, 2000: p. 86). Income controlled by women is more likely to be spent on children's needs (Badgett & Folbre, 1999: p. 317) – which can be seen as a proof of the fact that mothers are more altruistic towards children than fathers.

As mentioned above, Becker correlates the efficiency of the division of labor within the family with the exclusive specialization either in the labor market, or in the household. Ferber considers that this exclusive specialization in different fields represents 'a blatant justification and consolidation of the status quo' (Ferber 1995: p. 359). Moreover, Becker's specialization model represents a rejection of the modern family because it counts on the advantages of the traditional family and assumes that an egalitarian relation within the family (which would focus on sharing responsibilities and not on specializations) is not efficient because it cannot maximize the welfare of its members. Ferber stresses that Becker's models appeared contemporaneously with alternative forms of distribution and organization within the family (Ferber 2003: p. 10). This supports the idea illustrated above concerning the opposition between Becker and feminism.

According to Ferber, the specialization model cannot be taken into account when we talk about the future of the family as it describes (and prescribes) old, traditional models of family organization (Ferber 2003: p. 10). If in the past it could have been considered rational that women would exclusively dedicate to the household, this fact was determined by the high number of children and a lower life expectancy than was encountered in the U.S. after the 1950s: women spent most of their life giving birth and raising children (Ferber 2003: p. 14). The nuclear, modern family does not meet either of the two justificatory conditions, which reduces the utility of having women exclusively dedicated to the household. As Ferber and Birnbaum (1977: p. 21) note, it is tradition, not rationality, that 'dictates that household work and childcare are the woman's responsibilities, regardless of her other activities'.

Feminists draw attention to the disadvantages faced by women who specialize exclusively in household work, such as the devaluation of household work over time while the market earnings increase (Ferber & Birnbaum, 1977). Ferber (2003) mentions that research shows that individuals prefer to do anything else than to dedicate to household work (except child-raising). She considers that the interdependence between family members that results from the exclusive specialization is, in fact, a dependency of those that specialize in household towards those that bring income from the labor market (Ferber 2003: pp. 15-16). The sexual division of labor advantages only the male partner because power belongs to him as he can replace the other: 'it is much easier for the husband to replace the family care services of the wife than for the wife to replace the financial contributions of the husband' (Bergmann 2005: p. 185).

Julie Nelson (1996) highlights that dependency also means vulnerability: to be dependent includes depending on someone's power or goodwill. The interdependence that Becker considers as being the result of the family members' specialization in different fields can be also interpreted as responsibility: women are responsible for raising children and taking care of the household, men are responsible for financially supporting the family. Nelson links responsibility to power and, continuing the argument on the dependency of the housewives, discusses the situations where the family member who holds the power has the option of rejecting some responsibilities. Feminist economists prefer to focus rather on responsibility instead on altruism. The two concepts contrast. Responsibility 'means that actions may be taken quite apart from personal preference', even if 'the action will bring about no personal gain', whereas altruism 'moves one to act if another's misfortune makes one feel personally worse off' (Nelson 1996: p. 70). For Nelson, a theory on the family that does not take into account 'the concepts of responsibility and dependence' brings nothing new (Nelson 1996: p. 69).

The weight of individuals' power in making decisions is generated by their autonomy and the activities in which they are involved (Marion Young 1990: p. 27). Arneson believes that the main determinant of the distribution within the family is the bargaining power of each party (Arneson 1996: p. 11). The main effects of women's access to their own incomes are the increasing bargaining power of women and their share of the family resources (Weiss 1997: p. 99). These effects are neglected by Becker. This aspect was also noted by Pollak – women who specialize in household and devote less (or no) time to paid work and leisure activities have less bargaining power (Pollak 2005: p. 5).

In addition, according to Pollak, the advantages in negotiating within the family are not determined by the income of its members, but by the wage norm: individuals who work more hours in order to have the same income as those who work fewer hours have a reduced bargaining power. Linked to this, housewives do not meet the slightest condition to be agents in the negotiation process whereas the husbands have considerably more power in this process, which can be used as a threat (Ferber 2003: p. 17). Becker does not include negotiation in his models because decisions are made based on the altruistic model, which starts from the assumption that the family (although it has at least two members) behaves as a single agent who makes the decisions (Lundberg & Pollak, 1994: p. 132). In fact, this single agent is the male breadwinner.

Although Becker outlines his models (the altruist and the division of labor) based on the idea that they are Pareto efficient, he argues that negotiation within the family is not allowed. Thus, we encounter a contradiction because 'cooperative bargaining models assume efficiency, while non-cooperative ones allow inefficiency' (Pollak 2002: p. 22). Becker's models do not take into account negotiation, but they substitute it (based on the assumption that it is more efficient) with the altruistic model of sharing the resources within the family. His argument is that given the fact that the benevolent dictator takes all the decisions then the bargaining power is no longer a problem (Ferber 2003: p. 16). Ferber and other feminists raise the issue of the assumption of the altruist's benevolent intentions, especially given that he represents the image of the rational economic man.

4. The Altruistic Model or the Tyranny of the Sole Breadwinner

In chapter 8 of the *Treatise*, Becker develops the altruistic model. According to this model, a member of the family ('h'– husband) will be altruistic towards another member ('w' – wife) because his utility positively depends on the other's wellbeing. Thus, altruism maximizes both the altruist's utility, as well as the utility of the other members of the family (Becker 1993: pp. 278-279). Moreover, Becker considers that resource pooling will determine even the selfish members to behave in an altruistic manner – because it maximizes their consumption and utility. From this perspective Becker outlines the Rotten Kid Theorem – each beneficiary, no matter how selfish, will maximize the family's income generated by its benevolent family member and thus will internalize the effects of his/her actions on the other beneficiaries (Becker 1993: p. 288). It should be noted that 'the Rotten Kid Theorem applies to the interaction between all types of altruists and beneficiaries' (Becker 1993: p. 284), thus also to the wife.

As mentioned in a previous section, Becker embraces the neoclassical approach of applying altruism within the family and selfishness to the market. As such, he notes that 'altruism is less common in market transactions and more common in families' because altruism is less 'efficient' in the marketplace and more 'efficient in families' (Becker 1993: p. 299). But the model relies less on efficiency (as cooperative bargaining models perform better) and more on the fact that 'the rules [of the model] empower the altruist' (Pollak 2002: p. 23). The most important pre-existing rule is the sexual division of labor, discussed above. Becker (1993: p. 295) mentions that 'altruism encourages the division of labor and an efficient allocation of resources'. Thus, the two proposed models, the household production model and the altruistic one, reinforce themselves and are interdependent. As a result, Becker's models do not tackle the fact that the 'household head benefits from patriarchy', but, even more, they embed patriarchy and they provide a messianic portrayal of the husband: 'the head's power is attributed to altruism, rather to control over household resources' (Echevarria & Moe, 2000: p. 78).

The motivation of the altruistic behavior is precisely to increase the family's income (Becker 1993: p. 282). However, this does not say anything about who takes how much of the total. Although Becker states that 'families have harmony in production and conflicts in distribution' (Becker 1993: p.

292), the altruistic model is not the solution for conflict resolution or bargaining (Pollak 1994: p. 149), but rather a method of controlling and suppressing such conflicts and the need for negotiation.

Bergmann (1995) offers a sharp dismissal of Becker's altruistic model. She highlights that the altruistic husband will use 90%of the joint income for his own preferences, leaving only 10% to the wife. We should also note Moller Okin's (2003: p. 305) observation on the fact that men tend to keep a part of their income for themselves – mostly spending them on consumption vices and sexual services. For the same reason Nussbaum rejects resource pooling and the prioritization of family income as a whole because women are considered a simple element within the household, their interests are overridden by men and the latter are the sole decision-making agents (Nussbaum 2000: p. 227).

The altruistic model is a male biased one because the explanation of its efficiency relies also on a circular argument: putting on the first place the total income of the family favors husbands as they make decisions on the internal allocation of incomes between the members of the family. Bergmann stresses that 'Beckerian altruism does not necessarily mean a propensity to favor equal sharing, the same life style or standard of living for both partners', but rather that the 'wife is locked in the power of the petty tyrant: Make a move I don't like, and you'll suffer for it' (Bergmann 1995: p. 11). Feminists have preferred to emphasize the unequal position of the recipients of altruists that have little or no choice (Folbre 2004: p. 24). For feminists, the decision-making and the distribution of resources according to the preferences of a sole member does not denote truthful altruism, but rather a form of domination. Iris Marion Young (1990: p. 31) considers domination as the phenomenon that excludes some people from participating in the determination of their actions. This can also be applied to the altruistic model when women have to accept the husband's decisions since he has altruistic motivations.

It should be specified, however, that when using the term 'altruist', Becker does not refer to the usual sense of the word (equal consideration to all family members), but rather a vague attitude which is different from pure selfishness (Pollak 2002: p. 15) and in which 'agency issues [power] are arguably more central' (Nelson 1996: p. 74). As Folbre (2004: p. 24) notes, economists use the concept of altruism as specific to situations where 'someone derives satisfaction from another's well-being'. Thus, for Becker, altruism shares nothing with eradicating 'self-centered desire' nor with 'a life devoted to the good of others' (Lutz & Lux in Nelson, 1996: p. 135), but it is deeply 'linked to enhancing one's personal welfare' (Braunstein 2008: p. 970).

The altruistic model can be interpreted, according to Pollak (1994: p. 148), as a 'two-stage bargaining game in which the altruist moves first and confronts other family members with take-it-or-leave-it choices'. Besides this power asymmetry, we encounter another troubling aspect: the altruist and the beneficiary seem to also have different moral features. Thus, the former is depicted as a selfless, benevolent benefactor that shares his income with the family members for the utility of the whole family, whereas the latter are selfish and greedy 'rotten kids': 'the interests of altruistic benefactors and selfish beneficiaries are not identical. Selfish beneficiaries like larger contributions than their benefactors are willing to make' (Becker 1993: p. 284). This depiction favors and idealizes the altruist, because Becker 'implicitly assumes that all males are altruists' (Bergmann 1995: p. 12).

Pollak (2002) also highlights the inefficiency of the altruistic model: considering the family as a final game with two participants, where X is the altruist one and Y is the selfish one, the model is limited to two options at opposite parts – either Y accepts the division of income as established by X and both receive the shares proposed by the decision maker (X), or Y does not accept it, which leads to inefficiency because none of the two spouses receive anything. Pollak does not overlook the situation in which the proposal advantages the person who formulates it (X) so that the amount can be (almost) fully attributed to X, while the respondent (Y) either does not receive anything, or receives a share on the minimum level of utility. Hence the question: 'is Becker's altruist a dictator' (Pollak 2002: pp. 24-26)? The coexistence of the argument that all beneficiaries voluntarily maximize the family's income with that of the altruist who does not hold a dictatorial power on the decisions of the family members is based on Becker's assumption that, because the beneficiaries 'utility increases or decreases at the same time with the altruist's, the altruist is by no means a dictator, his decisions being favorable to the family as a whole' (Becker in Pollak 2002: p. 26). But this is an incomplete picture, as the decisions of the other members and the negotiation between them are missing, situations which might be more efficient than the decisions of the altruist.

5. Conclusion: Becker's Intrahousehold Allocation Models as a Backlash against Feminism

The constant opposition between the demands of the second wave of feminism and Becker's models suggests that Becker's theory emerged as a reaction against the feminist movement that supported the reconfiguration of the family. As Nelson (1996: p. 61) highlights, Becker's model of the family 'has been raising feminists' blood pressure since the mid-1970s when it first appeared'. Taking Becker's two models separately, we can say that the division of labor within the family and the exclusive specialization in different fields (public/private) justify discrimination on the labor market in the attempt to repel the increase of women's employment, whereas the altruistic model relies on the reinforcement of the patriarchal family.

The fact that Becker refused to address in detail[4] the feminist movements denotes the fact that he rejected them and attempted to undermine their goals. Moreover, the opposition between Becker and feminist claims is also present in his perspective on the biological-determined roles. According to the arguments presented above, Becker believes that biology determines the intrinsic differences that lead to comparative advantages (women in the household, men in the market). Contrary to feminist arguments, Becker fails to acknowledge the influence gender roles have on what he calls comparative advantage. Thus, he notes that 'biological comparative advantage cannot be readily disentangled from specialized investments' because 'specialized investments begin while boys and girls are very young they are made prior to full knowledge of the biological orientation of children' (Becker 1993: p. 40). This reason, early gendered specialization, is also recognized by feminists, but they address it in a totally opposite manner: feminists reject the sexist socialization of children, while Becker (1993) takes it as a natural, normal, unquestionable fact. He even goes further and proposes a rather radical sexist and homophobic measure:

'The optimal strategy would be to invest mainly household capital in all girls and mainly market capital in all boys until any deviation from this norm is established. In this manner investments in children with 'normal' orientations reinforce their biology, and they become specialized to the usual sexual division of labor. Investments in 'deviant' children, on the other hand, conflict with their biology, and the net outcome for them is not certain. For some, their biology might dominate and they would seek a deviant division of labor, with men in the household and women in the market.' (Ibid.: p. 40)

In contrast, second wave feminists have built their agenda based on the idea that 'biology is not destiny' (e.g., Friedan, Beauvoir). The fact that the Treatise fails to include into discussion feminism – or, in the few cases where it is taken into account, it is portrayed as having a negative role, namely that it leads to the dissolution of the family, to the increase of the households where women are the heads of the families and their correlation with an increase in poverty – especially taking into account that it was first published in 1981, during the promotion of the feminist idea of collective child-raising in the 70s and 80s (McRobbie 2009: p. 32) represents an additional argument supporting the claim that Becker was one of the backlashers of feminism[5].

The second core element of the dichotomy between feminism and Becker's ideas is represented by the state's intervention in the family and on

---

4 He talks about 'women's movements' only in three sections of the *Treatise*, namely at pp. 81-82, p. 356, p. 359.

5 The reduction of maternal responsibilities was one of the main arguments used by the opponents of feminism (see McRobbie 2009; Faludi 1991).

222

the labor market. Becker rejects the state's intervention in the family on the topic of the wife's dependency on the husband's income, but he accepts the state's intervention to mediate the arrangements between parents and children (Becker 1993: p. 379) only when the Rotten Kid Theorem does not apply (Becker 1993: p. 365). Thus, he joins the theorists that focus on the wellbeing of children and ignores the situation of caregivers.

Bergmann and Ferber note the polarization between feminism and Becker: the former considers that the traditional family is an impediment to achieving gender equality, while the latter considers that the conservation of the traditional family is the solution to all inequalities (Ferber 2003: p. 17). Bergmann contradicts Becker's findings according to which 'the presented institutions are benign and that governmental intervention would be, in the best case, useless and most likely harmful' (Bergmann in Pollak 2002: p. 7). Becker is aware of the powerful differences between spouses, but he supports their perpetuation precisely because women's autonomy (either through economic participation, or through financial support from the state) increases the chances of divorce. The second wave feminism demanded state intervention both in child-raising through public nurseries and kindergartens, social assistance, etc. (Bergmann 2005: p. 211), as well as on the labor market through programs aimed at helping women to become economic autonomous agents (through women's access to education and to professions considered as masculine). We should take into account the link between the *Treatise* (1981) and the emergence of governmental affirmative programs designed to increase the number of women on the labor market. Becker's model of the division of labor within the family is built as a rejection of any intervention that would aim at supporting the participation of women in the labor market. As Lundberg and Pollak stress, Becker believed that the state and the development of the market are key factors that alter the functions and the structure of the family (Lundberg & Pollak, 2007: p. 11).

The lack of empirical evidence to support the efficiency of the two models presented above has been used as a main argument against them. Both feminist economists (Ferber 2003: p. 12), as well as Becker's supporters (Hannan 1982: p. 71) observed the incongruity of the models with the current trends in the organization of the family. Thus, Becker's models are rather descriptive, not prescriptive, and specific to the period up to the nineteenth-century. As Lundberg and Pollak (2007: p. 14) highlight, exclusive specialization, the efficiency of resource pooling and their redistribution within the family based on the altruist's decision are not supported by empirical research, which made economists abandon these models.

Bibliography

America, Richard (1986) 'Affirmative Action and Redistributive Ethics', *Journal of Business Ethics*, 5(1): 73-77.

Arneson, Richard (1996) *Feminism and Family Justice*. Online. Available http://philosophyfaculty.ucsd.edu/faculty/rarneson/feminfa4.pdf (accessed November 27, 2016).

Badgett, Lee & Nancy Folbre (1999) 'Assigning care: Gender norms and economic outcomes', *International Labour Review*, 138(3): 311-326.

Becker, Gary S. (1993) *A Treatise on the Family*, Cambridge, Massachusetts, London: Enlarged Edition, Harvard University Press.

Ben-Porath, Yoram (1982) 'Economics and the Family – Match or Mismatch? A Review of Becker's A Treatise on the Family', *Journal of Economic Literature*, 20(1): 52-64.

Bergmann, Barbara (2005) *The Economic Emergence of Women*, New York: Palgrave MacMillan.

Bergmann, Barbara (1995) 'Becker's Theory of the Family: Preposterous Conclusions', *Feminist Economics*, 1(1): 9-12.

Bergmann, Barbara (1989) 'Does the Market for Women's Labor Need Fixing?', *The Journal of Economics Perspectives*, 3(1): 43-60.

Bittman, Michael, Paula England, Nancy Folbre, Liana Sayer & George Matheson (2003) 'When Does Gender Trump Money? Bargaining and Time in Household Work', *American Journal of Sociology*, 109(1): 186-214.

Braunstein, Elissa (2008) 'The Feminist Political Economy of the Rent-Seeking Society: An Investigation of Gender Inequality and Economic Growth', *Journal of Economic Issues*, 42(4): 959-979.

Echevarria, Cristina & Karine Moe (2000) 'On the Need for Gender in Dynamic Models', *Feminist Economics*, 6(2): 77-96.

Faludi, Susan (1991) *Backlash. The Undeclared War against American Women*, New York: Three River Press.

Ferber, Marianne (2003) 'A Feminist Critique of the Neoclassical Theory of the Family' in Karine Moe (ed.) *Women, Family and Work: Writings on the Economics of Gender*, Oxford: Blackwell Publishing Ltd., pp. 9-18.

Ferber, Marianne (1995) 'The Study of Economics: A Feminist Critique', *The American Economic Review*, 85(2): 357-361.

Ferber, Marianne & Bonnie Birnbaum (1977) 'The "New Home Economics": Retrospects and Prospects', *Journal of Consumer Research*, 4(1): 19-28.

Folbre, Nancy (2004) 'A theory of the misallocation of time', in Nancy Folbre & Michael Bittman (eds.) *Family Time. The social organization of care*, London: Routledge, pp. 17-34.

Folbre, Nancy & Julie Nelson (2000) 'For Love or Money–or Both?', *The Journal of Economic Perspectives*, 14(4): 123-140.

Hannan, Michael (1982) 'Families, Markets, and Social Structures: An Essay on Becker's A Treatise on the Family', *Journal of Economic Literature*, 20(1): 65-72.

Huber, Joan & Glenna Spitze (1980) 'Considering Divorce: An Expansion of Becker's Theory of Marital Instability', *American Journal of Sociology*, 86(1): 75-89.

Leonard, Jonathan (1989) 'Women and Affirmative Action', *Journal of Economic Perspectives*, 3(1): 61-75.

Lundberg, Shelly & Robert Pollak (2007) 'The American Family and Family Economics', *Journal of Economic Perspectives*, 21(2): 3–26.

Lundberg, Shelly & Robert Pollak (1994) 'Noncooperative Bargaining Models of Marriage', *American Economic Review*, 84(2): 132-137.

Marion Young, Iris (1990) *Justice and the Politics of Difference*, Princeton: Princeton University Press.

McRobbie, Angela (2009) *The Aftermath of Feminism*, London: Sage Publications.

Miroiu, Mihaela (2004) *Drumul catre autonomie. Teorii politice feministe*, Iaşi: Polirom.

Moller Okin, Susan (2003) 'Poverty, Well-being, and Gender: What Counts, Who's Heard?', *Philosophy and Public Affairs*, 31(3): 280-316.

Nelson, A. Julie (2005) 'Feminist Economics', in Steven N. Durlauf & Lawrence E. Blume (eds.) *The New Palgrave Dictionary of Economics*, London: Palgrave Macmillan, pp. 1-6.

Nelson, Julie A. (1996) *Feminism, Objectivity and Economics*, London: Routledge.

Nussbaum, Martha (2000) 'Women's Capabilities and Social Justice', *Journal of Human Development*, 1(2): 219-247.

Olson, Paulette (2007) 'On the Contributions of Barbara Bergmann to Economics', *Review of Political Economy*, 19(4): 475-496.

Pollak, Robert (2005) 'Bargaining Power in Marriage: Earnings, Wage Rates and Household Production', *Working Paper,* No. 11239, Cambridge, MA: National Bureau of Economic Research.

Pollak, Robert (2002) 'Gary Becker's Contribution to Family and Household Economics', *Working Paper,* No. 9232, Cambridge: National Bureau of Economic Research, pp. 1-42.

Pollak, Robert (1994) 'For Better or Worse: The Roles of Power in Models of Distribution within Marriage', *The American Economic Review*, 84(2): 148-152.

Shaw, Bill (1988) 'Affirmative Action: An Ethical Evaluation', *Journal of Business Ethics*, 7(10): 763-770.

Sowell, Thomas (2004) *Affirmative Action around the World. An Empirical Study*, New Haven: Yale University Press.

Weiss, Yoram (1997) 'The Formation and Dissolution of Families: Why Marry? Who Marries Whom? And What Happens upon Divorce', in Mark Rosenzweig & Oded Stark (eds.) *Handbook of Population and Family Economics*, Amsterdam: Elsevier, pp. 80-100.

Willis, Robert (1987) 'What Have We Learned from the Economics of the Family?', *The American Economic Review*, 77(2): 68-81.

CHAPTER XI

Consequences of Intimacy and Violence in the Couple Relationships of Young Romanians on Their Future Life Plans

Cristina FALUDI

1. Theoretical Background

Youth aged 19 to 22 are transitioning from adolescence into young adulthood, a time when individuals begin to make their own decisions about the path they will take in adulthood (Nagaoka et al., 2015). In the search for independence, young adults approach vocational, educational, and personal issues as major decisions.

One of the primary social developments in young adulthood is the entry into romantic and longer-term sexual relationships (Gutgesell & Payne, 2004). Recent studies pointed that, despite the spread of selfish individualism, there exists a continued high valuation of commitment within intimate relationships (Carter 2012). But at the same time, recent studies highlighted that intimate partner violence (IPV) is the most prevalent form of violence. Antecedents of violence in a couple are multifaceted and the negative outcomes are huge at a socio-psychological level (Vives-Cases et al., 2010; Roberts, Auinger & Klein, 2005; Plazaola-Castaño & Ruiz Pérez, 2004). Due to its serious long- and short-term mental, emotional and physical outcomes (Martsolf, Draucker & Brandau, 2013), violence within couples has become a serious public health concern.

Romantic relationships at a younger age are so profound that they have an undoubted impact on a youth's identity development (Eccles et al., 1993) and on educational achievements (Dégi & Faludi, 2015). Experiencing a positive and supportive couple relationship is associated with a happy and healthy life. On the contrary, living in a negative and abusive partnership brings harm to the individual's quality of life (Eccles et al., 1993). Abusive relationships lead to negative outcomes on self-concept, self-esteem and coping abilities in adulthood (Umberson et al., 2006).

According to the Center for Disease Control and Prevention (CDC 2012), intimate partner violence (IPV) is a type of violence occurring between two people in a close relationship, whose nature can be physical, emotional, or sexual. Different words to describe IPV are suggested by the CDC, such as:

teen dating violence; relationship violence; dating abuse; relationship abuse; domestic abuse; domestic violence.

When high levels of intimacy coexist with manifestations of violence it is difficult for a young person to develop and maintain a secure attachment to others and to learn how to select a healthy partner (Collins 2003).

Unfortunately, relationship abuse is a common problem (Foshee et al., 2009). However, IPV is usually underreported, because many young people are afraid or ashamed to confess it to friends and family (CDC 2012). The 2013 US Youth Risk Behavior Survey discovered that almost 10% of high school students were victims of physical violence and 10% reported sexual victimization from an intimate partner during the 12 months before the survey (Vagi et al., 2015).

Another form of teen dating violence is cyber dating abuse, i.e., the misuse of technology to harass, control, and abuse the dating partner. An empirical study showed that females register higher levels of non-sexual cyber dating abuse perpetration than males; young males report perpetrating sexual cyber dating abuse to a greater extent (Zweig et al., 2013). Moreover, victims of sexual cyber dating abuse had a much higher risk of also experiencing sexual coercion than non-victims (55% versus 8%), while perpetrators of sexual cyber dating abuse were much more likely to have also exerted sexual coercion than were non-perpetrators (34% versus 2%) (Ibid.).

2. Methodological Design

2.1 Aim and objectives

Taking into account these issues, the core purpose of the study is to investigate the interlink between levels of intimacy, the occurrence of violence within the current couple relationship, and plans related to personal development in the near future among Romanian youth, from a comparative gender perspective. The main assumption is that high intimacy encourages plans for personal achievement, while manifestation of violence in a couple discourages partners from assuming adult roles in their subsequent personal lives, for both genders. The structure of the study includes: an introduction about the theoretical background related to intimacy and violence in young couples; statements about the purpose, aims, and hypothesis of the study; a presentation of the methodology, containing explanations about the method of data collection, characteristics of participants, the measures used to fulfill the purpose of the study, and the methods of data analysis; a description of the main findings; a section of discussions and implication for practice; and a final section comprising concluding remarks.

In order to achieve the purpose and test the general hypothesis of the study, a few objectives are pursued in the analysis of the empirical data: 1. an investigation of the levels of intimacy and violence in the current couple relationship, decomposed on four constitutive items and differentiated by gender; 2. a comparison between genders of the levels of intimacy and violence by the duration of the romantic relationship; 3. an exploration of the association between the intimacy and violence scores and future life plans by gender; and finally, 4. a more complex inquiry on the effects of three different sets of explanatory factors on the intentions to assume four adult roles in the near future, among Romanian youth.

2.2 Methods

2.2.1 Design and participants

This study is based on the second wave of the online self-administered Outcomes of Adolescence Questionnaire. The investigation aimed at investigating: socio-demographic and family factors, educational and professional experiences, characteristics of adulthood (according to Arnett 2001), psychological factors (self-esteem, anxiety, depression, optimism), experiences as a student, intimate relationships, risk behaviors (drugs, alcohol, smoking), leisure time and volunteering, and future plans – organized in the eight sections of the questionnaire. The research has been designed to track the evolution of the risk factors (such as domestic violence, parental divorce, precarious socio-economic conditions, adverse life events, etc.) and protective factors over time, and the effect of life events from a life-course perspective (Schoon 2006). The starting assumption was that the factors influence and reinforce each other and may increase or decrease the likelihood of negative consequences in life (Roth et al., 2016).

A randomized stratified sampling type was used based on official data from the National Institute of Statistics. Four sampling layers were applied: a) the development region; b) the county – 14 counties were randomly chosen from the 7 development regions: Bihor, Sălaj, Sibiu, Covasna, Iaşi, Bacău, Galaţi, Constanţa, Argeş, Teleorman, Dolj, Vâlcea, Timiş, Caraş-Severin, including Bucharest and Ilfov; c) the place of residence; d) the profile of the class and school.

The questionnaire was completed by a total sample of 1509 Romanian young people, between October 2014 and February 2015. Among the participants, 59% were women, 61.9% originated from urban areas, 93.8% were Romanian, and 78.9 declared themselves as Orthodox. Using the European Commission definition of severe material deprivation, 16.6% of the respondents belonged to this category.

Of all the participants, only the respondents with a current romantic partner at the moment of the inquiry were selected; consequently, analyses were applied to 836 young people, of whom 66% were female. The age range was 19 to 23 years and the mean age was 20. About 90% of the participants with a romantic partner were sexually active, and 60% had been in partnership for more than a year.

2.2.2 Measures

The section on Intimate Relationships in the Outcomes of Adolescence Questionnaire used items synthesized and adapted from the following questionnaires and scales: Survey on the Sexual Behavior of University Students, 2001-2003 (Billari, Caltabiano & Dalla Zuanna, 2007); Reproductive Health Survey, 2004 (UNFPA et al., 2005); Maryland Adolescent Development in Context Study (MADICS 2000) – the section on Romantic Relationships; The Triangular Love Scale (Overbeek et al., 2007); Relationship Assessment Scale (Hendrick 1988); and Measuring Intimate Partner Violence and Victimization and Perpetration (Thompson et al., 2006).

In order to accomplish the objectives of the study, two sets of indicators measuring intimacy and violence in young couples were selected from the section on Intimate Relationships. These two indicators comprised four items and were measured on a 7-point Likert scale (Overbeek et al., 2007). Answers measuring intimacy items varied from 1 ('totally disagree') to 7 ('totally agree'). Taking into account the variability of scores for this scale, answers were grouped into two categories: total agreement, and all other answers which were included in the category of disagreement. Answers to items related to violence ranged from 1 ('not at all') to 7 ('very often'). Similarly, they were codified into two categories: the answer 'never' was transformed into the category 'no', while the answers 'sometimes' and 'often' were included in the category 'yes'. The respondents' answers on the 7-point Likert scale of both sets of items on intimacy and violence were used for calculating the mean scores.

Four future life events – moving in with the partner, separation from the partner, getting married to the partner, and giving birth to a child with the partner – were investigated in terms of intentions within the next three years. For the purpose of the study, answers to these questions were dichotomized in 'yes' and 'no'.

2.2.3 Data analysis

Descriptive and inferential analysis – Chi-square test and Independent-samples t-test – were used to investigate the levels of intimacy and violence in couples according to their constitutive items, by the duration of the couple relationship and by gender. Also, Independent-samples t-tests were applied in order to explore the consequences of intimacy and violence in young couples on future life plans.

In the multivariate analysis, binary logistic regression was implemented to investigate the role of three sets of covariates on the likelihood of undertaking four life events in the near future. Binary logistic regression is a model that uses one dichotomic dependent variable to examine the existence and intensity of the relation between the interest variable and one or more explanatory or independent variables. In this study, the binary dependent variable is represented by the intention to accomplish one of the four life-course events, where value 1 means a positive intention and 0 indicates the declination of undertaking a life event of adulthood. The logistic regression model quantifies the effects of the explanatory variables in terms of the *odds ratio*. When working with independent category variables, as is the case in this study, for each of them, results will be reported in terms of a reference category, codified by 1. Thus, an odds ratio higher than 1 will indicate a positive association, and a lower than 1 odds ratio will express a negative association (Greene 2002; Harrell 2001).

The data have been analyzed with the SPSS 19 programme.

3. Results of the Consequences of Intimacy and Violence in the Couple Relationships of Romanian Women and Men on Their Future Life Plans

3.1 Results of the descriptive and inferential analyses

Graph 1 illustrates the perceived levels of intimacy reported by young women and men who completed the Outcome of Adolescence Questionnaire. Both women and men perceived high levels of intimacy in their romantic relationship, and half or more than 50% of the participants declared a total agreement with all four items of the intimacy scale. However, women reported significantly higher levels of intimacy for three aspects of the scale (see Table 1). Thus, women felt very close to their partner most of the time to a much greater extent than men (70.2% versus 57.6%, Pearson chi-square=13.070, p<0.001). A higher volume of women than men declared they can tell everything to their partner (63.1% versus 54.5%, Pearson chi-square=5.696, p<0.017). Also, there was a larger share of women who confessed that some things they could tell only to their partner compared to men (60.6% versus 52.5%, Pearson chi-square=4.885, p<0.027).

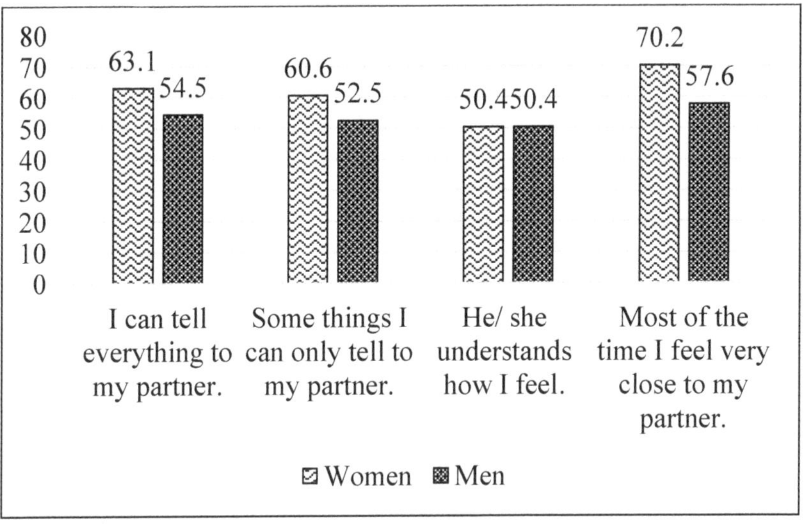

Source: author.

Remarkably, even though women felt closer to their partner, relying more on him when needing to speak to someone than men did with their partners, they were to a less extent convinced their partner really understood how they felt. Moreover, for this aspect of couple commitment, there was no gender difference; only half of both women and men felt their intimate partner understood them.

Graph 2 reflects the forms and the intensity of violence in couples by gender. In opposition to the results related to commitment, men reported significantly higher levels of violence in couples than women. However, when jealousy was investigated, surprisingly, it was reported as the most spread behavior associated to the spectrum of violence within a romantic relationship by over three quarters of both women and men. Apart from jealousy, young Romanian romantic couples were most exposed to the practice of addressing insulting or humiliating words to each other, with more men than women reporting such a behavior (46.6% versus 38.3%, Pearson chi-square=5.217, p=0.022) (Table 1). By far the most striking findings referred to the most severe forms of violence. Thus, men were three times more exposed to forced sexual intercourse than women (7.6% versus 2.4%, Pearson chi-square=12.810, p<0.001) and over two times more affected by being injured or harmed by the intimate partner as compared to women (9.9% versus 4.4%, Pearson chi-square=9.320, p=0.002) (Table 1).

Graph 2: Manifestation of violent behaviors in couples by gender

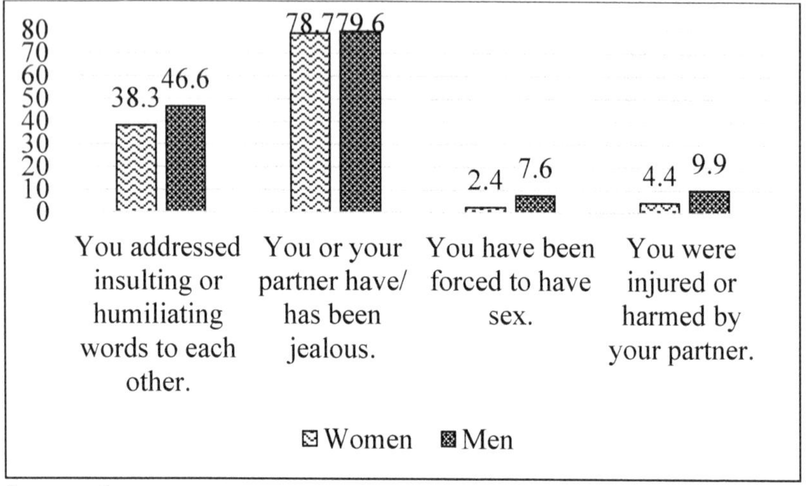

Source: author.

Table 1: Association between gender and items of intimacy and violence in couples

Scale	Category	W % (N)	M	Chi-square	Sig. (p)
Items on intimacy					
I can tell everything to my partner.	Totally agree	63.1 (349)	54.5 (151)	5.696	**0.017**
	Disagree	36.9 (204)	45.5 (126)		
Some things I can only tell to my partner.	Totally agree	60.6 (335)	52.5 (145)	4.885	**0.027**
	Disagree	39.4 (218)	47.5 (131)		
He/ she understands how I feel.	Totally agree	50.4 (278)	50.4 (139)	0	1
	Disagree	49.6 (274)	49.6 (137)		
Most of the time I feel very close to my partner.	Totally agree	70.2 (387)	57.6 (159)	13.070	**<0.001**
	Disagree	29.8 (164)	42.4 (117)		

Items on violence					
You addressed insulting or humiliating words to each other.	Yes	38.3 (*211*)	46.6 (*129*)	5.217	**0.022**
	No	61.7 (*340*)	53.4 (*148*)		
You or your partner have/ has been jealous.	Yes	78.7 (*435*)	79.6 (*219*)	0.105	**0.746**
	No	21.3 (*118*)	20.4 (*56*)		
You have been forced to have sex.	Yes	2.4 (*13*)	7.6 (*21*)	12.810	**<0.001**
	No	97.6 (*537*)	92.4 (*255*)		
You were injured or harmed by your partner.	Yes	4.4 (*24*)	9.9 (*27*)	9.320	**0.002**
	No	95.6 (*522*)	90.1 (*247*)		

Source: author.

As mentioned before, for 60% of the respondents who had a current romantic partner, the relationship was longer than a year old. Comparing couples older than one year with those having a shorter duration, we found significant differences regarding the intensity of intimacy and violence levels among the romantic partners. Thus, a longer relationship accentuated the perception of intimacy, but paradoxically, it intensified behaviors from the sphere of violence. The same tendency was apparent when all couples were taken into consideration and when the analysis was divided by gender (see Table 2 and Graph 3).

Table 2: Significance of differences between the mean levels of intimacy and violence by duration of relationship

Youth in couples	Scale	Duration of relationship	N	Mean difference	Standard deviation	Value of t test	Sig. (p)
All	Intimacy	Over 1 year	815	2.084	3.13	7.101	<0.001
		Under 1 year			4.67		
	Violence	Over1 year	811	0.704	3.40	3.158	0.002
		Under 1 year			2.90		
Women	Intimacy	Over1 year	545	1.868	2.87	5.199	<0.001
		Under 1 year			4.57		
	Violence	Over1 year	541	0.835	3.22	3.289	0.001
		Under 1 year			2.59		
Men	Intimacy	Over1 year	270	2.328	3.66	4.497	<0.001
		Under 1 year			4.69		
	Violence	Over1 year	270	0.664	3.76	1.538	0.125
		Under 1 year			3.26		

Source: author.

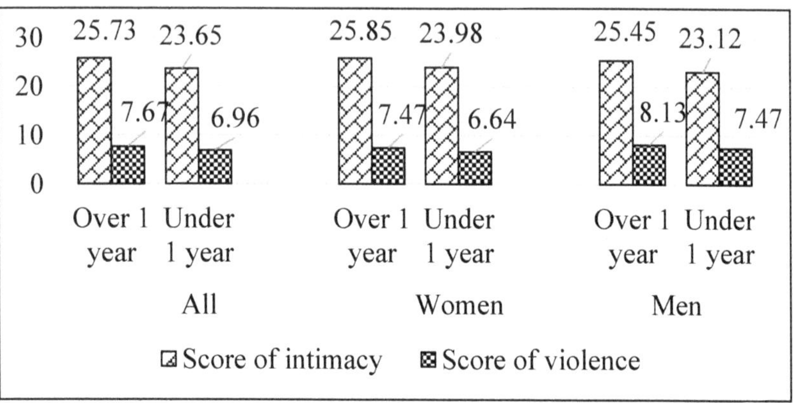

Source: author.

Again, women reported slightly higher levels of intimacy, while men made accusations of higher levels of violence, irrespective of the couple's duration. However, in the case of men, even if the violence increased with the extension of the couple's duration, this variation was not a significant one.

Independent-samples t-test was used to compare the differences between the partners' positive or negative intentions related to moving in together or separating from the partner, getting married and giving birth to a child, according to the mean scores on intimacy and violence in the current romantic partnership. The results, differentiated by gender, are exhibited in Tables 3 and 4.

Table 3: The interlink between intimacy and future life plans among women and men

Life plans with the partner	Intimacy score					
	Women			Men		
	Mean diff.	Value of t test	Sig. (p)	Mean diff.	Value of t test	Sig. (p)
Move	0.366	1.045	0.297	-0.232	-0.432	0.666
Separate	-1.135	-3.427	**0.001**	-1.702	-3.445	**0.001**
Marry	-0.771	-2.233	**0.026**	0.166	0.304	0.762
Child	-1.037	-2.516	**0.013**	-0.891	-1.476	0.142

Source: author.

Table 4: The interlink between violence and future life plans among women and men

Life plans with the partner	Violence score					
	Women			Men		
	Mean diff.	Value of t test	Sig. (p)	Mean diff.	Value of t test	Sig. (p)
Move	-0.291	-0.991	0.322	0.015	0.034	0.973
Separate	0.482	1.794	**0.073**	0.922	2.213	**0.028**
Marry	0.198	0.725	0.469	-0.420	-0.980	0.328
Child	0.396	1.286	0.199	-0.214	-0.492	0.623

Source: author.

According to the data from Tables 3 and 4, intimacy and violence in couples produced the strongest significant effect regarding separation in the expected way, for both genders. Both young women and men with lower levels of intimacy (t=-3.427, p=0.001, respectively t=-3.445, p=0.001) and with higher levels of violence in their couple (t=1.794, p=0.073, respectively t=2.213, p=0.028) intended to withdraw from the current partnership in the next 2-3 years.

Regarding the plan to move in with the partner within the next three years, women who perceived a lower intimacy and a higher level of violence in their current romantic relationship declined the intention to move in with their current intimate partner, but these tendencies were not statistically significant. Conversely, for men, a lower intensity of perceived intimacy is not a barrier in the plan to move in with the intimate partner. Again, however, these patterns lacked statistical significance. In addition, there was a similar level of perceived violence in couples between men who intended to move in with their romantic partner and those who did not have such a plan.

When a more serious commitment with the partner was put into question, divergent patterns were registered between genders. In an unexpected way, women with a lower level of intimacy and with a higher level of reported violence in the couple intended to marry the current partner within the next three years, but the results were significant only when intimacy was involved (t=-2.233, p=0.026). Among men, as expected, plans to formalize the current romantic relationship through marriage depended on a higher level of perceived commitment and a lower level of violence, although the findings were not statistically significant.

Also unexpectedly, women with higher levels of violence were more interested in having a child with the current intimate partner. A striking result was that both women and men with lower levels of intimacy in the couple expressed the intention to have a child in the next three years. But violence acted differently between genders: women with a higher level of violence in the couple were willing to give birth to a child, while the opposite was true for men. However, results were statistically significant only for the association between intimacy and intention to have a child for women (t=-2.516, p=0.013) (Table 3).

3.2 The results of the multivariate analyses

Table 5: Logistic regression analysis of intentions regarding personal life events in the next 2-3 years

Study variables	Move (N = 614)		Separate (N = 610)		Marry (N = 593)		Have a child (N = 609)	
	Exp(B)	p	Exp(B)	p	Exp(B)	p	Exp(B)	p
Gender Women (ref.) Men	1 0.993	0.972	1 1.423	**0.062**	1 1.035	0.853	1 1.803	**0.002**
Age (years) 19-20 (ref.) 21-23	1 0.714	0.219	1 0.973	0.921	1 1.289	0.363	1 1.141	0.641
Residential place Urban (ref.) Rural	1 0.627	**0.027**	1 1.007	0.975	1 0.598	**0.017**	1 0.787	0.294
Financial situation Good (ref.) Bad	1 0.704	**0.053**	1 1.162	0.398	1 0.949	0.769	1 0.928	0.694
In education No (ref.) Yes	1 1.722	**0.040**	1 0.690	0.175	1 2.242	**0.006**	1 0.686	0.161
Working status Never had a job (ref.) Have a current job Had a job in the past	1 1.392 1.136	0.155 0.559	1 1.202 1.753	0.407 **0.007**	1 1.032 1.024	0.886 0.909	1 1.287 0.780	0.272 0.285
Education of parents Secondary (ref.) Tertiary	1 1.454	**0.073**	1 0.653	**0.028**	1 1.277	0.192	1 0.787	0.254
Problems with parents No (ref.) Yes	1 0.955	0.821	1 1.164	0.437	1 1.155	0.463	1 1.376	0.118
Excessive use of substances in the family No (ref.) Yes	1 0.704	0.258	1 0.920	0.788	1 0.927	0.807	1 1.026	0.938
Duration of relationship Over 1 year (ref.) Under 1year	1 1.063	0.747	1 0.854	0.391	1 1.072	0.704	1 0.970	0.876

Level of intimacy in the couple High (ref.) Low	1 0.812	0.266	1 2.111	**<0.001**	1 1.042	0.818	1 1.551	**0.021**
Level of violence in the couple Low (ref.) High	1 1.021	0.911	1 1.330	**0.100**	1 1.147	0.428	1 1.012	0.949

Source: author.

Table 5 contains the results of four logistic regression models used to contrast positive to negative intentions to move in with the partner, to separate from partner, to marry the partner and to have a child with the partner, including all young people who participated in the study. Three typologies of covariates were included: a) background characteristics (gender, age, residential place, financial situation, educational and working status of respondent); b) life-course variables related to the family of origin (education of parents; problems with parents during the last year; whether a member of the family excessively consumed alcohol, drugs or other medicines during the last year); c) characteristics of the current couple (duration of relationship; level of intimacy in couple; level of violence in couple).

Data from Table 5 show that characteristics related to the current romantic partnership had an influence on some future life plans of Romanian young people, but they were neither the only ones, nor the most important ones. Hence, on the one hand, a low level of intimacy doubled the risk of separation from the current intimate partner (β=2.111, p<0.001), while on the other hand, it increased by half the willingness to have a child with the current partner (β=1.551, p=0.021). In addition, a high level of violence in the couple raised by a third the risk of separation from the current romantic partner (β=1.330, p=0.100). A shorter duration of the romantic relationship seemed to protect the couple from the risk of separation, but the result was not statistically significant (β=0.854, p=0.391).

A remarkable observation from Table 5 is that among all young people, future life plans were mostly influenced by background or individual characteristics. Regarding gender, young men had a higher propensity for separation from the romantic partner (β=1.423, p=0.062). At the same time, men's willingness to have a child with the current partner within the next three years was almost doubled, compared with young women's intention for this life event (β=1.803, p=0.002).

A positive intention to move in with the partner was more likely to be held by young people who were studying and by those who had a current job, although the effect was significant only for the former category (β=1.722, p=0.040, respectively β=1.392, p=0.155). Having the status of student increased more than twice the likelihood of marriage during the next three years (β=2.242, p=0.006), while not having a job anymore raised the risk of separation from the current partner (β=1.753, p=0.007) by more than one and a half. Residential place and financial situation also produced effects on the intentions to move in with and to marry the intimate partner within the next three years. More specifically, young people from rural areas and with a bad financial situation had a significantly much lower probability of moving in with the current intimate partner (β=0.627, p=0.027, respectively β=0.704, p=0.053), compared with their peers from urban areas and having no financial problems. Additionally, residing in the countryside reduced by almost a half the propensity to marry the current partner (β=0.598, p=0.017) (Table 5).

From the category of factors related to the family of origin, a prominent role was played by the education of parents. Namely, a young person who had at least one parent with a university education will be more inclined to move in with the romantic partner (β=1.454, p=0.073), and has less intention to separate from the partner in the near future (β=0.653, p=0.028), as compared to a counterpart whose parents achieved a lower level of education. Two other findings are worth noticing, although they are not statistically significant: young people who had problems with their parents during the last year were more willing to have a child during the next three years, and those who were confronted in the family of origin with a member who excessively consumed alcohol or other drugs had a higher desire to move in with their intimate partner (Table 5).

In order to identify the similarities and differences between genders as regards the effects of the three categories of covariates on future life plans, eight logistic regression models were constructed, separately for women and men, for each life event. Exposition of results issued from these multivariate analyses, which are illustrated in Tables 6 to 9, focused on the gender dimension. Young women who intended to move in with their intimate partner: were in education; had a job; and had higher educated parents. Conversely, women who declined the plan to move in with their partner: were older; resided in the countryside; claimed a bad financial situation; were confronted with excessive consumption of alcohol or drugs in the family of origin; and perceived a low level of intimacy in their own couple relationship. However, among all the mentioned factors, only current educational status produced significant results and, consequently, had the strongest impact on the plan to move in with the romantic partner. Hence, women enrolled in the educational system were almost three times more inclined to move in with their partner compared with women who had completed their studies (β=2.859, p=0.005). Also, a higher educational level of parents was associated with the intention to move in with the partner among women (β=1.570, p=0.092). In the case of men, the intention of moving in with the romantic partner was an acceptable life plan only for those who had a current job, although this tendency lacked statistical

238

significance. Most of the other covariates discouraged the plans of young men to move in with their romantic partner. The strongest negative effect was played by experiencing a bad financial situation, which decreased by half the likelihood of moving in with the partner (β=0.541, p=0.060). Without statistical significance, other discouraging factors among men were: residing in a rural area; having had problems with parents and being confronted with the excessive consumption of alcohol or drugs in the family of origin; and perceiving a low level of intimacy in one's own couple relationship (Table 6).

Table 6: Logistic regression analysis of the intention to move in with the intimate partner in the next 2-3 years by gender

Study variables	Women (N = 419)		Men (N =195)	
	Exp(B)	p	Exp(B)	p
Age (years)				
19-20 (ref.)	1		1	
21-23	0.574	0.136	0.935	0.876
Residential place				
Urban (ref.)	1		1	
Rural	0.651	0.102	0.541	0.110
Financial situation				
Good (ref.)	1		1	
Bad	0.839	0.437	0.541	**0.060**
In education				
No (ref.)	1		1	
Yes	2.859	**0.005**	0.965	0.930
Working status				
Never had a job (ref.)	1		1	
Have a current job	1.306	0.360	1.887	0.122
Had a job in the past	1.126	0.665	1.172	0.679
Education of parents				
Secondary (ref.)	1		1	
Tertiary	1.570	**0.092**	1.412	0.339
Problems with parents				
No (ref.)	1		1	
Yes	0.954	0.849	0.846	0.644
Excessive use of substances in family				
No (ref.)	1		1	
Yes	0.685	0.305	0.822	0.751
Duration of relationship				
Over 1 year (ref.)	1		1	
Under 1year	1.009	0.969	1.095	0.790
Level of intimacy in couple				
High (ref.)	1		1	
Low	0.757	0.235	0.880	0.697
Level of violence in couple				
Low (ref.)	1		1	
High	0.985	0.946	0.992	0.979

Source: author.

Table 7: Logistic regression analysis of the intention to separate from intimate partner in the next 2-3 years by gender

Study variables	Women (N = 411)		Men (N =199)	
	Exp(B)	p	Exp(B)	p
Age (years)				
19-20 (ref.)	1		1	
21-23	0.792	0.525	1.170	0.727
Residential place				
Urban (ref.)	1		1	
Rural	1.140	0.611	1.069	0.865
Financial situation				
Good (ref.)	1		1	
Bad	1.349	0.162	0.907	0.773
In education				
No (ref.)	1		1	
Yes	0.725	0.405	0.620	0.259
Working status				
Never had a job (ref.)	1		1	
Have a current job	1.521	0.122	0.598	0.222
Had a job in the past	2.186	**0.002**	1.118	0.775
Education of parents				
Secondary (ref.)	1		1	
Tertiary	0.830	0.436	0.412	**0.013**
Problems with parents				
No (ref.)	1		1	
Yes	1.019	0.935	1.445	0.328
Excessive use of substances in family				
No (ref.)	1		1	
Yes	0.846	0.647	1.243	0.730
Duration of relationship				
Over 1 year (ref.)	1		1	
Under 1year	0.954	0.830	0.585	0.133
Level of intimacy in couple				
High (ref.)	1		1	
Low	1.642	**0.022**	3.867	**<0.001**
Level of violence in couple				
Low (ref.)	1		1	
High	1.269	0.257	1.676	0.116

Source: author.

Table 7 presents the results of the logistic regression models regarding the intention to separate from the current romantic partner by gender. The risk of separation was twice as high among young women who had a job in the past compared with their peers who never had a job (β=2.186, p=0.002), and by more than a half as high among those who perceived a low level of intimacy (β=1.642, p=0.022), as compared with those perceiving a high level of commitment in the current couple relationship. Also, having a bad financial situation, having a current job and declaring a high level of violence in the romantic relationship increased the risk of separation from the intimate partner, but the regression's corresponding coefficients were lacking statistical significance. For young men, there were two opposite significant effects on plans to separate from the partner. Namely, perceiving a low level of intimacy in the romantic relationship increased by almost four times the risk of separation from the intimate partner (β=3.867, p<0.001), while originating from a family where parents had a higher educational level decreased by more than a half the probability of separation from the romantic partner within the next three years (β=0.412, p=0.013). Other factors which seemed to favor separation from the partner among young men, although not statistically significant, were related to having had problems in the family of origin (problems with parents and problems with alcohol or drugs of a family member) and with the manifestation of violent behaviors in the current romantic relationship. Instead, young men who were enrolled in education, who had a current job, and whose romantic relationship was shorter than a year were less likely to dissolve the current couple relationship. However, results were not statistically significant.

Table 8: Logistic regression analysis of the intention to marry the intimate partner in the next 2-3 years by gender

Study variables	Women (N = 408)		Men (N =185)	
	Exp(B)	p	Exp(B)	p
Age (years)				
19-20 (ref.)	1		1	
21-23	0.949	0.888	1.946	0.151
Residential place				
Urban (ref.)	1		1	
Rural	0.676	0.137	0.472	**0.074**
Financial situation				
Good (ref.)	1		1	
Bad	1.111	0.625	0.625	0.207
In education				
No (ref.)	1		1	
Yes	1.793	0.143	2.644	**0.034**
Working status				
Never had a job (ref.)	1		1	
Have a current job	1.061	0.827	0.953	0.907
Had a job in the past	1.371	0.214	0.508	**0.081**
Education of parents				
Secondary (ref.)	1		1	
Tertiary	1.375	0.171	1.036	0.921
Problems with parents				
No (ref.)	1		1	
Yes	1.127	0.613	1.127	0.751
Excessive use of substances in family				
No (ref.)	1		1	
Yes	1.131	0.737	0.366	0.131
Duration of relationship				
Over 1 year (ref.)	1		1	

	1.164	0.489	0.960	0.906
Under 1year	1.164	0.489	0.960	0.906
Level of intimacy in couple High (ref.) Low	1 1.138	 0.552	1 0.679	 0.254
Level of violence in couple Low (ref.) High	1 1.228	 0.326	1 1.086	 0.803

Source: author.

The plan to marry the current romantic partner among Romanian youth is exhibited in Table 8. For women, regression coefficients were not statistically significant, but most of the investigated factors produced a positive effect on the intention to marry the intimate partner. Young women who were studying, who had a job in the past and whose parents had university studies were more likely to engage in a marriage with their intimate partner within the next three years, compared with their peers who left the educational system, who never had a job and whose parents had a secondary level of education. Surprisingly, young women who experienced a high level of violence in the couple relationship were more open to marrying their actual intimate partner compared with those who had a romantic relationship characterized by a low level of violence. The only factor which seriously discouraged the plan to marry the partner was that of residence in a rural area. In opposition, for young men, a part of the analyzed factors acted as a brake for the plan to marry their romantic partner. Hence, a young man who had a bad financial situation, who had a job in the past, who experienced the excessive consumption of alcohol or drugs in the family of origin and who perceived a low level of intimacy in the current romantic relationship were less likely to plan a marriage with the partner within the next three years. For young men, the most negative effect on the intention to marry was played by residence in the countryside (β=0.472, p=0.074). In opposition, being older and being enrolled in education increased the likelihood of planning a marriage, but only the last factor was a significant one (β=2.644, p=0.034).

The last two regression models, illustrated in Table 9, reflect the results on the intention to have a child with the current intimate partner by gender. For young women, a positive intention to give birth to a child was associated with having a current job and with having problems with parents and a history of substance abuse of one member from the family of origin. Unexpectedly, a low level of intimacy in the couple increased by more than twice the willingness to have a child with the current partner in the near future, and the result had a strong statistical significance (β=2.094, p=0.002). Instead, young women who resided in the countryside, who were studying and with highly educated parents were less interested in conceiving a child within the next three years. Young men who had a job in the past and who had problems of substance abuse with one member from the family of origin had a significantly lower willingness to become a father within the next three years (β=0.385, p=0.018, respectively β=0.250, p=0.054). Fatherhood was

242

also undesired by young men who: had a bad financial situation; were enrolled in education; had highly educated parents; perceived a low level of intimacy in the current couple relationship, but these effects were not statistically significant. Young men who had problems with parents during the last year reported the desire to have a child with their current partner, although the effect was not significant.

Table 9: Logistic regression analysis of the intention to have a child with the intimate partner in the next 2-3 years by gender

Study variables	Women (N = 414)		Men (N =195)	
	Exp(B)	p	Exp(B)	p
Age (years)				
19-20 (ref.)	1		1	
21-23	1.142	0.734	1.208	0.664
Residential place				
Urban (ref.)	1		1	
Rural	0.628	0.130	0.988	0.975
Financial situation				
Good (ref.)	1		1	
Bad	1.038	0.877	0.706	0.291
In education				
No (ref.)	1		1	
Yes	0.867	0.720	0.555	0.142
Working status				
Never had a job (ref.)	1		1	
Have a current job	1.461	0.206	1.012	0.975
Had a job in the past	1.069	0.819	0.385	**0.018**
Education of parents				
Secondary (ref.)	1		1	
Tertiary	0.757	0.311	0.685	0.282
Problems with parents				
No (ref.)	1		1	
Yes	1.279	0.341	1.468	0.275
Excessive use of substances in family				
No (ref.)	1		1	
Yes	1.507	0.280	0.250	**0.054**
Duration of relationship				
Over 1 year (ref.)	1		1	
Under 1year	0.931	0.774	1.055	0.874
Level of intimacy in couple				
High (ref.)	1		1	
Low	2.094	**0.002**	0.876	0.685
Level of violence in couple				
Low (ref.)	1		1	
High	0.920	0.726	1.156	0.649

Source: author.

4. Concluding Discussions and Implications for Practice

One of the objectives of the study was to identify commonalities and divergences in the manifestations of intimacy and violence in romantic relationships by gender. As expected, women reported higher levels of intimacy in their couples than men. However, only half of both young women and men perceived that their intimate partner really understood how they felt. In the spectrum of violent behaviors, jealousy was by far the most prevalent manifestation in the couple, irrespective of gender. Strikingly, although forced sexual intercourse and inflicting harm on the romantic partner were rather rare practices, the empirical data revealed that young men were victims of such behaviors to a much larger extent than young women. One may ask how such tendencies can be understood. Two explanations could be possible: women may be inclined to under-declare such practices, while men tend to dramatize or to exaggerate behaviors in the area of violence; or a change in the pattern of courtship could have emerged, with a weakening of the double-standard rule for women and an increase of women's sexual emancipation, together with a change in the pattern of sexuality control by men. In any case, such patterns deserve further and more complex and investigation.

Findings of the present study showed that Romanian youth are inclined to get involved in stable and durable romantic relationships. Moreover, a longer couple relationship increased the perception intention to commit to the intimate partner for both genders, but accentuated the reported violence between partners in the case of young women. As for young men, the perception of violence in the romantic relationship did not depend on the couple's duration.

The connection between the intimacy and violence scores on the four future life plans reflected some significant tendencies. An expected and strong effect was noticed regarding the intention to end the current romantic relationship: for both genders, a low level of intimacy and a high level of violence predicted separation from the intimate partner within the next three years. Surprisingly, two opposite effects coexisted among young women: a low level of intimacy in the couple was significantly associated with the intention to marry and to give birth to a child with the current romantic partner within the next three years. A possible explanation might be the coexistence of two opposite attitudes of young women who live in a romantic partnership characterized by a low level of commitment: one in which commitment is highly valued but leads to a disposition to dissolve a partnership that is not fulfilling on this matter, and one in which there is an intention to secure a low-commitment partnership through marriage and a child.

The multivariate analyses revealed a more complex picture on three sets of factors which could influence the decisions regarding four important life events, including background or individual characteristics; variables related to the family of origin; and covariates regarding the couple's life (duration, intimacy and violence in the current couple). When the analysis included all participant young people, individual factors proved to play the major role in future life plans. Young men were more likely to take the decision to separate from the partner, but, at the same time, were more inclined to have a child with the current partner, compared with young women. Residing in rural areas and a bad financial situation discouraged plans to move in with and marry the current partner. This pattern could be a sign of a precarious relationship status and not an indicator of an emancipated behavior which could indicate a weakening of the importance of marriage. Instead, being enrolled in the educational system increased the probability of moving in with and marrying the intimate partner. Having highly educated parents was associated with the intention to move in with the romantic partner and with a lower risk of separation. It might be that more educated parents have a positive attitude towards the modern behavior of cohabitation among young romantic partners who are students, as a preceding period to marriage.

The multivariate analysis repeated for each gender and for each life plan revealed a series of remarkable results. When the intention to move in with the romantic partner was investigated, two different factors had a great impact among Romanian youth: for women, being enrolled in an educational institution, while for men, having a current job, represented the main catalyzers for such a future plan. Another pattern was that more disadvantaged young women and men had a lower propensity to move in with the partner, while the opposite was true for the more privileged young women. Also for women, a high level of perceived intimacy encouraged them to move in with the current romantic partner.

The results of regression reinforced the idea that the intention to separate from the partner was a plausible option for both young women and men who reported a low level of commitment in the current couple relationship. In addition, young women who did not have a job anymore intended to separate from the partner. Having at least one parent with a university education represented a protective factor against separation from the romantic partner among young men.

When the plan for marriage was investigated, an important result concerned the youth from rural areas. Irrespective of gender, residing in the countryside decreased the likelihood of marrying the current partner within the next three years. Instead, being enrolled in education was a factor that encouraged the plan for marriage for both genders. Although without statistical significance, it is important to point out the fact that young women reporting a high level of violence in the couple intended to marry their partner in the near future. This could indicate that accepting violent behaviors from the male intimate partner is still an acceptable practice for Romanian young women engaged in romantic partnerships.

When the most serious adult role – that of becoming a parent – was analyzed, different factors proved to matter from a gender perspective. Again, an unexpected effect regarding intimacy was reinforced in the multivariate analysis in the case of young women: namely, a lower level of perceived commitment in the couple increased the willingness to conceive a child with the current partner. Among young men, not having a job anymore and having experienced a history of substance abuse in the family of origin significantly discouraged fatherhood in the near future.

The present study showed that violence predicts separation from the intimate partner. Martsolf, Draucker & Brandau (2013) documented six ways of ending a violent couple relationship: deciding enough is enough; becoming interested in someone else; being on again, off again; fading away; deciding it's best for us both; and moving away. The same authors concluded that professionals working with young people can use the six ways of breaking up as a tool to initiate a discussion about the issues involved in ending violent couple relationships.

Young people should be supported to properly address IPV before it starts. In order to achieve this goal, young women and men must understand the associated psychological and behavioral consequences of IPV (Eccles et al., 1993). Additionally, they must be taught how to identify behaviors associated with IPV and how to prevent and intervene upon potential and ongoing abusive relationships (Booth, Van Hasselt & Vecchi, 2011). Also, they should learn to develop strategies to promote healthy and nonviolent relationships, such as: communicating with one's partner, managing uncomfortable emotions such as anger and jealousy, and treating others with respect. Although young people might receive messages from their peers, significant adults and the media that violence in a relationship is normal, they should be educated that violence is unacceptable and that there are reasons why violence occurs (CDC 2012).

A limitation of the present study is that it did not include a new form of IPV spread by the technological advance in social media and practiced by both young women and men. Called 'cyber harassment' or bullying, it includes 'teasing, telling lies, making fun of, making rude or mean comments, spreading of rumors, or making threatening or aggressive comments, that occur through e-mail, a chat room, instant messages, a Web site, or text messaging' (David-Ferdon & Hertz, 2007: p. 2).

This study found higher levels of experience of violence in the couple relationship reported by men than women. These findings should be interpreted cautiously, taking into account that the scientific literature constantly demonstrates the over-representation of females among the victims of couple and domestic violence.

Experiences in couple relationships heavily influence subsequent personal life plans. Healthy intimate relationships have a positive effect in assuming adult roles, while unhealthy, abusive, or violent relationships inhibit or postpone transition to main life course events during adulthood for both genders.

With the growing risk for young people of both genders of becoming victims of aggression perpetrated by their peers through new technology, electronic aggression has become an emerging public health problem. Therefore, new research about its prevalence and etiology are necessary to support the implementation of effective prevention programs (David-Ferdon & Hertz, 2007).

In order to build a comprehensive and efficient IPV prevention strategy, young people, families, organizations, and communities should mobilize their efforts to work together (CDC 2012). Professionals should provide opportunities for young women and men affected by IPV to find help and encourage them on their road to build positive and healthy relationships.

Acknowledgments

This work was supported by a grant from the Romanian National Authority for Scientific Research, CNCS – UEFISCDI, project number PN-II-ID-PCE-2011-3-0543.

Bibliography

Acosta, Marisa C., Brynn E. Balcom & Caitlin A. Conheim (2014) *Behind the Illusion: Addressing Adolescent Dating Violence in School*, A Project presented to the Faculty of the Graduate and Professional Studies in Education, California: California State University, Sacramento.

Arnett, Jeffrey L. (2001) 'Conceptions of the Transition to Adulthood: Perspectives from Adolescence through Midlife', *Journal of Adult Development*, 8(2): 133–143.

Billari, Francesco C., Marcantonio Caltabiano & Gianpiero Dalla Zuanna (eds.) (2007) *Sexual and Affective Behaviour of Students. An International Research*, Padova: Cleup Editrice.

Booth, Brandi, Vincent B. Van Hasselt, & Gregory M. Vecchi (2011) *Addressing School Violence: The Federal Bureau of Investigation*. Online. Available https://leb.fbi.gov/articles/featured-articles/addressing-school-violence (accessed June 2016).

Carter, Julia (2012) 'What Is Commitment? Women's Accounts of Intimate Attachment', *Families, Relationships and Societies*, 1(2): 137-153.

Centers for Disease Control and Prevention (2012) *Teen Dating Violence*. Online. Available https://leb.fbi.gov/articles/featured-articles/addressing-school-violence (accessed May 2016).

Collins, W. Andrew (2003) 'More than Myth: The Developmental Significance of Romantic Relationships during Adolescence', *Journal of Research on Adolescence*, 13(1): 1–24.

David-Ferdon, Corinne & Marci F. Hertz (2007) 'Electronic Media, Violence, and Adolescents: an Emerging Public Health Problem', *The Journal of Adolescent Health: Official Publication of the Society for Adolescent Medicine*, 41(6), Suppl. 1: pp. S1-5.

Dégi, L. Csaba & Cristina Faludi (2015) 'The Effect of Sexual Debut and Health Risk Behaviours on Baccalaureate Performance of Romanian Adolescents', *Croatian Journal of Education*, 17(2): 333-352.

Eccles, Jacquelynne S., Carol Midgley, Allan Wigfield, Christy M. Buchanan, David Reuman, Constance Flanagan & Douglas M. Iver (1993) 'Development during Adolescence. The impact of stage-environment fit on young adolescents' experiences in schools and in families', *The American Psychologist*, 48(2): 90-101.

Foshee, Vangie A., Thad Benefield, Chirayath Suchindran, Susan T. Ennett, Karl E. Bauman, Katherine J. Karriker-Jaffe, Heathe L. McNaughton-Reyes & Jasmine Mathias (2009) 'The Development of Four Types of Adolescent Dating Abuse and Selected Demographic Correlates', *Journal of Research on Adolescence: The Official Journal of the Society for Research on Adolescence*, 19(3): 380–400.

Greene, William H. (2002) *Econometric Analysis*, Upper Saddle River: Prentice Hall.

Gutgesell, Margaret E. & Nancy Payne (2004) 'Issues of Adolescent Psychological Development in the 21st Century', *Pediatrics in Review*, 25(3): 79-85.

Harrell, Frank E. (2001) *Regression Modeling Strategies. With Applications to Linear Models, Logistic Regression, and Survival Analysis*, New York: Springer-Verlag.

Hendrick, Susan S. (1988) 'A Generic Measure of Relationship Satisfaction', *Journal of Marriage and Family*, 50(1): 93-98.

Martsolf, Donna S., Claire B. Draucker & Melvina Brandau (2013) 'Breaking up Is Hard to Do: How Teens End Violent Dating Relationships', *Journal of the American Psychiatric Nurses Association*, 19(2): 71–77.

Ministerul Sănătății, Banca Mondială, UNFPA, USAID, UNICEF (2005) *Studiul sănătății reproducerii. România 2004. Raport sintetic*, Buzău: Alpha MDN.

Nagaoka, Jenny, Camille A. Farrington, Stacy B. Ehrlich, Ryan D. Heath, David W. Johnson, Sarah Dickson, Ashley C. Turner, Ashley Mayo & Kathleen Hayes (2015) *Foundations for Young Adult Success. A Developmental Framework, Concept Paper for Research and Practice*, Chicago: The University of Chicago CCSR's Publications.

Overbeek, Geertjan, Thao Ha, Ron Scholte, Raymond de Kemp & C.M.E. Rutger Engels (2007) 'Brief Report: Intimacy, Passion, and Commitment in Romantic Relationships – Validation of a "Triangular Love Scale" for Adolescents', *Journal of Adolescence*, 30(3): 523–528.

Plazaola-Castaño, Juncal & Isabel Ruiz Pérez (2004) 'Intimate Partner Violence against Women and Physical and Mental Health Consequences', *Medicina Clinica*, 122(12): 461-467.

Roberts, A. Timothy, Peggy Auinger & Jonathan D. Klein (2005) 'Intimate Partner Abuse and the Reproductive Health of Sexually Active Female Adolescents', *The Journal of Adolescent Health*, 36(5): 380-385.

Roth, Maria, Teodor D. Hărăguş, Mihai B. Iovu, Cristina Faludi, Ágnes Dávid-Kacsó, Anna E. Bernáth-Vincze, Florina Pop, Sergiu L. Raiu & Corina I. Voicu (2016) *Rezultantele adolescenţei. O viziune longitudinală, Seria Practica Asistenţei Sociale*, Vol. 9, Cluj-Napoca: Presa Universitară Clujeană.

Schoon, Ingrid (2006) *Risk and Resilience. Adaptations in Changing Times*, New York: Cambridge University Press.

Thompson, Martie P., Kathleen C. Basile, Marci F. Hertz & Dylan Sitterle (2006) *Measuring Intimate Partner Violence and Victimization and Perpetration: a Compendium of Assessment Tools*, Atlanta, GA: National Centre for Disease Control and Prevention, National Center for Injury Prevention and Control.

Umberson, Debra, Kristi Williams, Daniel A. Powers, Hui Liu & Belinda Needham (2006) 'You Make Me Sick: Marital Quality and Health over the Life Course', *Journal of Health and Social Behavior*, 47(1): 1-16.

University of Michigan (2000) *Maryland Adolescent Development in context Study* (MADICS). Online. Available http://www.rcgd.isr.umich.edu/pgc/ (accessed December 2015).

Vagi, Kevin J., Emily O. Olsen, Kathleen C. Basile & Alana M. Vivolo-Kantor (2015) 'Teen Dating Violence (Physical and Sexual) among US High School Students: Findings from the 2013 National Youth Risk Behavior Survey', *JAMA Pediatrics*, 169(5): 474-482.

Vives-Cases, Carmen, Maria T. Ruiz-Cantero, Vicenta Escribà-Agüir & José J. Miralles (2010) 'The Effect of Intimate Partner Violence and Other Forms of Violence against Women on Health', *Journal of Public Health*, 33(1): 15-21.

Zweig, Janine M., Meredith Dank, Jennifer Yahner & Pamela Lachman (2013) 'The Rate of Cyber Dating Abuse among Teens and How It Relates to Other Forms of Teen Dating Violence', *Journal of Youth and Adolescence*, 42(7): 1063–1077.

CHAPTER XII

Is My Reproductive Body Rightfully Mine? About Abortion and Individual Choice in Post-communist Romania

Andrada NIMU and Andreea ZAMFIRA

In this chapter we analyze juridical-ethical perspectives on the human body and women's perceptions of their own bodies. We tackle this endeavor by focusing on the case of Romania. The chapter is structured as follows: first, we present the issue of the human body in light of juridical and philosophical approaches, in order to understand the main theoretical aspects connected to the human body. Next, by connecting the issue of abortion with these two perspectives, we try to schematize people's perceptions according to these norms. Thirdly, we bring the discussion to empirical grounds, considering that the human body is a contextually dependent concept. Here, we analyze Romanian women's perceptions on abortion and sociologically explain how they are formed in one direction or the other. The empirical study is based on research conducted through an online platform. The data collection method was launched on CAWI (Computer Assisted Web Interview), covering 500 respondents, all women aged 18+ years old, and representative on the Romanian online population. We show that most women adopt a moderate liberal approach to abortion, despite the highly declared importance of religion in their lives.

1. The Human Body in Light of Juridical Ethics: Fundamental Premises

The discussion about abortion and about the right to interrupt a pregnancy is fundamentally related to the one regarding the individual's/the person's rights over his/her body. Two central notions are to be understood and explained within this discussion, namely 'the individual'/'the person' and 'the human body'.

Defining the person as an end in itself and not as a means to an end, Immanuel Kant first elaborated one of the core ideas on which dominant juridical-ethical discourses about the human body rely today. In the *Fundamental Principles of the Metaphysic of Morals* ([1785] 1949), Kant advanced a practical imperative based on this very idea: to treat oneself and all humanity as an end and never as a means. Hippocrates argued for a similar imperative (in point of fact, to physicians) even much earlier. One could consider that Hippocrates's Oath plays a crucial role in perceiving and defining the human body through medical ethics. But Hippocrates's Oath, dating from the fifth century BC, and all similar ancient medical pronouncements were massively influenced by mythology and legendary figures such as Asclepios (or Aesculapius, in Latin), the god of Medicine. Nowadays, medical practice needs unambiguous juridical definitions of the human body. From the juridical point of view, in the absence of such clear definitions and adjacent norms, medicine would be nothing but an abusive practice. In order to avoid such a situation, it is absolutely necessary that medical ethics should be based on common fundamental principles along with juridical ethics.

Beginning with Greek mythology, religious morals and totalitarian doctrines[1] and ending with contemporary post-materialist political ideologies, people's most intricate questions and answers about human nature (and particularly those posed by the dominant elites) have enormously influenced the codes of medical deontology and, also the sphere of medical activity. In other words, the source of different perspectives which have an impact on juridical and medical practices was always philosophy. Whereas general philosophy defines a person through the dichotomy means/purpose and does not develop a particular interest in the question of the human body, judicial philosophy fills this vacuum, trying to coherently link these two different objects of definition. From the perspective of judicial philosophy, the person's right over her/his body is theoretically non-discussable because 'the person' and 'the body' constitute a unique system; to define one part in the absence of the other becomes very problematic, interrogating the very existence of the system.

2. The Human Body: State Property or Private Property?

Concerning the person's rights over her/his body, it is generally admitted that the person has the right to offer a part of her/himself but solely through free will. Transposed into laws exactly in this form, this general desideratum might produce a lot of individual and social troubles. Next, by moving from abstract to more applied perspectives, we tackle some related issues by focusing both on judicial and philosophical approaches to the human body.

---

1   In 1971, in the Soviet Union, for instance, the *Oath* for medical doctors included the following phrase: 'I swear to follow the principles of the communist moral'.

Philosophical doctrine referring to the human body and underlying various European judicial codification insists on the importance of limiting the sphere of a person's rights over her/his body, offering arguments that one could only contest with difficulty the negative consequences of irresponsible or unethical acts, which could not leave even liberals and followers of post-materialist ideologies (of liberation) indifferent. In order to explain the limits of a person's rights over her/his body and their importance in line with juridical ethics, Bertrand Lemennicier (1991) analyzed four fundamental principles governing the field: inviolability, the act of giving, gratuity, and the healing purpose. In the following paragraphs, we summarize Lemennicier's arguments.

The first principle states that the human body is inviolable (because together with the person and the spirit it forms a coherent and indestructible unity). Moreover, the human body does not constitute an object, which the person can freely dispose of. Although it is forbidden to alienate parts of the body, the possibility of donating such parts is allowed. Therefore, the act of giving represents a condition *sine qua non* and it is affirmed by the second principle. In order to exclude any possibility of financial or commercial interest, the donation must be free of charge. The only acceptable purpose for such an act of donation is therapeutic.

Trying to demonstrate that this judicial doctrine is not perfectly sustainable and coherent, Lemennicier (1991: pp. 112-123) formulates some specific arguments.

In this sense, a first reproach would be that the concerned doctrine is socially noxious. Banning gene manipulation or the sale of organs, as well as artificial procreation or embryo freezing, could be seen as equivalent to hindering the chances humans may have of improving the physical characteristics of their offspring, and can endanger lives and even the human species itself. For instance, we could imagine, on the one hand, someone whose life depends on a kidney or a lung transplant and, on the other, a family that would consent to such a donation after the death of one of its members – but that does not take into consideration the respective act in the absence of material motivation. A second example is the one of a sterile mother that cannot enjoy an accomplished life, side by side with her children, and of a possible carrier mother, hindered by the law from earning money by helping the first one. All that being said, it becomes appropriate to ask ourselves whether the law discriminates sufficiently rigorously between the different possible utilizations of the human body. What about smokers or people working so hard to earn a living they endanger their health? Although the legislation in Europe does not totally ignore such cases, it continues to be fallible in some current inconsistent aspects.

The second reproach would be that this judicial doctrine is philosophically badly founded. We have observed that the philosophical postulate underpinning the law affirms the inseparability of the body and the person/personality. Consequently, they are both legally protected from any intrusion transgressing the principles of intangibility and of inviolability[2]. In line with Kant's definition of a person ([1785] 1949), also assumed by the legislator, a person is supposed to be conscious of herself/himself, rational, free to choose and to discern good from evil. But what about those individuals behaving inhumanly, committing criminal acts, who are presumably irresponsible and irrational? Should the same laws protect individuals with doubtful capacities of reason? Should they enjoy the rights to intangibility and inviolability of their body and of their intellectual products? Or should one formulate special norms for these cases?

Perspectives on the human body become even more complicated when referring to abortion. On the one hand, as the fetus is not considered a person, it does not enjoy the legal protection offered by virtue of the aforementioned principles. On the other hand, the law defends the mother's rights, because the mother is a person, and protects her to the detriment of the (potential) child. Although it does not legally constitute a person, the fetus is frequently defined as a prolongation of the mother's body. Therefore, we could justly ask ourselves what right entitles a woman to freely dispose of a part of her body, specifically when it comes to the fetus? In view of the fact of being renewable, cutting our nails and hair, donating blood or selling maternal milk and placenta do not equate to an alienation of parts of our body. According to Lemennicier (1991: p. 116), the body works as a 'biological machine' within which the spirit lives. Considering that the spirit is 'incorporated within this machine', and it is 'generally its unique occupant' and 'the spirit cannot change it', the author pleads for the judicial recognition of the person's private property over her/his body.

The last major reproach regarding the philosophical doctrine here in question points to the risk of confusing Law and Morality (Canto-Sperber 2002; Lemennicier 1991). In establishing and operating the separation between Law and Morality in matters related to the human body, the State plays a tremendous role. From a morality perspective, everyone can freely decide what 'human' and 'inhuman', 'good' and 'bad' means for herself/himself. In principle, everyone should have the right to live the way he/she likes, in the absence of any external intervention as long as he/she does not prevent others from living their lives the way they want to. In order to assure this condition for all people, the State necessarily has to impose important limitations on individual liberties. The way the State deliberates, taking a position on one side or another, brings interesting questions to the table: questions about what is supposed to be moral or immoral, and about

---

2   One has to understand that laws protect the products of the human body (hair, nails, placenta, cells, etc.), as well as the intellectual products (in line with the moral rights of the person).

the social construction of reality and its legality. Notwithstanding medical progress in discovering the pathological causes of a patient's malaise, the Law still focuses on evidently poor physical conditions, to the detriment of poor psychological conditions (which are more unlikely to be noticeable). Thus, judicial doctrine risks contradicting itself by dissociating from the very definition of a person as a system with two components. Sometimes, such an apparent internal inconsistency in judicial doctrine is wrongly understood and used as an argument by neoliberals and progressivists against the *status quo.*

3. The Central Controversy about Abortion

Most of the time, abortion constitutes a medical practice without a commonly accepted healing purpose. In other words, it is not aimed at procuring an antidote for a mother's physical or mental disease, but for her poor conditions or unwilled discomfort because the pregnancy or the baby is not convenient to her life plan. So-called abortion opponents (or, to be more precise, the people who are skeptical about the rightfulness of abortion) present such an act as an exercise of selfishness (Lemennicier 1991: p. 116). In contrast with this approach, pro-choice supporters try to draw attention to the dramatic situations women are confronted with. Today pro-life and pro-choice arguments, and the liberal and conservative viewpoints on this issue in intellectual or political debates, have become very sophisticated and challenging.

First, the subject of abortion brings into question the importance of separating Law and Morality – a difficult thing to do, given the fact that they represent two different normative systems (Canto-Sperber 2001). Within a given society, people naturally display more than one moral, but it is not possible for each moral to have an associated legal system. To give distinct legislation to every community sharing particular moral principles would be completely aberrant. An act contrary to morality may determine public disapproval but it is not implicitly legally penalized (for example, pregnancy interruption in Christian communities). Similarly, a moral act does not implicitly constitute a legal act (girls wearing a Muslim veil in those public schools where wearing this object is banned, for example).

When it comes to abortion, judicial and moral norms do not always dovetail.

The American Supreme Court legalized abortion on January 1973. In France, on the 18th of December 1975, the Veil Law exempted abortion from penalty. Nevertheless, the disputes continue even today, with each side formulating very powerful arguments. Even though abortion now constitutes a legal medical practice in most European countries, the ethical dimension of this act is still vividly contested. Accordingly to Canto-Sperber (2002: p. 23), the Veil Law was mainly based on considerations related to improving public health and to the affirmation of women's autonomy. From an ethical point of view, it would be preferable that no-one resorts to abortion; abortion is not at all a desirable experience. When one perceives abortion as a harmful act, the gravity of this essentially depends on the definition one uses for the fetus. An overwhelming number of factors influence our points of view regarding the fetus: religion, culture, personal experiences, our relatives' and friends' opinions, etc.

Excepting socio-cultural constraints, women are also conditioned by internal/subjective constraints, the personal *habitus*[3]. Religion also plays a tremendous role in the creation of these internal barriers. The Christian perspective on abortion and similar issues is very clear: the Christian Churches condemns abortion, euthanasia, love without commitment and all other acts conflicting with the basic rules of collective survival (Laurin 2011: p. 20). Nevertheless, despite the effort of the Christian Churches to preserve the traditional values and principles, people tend more and more to relativize and interpret the religious teachings in their own interest.

But it is not solely the Christian Churches which confront themselves with increasingly difficult situations. Juridical analysis and critical evaluation of the social effects of the law focus attention on more and more challenging dilemmas. The legislator has settled the judicial statute of the human embryo, for instance, relying on a specific principle: the conceived child is considered as viable every time this could represent an advantage for the baby. In France, if one wants to leave a legacy to a child as yet unborn, the law can arrange a succession case. On the contrary, in the case of a road accident ending with the death of a pregnant woman, the guilty car driver will be condemned for having provoked one death, that of the mother; in this case, the law cannot pronounce a condemnation for a double death because the child does not already possess a judicial statute. This type of double approach is susceptible to being easily critiqued; it shows that laws are sometimes based on weak definitions (of the human embryo, in this case).

Needless to say, the legality and the morality of abortion distinctly feature in political ideologies. Hursthouse (1987) summarizes the most important of such perspectives below.

---

3   Relying on Bourdieu's (1980) reflections, we consider that the *habitus*, as well as the *stable dispositions,* acquired through interaction with certain *structuring structures,* influence more or less consciously a woman's reasoning and decisions. A woman's *habitus* produces certain individual practices, induces certain feelings and moods, and encourages certain thoughts that superpose on the other social pressures.

Table 1: Classical ideological perspectives on the legality and the morality of abortion

Morality of abortion	Laws of abortion	Perspective
Wrong	Restrictive	Conservative
Innocuous	Restrictive	Totalitarian
Innocuous	Liberal	Liberal/Radical
Wrong	Liberal	Liberal/Moderate

Source: Hursthouse 1987.

The totalitarian perspective, indifferent to individual liberties, does not value the idea that women should have the right to choose. Some totalitarian regimes were preoccupied with rapidly increasing the population, while others of stopping population growth, both taking aggressive measures against under- or overpopulation. Therefore, in totalitarian countries, the discussion about the morality and the legality of abortion was never an authentic one.

In the classical conservative view, the fetus is nothing less than an unborn baby. Consequently, abortion constitutes an intentional homicide. For most conservatives, human life starts with conception. This approach is mainly based on two arguments. First, the theological argument, which affirm the existence of the soul before birth. This argument is shared by the Catholic Church and also by philosophers faithful to the Christian doctrine. Among them, Thomas Aquinas considered that the human soul is infused into the fetus in the moment of the creation of its human shape and basic organs. Second, the secular argument against abortion states that, from a moral perspective, there is no significant difference between an unborn baby and a six month old baby.

While the most important goal for moderate liberals is a woman's right to choose (admitting the limitations that ensure against the various negative consequences that may occur), radical liberals base their thinking on the idea that abortion is perfectly similar to an appendectomy. Thereby, there are people who consider the fetus a 'clump of living cells and hence the abortion is merely an operation which removes some part of one's body and hence is morally innocuous' (Hursthouse 1987: p. 27). The extreme liberal view or the most permissive one compares the fetus to a part of the human body that can be destroyed, the fetus having no moral characteristics (similarly to an animal). Consequently, an abortion is morally neutral and should not be more regrettable than killing animals.

4. The Case of Romania

In this section, we analyze how Romanian women, twenty-seven years after the legalization of abortion, perceive this issue, whether from a legal or moral perspective. Before presenting the results, we offer some contextual background to the development of abortion laws and practices in Romania.

When studying abortion, many researchers have cited the Romanian case in their studies (Mureşan 2008: p. 426). As a case study, Romania offers numerous insights, because throughout its history, it has witnessed both the ban and the legalization of abortion. In this sense, it presents data both on legal and illegal abortions, as well as underpinning important aspects regarding how people relate to and address this issue, in terms of perceptions, attitudes and beliefs.

Many factors influence the numbers of abortions that take place in a country: from individual factors (such as a woman's age, education and income, personal beliefs, religious affiliation, the environment of origin, and partner) to more contextual factors, that vary from country to country. Here we include national and local laws governing abortion, women's health insurance, the availability of contraception, sexual education, the state of public as opposed to private health care, the attitude of the medical community, or access to impartial and timely information and counseling (Claeys 2002). Looking at countries throughout the European Union, Claeyes suggests that there is no country where abortion is completely illegal, nor one where it is permitted under all circumstances. However, there are ranges of types of legislation, from the most restrictive to the most liberal.

In the next two sub-sections, we focus on offering contextual data regarding Romania and its special status when it comes to abortion. We present the main legislation regarding abortion, as well as data from national studies that take into account the number of abortions (legal/illegal), fertility rates and maternal deaths that occurred when abortion was illegal.

4.1 Abortion in Romania during the communist regime

Abortion has been a common and widespread form of fertility regulation throughout the formerly socialist countries of Central and Eastern Europe (Johnson, Horga & Andronache, 1996: p. 521). Abortion on request was legalized in the Soviet Union soon after the Czarist period ended in 1920, while in 1936 the abortion law was reversed by Stalin's government and then liberalized again in 1955. Abortion laws in Bulgaria, Hungary, Poland, Romania, and Czechoslovakia were liberalized by the end of the 1950s. However, in the 1960s and 70s, restrictions were reinstated in Romania, Bulgaria, Czechoslovakia and Hungary (Ibid.).

In Romania between 1957 and 1966 abortion on request was legal, and then in 1966 it became restricted. The abortion restrictions decreed in Romania in September 1966 were the most severe in the region (Ibid.). Government Decree 770 limited abortions to women who: had given birth to and raised four or more children; or were over 40 years of age; or suffered from (or had a spouse who suffered from) a severe disease that might be transmitted hereditarily and/or cause severe congenital malformations; or had severe physical, psychological, or sensorial disabilities that would prevent them from caring for the newborn; or whose life was endangered by the pregnancy; or whose pregnancy was the result of rape or incest (Ibid.).

At the same time, several pro-natalist policies were also implemented. These included a ban on contraceptives, the divorce process was lengthened, and later, tax incentives and monetary allocations were given to couples who had children and disincentives were levied on childless couples and unmarried individuals (Ibid.). According to Kligman (1992: p. 264), during the communist regime, the 'marriage' between demographic concerns and nationalist politics turned women's bodies into instruments to be used in the service of the state.

In December 1985, Ceauşescu further restricted access to legal abortion. Having four children was no longer sufficient grounds for abortion on request; to qualify, a woman had to have five living children, all under the age of 18 (David & Baban, 1996: p. 237). He proclaimed that: 'the fetus is the socialist property of the whole society. Giving birth is a patriotic duty. Those who refuse to have children are deserters, escaping the law of natural continuity' (Ibid.). This portrays what we call *the totalitarian position*, one that does not give an inch on women's right to choose, or even on the limits of exercising this right but, indifferent to both, is preoccupied with quickly increasing the population, particularly when the country is underpopulated.

Additionally, employed women between the ages of 16 and 45 were required to undergo regular gynecological examinations and those who refused to appear were told they could lose their right to dental and medical care, pensions, and social security (Ibid.). Self-induced abortion was punishable by imprisonment from six months to two years or by payment of a specified fine. Women known to have had abortions, whether induced or spontaneous, were officially registered at medical dispensaries and examined at three-month intervals to discourage repeated pregnancy terminations (Ibid.). Many women suffering medical complications from clandestine abortions were forced to stay away from hospitals for treatment, thus risking permanent injury to their health or, often, death; while physicians who performed abortions risked prison terms of up to twelve years and loss of the right to practice medicine (Ibid.). Hospitalization for what was called *spontaneous* abortion required police notification and a call to a public prosecutor, followed by a formal inquiry (Ibid.: p. 241). On top of that, a

258

large amount of money was necessary, usually the equivalent of two to three months' salary (Ibid.). It has been reported that 9,452 women died from illegal abortions between 1966 and 1989 (Kligman 1992: p. 406).

Following the 770 Decree, data shows that female mortality increased dramatically. The number of maternal deaths from septic abortion jumped from 64 in 1966 to 173 in 1967, the year after new restrictions were in place, and to 192 in 1968. During the four years from 1969-72 there were only 11 deaths that resulted from legal abortions – less than 1% of all maternal deaths due to abortion (Johnson, Horga & Andronache, 1996: p. 522). Moreover, there were an average of 341 maternal deaths per year from illegal abortion during the 1969-89 period (Ibid.). The maternal mortality rate rose from 86 deaths per 100,000 live births in 1965 to almost 150 in 1984, when 86% of maternal deaths were due to abortion. By 1989, there were 170 maternal deaths per 100,000 live births, ten times higher than the highest figure ever recorded in Europe (David & Baban, 1996: p. 238)

4.2 Abortion in Romania after 1989

In 1989, a year that ended with the collapse of the communist regime and the re-legalization of abortion on request, there were at least 445 maternal deaths attributable to illegal abortion (Johnson, Horga & Andronache, 1996: p. 522). Moreover, in 1990, the rate of maternal deaths due to illegal abortion decreased 67% to 145 (Ibid.). In 1991, there were 789,096 reported abortions on request; that is, nearly three abortions for every live birth (Ibid.: p. 525).

Nowadays, in Romania, abortion can be performed at any time by a gynecologist if it is necessary to save the life, health or bodily integrity of a pregnant woman from serious and imminent danger which cannot be avoided by other means; or if the abortion is necessary for therapeutic reasons and the pregnant woman cannot express her will (WHO 2004). There are no specific laws concerning the sale and distribution of contraceptives and the laws and regulations for drugs in general apply to contraceptives as well. All contraceptives sold in Romania are registered as drugs obtainable by medical prescription (Ibid.).

Below, we present a graph that shows the average number of abortions from 1984 to 2014 in Romania, as compared to the European Union. The data shows that between 1988 and 1992 the average rate of abortion in Romania was at higher levels compared to the European Member States. According to some authors (Johnson, Horga & Andronache, 1996: p. 529), the former ban on information and education about contraception, along with Romania's long history of little or no high-quality contraceptives, has contributed to the recent high rates of abortion. Lack of knowledge of issues related to sexuality and contraception, and the issues regarding access to medical care are also important triggers that affect the rates.

Chart 1: Abortions per 1000 live births in Romania and EU

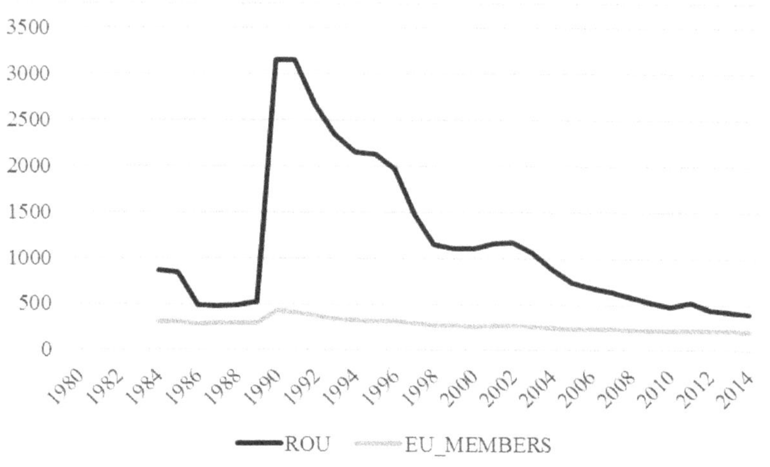

Source: European Health Information Gateway, Abortions per 1000 live births.

The repeal of the law banning abortions on request led to a surge in the number of legal abortions from 109,819 (reported in 1989 as incomplete but including many illegally induced abortions) to 913,973 in 1990. At the same time, maternal deaths due to illegal unsafe abortion decreased from 447 (in 1989) to 142 (Johnson, Horga & Andronache, 1993: p. 875). In this sense, in 1991 there were 789,096 reported legal abortions compared with around 275,000 live births, suggesting that almost three women induced abortions for every live birth (Ibid.: p. 876).

However, during more than ten years of free access to family planning, while the registered number of abortions fell systematically, only in 2004 did it fall for the first time below the number of live births (Mureşan 2008: p. 428). Although modern contraceptive methods are known, most Romanians consider them dangerous to their health (Johnson, Horga & Andronache, 1993); the lack of information on the availability of contraceptive devices and of advisory services in family planning clinics are also contributing factors to this situation. Religious and civic organizations and overall cultural factors are also influential.

As already mentioned, after the downfall of the Ceauşescu regime in December 1989, the new Government of Romania abolished the law that prohibited abortions on request and the policy that forbade the commercial importation of modern contraceptives. This repeal was followed in 1996 by formal legislation which allowed women to freely request a termination of pregnancy within twelve weeks of conception. Beyond twelve weeks gestation, elective abortion can only be performed to preserve the life or physical integrity of the woman, while all abortions must be performed by a gynecologist in an approved institution (Benson, Andersen & Samadari, 2011: p. 3). Moreover, the Romanian government improved family planning and reproductive health policies and services and increased access to safe abortion. Furthermore, in 2000 the Romanian government, with support from USAID and John Snow, Inc., established the Romanian Family Health Initiative, which increased access to family planning and reproductive health services, particularly for vulnerable populations (Ibid.). Subsequently, the rate of legally induced abortions increased significantly while the rate of maternal mortality declined dramatically (Johnson, Horga & Andronache, 1993: p. 875).

Due to the efforts of the Ministry of Health, the World Bank and the Romanian Family Health Initiative, modern contraceptive use steadily increased in Romania from 13.9% in 1993, to 29.5% in 1999 and 38.2% in 2004. Improvements in contraceptive use in rural areas showed a rise from 20.9% in 1999 to 33.0% in 2004, while the abortion rate also declined to a low of 27.1 per 1,000 women in 2006 (Benson, Andersen & Samadari, 2011: p. 3). According to the authors (Ibid.: p. 4) abortion-related mortality continued to decline steadily in subsequent years, as access to safe abortion and comprehensive family planning improved; and by 2006, the overall maternal mortality ratio dropped to 15 per 100,000 live births, and the abortion-related mortality ratio fell to 5 per 100,000 live births.

5. Romanian Women's Perceptions on the Human Body and Abortion

In this section we present the main findings regarding how Romanian women perceive abortion, and implicitly the human body. Here, we try to understand how these perceptions relate to the judicial-ethical perspective.

In order to do so, we conducted an online survey. Online polling has the advantage of offering respondents the possibility to answer directly to questions that are more 'sensitive' or uncomfortable, such as the issue of abortion, by eliminating the presence of the interviewer. In this sense, the study is based on research conducted through an online platform. The data collection method was created with CAWI (Computer Assisted Web Interview), and covered 500 respondents, all women aged 18+ years old, and representative of the Romanian online population. The research was conducted between 27-29 November 2017, on the online panel of Questia Group, an independent Romanian company that conducts online polling. The research has +/- 4% margin of error, at a 95% confidence level. The margin of error takes into account the probability of an individual being a part of the respective sample, and expresses the maximum expected difference between the true population parameter and the sample estimate of that parameter. For results based on the full sample, one can say with 95% confidence that the error attributable to sampling and other random effects is plus or minus the margin of error. The margin of error is larger for results based on subgroups in the survey. Below, we present the main socio-demographical characteristics of the sample.

Table 2: Key sample characteristics
(age, urbanization level, marital status, education)

Characteristic	Percent
Age	
18-24	16.4%
25-34	30.8%
35-44	25.6%
45-54	14.6%
55-64	11.0%
65+	1.6%
Urbanization level	
Rural	12%
Urban	86%
Marital status	
Single	15.4%
Living with my partner	17.8%
Married	57.9%
Divorced	5.6%
Widow	3.2%
Education	
Middle school	1.40%
Professional school	3.81%
High-school	31.26%
Post-secondary school or college	5.61%
University level (Bachelor's Degree)	36.47%
Post-university level (Master's Degree)	19.64%
Ph.D. level	1.20%
Sample size -500; Mean age (years) 37.5; Min. 18, Max. 68	

Source: authors.

The first question we addressed tackled the issue of abortion, euthanasia and cloning (humans/animals) in order to highlight respondents' spontaneous view on abortion in a general context, by comparing other ethical issues. In this sense, respondents were asked whether these issues should be legal or illegal. Abortion was perceived as legal in all cases by more than half of the respondents (67.1%), while euthanasia had mixed approaches, with the proportion of respondents supporting it similar to those who opposed it. On the other hand, opinion on cloning is less polarized, with almost all respondents considering it to be illegal. As previously mentioned, many factors influence opinion on abortion: age, education and income, personal beliefs, religious affiliation, the environment of origin, and knowledge on the issue of prevention (contraceptives), as well as more legal attributes, such as the legislation of a particular country. Here we add previous historical experiences of women, by referring to the communist past.

The second question asked respondents directly how they consider abortion, on a scale from 1 to 5, where 1 means legal in all cases, and 5 means illegal in all cases. Most respondents (77.1%) consider that abortion should be legal in all and in some cases. Those who say abortion should be illegal are generally young married women (18-34), Orthodox, who consider that religion is important to them. In this manner, religion and age play a crucial role in shaping one's perception. Religion imposes a coherent system of norms that aim to facilitate life in society by prohibiting behavior that could be prejudicial for the collective. As mentioned, despite this effort to maintain a certain traditional or parochial order, people relativize and interpret in the service of their own interests not only sexual morals, but all Church teachings.

Chart 2: Women's perspective on abortion, euthanasia and cloning

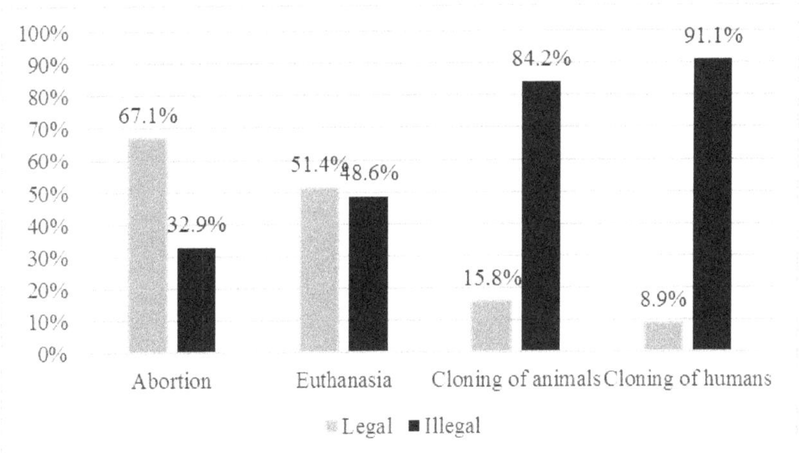

Source: Online polling data, November 2017.

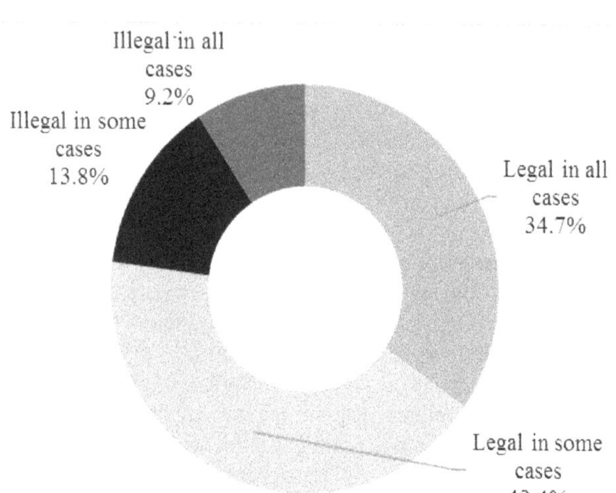

Source: Online polling data, November 2017.

Asked whether they agree or disagree with the statement 'Any woman has control over her body, no matter what decisions she takes', 85.9% said they agree with the statement. This shows that on most issues women view their bodies through a liberal perspective, while perceptions on abortion are connected to one's religious beliefs, age and marital status. Here, we see that most women fall into a moderate liberal category, where one's own deliberate decisions play a more important role than religious beliefs.

Chart 4: Women's perception of the human body

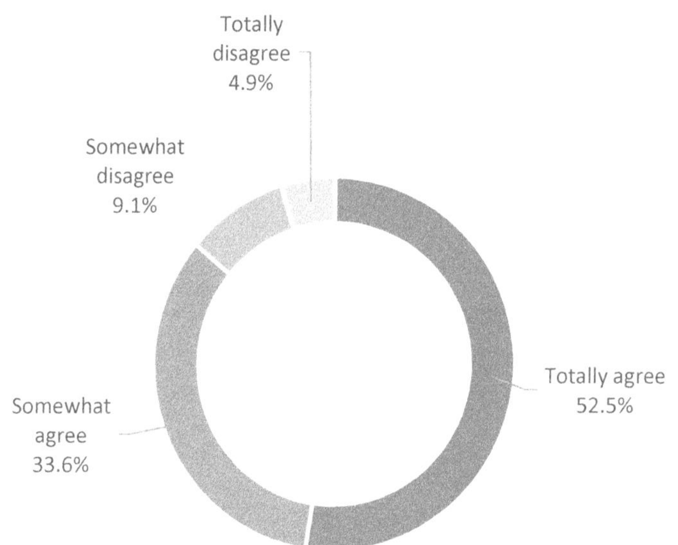

Source: Online polling data, November 2017.

When it comes to assessing whether they agree or disagree with the statement 'There are some situations that morally justify abortion', 84.4% said they agree with this statement. As before, religious beliefs, age and marital status play a significant role when there is disagreement with the statement. This shows that, at least to some extent, the negative implication of the previous illegality of abortion during communism seems to have diffused among the younger generation. In this sense, the experience of communist and post-communist history is starting to play a more marginal role in how women perceive abortion.

Chart 5: Women's perception of the morality of abortion

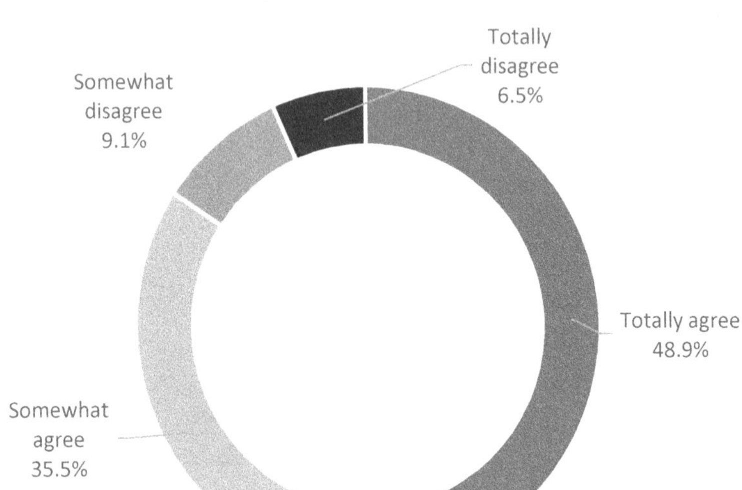

Source: Online polling data, November 2017.

Quite interestingly, when asked whether they agree or disagree with the statement 'Abortion is murder', more than half (64.1%) said they agree. In this case, religion plays a significant role in assessing women's perceptions on abortion. In the sample, 88.2% of the respondents consider that religion plays an important role in their life. The respondents' religious affiliation influences their perceptions on abortion positively from a legal standpoint, but negatively from a religious perspective. This finding best highlights the theoretical aspects presented in the first part of the chapter, in the relationship between legal and ethical perspectives and the tensions that arise from these approaches.

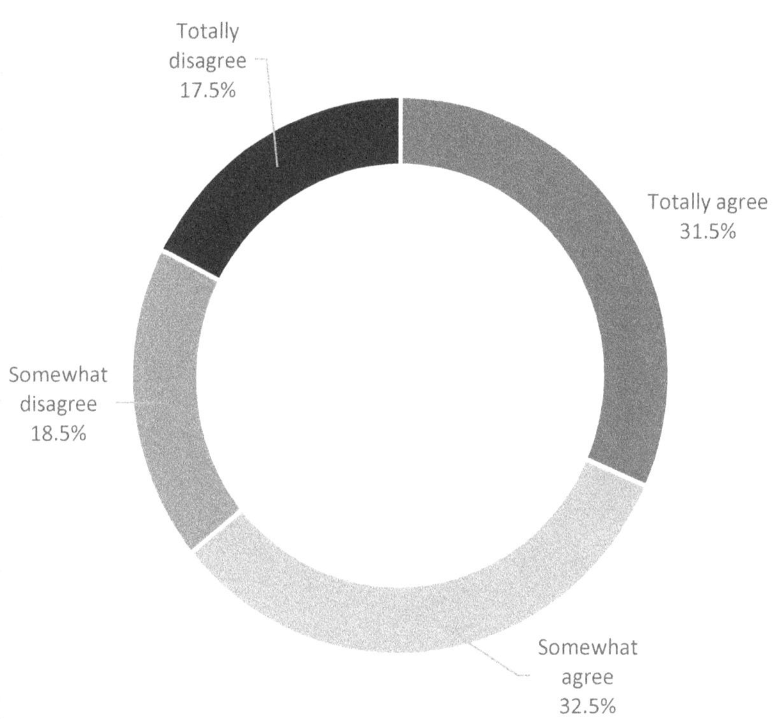

Source: Online polling data, November 2017.

Asked whether they know someone in their social circle who has had an abortion, 80.2% said they did. This data further portrays what we have presented in the contextual part about Romania, i.e., that abortion was and continues to be a common issue for Romanian women. In some previous studies (1993, 1996) Johnson, Horga & Andronache showed that most women said that it was very rare for a woman not to have at least one abortion in her lifetime. In this sense, in their study 47% of the women said that they had had a previous legally induced abortion and 25% reported having had a previous illegal abortion (Johnson, Horga & Andronache, 1993: p. 876). Since 1993, the abortion rate has come closer to that of other

European Union Member States, generally showing that women are better informed about contraceptives.

**Chart 7: Women's declared knowledge that a woman
in their social circle that has been through an abortion**

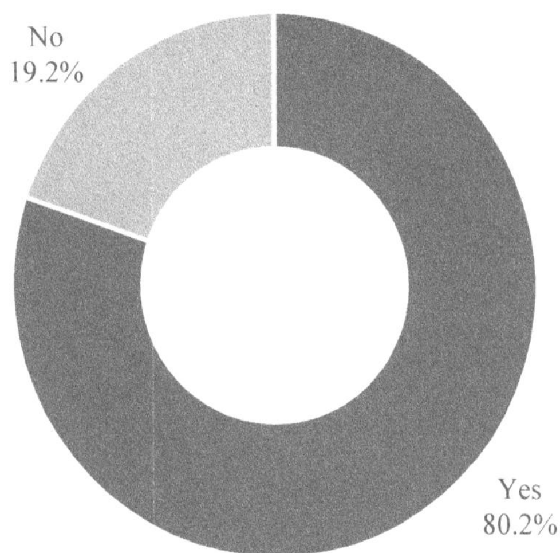

Source: Online polling data, November 2017.

Finally, we wanted to find out what women's attitudes about some other issues were, such as contraceptives, sex education and family planning. In this sense, almost all respondents agreed to the statements regarding contraceptives: the fact that women should be able to afford what contraceptives they want and that there should be more awareness campaigns about contraceptive methods. Sex education and family planning are also considered priorities that could enhance women's health. Therefore, data shows that women value modern contraception, information and counseling instead of abortion. This is in line with previous studies conducted in Romania (Johnson, Horga & Andronache, 1993: p. 875). Women need a wide choice of dependably available high-quality contraceptives; they need to be able to obtain information, counseling, and methods from a wide range of sources/health-care providers (Ibid.). As the above authors point out, women's positive perceptions about sex education and contraceptives, in contrast to their negative perceptions on abortion (as a 'murder', see above) highlight the fact that religion plays an important effect on their attitudes related to abortion.

Chart 8: Women's attitudes towards contraceptives
and sexual education

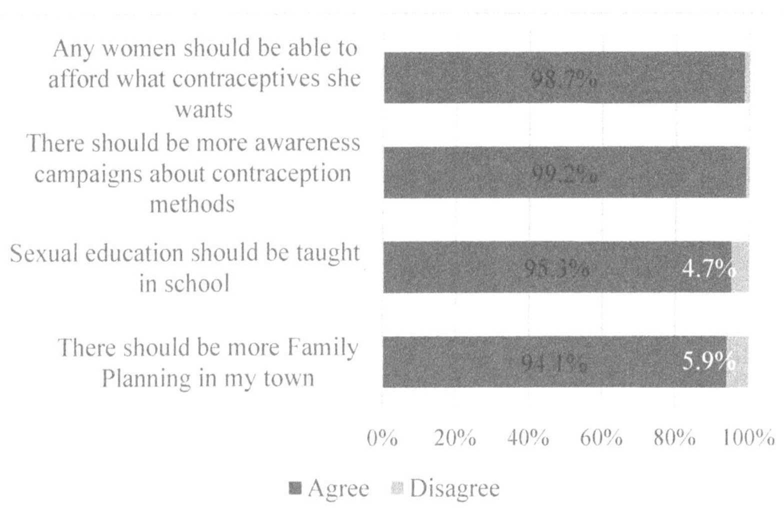

Source: Online polling data, November 2017.

6. Conclusions

The topic of the human body is appropriate for many theoretical debates, ranging from anthropology and sociology to political science, because it rightfully belongs to the analysis of human identity. Without the body, which offers an individual a face, human beings would not exist (Le Breton 2009: p. 10). The social and cultural amendments that the body is subjected to shows us the numerous values, images and definitions that the human body takes. Because it is situated at the center of individual and collective action, and of social symbolism, the body is an important concept in how we understand our societies, in present time.

Our conceptions of the body highly depend on numerous factors, from the rise of individualism as a social structure, to rational positive and secular thinking about nature, local traditions, and the history of medicine, philosophy and law. In our chapter, we tried to offer a perspective that combines judicial and philosophical approaches to the human body, as well as offer a model in order to understand how they affect women's perceptions, in the case of Romania. By choosing this country, which witnessed very different approaches to the human body pre- and post-1989, we highlighted how the state deliberates and how it shapes women's perceptions regarding the issue of abortion. Moreover, we also analyzed how these changes shape women's perspectives of their own bodies in today's society.

Firstly, we started our inquiry with the consideration that, in accordance with the principles of juridical ethics, the human body is unassailable and inviolable because the body and the person form a single whole, and therefore they are inseparable. Moreover, by following Lemennicier's approach (1991), we pointed out some important weaknesses of current judicial ethics and discussed the specific issue of abortion. Finally, we addressed the views that combine Law with Morality, trying to emphasize the difficulty of separating them. We showed that, when it comes to abortion, the judicial and the moral norms do not always dovetail. We summarized three types of perspectives on abortion, taking into account the moral, the legal and the ideological criteria. Having described the theoretical framework, we presented how the Romanian state deliberated in the case of women's bodies in two political regimes: the communist one (1947-1989) and the democratic one (1989 - onwards). Between 1957 and 1966 abortion on request was legal, and then in 1966 it became restricted, only to become legal again after 1989. Abortion restrictions imposed by the Ceaușescu government had a devastating effect on women's lives, as evidenced by extremely high rates of mortality and women's admissions of inhibited sexual relations and increased family tensions (Johnson, Horga & Andronache, 1996: p. 528). Moreover, the changes in the legislation after 1989 had tremendous influence on the abortion rate and subsequently on how women relate to their bodies. By identifying attitudes to abortion from a moral perspective we could better understand how women relate to abortion and implicitly to their bodies.

The findings are in line with what we know about those factors which affect women's perceptions when it comes to abortion. Some of the factors that play an important role are related to age, education, income, personal beliefs, religious affiliation, the environment of origin, and a woman's partner, as well as national and local laws governing abortion, public policies, the level of health insurance, the availability of contraception, and sex education, as well as the medical community's attitudes. In Romania, factors such as age, religion and, to some extent, women's perceptions and the realities of the communist past shape their current opinion on abortion. Generally, women fall into the category of a moderate liberal perspective on how they relate to their bodies and the issue of abortion. Tensions rise when taking up position between the legal and ethical perspectives on abortion, in which age, religious affiliation, education and marital status play their role:

young (25-44), somewhat religious women, with higher education (B.A or M.A level) and married fall into the liberal category. However, young married women (18-34), who declare that they are Orthodox, and consider that religion is important to them, have adopted negative perceptions on this issue. Moreover, when it comes to this particular sub-group, the negative implication of the previous illegality of abortion during communism seems to have diffused. This points to a rather interesting perspective and positions numerous questions that future studies should tackle. How much do previous social, economic and cultural norms affect women's attitudes towards abortion? Are past institutions still a strong predictor of today's perceptions? Are there similar trends regarding women's perceptions of abortion in the Central and Eastern European region? Tackling the specificities of geographical, legal and cultural dimensions, together with socio-demographical attributes could offer numerous highlights in understanding, in a holistic approach, women's knowledge, perceptions and attitudes about their bodies.

Acknowledgments

Some theoretical parts of this chapter were previously published: Andreea Zamfira (2010), 'What Rights do People have over their Own Body? A Discussion about Jurisprudence, Private Law, Rational Choice and Bioethics', *Sfera Politicii*, XVIII (4/146): pp. 31-46.

Bibliography

Benson, Janie, Kathryn Andersen & Ghazaleh Samadari (2011) 'Reductions in Abortion-Related Mortality Following Policy Reform: Evidence from Romania, South Africa and Bangladesh', *Reproductive Health*, 8(39): 1-12.

Bourdieu, Pierre (1980) *Le sens pratique*, Paris: Minuit.

Canto-Sperber, Monique (2002) 'Séparer droit et pensée morale. La question de l'avortement', *Res Publica*, Vol. 'Bioéthique et éthique médicale', Hors série, 1.

Canto-Sperber, Monique (2001) *L'inquiétude morale et la vie humaine*, Paris: Presses Universitaire de France.

Claeys, Vicky (2002) *Abortion Legislation in Europe*, 7th Congress of the ESC, Online. Available www.escrh.eu/sites/escrh.eu/files/g6.ablegislation.ppt (accessed October 2017).

David, Henry P. & Adriana Baban (1996) 'Women's Health and Reproductive Rights: Romanian Experience', *Patient Education and Counseling*, 28(3): 235-245.

European Health Information Gateway (2016) Online. Available
    https://gateway.euro.who.int/en/indicators/hfa_586-7010-abortions-per-1000-
    live-births/ (accessed October 2017).
Hursthouse, Rosalind (1987) *Beginning lives*, New York: Basil Blackwell.
Johnson, Brooke, Mihai Horga & Laurentia Andronache (1996) 'Women's
    Perspectives on Abortion in Romania', *Social Science & Medicine*, 42(4): 521-
    530.
Johnson, Brooke, Mihai Horga & Laurentia Andronache (1993) 'Contraception and
    Abortion in Romania', *The Lancet*, 341(8849): 875-78.
Kant, Immanuel ([1785] 1949) *Fundamental Principles of the Metaphysic of Morals*,
    translated from German by Thomas K. Abbott, introduction by Marvin Fox,
    Indianapolis, NY: Bobbs-Merrill.
Kligman, Gail (1992) 'Abortion and International Adoption in Post-Ceauşescu
    Romania', *Feminist Studies*, 18(2): 405-419.
Laurin, Nicole (2001) 'Si l'Église cessait d'interdire', *Relations*, 671: 20-22.
Le Breton, David (2009) *Antropologia corpului si modernitatea*, Cartier: Chişinău.
Lemennicier, Bertrand (1991) 'Le corps humain: propriété de l'État ou propriété de
    soi?', *Droits*, 13: 112-116.
Mureşan, Cornelia (2008) 'Impact of Induced Abortion on Fertility in Romania',
    European Journal of Population/Revue Européenne de Démographie, 24(4):
    425-446.
World Health Organization (2004) *Abortion and Contraception in Romania A
    Strategic Assessment of Policy, Programme and Research Issues.* Online.
    Available http://apps.who.int/iris/bitstream/10665/43113/1/9739953166.pdf
    (accessed November 2017).

PART FOUR

SOCIAL, POLITICAL AND INSTITUTIONAL CONSTRAINTS ON WOMEN

CHAPTER XIII

The Influence of Academic Self-concept on the Study Program Choice of Computer Scientists

Silvia FÖRTSCH and Ute SCHMID

1. Introduction

Gender and gender relations are not seen as a natural phenomenon, but as a predominant social phenomenon, which is constructed by social and cultural practices and structures. A deterministic relation between biological gender and gender role in society cannot be established. Biological gender is generally fixed. However, the term gender refers to a socially and culturally shaped identity that can also be changed (Frey, Rosenthal & Väth, 2004: pp. 11ff). Gender is a social practice that takes place or not. This fact makes it necessary and interesting to carry out gender studies.

Gender studies look at the diversity between 'male' and 'female'. The image of masculinity and femininity is analysed in the sense of stereotypical perceptions. The aspect of the importance of gender, which is addressed to one gender within society and the cultural field, plays a major role. At the same time, gender role conflicts are produced, which are felt more by women than by men (Rustemeyer & Thrien, 2001: pp. 34-35). Gender studies are able to discover the mechanisms which lead to gender differences. We can recognize gender differences in many areas, for example in education, in the choice of study courses and careers, in the labor market, and within the family, etc. (Lenzen et al., 2009).

This chapter deals with the choice of study program within the male connoted field of computer science in Germany, specifically at the University of Bamberg. It is assumed that gender differences are to be found. Of course, different occupational fields and study programs have different gender-typical images. The image of the occupational profile depends on the male and female rate in the professional field as well as those male and female characteristics which are associated with the profession. In addition to the image of the professional field and to the gender fit, the personal abilities and characteristics of men and women play an important role in choosing the study program (Lenzen et al., 2009: p. 35). It is a fact that women continue to be under-represented in computer science in Germany (Kempf 2012). Furthermore, the low proportion of women in computer science influences the deficit of skilled workers. In Germany, 43,000 IT-specialists are currently missing (Bitkom 2015).

The lack of qualified professionals in the field of computer science is a topic of focus that affects more than the economy. Government-controlled measures to counteract the current lack of qualified personnel have not led to the desired results. Women in particular have benefited from the expansion of education during the last century, which began in Germany in the 1960s. Furthermore, the proportion of women in the field of computer science is increasing. In 1997, the rate of female students in computer science was 18.5%. However, in 2014, the rate of female students was 22.4% (Statistisches Bundesamt 2015)[1]. Nevertheless, specialists are still missing.

The possible causes and factors influencing the situation are manifold. One reason is that computer science is perceived as a male dominated area (Broy, Denert & Engeser, 2008: pp. 619-628). Furthermore, there is a lack of qualified female managers who represent female role models. The path leading to the field of computer science is more difficult for women, due to this absence of female role models. Therefore, young women have problems in identifying with this career field. They are in conflict with their gender self-image. In addition, they have no confidence in their academic performance, which is necessary when studying computer science. According to our findings, a high self-concept is directly related to high academic performance (Hannover 2007: p. 16).

The following analysis examines how gender differences in behavior influence choosing a degree program in computer science. This is due to stereotypical perceptions, different self-concepts and factors that usually affect the importance of gender in special situations.

The main objectives of this research project were to examine whether there are gender differences with regard to the choice of degree program in computer science, as well as in academic achievement and motivational aspects. Numerous studies confirm that women underrate their academic abilities, particularly in mathematics, in contrast to men (Skorepa & Fuhrmann, 2009: pp. 191-199; Hannover 2007: p. 16; Zimmer, Burba & Rost, 2004: pp. 218-222; Kessels 2002: pp. 21ff; Hannover & Bettge, 1993: pp. 1-170; Heatherington et al., 1993: pp. 739-745). Spatial visualization and mathematical competence in particular are areas where consistent gender differences can be found (Quaiser-Pohl 2012: p. 216). The results from the Bavarian Baccalaureate (the Abitur examination) from 2011, 2012 and 2013 show that girls received a better average high school finale grade than boys. However, their average high school grade in mathematics was lower (Bavarian State Ministry of Education and Culture 2013).

---

1   German Federal Statistical Office.

2. Theoretical Framework and Empirical Implications

2.1 Theoretical background and state of research

Previous research has also demonstrated the relationship between academic self-concept, academic achievement and course selection. Additional factors influencing the choice of degree program are also socioeconomic factors, professional interest and motivational aspects (Abel 2002: pp. 192-201; Guggenberger 1991: pp. 88 ff. and 129 ff.). Academic achievement and academic self-concept are analyzed with the theoretical background of the Internal/External Frame of Reference Model (Marsh 1986: pp. 129-149). An important part of this model is the development of an academic self-concept on the basis of internal and external academic performance comparisons. When using the Internal Frame of Reference Model, academic achievements are compared in various school subjects. Those who perform better in German than in mathematics evaluate their academic skills in mathematics lower because their grades in German are better, for example. The External Frame of Reference Model compares the performance between people in a specific domain, for example in mathematics (Marsh 1986: pp. 129-149). Marsh and colleagues argue that an academic self-concept is determined by students' Frame of Reference. Thus students underestimate their academic achievement because they compare their abilities with the top of their peer group.

Köller et al. (2006) reported that in addition to a high or low academic self-concept other factors pertain, such as motivational aspects, professional interests, and the impact of an academic career (Hachmeister, Harde & Langer, 2007: p. 55; Köller et al., 2006: pp. 27-39). A questionnaire organized by the Higher Education Information System (HIS) confirmed the findings that intrinsic, extrinsic and social motives influence the choice of degree program (Heine et al., 2005: pp. 129-141). Intrinsic motives, over and above extrinsic motives and social motives, are an influencing factor for 50% of both men and women. In this context, the question to be addressed is how motivational aspects, mindsets, expectations, and goals influence the choice of degree program? The answer is that gender plays an important role in all these elements of subjective evaluation processes (Deaux & LaFrance, 1998: pp. 788-827). Gender differences in the behavior of men and women are determined by the following: gender stereotypes (Steele 1997: pp. 613-629), one's own knowledge of oneself, and factors which can generally influence the significance of gender in special situations. Also self- and external-perception has a significant impact on academic achievement. Therefore, it is possible that a negative self-assessment leads to poorer career opportunities (Deaux & LaFrance, 1998: pp. 788-827).

2.2 Research questions and hypotheses

While the research on the validity and reliability of the Internal/External Frame of Reference Model, as well as other theoretical models, are valuable and the reports on the predictors of motivational aspects are interesting, there is a lack of research that focuses on the academic self-concept and academic achievement of students enrolled in computer science programs. Based on these theoretical assumptions, as well as the implications of the empirical results and the specifications of the male-dominated area of computer science, the following research questions have been investigated by analyzing students' academic self-concept and their choice of degree program in the field of computer science at the University of Bamberg[2]: 1. Are there differences between male and female students studying computer science with regard to their academic self-concept? 2. Is there a relationship between the self-concept of individual students and their specific objectives and expectations? 3. Is there a difference between male and female students?

Overall, it is assumed that students studying computer science achieve good academic results, particularly in mathematics. Based on gender stereotypical discrimination, female students show poorer performance in maths. In compliance with Köller et al. (2006: pp. 27-39), an additional assumption is that the decision to enroll in computer science programs that focus either more heavily on the technical aspects or less depends on the performance-rating in mathematics and the individual's own motives. It is assumed that more male students in comparison with female students choose a strong technically-oriented degree program in computer science even with an average performance in mathematics. Women choose a more technically-oriented degree program only if they have an above-average final high school grade in mathematics. In this way, internal and external performance comparisons lead to paradoxical conclusions regarding talent (Möller 1999: pp. 11-17). In the male-dominated field of computer science, students show high performance in their course of study. Female students underestimate their academic achievement, because they compare their abilities with the top of their peer group. Based on the theoretical models discussed the following hypotheses are formulated:

1. It is assumed that the academic performance of male and female students is different in computer science.
2. In terms of the motivational aspects for enrolling in their chosen degree program male and female students differ.
3. It is also assumed that students choose their degree program based on internal and external comparisons and motivational aspects.

---

2 Otto-Friedrich-Universität Bamberg.

Generally, the better the academic performance, the higher the academic self-concept of a person. Women also benefit from their academic performance. When attaining a high academic performance in mathematics, they more often than men choose a degree program that focuses more heavily on technical aspects.

3. Research Method and Operationalization

3.1 Research method

This article aims to shed light on the research questions by utilizing a data source unique to Germany, namely the Bamberg Alumnae Tracking Study. This study offers detailed information on students and graduates of the Faculty of Information Systems and Applied Computer Sciences at Bamberg University. For the purpose of this article, which aims to investigate gendered specific choice of study program and academic self- concept in computer sciences, we make use of the students' subsample of the Bamberg Alumnae Tracking Study[3].

The sample for the survey of students was conducted in two waves. The first questionnaire was conducted in 2013 with a return rate of 18.59% (116 out of 624 students) and the second questionnaire was conducted in 2014 with a return rate of 13.07% (106 out of 811 students). Descriptive statistics, Wilcoxon rank-sum test and regression analysis were used to analyze the data (Long 1997: pp. 34ff.).

3.2 Operationalization

In this survey the reasons for studying computer science were determined by the following question: What role did the following reasons play for you when choosing to study computer science? The possible answers included motivational aspects such as intrinsic, extrinsic and social motives. In addition, academic self-concept and academic achievement were analyzed.

---

3   The research period was from 10.01.2012 to 03.31.2015. Alumnae Tracking researched the life and career paths of women in the Faculty of Information Systems and Applied Computer Science at the University of Bamberg (Otto-Friedrich Universität Bamberg).The project was funded by The European Social Fund; the Bavarian State Ministry of Employment and Social Order, the Family and Women ; and the Technology Alliance of Upper Franconia. Online. Available:
[https://www.uni-bamberg.de/wiai/gremien/frauenbeauftragte/projekte/alumnaetracking/].

Academic self-concept was constructed by analyzing the final average grade in mathematics received in high school and the final average grade received in high school. The following table gives an overview of the operationalization:

Table 1: Operationalization of socio-demographic variables and theoretical constructs

Theoretical construct	Operationalization	Scale/Characteristics
Socio-demographic variables		
Gender	Gender	Male
		Female
Year of birth	Age	19-32
Skills		
Objective assessment	Mathematics grade	1.0 to 6.0; dichotomized
	High School final grade	1.0 to 6.0; dichotomized
Motivational aspects		
Extrinsic motives	Income	5-point Likert-scale (1: not any role; 5: very important role); dichotomized
	Reconciling career and family life	5-point Likert-scale (1: not any role; 5: very important role); dichotomized
	Career opportunities	5-point Likert-scale (1: not any role; 5: very important role); dichotomized
	Secure field of work	5-point Likert-scale (1: not any role; 5: very important role); dichotomized
Intrinsic motives	Aptitude for the subject	5-point Likert-scale (1: not any role; 5: very important role); dichotomized
	Professional interest	5-point Likert-scale (1: not any role; 5: very important role); dichotomized
Social motive	Opportunity to help other people	5-point Likert-scale (1: not any role; 5: very important role); dichotomized
Choice of study program **Bachelor's and Master's Degree Programs**		
Strong technically oriented program	Bachelor Applied Computer science	Nominal
	Bachelor Software System Science	Nominal
	Master Applied Computer science	Nominal
Less technical oriented program	Bachelor International Information Systems	Nominal

	Managements	
	Minor subject Applied Computer Science	Nominal
	Master Education in Business and Information Systems	Nominal
	Master Computing in the Humanities	Nominal
Information Systems	Bachelor Information Systems	Nominal
	Master Information Systems	Nominal

Source: authors' analysis of data from Alumnae Tracking, 2015.

4. Results

Table 2 shows the results of the Wilcoxon rank-sum test for males and females regarding high school final grade, mathematics final grade and motivational aspects. The different sample sizes are based on 'Non response' for this item. The results were rounded. The significant level */**/*** is of 10/5/1%.

Table 2: Results of the Wilcoxon rank-sum test on gender and academic performance as well as motivational aspects for all students in computer science

Sample size	Academic performance	Motivational aspects	Male $\bar{x}$	Female $\bar{x}$	WRS-Test	p-value
n=211 (men=133)	Mathematics final grade		2.25	2.28	-0.409	0.68
n=203 (men=129)	High school final grade		2.40	2.18	2.037	0.04**
n=215 (men=136)		Income	3.94	3.86	0.611	0.54
n=214 (men=135)		Reconciling career and family life	2.63	2.77	-0.775	0.44
n=214 (men=136)		Career opportunities	3.84	3.94	-0.788	0.43
n=215 (men=136		Secure field of work	3.70	3.67	-0.016	0.99
n=214 (men=136)		Aptitude for the subject	3.90	3.53	3.262	0.001***

| n=215 (men=136) | | Professional interest | 4.29 | 4.23 | 0.706 | 0.48 |
| n=214 (men=136) | | Opportunity to help other people | 2.74 | 2.78 | -0.379 | 0.70 |

Source: authors' analysis of data from Alumnae Tracking, 2015.

With regard to the overall academic performance of undergraduates in computer science, gender differences can be found. Therefore, hypothesis 1 and 2 (see above) are partially supported. A statistically significant result is found for high school final grade at the 5% level (average men 2.40 vs. average women 2.18; n=203; U= 2.037; p = 0.04**). Female students have a better average final grade in high school than male students. This result is congruent with findings from the Bavarian State Ministry of Education and Culture, Science and Art[4] (2013) in 2011, 2012 and 2013. Furthermore, the intrinsic motive 'Aptitude for the subject' shows a significant outcome level (average men 3.90 vs. average women 3.53; n=214; U= 3.262; p = 0.001***). This motivational aspect was considered to be more important to men than women. It is also interesting to note that male and female students consider the motivational aspect 'Professional interest' as particularly important (average men 4.29 vs. average women 4.23; n=215; U= 0.706; p = 0.48). The present data suggest that intrinsic and extrinsic motives are more important than social aspects in choosing a degree program in computer science. The results are comparable with the values found by Köller et al. (2006: 27-39).

In Table 3 the results of the Wilcoxon rank-sum test on gender and academic performance in relation to the choice of a degree program in computer science are shown.

Table 3: Results of the Wilcoxon rank-sum test on gender and academic performance in choosing a degree program of computer science

Study program	Sample size	Academic performance	Male $\bar{x}$	Female $\bar{x}$	WRS-Test	p-value
Less technically oriented bachelor program	n= 22 (men=12)	Mathematics final grade	2.75	2.4	0.380	0.70
	n= 22 (men=12)	High school final grade	2.58	2.2	1.174	0.24
Strong technically oriented bachelor program	n= 51 (men=34)	Mathematics final grade	2.35	2.06	0.731	0.46
	n= 47 (men=32)	High school final grade	2.25	1.93	1.114	0.11

---

4   Bayerisches Staatsministerium für Bildung und Kultus, Wissenschaft und Kunst.

Bachelor information systems	n= 45 (men=33)	Mathematics final grade	2.0	2.25	-0.620	0.54
	n= 46 (men=34)	High school final grade	2.53	2.67	-1.344	0.18

Source: authors' analysis of data from Alumnae Tracking, 2015.

When examining the outcome there is no significant influence regarding gender differences, but the findings are still interesting. Women with high academic achievement seldom choose the information systems study program. However, the men enrolled in this degree program have a better final grade in mathematics than those in a less technical or strongly technical study program. Taking into account the small sample size the data must always be interpreted carefully.

Multinomial logistic regression was used to analyze the relationships between choosing a degree program in computer science and academic self-concept, as well as motivational factors (Table 4).

Table 4: Estimation results of the multinomial logistic regression for choosing to enroll in a computer science program, and interaction effects for gender and mathematics final grade

	Model 1		Model 2	
Less technically oriented Bachelor program (4)				
Women (1)	**0.591**	(0.699)	0.650	(0.705)
Age	**0.828**	(0.113)	0.835	(0.105)
Skills				
Mathematics final grade (2)	**0.120****	(0.117)	0.158*	(0.145)
High school final grade (2)	**1.97646**	(1.439)	2.160	(1.471)
Extrinsic motives				
Income (3)	**1.759**	(2.095)		
Reconciling career and family life (3)	**3.618****	(2.378)	2.999*	(1.849)
Career opportunities (3)	**1.220**	(1.339)		
Intrinsic motives				
Aptitude for the subject (3)	**2.373**	(1.830)		
Secure field of work (3)	**0.416**	(0.343)		
Professional interest (3)	**3.94e+07**	(4.82e+10)	79152	(5.88e+09)
Social motive				
Opportunity to help other people (3)	**4.342***	(3.338)	2.787*	(1.927)

Interaction Women (1) x Mathematics final grade (2	**3,147**	(-4621)	4,484	(-6.122)
Constant	**8.95e-07**	(0.001)	5.00e-06	(0.003)
Strong technically oriented Bachelor program (4)				
Women (1)	**0.586****	(0.734)	0.754**	(0.852)
Age	**0.756****	(0.090)	0.767**	(0.090)
Skills				
Mathematics final grade (2)	**0.618*****	(0.561)	0.709***	(0.599)
High school final grade (2)	**8.409*****	(6.133)	7.180***	(4.771)
Extrinsic motives				
Income	**0.370**	(0.376)		
Reconciling career and family life (3)	**5.536*****	(3.248)	5.236***	-2,900
Career opportunities (3)	**1.451**	(1.287)		
Intrinsic motives				
Aptitude for the subject (3)	**1.335**	(0.912)		
Secure field of work (3)	**0.314**	(0.226)		
Professional interest (3)	**6.448****	(5.966)	5.897**	(4.917)
Social motive				
Opportunity to help other people (3)	**5.254****	(3.654)	4.000**	(2.486)
Interaction Women (1) x Mathematics final grade (2	**20.182****	(-29252)	32.700**	-44,547
Constant	**208.755**	(602.074)	52.187	(139.948)
Log.Like.	**-80,963**		-87,472	
Iterations	**10**		9	
Pseudo-r2	**0.2922**		0.2521	
*/**/*** significant at 10/5/1% level				
Number of observations = 109				

Source: data from Alumnae Tracking, Student Survey first and second wave; Odds Ratios shown; SE in brackets. Reference categories: (1) Men; (2) average/low achievement; (3) less important; (4) Information Systems Bachelor program.

Model 1 includes the predictor variables for academic performance and all variables which reflect motivational aspects. Due to the small number of observations, the first model was reduced to statistically significant variables. This method is called 'Backward Selection' (Nold 2014: pp. 111-114). After the initial estimate, non-significant variables were excluded. However, only the first and last model is plotted. In both model 1 and 2, there are interaction-effects. All results are displayed in Relative Risk Ratios (RRR). Values greater than 1 represent a higher chance of choosing a less technically oriented or strong technically oriented degree program than a program in information systems. Values between 0 and 1 indicate a lower chance of choosing a degree program mentioned above.

In view of the results presented, it can be concluded that women are significantly less likely than men to choose a Bachelor program that focuses heavily on technical aspects, and choose information systems instead (sig. at 5% level). Students with a high performance in mathematics are significantly more likely to study information systems than a less technical or strongly technical Bachelor program (sig. at 1% and 5% level). The effect of the mathematics final grade on choosing a less technically oriented course in model 2 is slightly weaker than in model 1 (sig. at 10% level). These findings can be attributed to the high rate of men in the sample.

Moreover, an above average final grade in high school was significant for students enrolled in a strong technically oriented program (sig. at 1% level). Interest in enrolling in a strongly technical program decreases with student age (sig. at 5% level). This outcome is attributed to the high fluctuation between programs of studies in computer science. For example, after completing a bachelor's degree in applied computer science, students choose the less technical oriented master program like International Information Systems Management.

Additionally, in models 1 and 2, motivational aspects are considered. It can be observed that the extrinsic motive to reconcile career and family life, is significantly more important for students enrolled in both strong and less technical programs of study than it is for students in information systems. This is also true for the social motive of the ability to help others through their chosen profession. It should be noted that in model 2 the effect is slightly weaker for persons who are enrolled in a less technically oriented course (sig. 10%). Also, intrinsic motive, such as professional interest, is significantly relevant for undergraduates in a strong technically oriented program (sig. 5%).

The integration of interaction-effects confirms the hypothesis that the effects of gender are bound to academic self-concept and academic achievement, because the interaction-effects in model 1 and 2 are significant at an intermediate level. This means that those women who demonstrate a high academic performance in mathematics are, in comparison to men, significantly more likely to study a computer science program that is strongly technically oriented than they are to study information systems.

5. Discussion and Conclusion

This study analyzed the choice of study program in computer science at the University of Bamberg for the first time. The analysis will help in understanding the academic self-concept of women and their motivation for choosing a study program in computer science.

The analysis is concerned with the question how gender differences in behavior influence the choice of a degree program in computer science, which are due to stereotypical perceptions, different self-concepts and factors that usually affect the importance of gender in special situations. The main objective of this chapter is to find out whether there are gender differences with regard to the choice of degree program in computer science, as well as aspects of academic achievement and individual motivation. In doing so, the reasons for the underrepresentation of women in the field of computer science may be identified. Certainly, the discussed results should be interpreted carefully due to the small sample and the low proportion of women in the sample. In order to be able to make a general statement about the stated hypotheses, a larger sample size is required. Within the framework of the research project, further survey waves are planned to get deeper insights.

In the primary analysis, we took a look at the following research question: What are the differences between male and female students studying computer science with regard to their academic self-concept? The descriptive findings show that male and female students differ in their general academic self-concept, as women have significantly better average grades in high school. This result is in line with earlier studies conducted by the Bavarian State Ministry of Education and Culture, Science and Art[5] (2013).

However, there were no significant gender differences with regard to high school final grades in mathematics. This is due to students being aware of the fact that an above average grade in high school in mathematics is necessary if one is interested in studying computer science. According to Eccles (2007: pp. 199-210), the gender gap is attributed to a lack of information and not to the differences in academic self-concept.

Based on these results, it could be assumed that women should have a high academic self-concept. Female and male students who study computer science certainly choose such a program only if they have an above average grade in mathematics. Good performance in mathematics is especially important for women enrolled in a strong technically oriented degree program.

---

5   Bayerisches Staatsministerium für Bildung und Kultus, Wissenschaft und Kunst.

By using multinomial regression and the control of sociodemographic and motivational aspects, an analysis was carried out as to whether academic self-concept influences choosing a study program in computer science. The aspect of gender leads to a significant result. Compared to men, women have a significantly lower likelihood of choosing a strong technically oriented degree program than of choosing information systems. These findings can be linked to an absence of female role models (Hannover 2007: pp. 54-56). Similar to the findings of a study conducted by Broy et al. (2008) women recognized that a strong technically study program of computer science was a male dominated area which did not correspond to their gender-specific self-image (Broy 2008: pp. 619-628). However, the interaction-effect shows that women in strong technically oriented study programs are convinced of their academic self-concept and demonstrated a high performance in mathematics. They are, as compared to men, more interested in studying a strong technically oriented program of computer science. The interest and motivation to study a program of computer science is so high that negative stereotypes are being overcome. The mechanism of stereotypes is resolved (Steele 1997: pp. 613-629).

Nevertheless, it seems that women are very much interested in careers. They prefer information systems study programs over strong technical study programs. In the area of information systems, career opportunities are seen as very good, because the income is high.

Moreover it seems that women, rather than men, choose their degree program based on internal and external comparisons. Men opt for a strong technically oriented program even with a lower academic performance in mathematics. For male students, the priority lies rather in a professional interest for the subject. Regarding all study programs of computer science, it is assumed that women have a lower academic self-concept, even though they have a better average in their academic achievements.

In addition to academic self-concept, motivational factors also explain the reason for choosing a program of study in computer science. This result agrees with earlier studies (Hachmeister et al., 2007: p. 55; Köller et al., 2006: pp. 37-39; Heine et al., 2005: pp. 129-141). The analyses of multinomial logistic regression show that those students who enrolled in a degree program that focuses both more heavily and less heavily on the technical aspects of computer science, also focus more on the social goal of helping others through their chosen tant for them. In their future careers they would like to be able to reconcile work and family life. Based on this it can be interpreted that students who enrolled in a either stronger or less technical program are more interested in work life-balance than in career opportunities. Furthermore, it is possible that the students sampled are aware that those with a computer science degree focusing heavily on technical aspects will receive better offers from companies, as there is a lack of professionals in the field of computer science.

On the whole, the overall academic performance of women is higher. However, the impression remains that they have less confidence with regard to their academic self-concept. The question that arises is how we can motivate women to study computer science if they have an interest in this field. First, it is necessary that parents and teachers provide positive feedback for good academic achievement, starting in pre-school, continuing in elementary school and all through high school. In this way girls can learn to rate their academic achievements positively (Möller 1999: pp. 11-17).

But interestingly, other cultures in regions like India or Eastern Europe have no problems with the lack of professionals and with negative stereotypes in STEM[6] professions (Quaiser-Pohl 2012: pp. 19f). One point is that in less industrialized cultures, reservations about women and technology are often lower. A further point is that in some cultures, STEM professions are considered attractive because of they have a different image. In India, for example, it is quite normal for women to study natural sciences or engineering sciences. And there are more women in management positions than in Germany. The assignment of jobs is oriented towards the prestige of the university in which the examination was taken. Study places in prestigious universities are strictly awarded according to the performance principle. The often powerful female students benefit from this (Walitzek-Schmidtko 2013). Another example is young women in Eastern Europe are, compared to female students from Western Europe, less afraid of difficult technical study programs. This may be due to the fact that there is no lack of role models in socialist countries (Walitzek-Schmidtko 2013).

In Germany, the image of STEM is still that of being male-dominated, and women always feel alone in this area. Female students tend to change their study program more than male students, even though women are very successful in their studies. So it could be important to create courses in computer science only for women. In doing so, the aspirations and goals of women will be focused on, making it possible to counteract gender stereotypes. A good example is a German university in Berlin. This university has introduced a Bachelor program in computer science and information systems only for women. Lectures take place from 8.00 a.m. to 4.00 p.m. During this time slot, childcare is ensured (Rentsch 2014). But it is possible that study programs only for women could be misinterpreted. It very often happens that human resources departments do not know the concept of such study programs. They suppose that women have a lack of assertiveness in usual study programs. It is assumed that the problem of gender stereotypes

---

6   Science, Technology, Engineering and Mathematics.

is postponed until later and when working life starts, the problem appears again (Ibid.).

Furthermore, it is important to analyze why so many women do not want to climb the career ladder. It is not because women are less qualified or less intelligent, but because of the glass ceiling, an unseen barrier set up consciously or unconsciously by a traditionally male-dominated ruling class. The question is: what is necessary on the part of companies and society so that women become more interested in career opportunities? The first step may be to reduce the pressure of expectations. Women fear that they will have to perform better than men holding an equivalent position (Wippermann 2010: p. 9). They represent a minority in a male domain. Therefore, they will have to fight some established habitual 'male' rituals and will exhaust themselves. Above all, the increase of workload and lack of time will make it even more difficult to reconcile job and family. It is a negative stereotype that women in leadership positions have no time to raise children and to organize a household. However, for men in leadership positions the background of a strong family is seen as advantageous for planning their career. Here a change of thinking and a clear message are necessary: family and leadership positions are compatible with women in the company. The compatibility of work and family life is also a task for men in management positions (Ibid.: p. 10). Role models which show that a leadership position is quite compatible with the family must be accepted. The management floor and the corporate culture will only change when barriers have been overcome and women have reached the goal of leadership positions. Companies should rethink their business structure and they need support measures to recruit more women into management positions.

Longitudinal data offers the opportunity to empirically model causal relationships and thereby provide evidence for the argument that academic self-concept, academic performance and motivational factors are important when choosing a degree program. It is our future goal to analyze whether an academic self-concept can be changed. Therefore, a longitudinal study is planned to analyze the academic self-concepts of graduates and professionals after their first job-experience in the field of computer science. The basis for that is the Hannover's theoretical concept of 'The Dynamic Self'. The central thesis of this approach is that the self is not static but dynamic, and that it is controlled by the social context (Hannover 2002: pp. 1-160).

Acknowledgments

We thank Mrs. Dr. Anja Gärtig-Daugs very warmly for the interesting discussion and critical feedback. We continue to thank Mr. Dr. Wolfgang

Ellegast and Mr. Nico Waibel from the Bavarian Ministry of Education and Cultural Affairs, Science and Art for the transmission of the final grade scores and the mathematics notes. Part of this work was the project 'Alumnae-Tracking', sponsored by the ESF, the Free State Bavaria and Technology Alliance of Upper Franconia.

Bibliography

Abel, Jürgen (2002) 'Kurswahl aus Interesse? Wahlmotive in der gymnasialen Oberstufe und Studienwahl. Die deutsche Schule', *Zeitschrift für Erziehungswissenschaften, Bildungs-politik und pädagogische Praxis*, 94(2): 192-204.

Bavarian State Ministry of Education and Culture (2013) *Durchschnittliche Mathematikergebnisse und Abiturergebnisse in Bayern in den Jahren 2011, 2012 und 2013*, persönliche Mitteilung des StMUK am 16.10. 2013 und am 28.11.2013, personal communication of StMUK at 16.10. 2013 on 28.11.2013.

Bitkom (2015) *Beste Aussichten für IT-Spezialisten*. Online. Available https://www.bitkom.org/Presse/Presseinformation/Beste-Aussichten-fuer-IT-Spezialistinnen.html (accessed August 21, 2016).

Broy, Manfred, Ernst Denert & Stefan Engeser (2008) 'Informatik studieren! – Warum nicht?', *Informatik Spektrum*, 31: 619-628.

Deaux, Kay & Marianne LaFrance (1998) 'Gender', in Daniel T. Gilbert, Susan T. Fiske & Lindzey Gilbert (eds.) *The handbook of social psychology*, New York: McGraw Hill, pp. 788-827.

Eccles, Jacquelynne S. (2007) 'Where are all the women? Gender differences in participation in physical science and engineering', in Stephen J. Ceci & Wendy M. Williams (eds.) *Why aren't more women in science? Top researches debate the evidence*, Washington, DC: American Psychological Association, pp. 199-210.

Frey Steffen, Therese, Caroline Rosenthal & Anke Väth (2004) *Gender Studies: Wissenschaftstheorien und Gesellschaftskritik*, Verlag: Königshausen & Neumann.

Guggenberger, Helmut (1991) *Hochschulzugang und Studienwahl. Empirische und theoretische Ergebnisse von Hochschulforschung*, Klagenfurt: Kärtner Druk–u. Verlag-Ges.

Hachmeister, Cort-Denis, Maria Harde & Markus Langer (2007) 'Einflussfaktoren der Studienentscheidung. Eine empirische Studie von CHE und EINSTIEG', *Arbeitspapier*, No. 95. Gütersloh: CHE Centrum für Hochschulentwicklung gGmbH.

Hannover, Bettina (2007) 'Vom biologischen zum psychologischen Geschlecht', in Alexander Renkl (ed.) *Die Entwicklung von Geschlechtsunterschieden*, Bern: Verlag Hans Huber, pp. 1-150.

Hannover, Bettina & Susanne Bettge (1993) *Mädchen und Technik*, Gottingen: Hogrefe.

Heatherington, Laurie, Kimberly Daubman, Cynthia Bates, Alicia Ahn, Heather Brown & Camille Preston (1993) 'Two investigations of female modesty in achievement situations', *Sex Roles*, 29(11-12): 739-754.

Heine, Christophe, Heike Spangenberg, Jochen Schreiber, Dieter Sommer (2005) 'Studienanfänger 2003/04 und 2004/05 Bildungswege, Motive der Studienentscheidung und Grunde der Hochschulwahl', Hochschul Informations System (HIS) A 15, Hannover: Bundesministerium für Bildung und Forschung.

Kessels, Ursula (2002) *Undoing Gender in der Schule. Eine empirische Studie über Koedukation und Geschlechtsidentität im Physikunterricht*, Weinheim und München: Juventa Verlag.

Kempf, Dieter (2012) *Dauererbrenner Fachkräftemangel*, Bitkom-Umfrage. Online. Available http://www.computerwoche.de/a/dauerbrennerfachkraeftemangel,2526474 (accessed April 17, 2014).

Köller, Olaf, Ulrich Trautwein, Olivier Lüdtke & Jurgen Baumert (2006) 'Zum Zusammenspiel schulischer Leistung, Selbstkonzept und Interesse in der gymnasialen Oberstufe', *Zeitschrift für Pädagogoische Psychologie*, 20(1-2): 27-39.

Lenzen, Dieter, Hans-Peter Blossfeld, Wilfried Bos, Bettina Hannover, Detlef Müler-Böling, Manfred Prenzel & Ludger Wößmann (2009) *Geschlechterdifferenzen im Bildungssystem*, Wiesbaden: Vereinigung der Bayerischen Wirtschaft e. V.

Long, Scott J. (1997) *Regression Models for Categorial and Limited Dependent Variables (Advanced Quantitative Techniques in the Social Sciences Series)*, Thousand Oaks, London, New Delhi: Sage Publications.

Marsh, Herbert W. (1986) 'Verbal and math self-concepts: An inte nal/external frame of reference model', *American Educational Research Journal*, 23(1): 129-149.

Möller, Jens (1999) 'Soziale, fachbezogene und temporale Vergleichsprozesse bei der Beurteilung schulischer Leistungen', *Zeitschrift für Entwicklungspsychologie und Pädagogische Psychologie*, 31(1): 11-17.

Nold, Mariana Sasha (2014) *Behavior of convergence in logistic regression models*, Dissertation, Bamberg, Fakultaät der Sozial- und Wirtschaftswissenschaften der Otto-Friedrich-Universität Bamberg.

Rustemeyer, Ruth, Sabine Thrien (2001) 'Das Erleben von Geschlechtsrollenkonflikten in geschlechtstypisierten Berufen', *Zeitschrift für Arbeits- und Organisationspsychologie*, 45(1): 34-39.

Quaiser-Pohl, Claudia (2012) 'Mädchen und Frauen in MINT: Ein Übeblick' in Heidrun Stöger, Albert Ziegler, Michael Heilemann (eds.) *Mädchen und Frauen in MINT. Bedingungen von Geschlechtsunterschieden und Interventionsmöglichkeiten*, Berlin, Münster, Wien, Zürich, London: Lit Verlag, pp. 13-39.

Skorepa, Martina & Bettina Fuhrmann (2009) 'Studienziele und -interesse, Lernmotivation, Lernstrategien und Fähigkeitskonzept von Erstsemestrigen an der Wirtschaftsuniversität Wien', in Michaela Stock (ed.) *Tagungsband zum 3. Österreichischen Wirtschaftspädagogik-Kongress. Festschrift für Dieter Mandl & Gerwald Mandl*, Wien: Manz-Verlag Schulbuch, pp. 191-199.

Statistisches Bundesamt (2015) *H 201-Hochschulstatistik. Schnellmeldungsergebnisse der Hochschulstatistik Vorläufige Ergebnisse-Wintersemester 2014/2015*. Online. Available

https://www.destatis.de/DE/Publikationen/Thematisch/BildungForschungKultur/
Hochschulen/SchnellmeldungWSvorlaeufig.html;jsessionid=00E63A5E4BAF3C
662FFC5BCE4F2796C3.cae3 (accessed September 5, 2016).

Steele, Claude M. (1997) 'A Threat in the Air: How Stereotypes Shape Intellectual Identity and Performance', *American Psychologist*, 52: 613-699.

Walitzek-Schmidtko, Eva (2013) 'MINT Frauen im Ausland', *MINT Magazin*. Online. Available www.mint-magazin.net/artikel/mint-frauen-im-ausland-201453 (accessed October 28, 2016).

Wippermann, Carsten (2010) *Frauen in Führungspositionen. Barrieren und Brücken, Bundesministerium für Familie, Senioren, Frauen und Jugend*, Heidelberg: Beauftragtes und durchführendes Institut: Sinus Sociovision GmbH.

Zimmer, Karin, Désirée Burba & Jürgen Rost (2004): 'Kompetenzen von Jungen und Mädchen', in Manfred Prenzel et al. (eds.) *PISA 2003. Ergebnisse des zweiten internationalen Vergleichs. PISA-Konsortium Deutschland*, München: Waxmann, pp. 211-222.

CHAPTER XIV

Women in Academic Medicine: The 'Leaking' Process in Italy

Rita BIANCHERI and Silvia CERVIA

1. Introduction

The interest in the sociological approach to science has grown since the 1970s and has led to interesting interpretations that define science as a 'complex, cognitive, cultural and social phenomenon' (Merton 1973). This co-construction, together with the key contribution of feminist studies, has provided a broader framework in which to identify the conditions and processes that form the basis for the reproduction of the characteristics related to the history of scientific knowledge and of scientific institutions, where women are excluded as both subjects and objects. This chapter clearly shows how women's subordination to male rationality is present today in the organization of universities and in the teaching staff recruitment policies.

This phenomenon refers to the polarization that has marked the relationship between men and women, the dichotomy and the conflict between opposing poles, such as the public and private sectors, body and mind, sense and sensibility, which have turned science into a man's job. In addition, the separation between nature and culture has raised rigid disciplinary boundaries. A critical review is, therefore, necessary to acquire a common language of reference and for more fruitful contamination and intersection (Biancheri 2014).

As highlighted by Merchant (1983), questioning the founding core of scientific conception, typical of modern Western culture, means refuting the ideology of objectivity, and thereby allowing us to reveal the conditioning that symbolic structures impose on intellectual attitudes and consequently, use to subvert the influence of social roles on the production of science. This means that to eliminate the barriers that have stopped the rise of women, greater attention must be paid to the positive consequences associated with a large presence of women in scientific professions; moreover, some thought must go into the conceptual categories, tools and methods of research (Biancheri & Tomio, 2015).

Equity in science and gendering of research content, tools and methods – put simply, the promotion of gender mainstreaming – have become crucial, the main way to promote science innovation and to maximize the impact and social benefits of research (Horizon 2020). We are talking about structural change, which is emphasized in the objectives of our European project, as indicated by the acronym itself: TRIGGER (Transforming Institutions by Gendering contents and Gaining Equality in Research). The project aims to trigger the dynamics able to permeate science, especially 'hard science', and create new career prospects.

That is why we have defined the concept of gender mainstreaming as a general strategy that allows for the connection of the diverse meanings linked to the issue of 'gender in research', particularly research carried out by women, research for women, research about women (CEC-WYS, 2007). However, to properly address all issues related to the social assumption that men represent a neutral/universal choice in the world of science, we must adopt a critical perspective that allows us to highlight the many competing dynamics that contribute to gender exclusion in science.

The research that we are presenting today is part of a detailed Action Plan that combines the analysis of the dynamics of female exclusion from and marginalization in top academic positions, especially in scientific areas, with the implementation of measures devoted to increasing institutional awareness on the importance of gender mainstreaming (Horizon 2020). For the purpose of brevity, we shall refrain from explaining the entire Action Plan, and instead go into the research method adopted and identified as a singular course of action.

2. Research Method

Assumptions. We focused on academic careers in medicine at the University of Pisa. We selected medicine as our field of interest, because it has a high internal resistance rate. Indeed, as we shall see below, the field of medicine is the scientific area with the highest rate of 'leaky pipeline'[1]. We also chose the University of Pisa as our case study, both because its theoretical framework requires that the institutional/organizational aspects of the university be analyzed further, and because the statistical data, provided below, qualifies the University of Pisa as a representative of female presence in Italian Universities.

---

1   The metaphors of the 'leaky pipeline' have been introduced in a context in which academic careers develop according to a rigid 'tenure track', such as the regime in the United States, in order to underline the significant 'loss' of female talent at each step of an academic career (Berryman 1983).

Theoretical Framework and Objectives. Our research aims to analyze the dynamics of exclusion, as a result of a multidimensional process (individual behaviors that add to the interactional dynamics and organizational rules) and of social construction of gender (Wharton 2005) and science (Fox-Keller 1985; Merchant 1983).

With regard to the process of gender identity construction, the implications of belonging to one sex in terms of development of attitudes, behaviors and desires more or less conform to cultural and social expectations (Ruspini 2003). We therefore aim to focus on the implications of the connection between these expectations and the expectations associated with the contents of science from a social standpoint.

We would like to examine from an interactional perspective, how these expectations and perceptions have changed during people's professional careers, by focusing primarily on the choices made in both their private and professional lives (e.g., research methods and priorities, power, leadership style, presence in the scientific world and in science networks, etc.).

Lastly, in keeping with the contextual perspective, we wish to analyze the role of facilities and the practices of organizations and research institutions (with the University of Pisa as a case study) in defining the relationship between gender (i.e., female) and science. The institutional perspective allows us to direct our attention to organizational practices and policies, which at the material and symbolic level, incorporate and strengthen gender categories, thereby helping to confirm exclusion and inequality (Acker 1992).

Research Design. According to the theoretical framework, a quantitative and qualitative analysis was designed to examine female careers in Medical Faculties. By assessing the gender asymmetry present in the top academic positions in Medical Faculties, the aim of our research is to analyze the dynamics of exclusion as a result of a multidimensional process (individual behaviors that add to interactional dynamics and organizational rules).

The study of academic positions and of retention in terms of gender has been articulated in two different steps. The first step is an analysis of the administrative database (of the University of Pisa - UNIPI) to determine the female and male status quo in the Medical Faculty vs. the average of the other faculties of the University of Pisa. The key points of the study are: the age of people in different academic positions; the average age at time of appointment; the average period of time in the position; academic duties, etc. The results of the quantitative analysis are utilized as stimulus for the second step (qualitative analysis). The qualitative analysis of women in science, aimed to consider an individual and interactional perspective, is conducted through semi-structured interviews[2]. The set of open questions are connected

---

2 Considering the small number of universe of reference, the respondents are identified as the whole universe of female Full Professor (n.5) and a random sample of the female Associate

to: the process of socialization, gender socialization, family of origin (class, family structure and gender model), education, private and public choices, crucial events, work-life balance, work organization, etc.

The next step intends to integrate the contextual perspective by analyzing the rules and practices developed by each medical school department, with particular attention paid to the practices of the Boards, Councils and meetings (i.e., convening power and definition of the agenda), and to the decision-making process and to the allocation of functions and powers.

3. The Feminization of Medicine: The Italian Situation

All over the world, women have made significant progress in the medical profession (Boulis & Jacobs, 2010). They represent 32% of the total medical workforce in the United States (OECD 2013), while in Western Europe they range from more than 56% of all practitioners in Finland to around 40% in France, Germany and Italy (OECD 2013). However, despite such strong feminization of the medical workforce, gender disparities persist in the profession. Empirical research has shed light on gender inequalities in fields of specialization (Boulis & Jacobs, 2010; Baxter et al., 1996), leadership (Boulis & Jacobs, 2010; Carnes et al., 2008) and at remuneration level (Sasser 2005; Hoff 2004; Baker 1996).

Worth highlighting is the statement by the Medical Women's International Association that the feminization of the medical profession is linked to the threat of medicine becoming a 'pink collar profession', and therefore losing the status and influence and monetary compensation traditionally attached to the practice of medicine (Ross 2003).

In Italy, the feminization of medicine came about in a profession characterized by overcrowding. In 1969, the year when entry into university from all secondary schools was liberalized, graduates in medicine numbered 3,350; in 1979, the figure was 14,792; in 1982, it was 15,171 (Cammelli & di Francia, 1996: p. 70). Once a ceiling was reached in 1986, students had restricted access to medical schools. In relation to the overall increase in graduates, that of women was initially modest, but it then rapidly accelerated during the 1980s. In 1959, female graduates represented 10.7% of the total number of graduates; in 1994, 45.3%, and in 1999, 53.3%. Hence, it may be surmised that restricted entrance and an admission examination did not penalize women, on the contrary (Malatesta 2011: pp. 153-154).

Professors (n.9 interviews on 23 Associate Professors) the sample will be defined in accordance with the quantitative results in charge in the medical Departments.

Despite the above, the feminization of the profession and of academic careers happened even more slowly. With regard to the former, in 1961, around 5% of Italian doctors were women; 17.7% in 1981; 28.4% in 1995. In 2005, there were 119,070 women out of 351,658 doctors, which is equal to 33.8% (Malatesta 2011: pp. 153-154). In terms of the latter, we must take into account the trend since 1998, at which time Law 210 was approved, giving rise to a recruitment process based on the autonomy of the Research Institution. As you can see in Figure 1, a very slow growth has been registered that, in relation to male presence, has been particularly significant in recent years. However, this has to be read in light of the high incidence of retirement of mainly male professors.

Figure 1: Number of Professors in Italian Universities, Medical Field (1997-2013)

Source: Authors' Elaboration of the MIUR (Italian Ministry for University and Research), Database of tenured Faculty.

However, if we observe the trends related to the different positions in academic careers (Figure 2), it is clear that the upward trend is due to an increase in the number of women occupying the lowest hierarchical position (i.e., Associate Professor), as opposed to the stable number of women working as Associate Professors or Full Professors. There is evidently a strong male hierarchy (the number of female Full Professors is too low) in the field, but also a high number of female researchers, clearly more than for other scientific fields, especially if compared to the number of students (Frattini & Rossi, 2012).

297

**Figure 2: The Presence of Women in Academic Careers
in the Field of Medicine (Italy: 1996-2012)**

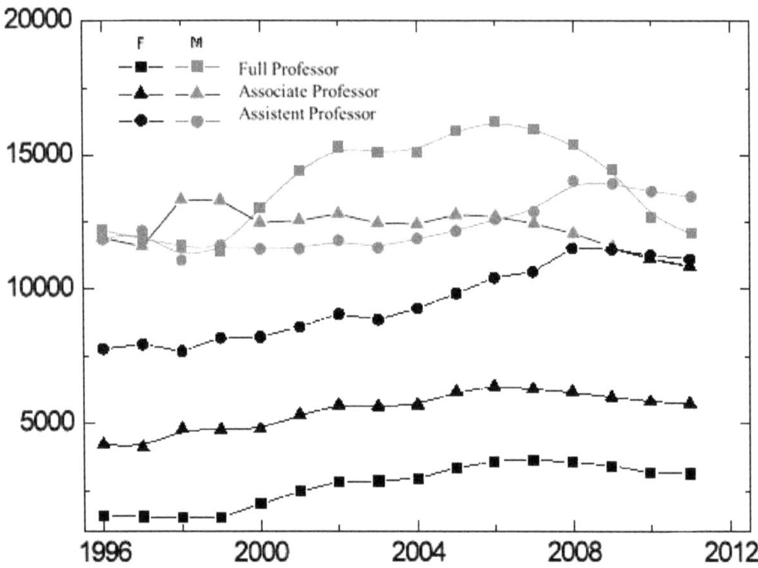

Source: Frattini & Rossi, 2012: Fig. 6.

The University of Pisa has been used as a case study, as its female presence in academic careers is in line with the national average (see Figure 3).

Considering the varying weight of the female population on academic careers, it must be said that the extremely positive end of the scale comprises universities like 'L'Orientale' in Naples, with solely Humanities Departments, while on the opposite end we find the Polytechnics, most of which focus on Engineering. In a nutshell, the universities with both Humanities and Natural Science Departments tend to have a female representation in academic careers that ranges between 30% and 39%. Pisa, with 34%, is a good average and can therefore be used as a case study.

**Figure 3: The Presence of Women in Academic Careers
in Italian Universities (2011).**

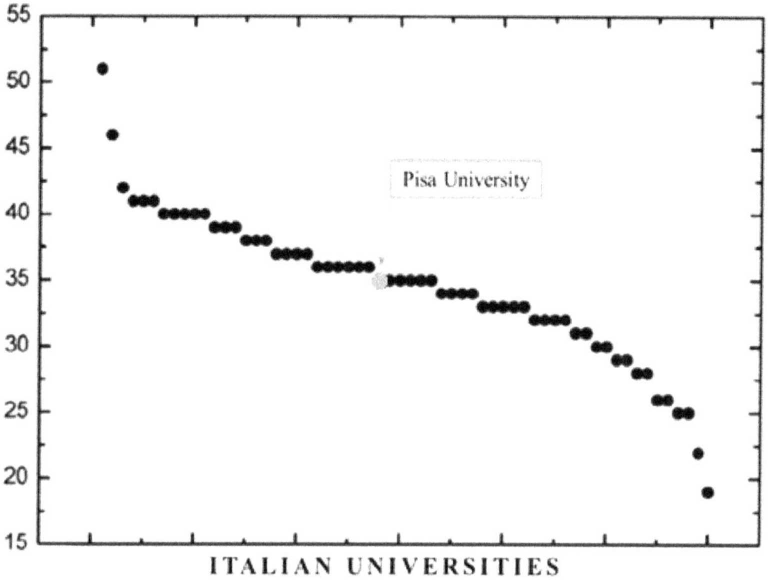

Source: Frattini & Rossi, 2012.

4. Results

4.1 Indicators of a gender-insensitive context

4.1.1 The leaky pipeline

Data reveal that Italian Medical Departments are one of the most problematic areas in terms of gender equity. The situation at the University of Pisa is in keeping with the national data. In fact, although the numbers of women entering Medical School has increased, their career opportunities are much more limited. In the Master's Degree in Medicine and Surgery, women get better results than men. Take 2013 for example: 135 women doctors graduated from the University of Pisa, compared to 84 males, with a final average of 107.8 vs. 106.4/110 respectively and with the female students graduating at a slightly younger age than their male counterparts, albeit with only a slight difference, i.e., 27.2 years compared to 27.6.

Indeed, the Medical Faculty of the University of Pisa has a record 'leaking' rate, with the number of women decreasing by 50% at each step of their careers. The female Researchers/Professors are double the Associate Professors (49% vs. 24.5%), who in turn account for more than double the number of Full Professors (24.5% vs. 11.5%).

Figure 4: Ratio of Men and Women in a Typical Academic Career in Medicine, Students and Academic Staff at the University of Pisa (2013)

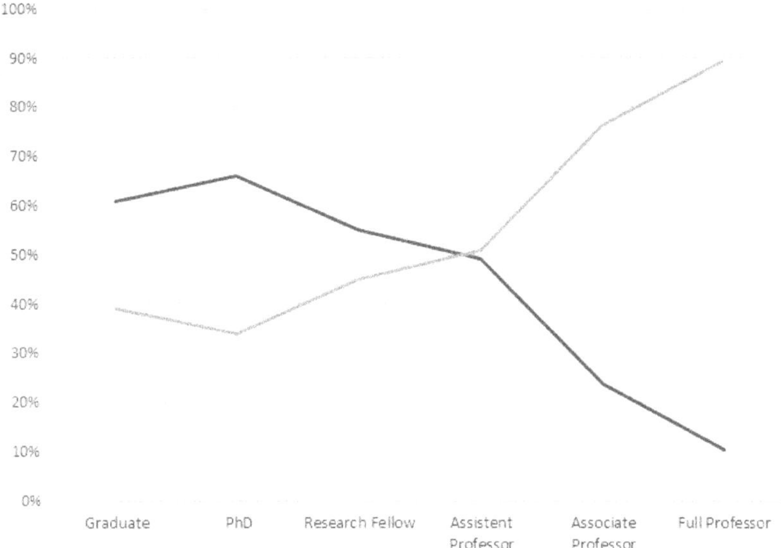

Source: Authors' Elaboration of the Administrative Database of the University of Pisa.

4.1.2 Gender gap in retention

Our analysis shows an additional element of gender inequality, and that is the average retention of professors promoted from a lower to a higher academic position. In terms of the Professors employed by the University of Pisa (as at 31/12/2013), female Assistant Professors who became Associate Professors had spent an average of 12 years in their previous role, and their average recruitment age was 43.2 years, whereas male Assistant Professors promoted to Associate Professors had spent an average of just 10.2 years in their former position and their average recruitment age was 41.6 years. The situation changes during the second promotion phase: data show a similar retention average for men and women (10.4 years for men and 10.6 for women); the difference in recruitment age (46.6 years for men vs. 48.8 for women) is mostly due to the age gap in the previous position. For both Assistant Professors that become Associate Professors and Associate Professors that become Full Professors there is a higher variance in male retention, which is an indicator of a higher degree of similarity in female careers (the standard deviation is of 8.8 for men and 7.0 for female in the first step, and 7.9 vs. 6.1 in the second step).

To complete the information provided, we have included a table below, featuring data related to the Medical Faculty (see Table 1). However, the low universe of reference (N=26) compels us to be cautious when identifying trends and specificity for this specific field. For this reason, the information gathered through the analysis was used only as input information during the interviews conducted with female Full and Associate Professors.

Table 1: Gender Gap in Academic Career Progression

	Retention		Recruitment Age – Top Position		Universe of Reference	
	Average		Average		N	
	M	F	M	F	M	F
University of Pisa						
Assistant Professor	10.2	12.0	41.6	43.2	290	148
Associate Professor	10.4	10.6	46.3	48.8	235	57
Medicine						
Assistant Professor	12.8	11.2	43.6	43.5	46	20
Associate Professor	11.9	13.0	51.2	49.5	34	6

Source: authors' analysis from UNIPI DataBase.

4.1.3 Vertical and horizontal segregation

Vertical segregation becomes evident when we consider the assignment of roles. No woman is Director or Deputy of the Medical Department (the ratio at the University of Pisa is 7M: 1F); none of the three doctoral courses are chaired by a woman (in the rest of the University of Pisa, the ratio is 5M: 1F). Only one degree of the twelve available is chaired by a woman (the ratio in the whole University is 6M: 4F) and also the coordination of post-graduate schools is assigned almost nine times out of 10 to men (in this case, the comparison with the whole University is not possible, because the postgraduate schools are, for the most part, in the medical field).

This high level of vertical segregation is connected both to the numerical scarcity of female Full Professors and to another fact, related to the high incidence of female biologists working in Medical Schools. It is by no means a coincidence that the two cases of female Presidents of a Graduate or Post-graduate Program coincide with the cases of two female Full Professors from the natural sciences (Biology).

The presence of women is characterized by a high incidence of female professors in the related subject areas. This means, with regard to Medicine, that female Full Professors stand at a ratio of 2:1 in biology (of the six female Full Professors, four are biologists and two studied Medicine); this ratio drops to less than 1:10 in male Full Professors (three of them studied Biology, 34 something related to Medicine). There is a higher incidence of biologists, albeit to a lesser extent, in the passage from one role to another. In this case, the ratio for women is inverted – 1:2 (because 7 in 20 were biologists) and the ratio for males increases, reaching1: 4 (9 out of 46 Associate Professors are biologists).

4.2 Female professors' profile

In view of the data presented above as indicators of a gender-insensitive context, we shall now briefly present the results of the qualitative assessment, by aggregating the results on two levels – individual and interactional. We shall also provide a number of suggestions related to the contextual approach, which shall be investigated in greater detail in the next phase of our research.

We have conducted 14 in-depth interviews with all female Full Professors, giving us a total of five interviews[3], and with nine female Associate Professors[4].

Individual Level. The interviewees share many elements of the ascriptive and acquisitive spheres: a high economic, social and cultural capital also deriving from family of origin and which is reflected in the current family setup (the presence of other academics in the family is not uncommon), a significant investment in training and education during the first phase of their education, a high degree of dedication to their work, the possibility to employ domestic staff, etc.

As to the process of socialization, what is interesting is that their stories reflect a strong orientation towards professional achievement. Often, this

---

3   At the time of our study, there were five female Full Professors due to those retiring in 2014.

4   At the time of our study, the female Associate Professors had increased from 20 to 23 due to the results of the first edition of the new recruitment process (Law 240/2010). The new process includes a national call for qualified professors and then a second phase, during which each university can appoint new Professors from those deemed qualified (the total amount of new professors to be appointed is determined by the ranking of the University and its financial situation). Given the importance of innovation introduced by Law 240 of 2010, our research group has chosen a specific research path devoted to the analysis of the impact of this new selection process. It is for this reason that at this stage of our work, we have ruled out the three newly-appointed professors. Moreover, of the 20 Associated Professors, two were excluded as they were appointed under the old national selection process. We finalized the remaining 18 interviewees, according to the following criteria: age, seniority, disciplinary field and membership.

orientation is strengthened by the existence of similar strong female models in the family (frequently mothers are teachers or professionals). Medicine, socially perceived as a vocation rather than as a profession, is a recurring feature of their stories and permeates throughout their tales of educational and professional choices.

Scholars have shown how the gendered 'separation of labor' in science causes women to be better represented in the biological sciences and medicine, and men in the physical sciences and engineering. Similar phenomena may be observed at more fine-grained levels within particular medical, nursing and engineering subfields. One explanation for this is the phenomenon of 'territorial sex segregation' and 'ghettoization' (Rossiter 1995).

When analyzing female academic careers, it is important that we underline how women who have chosen medicine and biology, despite having chosen to specialize in a field that is inextricably linked to the social construction of gender roles, have to face the challenge of professional status (Etzkowitz 1971), whereby they aspire to reach the top of the hierarchy. According to the theories on the processes of socialization, it is not surprising to find a significant number of professors whose fathers were also university professors (among the interviewees, the rate is approximately half).

The presence of a mother with significant cultural capital is also fundamental; indeed, the average interviewee's mother was a teacher or has a bachelor's. International literature has stressed this as a key factor for a successful educational path for women (Osborne, Simons & Collins, 2003). This appears to be essential for our interviewees too, especially in terms of encouraging self-confidence and motivation. Where the mother was a housewife, this condition was perceived as a deminutio. These mothers complained of not being able to follow their own dreams and put pressure on their daughters not to forsake their careers. In one specific case, the mother cultivated in her daughter the same passion she had once had, to become a doctor, which her daughter did (she is now a Full Professor in Medicine).

'They spurred me on … I think I would say that for them it was a bit of a given that I would study and move ahead in life … actually, it was my mom … perhaps she was excessive … she pushed a lot … because she couldn't study due to family problems, because her father died young … so she had to roll up her sleeves, she had three brothers, she had to stay home and she would have liked to have studied medicine, of course … so she had high expectations of me, and she kept a close eye on me … I would say she expected a lot of me, so I was under a lot of pressure.'

(COD_15, Full Professor, MED)

Interactional Level. Approaching the meso level of the analysis means considering the work-life interface as the intersectional and frictional point between the public and private spheres as a result of the social construction of gender roles. Research has in fact highlighted how, in crucial moments of their scientific careers, women tend to choose to abandon academia ('fight or flight response') for reasons outside the professional realm, citing, instead reasons of a private nature (Joecks, Pull & Backes-Gellner, 2014; Xie & Shauman, 2003). Not surprisingly, the dynamics of a couple and the demands of reconciling work and private life have been identified by women scientists as the primary obstacles to the advancement of their careers (Biancheri 2013; Rosser 2004; Barnes et al., 1998; Riger et al., 1997; Aisenberg & Harrington, 1988). Working in a university requires a competitive attitude, flexible working arrangements, the setting aside of one's private life and total dedication to work. International research has confirmed that it is difficult for women scientists to combine work and family life. Becoming a mother under such circumstances can jeopardize a woman's career prospects (Julkunen 2004).

It is therefore not surprising that, by dividing our interviewees into age cohorts, we noticed that childbearing rates are lower than the average. When examining why and when a woman chooses to have a family, based on her career, we realized they do not have any children because of their dedication to their work.

'So, it's not a choice, it's not … I'm not getting married … and that things then happen in life … and that's the way things go … in some way, maybe, I think … because … I was born … yes, a doctor, I am a surgeon, I am an orthopedist and I was born a doctor. And there you have the whole man/woman debate, because … yes, but it's different. I am specialized in 3 things: firstly, orthopedics, and physiatry, which we all did back then. I am an associate professor in physiatry, physical medicine and rehabilitation and health resort medicine. I … what I can say is that, firstly, the mentality of today is very different … at least I … we conquered certain things … now, but not because I am against the family, on the contrary, I had always said that if I have children I will stop working. But I see that a family … well … being a surgeon is tough, in my opinion.'

(COD_20, Associate Professor, MED)

In some cases, motherhood was programmed, depending on the woman's career. Indeed, we have a full professor who waited to complete her Ph.D. before having children, examples of women whose first child was born immediately after securing a permanent position (in some cases, even the birth of the second child came after making progress in their careers), and examples of women for whom motherhood can prevent a scientific career from developing (this means that the most difficult years in terms of work-life balance are spent outside of the academia):

'Thankfully, I already had one … a child, because determination, after graduating …   in your career makes you postpone motherhood and then maybe … but luckily, I already had a child.'

(COD_06, Full Professor, MED)

'So in 2001, I started my open-ended research at the university. In 2003, I became an associate professor … I was supposed to start on 1 January 2005 … but I couldn't, because I was on maternity leave … so I actually started in May 2005.'

(COD_13, Associate Professor, MED)

'I was hired in August 2001 … my girls were born in 2004 and in 2008.'

(COD_16, Associate Professor, MED)

If you become a mother, you need a secret weapon: grandparents! They need to live close by and be available. All our interviewees cited this resource as being crucial for their work-life balance. Grandparents are essential. Public services are also considered useful and have been used, in some cases; partners can be cooperative, helping when they can and when they are asked '… my husband helped … when he could!' (COD_01, Associate Professor, MED), but in daily management, especially with small everyday emergencies, the help and constant presence of grandparents makes all the difference. It allows these women to quickly resume their research and respect their work commitments.

'But my son did not hinder my career, because his paternal grandmother, a truly delightful … all my friends were envious … such a kind and helpful woman, she only had the one son… she dedicated herself fully to her grandchild, because she didn't work. She also had a high regard for my work … So, I continued to study as before. It might have been a problem if I hadn't been able to keep up my standards because of my family … instead, I managed to maintain them.'

(COD_06, Full Professor, MED)

'The holy grandparents … every now and again, a babysitter, because of course we also needed babysitters … but not a lot! We were really lucky to have such a great support system!'

(COD_03, Associate Professor, MED)

'My mom, who helped me a lot here too, because she would come often, even though I have a brother, but back then he didn't need as much help. So she would come often, especially in the first few years of my child's life, which were problematic because he was often ill. I decided to take him to crèche early on, because I didn't like the idea of having a woman who would look after him from morning till night without anyone to watch her, the idea scared me. Crèche seemed like a complete and important form of socialisation for my child. But at first he didn't fit in well, maybe because he was already 11 months. But in the end, he adapted quite well, even if he was ill every week. So those were difficult years and luckily, I had my mother and my mother-in-law who came every week.'

(COD_08, Associate Professor, MED)

Contextual Approach. At the macro level we focused on the dynamics of exclusion and discrimination resulting from the way in which work is organized in science and academe (Rosser 2004; Rosser & Lane, 2002; Rosser 1999). International literature has stressed the existence of organizational mechanisms, which, at both formal and informal level, would offer women scientists less opportunities, thereby creating a barrier to the advancement of their careers, reducing their level of job satisfaction, and as a result, their interest in pursuing an academic career (Settles et al., 2006). Female professors in medicine, especially those who are physicians, perceive work-time duties as demanding and pervasive.

'I love my job so much that I work almost 11 hours a day, something else not everyone can do. So this is also important, if a woman has certain time limits, for example, because she has to be home by 6pm … because it is normal … and that's ok … but it makes it difficult! Because … certain jobs don't have a time card … you can't have a time card … do you understand?! When I start research or scientific work or something similar, I can't leave at 5pm. If I have to stay until 8pm, I will stay until 8.'

(COD_07, Associate Professor, MED)

We have already emphasized the close connection between career and private life, and the fact that women wait to have children until they have secured a permanent position. We have also introduced an opposing issue, i.e., the effect of motherhood on a woman's career. It is, as we will see from our analysis, an indirect effect, due to the reduction in working hours because of childcare duties. In other cases, the dynamics of exclusion are more underhanded.

'And that's something that really struck me that I had to make up all the shifts I had missed while on maternity leave. I was basically made to feel guilty for being absent for five months.'

(COD_07, Associate Professor, MED)

'In other words … if you dedicate yourself heart and soul to something, then even if you are a woman you may very well succeed … but I still think it's difficult … not because women are not collaborative, intelligent, eloquent … there's this legacy … a cultural legacy … that in my opinion, needs to be eliminated.'

(COD_13, Associate Professor, MED)

'When I said I was, when in actual fact I wanted to fall pregnant because I was 33, I informed them and it caused problems … because I was the only young person running the lab and I understood my superiors, if I were gone for a few months, then things in the lab would come to a halt, and also in the field of teaching, because at the time I was following a number of practicals … I saw that this thing was not appreciated, especially because back then one of my colleagues, who was a grade higher than me, was due to become a full professor and he needed to publish more and so it wasn't accepted.'

(COD_24, Associate Professor, MED)

These extracts point out how women have been relegated to the lower grades: 'women were utilized as research associates or side-lined into fields that were low in status and lacking in resources' (Etzkowitz & Ranga, 2011: p. 134).

What is more, pregnancy is perceived as a betrayal of the fiduciary relationship.

Scientific work continues to be organized according to a relatively inflexible academic format, with a persistent 'male model' of scientific career as the norm to which women must conform (Etzkowitz & Ranga, 2011). Academic life is a 'long hours' culture that makes work-life balance difficult.

What emerges from this approach is that it is particularly difficult for women professors and physicians to manage the 'quadruple presence' that characterizes their private and professional lives. Physicians/Professors (both men and women) have to face a triple presence: they have to teach, do university research, and perform their hospital duties. This leads to a so-called 'triple engagement', which, in the case of female physicians, is added to the phenomenon known in Italy as double presence, i.e., professional work and domestic chores (Balbo 1978), and termed in America as the shift presence (Hochschild & Machung, 1990). This means that these female professionals reach a superhuman goal, which, for the purposes of our study, could be called 'quadruple presence'. The workload of a biologist, on the other hand, does not foresee any hospital work.

'I basically think that … a university career in medicine is very, very tiring … in the fields of medicine. Why? Obviously because you want to do everything well, to the best of your ability! You have patients, your academic activities: meetings, faculty meetings and teaching. So, how can a woman doctor launch her career if she wants to have a family, I mean children, right? There are many ways to have a family, of course … So how do you reconcile these three things: healthcare, academia, research, and family life? But if we only talk about work … a job like freelancing … work that you organize as you please, that you manage based on family needs … so … I probably have a number of friends who at times … A dear friend of mine comes to mind, she worked at the National Research Centre, she was under so much pressure from all directions … she now works as a freelancer! She left! So a lot of people cannot cope! You just can't cope! Because the load is too heavy … possibly in the fields of Biology, because there is no healthcare involved … it is … it is … a job you can do well and still reconcile with your family life … perhaps that's the thing.'

(COD_03, Associate Professor, MED)

'Why women like Biology more, quite honestly, is not a question I can answer. Perhaps because it is so similar to medicine but it doesn't require the same responsibilities, the same dedication, the same skills, and perhaps women with a family are less suited to medicine, because it demands all your time. I see it more as a man's profession, even though I would not have a problem being treated by a woman doctor … A biologist works in a lab, he has his office hours.'

(COD_04, Associate Professor, MED)

'Of course… but I could explain it as follows … that a clinic is a lot more … for a woman, it implies a lot more difficulty in reconciling family and work life… because having to be frequently in an operating room … I don't know … if we're talking about a woman who also wants a family … because you have women who have chosen not to have a family and perhaps they could manage …'

(COD_14, Full Professor, MED)

5. Discussion and Conclusions

Despite being transversal processes typical of Italian universities, vertical segregation and the 'leaking pipeline' are occurring at a worrying rate in the Departments of Medicine. Our data underline how, when examining the reason behind the 'leaky pipeline' (Berryman 1983), the private life of women becomes relevant. When focusing on the factors of retention or advancement of women researchers, rather than considering an increase in the number of women qualifying in the sciences or technology – as suggested by Fielding and Glover (1999) – a key factor (although certainly not the only one) should be taken into account: motherhood. Introducing a life course approach has allowed us to highlight the existence of a high level of attrition between care giving and work commitments, which has a negative impact on the career prospects of women. The sustained asymmetries arising from the social construction of gender roles and obligations – in the management of private care, household responsibilities and working hours – significantly alter the opportunities for the affirmation of women, especially in a workplace like academia, which is highly competitive and time-consuming.

Our analysis reveals the effect of the interaction of the dynamics at the three different levels. The micro level is crucial for us to understand gender role socialization, aspirations in both the private and public sphere, and how people build confidence in themselves and their abilities. However, even if the socialization process has succeeded in constructing alternative beliefs to counter existing hegemonic beliefs about gender roles and attitudes, women still have to face the effects of traditional roles at meso and macro level.

At meso level, which involves tackling everyday life and time management, we determined that despite a demanding job and the socialization process, women tend to take on the more time-consuming household duties and care giving activities. Female professors continued to be the primary caregivers in their families, with the help of their partners, or "when they can", with the help of the grandparents. Clearly, this introduces an external variable, originating outside the walls of the family home, which goes over and beyond their merits or abilities. It is therefore not surprising that the child bearing rates of female professors are lower than the average rate (as opposed to men). On the one hand, women who remain in academia tend to get married and become mothers only after reaching a stable position in their careers, because they know that motherhood will have a negative impact on their career opportunities (particularly in the short term). Indeed, the life histories we heard revealed how maternity leave has been stigmatized by research teams and by their superiors in particular, especially when work schedules were tight. On the other hand, in the case of women who flee ('flight'), the highly demanding workload of a physician tends to discourage women wanting a family with more than one child. They often end up abandoning their academic careers and are unable to find an equally satisfying career outside the University, meaning their only choice is to settle down (this is an excellent example of the 'leaking pipeline').

The data at macro level clearly show that female careers are more unorthodox and slower, frequently less recognized and without any relevant assignment of roles. Even if it is true that fewer women apply in the first place, and that the issue of time management is crucial, it is also a matter of fact that the working environment is not particularly favorable, and institutional rules and arrangements do not help. In this regard, we have to stress the situation in Italy, which was aggravated by the introduction of the new rules on recruitment and career advancement (Law No. 240/2010, better known as the 'Gelmini Reform').

The new regulatory framework, which has introduced new rules and regulations about academic careers, could further penalize female scientists, not only hindering their scientific careers, but also increasing the perverse effects on their private lives. In many of the interviews we conducted, we heard that one such risk is the time needed to reach a permanent position, which is seen as an almost insurmountable odd in a woman's career. It is an issue that must be examined closely and that has been stressed in international literature, calling upon us to protect and defend women in science in their mid to late 30s and early 40s (Hewlett et al., 2008; Julkunen 2004).

Recent analyses of the consequences of the new rules on recruitment and career advancement introduced by the 'Gelmini Reform' have shed some light on the persistence of certain mechanisms that aggravate the recruitment and selection processes. The results of the first National Scientific Qualification Procedure pointed to a lower presence of Italian female researchers who are qualified to apply for permanent positions (associate and full professors). The results are mainly due to the lower number of female applications, rather than lower female success rates. Indeed, the gender-based difference in the probability of success is negligible, whereas the proportion of applicants out of the total number of 'potential candidates' is 48% women and 54% men (Pautasso 2015).

In terms of the impact of this reform on the University of Pisa, it is worth mentioning, as it is likely to have a positive effect on promotions from Grade C to Grade B (female associate professors stood at 42% at the end of 2013, and 49% at the end of 2015). As for the following step, Grade B to Grade A, we noticed a more conservative increase (+1%), mainly due to the retirement of male professors in the reference period. The number of female researchers in fixed-term positions is dramatically low (as at 31 December 2014, only 28% of Type A temporary re-searchers were female). Even if these data are not taken seriously, we are describing a situation that has not yet been consolidated, meaning that the signs are worrying and that the current trend must be monitored closely.

We also have to consider how extending a temporary employment period could have a negative effect on the possibility to meet expected research performance standards and how it could amplify the effects of competition and uncertainty, thereby making careers more vulnerable to early termination. This could occur for a number of reasons. On the one hand, the need to find a new job before the current position expires overlaps with key research and writing activities (Toscano et al., 2014). On the other hand, unexpected events such as health problems, childbirth, or other events that force the employee out of work-related activities (Falcinelli & Guglielmi, 2014; Petersen et al., 2012).

With a lack of resources and a seemingly gender-blind regulatory system, we may have to deal with a 'crotch' shortage, like the one following the economic crisis (Rigney 2011). A 'crotch' shortage is a process by which gaps are created in the system. It is a worrying phenomenon, inflamed by failing to consider merit and talent, and which could very well exacerbate the gap between 'rich' and 'poor', leaving the 'middle tier' to slip through the cracks and into the 'poor group'. This is the so-called Matthew Effect, or accumulated advantage, under which the 'rich' get 'richer' and the 'poor' get 'poorer' (Merton 1968). At University level, females are the 'poor' and males are the 'rich'. Therefore, Italian universities could emerge from this phase of scarce resources and the reform of the system as even more unequal and unfair universities, where the loss of female talent is likely to be even more pronounced than before the reform (of 2010).

Bibliography

Acker, Joan (1992) 'From Sex Roles to Gendered Institutions', *Contemporary Sociology*, 21(5): 565-569.
Aisenberg, Nadia & Mona Harrington (1988) *Women of Academe: Outsiders in the Sacred Grove*, Amherst: the University of Massachusetts Press.

Baker, Laurence C. (1996) 'Differences in Earnings between Male and Female Physicians', *New England Journal of Medicine*, 334(15): 960-964.

Balbo, Laura (1978) 'La doppia presenza', *Inchiesta*, 32: pp. 3-6.

Barnes, Laura B., Menna O. Agago & William T. Coombs (1998) 'Effects of job-related stress on faculty intention to leave academia', *Research in Higher Education*, 39(4): 457–469.

Baxter, Nancy, Robert Cohen & Robin McLeod (1996) 'The impact of gender on the choice of surgery as a career', *American Journal of Surgery*, 172(4): 373-76.

Berryman, Sue E. (1983) *Who will Do Science? Minority and Female Attainment of Science and Mathematics Degrees: Trends and Causes*, New York: Rockefeller Foundation.

Biancheri, Rita & Patrizia Tomio (2015) *Lavoro e carriere nell'università*, Pisa: ETS.

Biancheri, Rita (ed.) (2014) *Genere e salute tra prevenzione e cura*, Milano: Franco Angeli.

Biancheri, Rita (2013) *Famiglia di ieri, famiglie di oggi. Affetti e legami nella vita intima*, Pisa: ETS.

Boulis, Ann K. & Jerry A. Jacobs (2008) *The changing face of medicine. Women doctors and the evolution of health care in America*, New York: Cornell University Press.

Cammelli, Andrea & Angelo di Francia (1996) 'Studenti, università, professioni: 1861-1993', in Maria Malatesta (ed.) *Storia d'Italia, Annali 10, I Professionisti*, Torino: Einaudi, pp. 21-72.

Carnes, Molly, Claudia Morrissey & Stacie E. Geller (2008) 'Women's health and women's leadership in academic medicine: hitting the same glass ceiling?', *Journal of Women's Health*, 17(9): 1453-1462.

Etzkowitz, Henry & Marina Ranga (2011) 'Gender dynamics in science and technology: From the "Leaky Pipeline" to the "Vanish Box"', *Brussels Economic Review*, 54(2-3): 131-148.

Etzkowitz, Henry (1971) 'Sexual Separation of Labor in Society: The Precarious Identity of the Male Nurse', *Journal of Marriage and the Family*, 33: 431-434.

Falcinelli, Daniela & Simona Guglielmi (2014) 'Genere, precarietà e carriere scientifiche', in Elena Armano & Annalisa Murgia (eds.) *Generazione precaria, nuovi lavori e processi di soggettivazione*, Bologna: Odoya, pp. 81-101.

Fielding, Jane & Judith Glover (1999) 'Women Science Graduates in Britain: the value of secondary analysis of large scale data sets', *Work, Employment & Society*, 13(2): 353-367.

Frattini, Romana & Paolo Rossi (2012) 'Report sulle donne nell'università italiana', *Meno di zero*, 8-9.

Hewlett, Sylvia A., Carolyn B. Luce, Lisa J. Servon, Laura Sherbin, Peggy Shiller, Eytan Sosnovich & Karen Sumberg (2008) *The Athena Factor: Reversing the Brain Drain in Science, Engineering and Technology*, Cambridge, MA: Harvard Business Review Research Report.

Hochschild, Arlie & Anne Machung (1990) *The Second Shift*, New York: Avon Books.

Hoff, Timothy J. (2004) 'Doing the same and earning less: male and female physicians in a new medical specialty', *Inquiry*, 41(3): 301-315.

Joecks, Jasmine, Kerstin Pull & Uschi Backes-Gellner (2014) 'Childbearing and (female) research productivity: a personnel economics perspective on the leaky pipeline', *Journal of Business Economics*, 84(4): 517-530.

Julkunen, Raija (2004) *Hullua rakkautta ja sopimustohtoreita*, Jyväskylä: University of Jyväskylän.

Fox Keller, Evelin (1985) *Reflections on Gender and Science*, New Haven: Yale University Press.

Malatesta, Maria (2011) *Professional Men, Professional Women: The European Professions from the 19th Century until Today*, Thousand Oaks: Sage.

Merchant, Caroline (1983) *The Death of Nature: Women, Ecology and the Scientific Revolution*, San Francisco: Harper & Row Paperback Edition.

Merton, Robert K. (1973) *Sociology of Science: Theoretical and Empirical Investigations*, Chicago: University of Chicago Press.

Merton, Robert K. (1968) 'The Matthew Effect in Science, II: Cumulative advantage and the symbolism of intellectual property', *ISIS*, 79: 606–623.

Organization for Economic Cooperation and Development (2013) *OECD Health Data 2013*. Online. Available http://www.oecd.org/health/healthsystems/oecdhealthdata.htm (accessed January 10, 2014).

Osborne, Jonathan, Shirley Simon & Sue Collins (2003) 'Attitudes towards science: A review of the literature and its implications', *International Journal of Science Education*, 25(9): 1049-1079.

Pautasso, Marco (2015) 'The Italian University Habilitation and the Challenge of Increasing the Representation of Women in Academia', *Challenges*, 6(1): 26-41.

Petersen, Alexander M., Massimo Riccaboni, Eugene H. Stanley & Fabio Pammolli (2012) 'Persistence and Uncertainty in the Academic Career', *Proceedings of the National Academy of Sciences*, 109(14): 5213-5218.

Riger, Stephanie, Joseph Stokes, Sheela Raja & Megan Sullivan (1997) 'Measuring perceptions of the work environment for female faculty', *The Review of Higher Education*, 21(1): 63–78.

Rigney, Daniel (2011) *Sempre più ricchi, sempre più poveri. Effetto San Matteo: perché il vantaggio genera altro vantaggio*, Milano: Etas.

Ross, Shelby (2003) 'The Feminization of Medicine', *Virtual Mentor*, 5(9), American Medical Association Journal of Ethics.

Rosser, Sue V. (1999) 'Different laboratory/work climates: Impacts on women in the workplace', *Annals of the New York Academy of Sciences*, vol. *Women in Science and Engineering: Choices for Success*, 869: 95-101.

Rosser, Sue V. (2004) *The Science Glass Ceiling: Academic Women Scientists and the Struggle to Succeed*, New York: Routledge.

Rosser, V. Sue & E. O'Neal Lane (2002) 'Key barriers for academic institutions seeking to retain women scientists and engineers', *Journal of Women and Minorities in Science and Engineering*, 8(2): 163-191.

Rossiter, W. Margaret (1995) *Women Scientists in America: Before Affirmative Action 1940-1972*, Baltimore: Johns Hopkins University Press.

Ruspini, Elisabetta (2003) *Le identità di genere*, Roma: Carocci.

Sasser, Alicia (2005) 'Gender Differences in Physicians Pay: Trade-offs between Career and Family', *Journal of Human Resources*, 40(2): 477-504.

Settles, Isis H., Lilia M. Cortina, Janet Malley & Abigail J. Steward (2006) 'The climate for women in academic science: the good, the bad, and the changeable', *Psychology of Women Quarterly*, 30(1): 47–58.

Toscano, Emanuele, Francesca Coin, Orazio Giancola, Barbara Gruening & Francesco M. Vitucci (2014) *RICERCARSI - Indagine sui percorsi di vita e lavoro del precariato universitario*. Online. Available www.ricercarsi.it (accessed January 2016).

Wharton, Amy S. (2005) *The Sociology of Gender. An Introduction to Theory and Research*, Backwell: Malden.

Xie, Yu & Kimberlee A. Shauman (2003) *Women in Science. Career Processes and Outcomes*, Cambridge, MA: Harvard University Press.

CHAPTER XV

Female Labor Market Participation in Serbia

Natalija PERIŠIĆ and Jelena TANASIJEVIĆ

1. Introduction

Female labor market participation has become an increasingly important topic in public debates, policies, and regulations worldwide. The focus has been on obstacles to female labor market participation, their reduction and facilitation, as well as on practices for the improvement of opportunities for the realization of gender equality in the labor market. Starting from the International Labor Organization's view (2013) on gender equality as a fundamental human right, it is rather disappointing to come to the conclusion that:

'… despite some progress over the last few decades, gender equality in employment remains an elusive goal in all societies. Women continue to face disadvantage and discrimination in all areas of economic life.' (p. 7)

The consequential challenges societies have to face are manifold. Gender inequality in the labor market presents a threat to development on the whole. Furthermore, gender equality contributes to:

'… poverty reduction, increased productivity and aggregate output, reduced fertility, lower infant mortality, less child labor, greater decision making and bargaining power for women within households. All these factors contribute to economic growth either directly or indirectly.'

(International Labor Organization 2013: p. 5)

This chapter is structured in five sections. It seeks to analyze women's participation in Serbia's labor market. Following Section 1, Section 2 presents the theoretical framework, which begins with the segmented labor markets. The study of labor markets, which challenges changing social reality, has been enriched and influenced significantly by the theory of labor market segmentation. Pursuant to this theory, one of the key labor market developments worldwide in the recent period has been the phenomenon of the division of the labor market into separate segments that vary from the point of view of their manifestations, characteristics and behavioral rules. One of the main points of the theory is the existence of gender segregation in the labor market. Even though the econometric data do not support the theory, it presents a useful framework for the analysis of the dimensions of female labor market participation in Serbia.

Ever since 2000, the topic of female labor market participation has been attracting heightened attention in the national context, both from researchers and policy makers. Findings of some of the most comprehensive national studies are briefly presented in Section 3. The authors of this chapter tried to summarize the findings of the research conducted on the topic so far, to present and to analyze the most recent data and to contribute in that way to the ongoing discussion on the positive and negative aspects of female labor market participation in the national labor market.

Accordingly, Section 4 is concentrated on the actual characteristics of the labor market, from the point of view of the female labor force and gender segregation. This section presents data on female employment and female unemployment, in order to enable the authors to discuss the opportunities women have in terms of engaging with employment and also their unequal positions compared to men, once they are engaged in paid employment. Therefore, the indicators presented and analyzed are: female employment rates in the formal and informal economy, female educational attainments, female dominated sectors of employment and occupations, the gender pay gap, and female unemployment rates.

The discussion of the data is presented in Section 5, followed by the concluding section of the chapter. Our conclusions are in line with those of previously conducted research on the topic in the national context. A clear deficiency of our chapter is the lack of longitudinal data. However, one of the justifications for the absence of a long time study, that would enable us to come to more solid conclusions, is the lack of harmonized data in different time periods in Serbia.

The methodological framework consists of the analysis of the data of two national statistical services: the Republic Statistical Office and the National Employment Office. The different methodologies which the two national services apply in their reports proved useful for the authors, in order to come to conclusions. Qualitative data were sourced from the relevant literature on the topic, first of all from available empirical studies which comprised surveys and inspections, as presented in Section 3.

2. Theoretical Approach

Strictly speaking, the theory of Segmented Labor Markets (SLM) has been challenging classical economic explanations of the labor market ever since the 1960s. Attempts to apply the segmentalist approach can be traced back even earlier, to John Cairnes, John Stuart Mill and Arthur Cecil Pigou (Leontaridi 1998). Its core hypothesis is that differentials in wages are a result of the dual and segmented nature of the labor market, and not of differentials in skills. The labor market is divided 'into separate submarkets or segments, distinguished by different characteristics and behavioral rules' (International Labor Organization 2016: p. 1). Segmentation in four key forms was identified as shaping labor markets: segmentation between the primary and secondary labor market sectors; between primary independent and primary subordinate segments; racial segregation; and gender segregation (Babović 2010; Leontaridi 1998).

Segmentation between the primary and secondary sectors contrasts the two so that the primary sector is the high-wage and the secondary is the low-wage sector[1]. The consequential characteristic of the primary sector is that it is made up of the so-called *good* jobs, contrary to the secondary sector, that is made up of *bad* jobs:

'... good jobs make up the primary sector of the dual economy, while bad jobs and the workers frozen out of the primary sector compose the secondary sector. In that sector jobs are sufficiently plentiful to employ all workers, but they are low paying, unstable, and generally unattractive. Workers are barred from the primary sector not so much by their own lack of human capital as by institutional restraints (such as discrimination) and by a simple lack of good jobs. As such, workers in the secondary sector suffer from underemployment'

(Wachter 1974: pp. 638-639)

Some authors go further to argue that segmentation trends can be observed even within the primary sector, so that there are independent primary and subordinate primary segments. These segments differ in terms of earnings, employment stability and status (Leontaridi 1998). The subordinate primary segment is composed of routine jobs, such as those in industry and administration. It encourages the development of dependency, discipline and respect of the employed. Contrary to that, the independent primary segment requires creativity, problem solving skills and initiative. It is connected with high, however voluntary, rates of fluctuation, while individual motives and achievements are highly valued (Babović 2010).

Thirdly, some segments or submarkets are racially labeled, frequently based on discriminatory institutions in the labor market and the prejudices of employers, i.e., there are 'mechanism or institutional barriers which truncate

---

1   Graham and Shakow attributed the following to the primary sector: high wages, job stability, good working conditions, seniority rights and benefits, unions, low unemployment, a monopoly sector industry, white prime age males, and skilled employees. The following were attributed to the secondary sector: low wages, job instability, poor working conditions, no seniority rights and benefits, no unions, high unemployment, a competitive sector industry, disadvantaged groups (minorities, women, youth, older workers), and unskilled employees (Graham & Shakow, 1990).

competition by precluding mobility between the various labor market segments' (Flanagan 1973: p. 253). This results in lower wages for blacks, contrary to whites, even 'when individual differences in human capital are held constant' (Ibid.: p. 256).

Similar to racial segregation, gender segregation exists as well, and 'access to certain jobs is reserved for the members of another gender' (Babović 2010: p. 89). According to Emerek (2008) the key factors contributing to it are:

'… comparative biological advantages, under-investment in human capital (schooling or training), differential income roles, preferences and prejudices, socialization and stereotypes, entry barriers and organizational practices.' (pp. 5–6)

Even though evidence on the explanatory potential of all of the above-mentioned factors varies, in support of this, a survey in the European Union reported the six occupations with the largest number of men and women, and none of them overlap:

'… shop salespersons and demonstrators, the top occupational category for women employing 8% of those in work, accounted for under 3% of men in employment. The next three largest categories for women – "domestic helpers", "personal care workers" and "other office clerks" – between them employed a further 19% of women, but only 3% of men'

(Burchell, Hardy, Rubery & Smith, 2014: p. 30)

Gender segregation is thought of in terms of occupational versus sectoral, horizontal versus vertical, vertical versus hierarchical (Bettio & Verashchagina, 2009: p. 30), as well as absolute versus relative (Burchell, Hardy, Rubery & Smith, 2014). Furthermore, there are different measures of gender segregation in the labor market, and some of the most commonly used are: the ID index, the IP index and SR ratio[2]. The ID index, i.e., the index of dissimilarity was introduced by Duncan and Duncan in 1955 (Blackburn 2012). It presents the difference in the distribution of female and male employment across occupations or sectors. The less equal the distribution, the higher the level of segregation. It varies between 0 and 1 (0 and 100 if expressed as a percentage) (Burchell, Hardy, Rubery & Smith, 2014). The IP index, introduced by Karmel and MacLachlan, takes into account the total employment and the number of employed men and women, as well as their occupations or sectors of employment:

'The index ranges from 0 in the case of complete equality to twice the male share of employment multiplied by the female share in the case of complete dissimilarity … The

---

2   On top of the aforementioned, Blackburn revised the following indicators: the Women in Employment index (WE), the standardized sex ratio (SR*), the marginal matching measure (MM), and also the Gini coefficient (G) (Blackburn 2012).

317

absolute maximum for the index is 0.5 (50 if expressed in percentage), and it is reached when the female and male shares are equal.'

(Burchell, Hardy, Rubery & Smith, 2014: p. 103)

Finally, SR was used by Hakim, to measure 'the difference between the level of over-representation [of women] in typically female jobs and the level of under-representation in typically male jobs' (Blackburn 2012: p. 182). Hakim identified female-dominated, male-dominated and mixed occupations in the following way:

'… female-dominated occupations are those where the share of women exceeds their mean share in employment +15%; conversely for male-dominated occupations. Mixed occupations are comprised in the ± 15 points interval around the mean.'

(Burchell, Hardy, Rubery & Smith, 2014: p. 103)

3. Research into Female Labor Market Participation in Serbia

Female labor market participation has been in a focus for research in Serbia in the recent period, predominantly with feminist-oriented researchers. Along with that, research into the labor market in general, as well as into poverty and social exclusion, sheds light on the female 'dimension' of the topic.

Research into the female labor market position by the Government of the Republic of Serbia and the United Nations Development Program in Serbia (UNDP) was conducted in 2006, with a view to gaining a holistic insight into the situation and recommending guidelines for future strategies and reforms in the field. Research methodology was twofold. On the one hand, evidence was sourced from the available data of the Republic Statistical Office and the National Employment Office, along with analysis of the related legislation. On the other hand, female focus groups were organized in several cities and towns across Serbia. The main findings from the research were as follows: although there have been legislative improvements, they have been followed by an implementation trap; there are differences in the levels of earnings between women and men performing the same jobs; there are no widespread possibilities for the promotion of either women or men; women have been dominantly engaged in unpaid work in households, including obligations regarding their children (Babović 2007).

Three years later, in 2009, the European Movement streamlined its research into the adaptation of women to new labor market demands, in the search for the level of changes regarding female economic activity, their professional paths and resulting social positions. The methodology was designed similarly to that of previous research, with analysis of the relevant legislation and data held by the Republic Statistical Office as well as the use of focus groups (organized in three cities and towns). Findings pointed to decreasing female economic activity rates; high levels of gender inequality in the national labor market; a low percentage of women occupying managerial positions and higher paid positions; and strict divisions between jobs perceived as masculine or feminine. Furthermore, women were recognized as the gender with a higher risk of poverty in general, with a special vulnerability of women belonging to certain national minorities, such as Roma, lone mothers, women with disabilities, women refugees and internally displaced and older women (Kolin 2009).

Discrimination against the female labor force was tackled by the Victimology Society of Serbia and the United Nations Agency for Gender Equality and Empowerment of Women in 2011. The research included 706 female respondents living in seven of Serbia's cities and towns, of whom:

'431 (61.0%) were exposed to some form of discrimination in the labor market: 242 (56.1%) women experienced discrimination in the process of gaining employment and 342 (79.4%) experienced discrimination at work. In addition, 72.2% (510) of the respondents had knowledge that a woman they knew (a friend, relative, colleague) was discriminated against in the labor market – 464 (65.7%) women had indirect knowledge of other women being discriminated against while gaining employment, and 372 (52.7%) had indirect knowledge of discrimination against other women at work.'

(Nikolić, Nikolić-Ristanović, Ćopić & Šaćiri, 2012: p. 10)

Furthermore, discriminatory practices were closely related to age (mainly for the age group 18 to 34), civil status (mainly for divorced and separated women), education (mainly for women with a lower education level), duration of employment (mainly for those employed between one and two years) and employment sector (64.8% respondents in private and 48.7% respondents in public sector reported discrimination) (Nikolić, Nikolić-Ristanović, Ćopić & Šaćiri, 2012).

4. The Female Labor Market in Practice

After World War II, the then socialist Serbia (being one of the Republics of the former Yugoslavia) saw rapidly increasing female labor force participation rates in the context of overall increasing labor force participation driven by the full employment policy. Even though economic growth trends had already slowed down in the 1960s when the socialist Government designed measures to facilitate the employment of redundant workers abroad, the officially-led employment policy was declaratively in favor of full employment. Therefore, all the way until the 1990s, there was female emancipation in the labor market in Serbia (Perišić & Vidojević, 2015a) in part as a result of female participation in socialism of around 70% (Arandarenko 1997 in Babović 2010)[3]. Contrary to that, due to the complete economic collapse of the 1990s, the transition was extremely disadvantageous for women. In general, it was characterized by:

'… extremely low levels of employment … hidden unemployment … weak labor force mobility, the huge share of informal markets (gray economy), low earnings, extremely high rates of unemployed young and the female labor force.'

(Vuković 2009: p. 178)

The economic decline pushed women back into families:

'… certain female authors describe this phenomenon in terms of 'self-sacrificing micro-matriarchy' because the power of women is transferred primarily to the private sphere, with an intensive consumption of female resources in their households in order to reduce the negative effects of aggravated transition.'

(Blagojević 2002 in Babović 2010: p. 122)

Employment reduction and consequent growth in unemployment which was characteristic of the 1990s, continued in the next decade, despite economic growth. The reasons for that were the privatization process and structural adjustments which left many unemployed, the numbers of which could not be absorbed by the emerging and weak private sector (Perišić &Vidojević, 2015b). This period of jobless growth, as generally referred to in the national economic literature, was followed by the world economic and financial crisis that severely hit Serbia.

It was in this context in which the number of the employed in Serbia, according to data from the Labor Force Survey, amounted to 2,421,270 in 2014, representing an employment rate of only 39.7% (Republički zavod za statistiku 2015). Along with a highly unfavorable employment rate in general, the structure of the labor market is equally unfavorable. Certain demographic characteristics, first among them gender and age, have strong correlation with their labor market position. Male employment of 46.9% clearly dominates over female employment of 33% (Republički zavod za statistiku 2015). This gap is certainly the indicator of prominent gender segregation in the labor market in Serbia. The period of the last fifteen years has seen the reduction of the employment gap between the genders, but the trend was oscillating, i.e., there were huge variations from one year to

---

3   The position of women in Serbia during socialism was rather contradictory and therefore straightforward conclusions cannot be made based on their high activity and employment rates.

another[4]. At the same time, this reduction was not sufficient to conclude that the gap is moderate, especially with the resulting figure of a 13.9 percentage point in 2014. Another unfavorable fact is that the reduction of the employment gap between the genders was in the context of overall employment rate reduction. Furthermore, the informal employment rate of 22% is somewhat unequally distributed between the male and female labor forces, with the female labor force (23.5% versus 20.9% of the male labor force) prevailing in those informally employed (Republički zavod za statistiku 2015).

The unfavorable labor market position of women is also reflected in their educational attainments, which are *de facto* higher, compared to men. However, certain contradictions persist, first of all regarding the proportion of females without primary school education, which is higher than that of males, both in urban areas (10% women and 4% men) and especially in other areas (30% women and 17% men) (Republički zavod za statistiku 2014). Regarding literacy, the situation is similar: on the whole, '1.96% of the population is illiterate (aged 10 and over). Illiteracy is most common among women (82.1%) and in the age group 65 and over (70.5%)' (Republički zavod za statistiku 2016: p. 32). Technological literacy is also lower among women. The gap between the genders is unsurprisingly small, almost negligible, in younger generations (aged 16-24), and increased age increases the gap (Republički zavod za statistiku 2014). However, a higher proportion of girls has enrolled and graduated from secondary schools and universities. The proportion of female students to male students on both secondary and tertiary educational levels is the same: 58% female students and 42% male students (Ibid.). However:

'... in 2012 the structure of graduate studies was dominated by women in the areas of education (87%), health care and welfare (73%), art and humanities (71%), social sciences, business and law (61%). Men represented the majority of university students in engineering, production and construction (65%), sciences, mathematics and information sciences (54%), agriculture and veterinary medicine (54%) and services (51%).'

(Ibid.: p. 36)

Sectors with higher female employment are a reflection of the areas of their educational attainments, resulting in their dominance in the sectors of education, health care and welfare, financial services and insurance, and retail and wholesale. Professional positions which more women statistically occupy are not the managerial ones (Republički zavod za statistiku 2015).

---

4 In the last ten years, female employment rates have been oscillating, with their peaks in 2004 and 2008, when they accounted for 36.3% and 36.5% respectively. The lowest rate was in 2012, when it accounted for 28.7% (Republički zavod za statistiku 2015).

Female dominated occupations[5] are elementary occupations (51%), service and trade occupations (52%), assistants and technicians (54%), administrative workers (58%) and experts and artists (58%)[6].

The gender gap is significant regarding self-employment and private entrepreneurship – only 20% of women were recorded as owners of private companies (Republički zavod za statistiku 2016). Working hours for females are dominantly full – 1/5 of women employed in the private sector and only 3% of women employed in the state sector have shorter working hours. Women are absolutely dominant (comprising approximately 90%) in those working shorter hours due to the need to take care of a child or an incapacitated adult member of the family (Republički zavod za statistiku 2015).

The average earnings in the last ten years (from 2004 to 2013) were consistently lower among female employees by about 10 percentage points on the average (Republički zavod za statistiku 2014). Data on average salaries per sector point to only three sectors (i.e., construction, administrative and supporting services, and 'other') in which female employees earn higher salaries (Table 1). Their higher salaries in the aforementioned sectors could be correlated with their higher educational attainments, compared to men employed in those sectors. On the other hand, the sectors characterized by higher female employment are sectors which have lower earnings (Table 1).

Table 1: Average earnings (in RSD[7]), per sectors and gender, March 2014

Sectors	Women	Men	Total average earnings = 100	
			Women	Men
Total	60,185	68,026	94	106
Agriculture, forestry and fishing	48,850	49,930	98	101
Mining	87,971	95,571	93	101
Processing industry	49,962	57,861	87	108
Power, gas and steam supply	90,082	108,236	86	104
Water supply and waste water management	54,677	55,603	99	100
Construction	57,368	50,963	110	98
Retail and wholesale	54,923	74,018	86	106
Traffic and warehousing	60,115	61,479	98	101
Provision of accommodation and food	39,282	46,101	93	109

---

5   Female dominated occupations were calculated by the authors, starting from the data of the Labor Force Survey, and pursuant to Hakim's definition. According to the same principle, 'mixed' occupations are farmer occupations in Serbia.

6   The latter can be correlated with their higher representation in the graduate population (Pokrajinski ombudsman 2012).

7   In March 2014, as per the exchange rate 1 EUR = 115 RSD.

Information and communication	95,671	104,751	95	104
Financial and insurance services	91,144	120,518	89	118
Estate business	68,115	72,027	96	102
Expert, scientific, information and technical activities	93,852	97,178	98	102
Administrative and supporting services	47,252	44,530	104	98
State administration and obligatory social insurance	75,626	80,742	97	104
Education	56,550	65,507	95	110
Health care and welfare	57,871	70,823	95	117
Art, entertainment and recreation	55,360	57,134	99	102
Other services	72,386	59,089	113	92

Source: Republički zavod za statistiku 2014.

On average, the unadjusted wage gap stands at 3.3%. However, the comparatively better labor characteristics of female employees (first of all, their education) hide the real gap. 'The main reason for this female "advantage" is the low employment rate of women with lower educational attainments' (Fond za razvoj ekonomske nauke 2013: p. 2), with a resulting adjusted wage gap of 11%[8]. The gap is more prominent in the private sector (11%), compared to the public one (7.5%) (Ibid.).

General unemployment rates have been consistently high, ever since the beginning of the transition in the 1990s. Currently, the unemployment rate stands at 18.9% (Republički zavod za statistiku 2015). Gender segregation is present: 19.6% of women are unemployed; however, the difference is not that immense when compared to that of men (18.3%). The magnitude of the problem can be grasped only when the data on unemployment rates are matched with the data on inactivity rates. Namely, the inactivity rate of women in Serbia is 78.8% (Ibid.). Furthermore, women clearly prevail among those who would like to work, but cannot due to personal and family reasons – out of the total number of persons in this category, men occupy only 12%; while women dominate in the category of caring for children or incapacitated adults in the family, representing 96% of the total number (Ibid.).

Women's prevalence in the category of unemployed persons is not evident at all levels of educational attainment. Firstly, a negligible difference is discernible in the number of unemployed women and men with incomplete and complete primary school educations. Their chances for employment are in general slim, i.e., they normally belong to vulnerable groups in the labor market. The same difference is present at the level of Ph.D. studies – there are almost identical numbers of women and men with a Ph.D. degree. The difference is small at the level of secondary school studies with men prevailing only by 2 percentage points compared to women. At the level of

---

8   In another words, a woman in Serbia works "for free" 40 days per year compared to a man having the same labor characteristics (Arandarenko 2012).

two-year post-secondary and faculty education, women prevail in those unemployed (Nacionalna služba za zapošljavanje 2015).

5. Contextualizing Data

The National Strategy for the Improvement of the Position of Women and Gender Equality of 2009 was the first strategic document with a view to improving the social and economic position of women in Serbia. It was followed by The National Strategy for Gender Equality in the Period 2016-2020, the aim of which is to improve the economic position of women and their labor market status (Vlada Republike Srbije 2016). Some of the measures designed are as follows: encouraging female trade unions, recognizing and fighting female labor market discrimination, developing flexible forms of employment, and recognizing the principle of equal pay for equal work or work of equal value. The need to reconcile national regulations with the relevant international and especially European regulations is highlighted (Ibid.). National legal instruments are in favor of equal treatment of women and men in the labor market, the most important being the Labor Law of 2005, the Law on Employment and Insurance against Unemployment (2009), the Law on Discrimination Prohibition and the Law on Gender Equality (2009). Still, the main characteristics of the national labor market have remained long-standing high unemployment rates, a large number of participants in the informal market, slim chances for pre-qualification, and a high share of unemployed female labor compared to males.

As regards the future:

'... more detailed labor market projections, up to 2020, show that even in the case of an optimal scenario, one cannot expect spectacular results in the national labor market, almost until the end of the following decade ... we could argue that the fulfillment of this optimistic scenario would contribute to a significant convergence toward the average indicators of the EU labor market, but with significant lagging behind the EU.'

(Arandarenko, Krstić, Golicin & Vujić, 2013: p. 52)

The demographic situation in the future will lead to a faster reduction in unemployment rates but a slower increase in employment. The percentage of unemployed women could be expected to be reduced along with the overall reduction of the unemployment rate to 10.84% in 2020 (Arandarenko, Krstić, Golicin &Vujić, 2013).

National statistic indicators stand in sharp contrast to those of the EU (28). In 2014, the Serbian female employment rate of 33% is almost two times lower than the EU average of 63.5% (Eurostat 2016), and is not comparable even with the new member states. Surprisingly, the female informal employment rate is higher than that of males, in contrast to the European Union (Babović 2010). The adjusted wage gap of 11% in Serbia is lower than the EU (28) average of 16% (Evropska komisija 2014). The female unemployment rate of 19.6% in Serbia is almost two times higher than that of the EU (10.3%) (Eurostat 2016).

The number of women without primary school education is higher than the number of men, and women prevail among the illiterate population. However, women have been outnumbering the men regarding secondary school and university education. This is especially important in terms of matching the data on education to age. Females belonging to an older age cohort have lower educational attainments and vice versa. Men have been outnumbering women at the level of Ph.D. study, which can be interpreted in terms of higher aspirations among men, in contrast to women. Consistently with this, research conducted by the European Movement in Serbia showed lower professional aspirations among women (Kolin 2009). This can partially explain their under-representation in managerial positions, in the positions with higher potential for very high earnings and social power, as well as their reluctance to start their own business. However, female professional choices are rather stereotyped, as well as their educational paths, with strong implications for the possibilities of promotion. Consequently, they occupy lower ranged employment positions. The data from the Labor Force Survey points to gender segregation in terms of occupations and sectors of female employment. Even those women with their own private entrepreneurships opted for their own business because of the lack of other employment options (66% of them). They mainly work in the local market and in the area of services (Poverenik za rodnu ravnopravnost 2014). The professions are divided to female and male ones[9], with women prevailing in those requiring manual coordination, attention and patience. Women have been traditionally directed toward jobs which do not require overtime work and frequent absences from home (Pokrajinski ombudsman 2012). More frequently than men, women perform other tasks at work which are not within the scope of their work position, such as making coffees, cleaning the premises, etc. (Nikolić, Nikolić- Ristanović, Ćopić & Šaćiri, 2012). Women also prioritize

---

9   'The division of jobs to typically female or typically male is more rigid and prominent in developing countries, where gender inequality is also more visible. In such societies, inequality is manifested through assigning higher social importance and productivity to male labor, and at the same time, to greater visibility and recognition of men. They are paid for their working engagement and they rarely perform unpaid tasks in their households. The roles played by women most frequently are jobs in the household, the reproductive role, as well as public jobs, meaning that they are either not paid for their work or that they are underpaid, compared to men. Therefore, they are less visible in society, and their contribution is not valued in the same way as that of men' (Petrušić 2007, in Tanasijević 2012: pp. 29–30).

family over employment in terms of their justifications for working shorter hours.

'It is not that women are willing to forgo pay because they enjoy flexible hours whilst men do not; rather, women are more likely to accept lower (per hour) wage offers if this is the only way that they can combine the roles of mother and wage earner.'

(Bettio & Verashchagina, 2009: p. 41)

The character and qualities of female labor are arguably less valued by employers. The reasons could be women's alleged lower capability for adaptation to work requirements (as already mentioned, their inability to travel from home and to work longer hours, due to work obligations) and in combination with more frequent absence from work (due to family reasons), and unsurprisingly they have lower earnings.

'The analysis shows that the pay gap between men and women exists mainly due to the differences in characteristics between them that cannot be noticed – i.e., the characteristics that are not recorded in the Labor Force Survey.'

(Fond za razvoj ekonomske nauke 2013: p. 3)

On the other hand, the position of unemployed women is determined by weaker chances of finding employment, low and stigmatizing social welfare benefits, almost non-existent active labor market programs and finally greater opportunities to participate in the informal economy and to engage in unpaid household activities. The high female inactivity rate, showing that they are discouraged from searching for a job, is connected with female prevalence in the structure of contributing household members. This points to very traditional division of roles between the genders in the families (in other words: women are responsible for the family) and unequal division of caring obligations. This has at least two important implications. First, as Bettio and Verashchagina (2009: p. 41) outline, 'women's bargaining position tends to be lower, primarily because of unequal distribution of care work and unequal commitment to securing monetary income for the family'. Thus, women become 'punished' for the work they do in households. Second, this makes them even more distant from the labor market, with their skills objectively becoming obsolete, and their confidence that they will be engaged in paid employed subjectively becoming lower. The female cohort from ages 18 to 34 is dominant in the search for jobs. This age cohort is the most educated and probably less prone to traditionalism. However, research finds the most persistent discrimination in the labor market directed toward women of this age cohort (Nikolić, Nikolić-Ristanović, Ćopić & Šaćiri, 2012).

6. Conclusion

The socialist legacy regarding the female labor market in the national context is controversial because of, among other things, the issue of gender segregation. On the one hand, female employment and educational rates were significantly improved, both in legislative and practical terms, during socialist rule. On the other hand, socialism did not liberate women from domestic unpaid work. The transition 'test' which started with the breakdown of socialism pointed to the fragility of socialist progress regarding all labor market indicators.

In the last fifteen years, there have been a lot of activities in terms of defining and redefining the national legal framework concerning gender equality in general, and among other things, the female labor market position. Currently there are laws, strategies and policies in support of the female labor market position, which are in compliance with EU regulations and recommendations. However, there are two important challenges. The first one refers to the still-missing approach of gender mainstreaming in the national context. Despite evidence on the success of gender mainstreaming in the EU, Serbia is clearly at the very beginning regarding the design of this kind of approach. However, based on existing differences between national and EU labor market characteristics, national policy makers should scrutinize in more detail the issue of the transfer of the EU approach. The second challenge refers to the implementation of laws, papers and documents in order that there is no doubt about the legal guarantee of the equality of women and men in the labor market. However, even though the importance of the legal context cannot be over-emphasized, it is not sufficient for the improvement of the female labor market position. More precisely, despite certain improvements, initiated by legal and strategic reforms as well as by the consequential changes in the way in which institutions function, a clear inconsistency can be found between the laws and their implementation. There is a gap between declared rights and the situation in the field, which reflects the deteriorated labor market position of women. Therefore, the emphasis should be on efforts aimed at overcoming the implementation trap.

Further efforts should also be put into the creation of suitable and reliable data, i.e., evidence on which to base policy. Firstly, much data is missing, and that which exists is not sensitive enough. Secondly, the system of monitoring currently held data should be further improved.

In Serbia, women have been in an unfavorable position, in comparison to men, in almost all segments of family and societal life. One of the reflections of this is their disadvantaged position in the labor market. The finding in this chapter is that national labor market segmentation can be observed in each of four dimensions (presented in Section 2), when seen from a female labor perspective. That is to say, gender segregation *per se* not only exists, but it can also be found within the segmentation between the primary and secondary labor market sectors, between primary independent and primary subordinate segments, and finally in racial segregation.

The segmentation between the primary and secondary labor market sectors and female "attachment" to the secondary one in Serbia is demonstrated based on women's overall employment in low-wage sectors. Additionally, sectors of higher female employment are those universally denoted as less competitive than elsewhere; there is and there will be a sharp distinction between the economy of knowledge (primary labor market) dominantly populated by men, and the economy of care and economy of services (secondary labor market) dominantly populated by women in Serbia. The dominance of women in the subordinate primary segment is further documented by their earnings, employment stability and status. Average earnings have been consistently lower among female employees, compared to men, for about 10 percentage points on the average, with a resulting adjusted wage gap of 11%. Employability status, as demonstrated by fixed term contracts in Serbia, shows that flexible working hours are, as a rule, "reserved" for women, primarily due to family care obligations. Finally, when in the primary labor market, women disproportionally occupy fewer managerial positions. The combination of female gender and ethnicity, such as in case of Roma women, brings another challenge: that of racial segmentation, when the female labor market position is additionally aggravated.

Along with the abovementioned, gender segregation can be observed in lower female employment and higher unemployment, compared to men. Additionally, the female employment rate of 33% is low when put into the EU framework. Women are tremendously discouraged from getting into employment, which is reflected in their high inactivity rate of 78.8%.

The issue is further demonstrated when the data are contextualized with reference to higher female educational attainments. Segregation is observed from the point of view of the areas of female study, rather than the level of their education. There is also a subsequent stereotypical division of occupations to those pertaining to males and females, respectively. Women are doubly discouraged: both objectively and subjectively. Objectively, since their chances for employment and after that for employment promotion are weaker, due to their occupational choices. These were, in turn, mediated by stereotypes, which could be interpreted as a subjective obstacle for emancipation in employment. All the described developments have their clear consequences for women's future: being further unemployed, or employed in the informal economy or with lower earnings, they will also have lower or no earnings in old age. The sure and certain consequence is the feminization of poverty. To a certain extent, this can be construed so as to mean a punishment for female fertility.

Obstacles to higher female labor force participation rates can be correlated with the values and forms of family life in the national context. The Serbian transition increased the responsibility of female members of the population, and the majority of women started to take care of their families, thereby withdrawing from the formal labor market. Additionally, the current crisis, which started in 2008, and which is yet present in Serbia, favored the strengthening of still-conservative values, with a similar outcome. It has become widely accepted that women should be directed toward family tasks, taking away the possibility of choices regarding their educational advancement, employment, promotion in their profession, and so on. Therefore, employment in traditionally 'female' sectors enables women to fulfill their obligations toward family members. Their unemployment and underemployment, on the other hand, could be a consequence of their burden of family and household work. A strong and objective pressure to increase female labor market participation rates is primarily, if not only, driven by increased economic pressure for households to have multiple breadwinners (not only male). Such a situation does not contribute to the devotion of public policies to a genuine improvement of the female labor market position. This refers to all policies in support of female employment – not only employment policy, but also for education, social welfare, pensions and other public policies. Additionally, there seems to be a lack of motivational events – career planning and counseling that would target occupational segregation. Gender-sensitive measures and affirmative action when it comes to employment practices are also absent. The public sphere is governed to the highest extent by economic interests which have been undermining many efforts to strengthen the female labor market position and combat gender segregation. In general, Serbian national policy design has been mainly following the logic of general labor market participation rate improvement, but the expected effects seem to be absent.

Bibliography

Arandarenko, Mihail, Gorana Krstić, Pavle Golicin & Vukan Vujić (2013) *Studija: Procena uticaja politika u oblasti zapošljavanja*, Belgrade: Fond za razvoj ekonomske nauke.

Arandarenko, Mihail (2012) *Results of the New Study on the Gender Pay Gap in Serbia: Working Women Better Qualified but Still Paid Less than Men*. Online. Available http://www.rrpp-westernbalkans.net/en/News/Gender-Pay-Gap-in-Serbia.html (accessed September 1, 2013).

Babović, Marija (2010) *Rodne ekonomske nejednakosti u komparativnoj perspektivi: Evropska unija i Srbija*, Belgrade: Sociološko udruženje Srbije i Crne Gore, Institut za sociološka istraživanja Filozofskog fakulteta u Beogradu i SeConS – Grupa za razvojnu inicijativu.

Babović, Marija (2007) *Položaj žena na tržištu rada*, Belgrade: Program Ujedinjenih nacija za razvoj.

Bettio, Francesca & Alina Verashchagina (2009) *Gender segregation in the labor market: root causes, implications and policy responses in the EU*, Luxembourg: Publication Office of the European Union.

Blackburn, Robert (2012) 'The measurement of occupational segregation and its component dimension', *International Journal of Social Research Methodology*, 15(3): 175–198.

Burchell, Brendan, Vincent Hardy, Jill Rubery & Mark Smith (2014) *A New Method to Understand Occupational Gender Segregation in European Labor Markets*, Luxembourg: Publication Office of the European Union.

Emerek, Ruth (2008) *Gender segregation in the labor market: roots, implications and policy responses in Denmark*, Luxembourg: Publication Office of the European Union.

Eurostat (2014) *Labor Force Survey*. Online. Available http://ec.europa.eu/eurostat/web/lfs/data/main-tables (accessed November 26, 2016).

Evropska komisija (2014) *Smanjivanje razlike u platama muškaraca i žena u Evropskoj uniji*, Luxembourg: Ured za publikacije EU.

Flanagan, J. Robert (1973) 'Segmented Market Theories and Racial Discrimination', *Industrial Relations*, 12(3): 253–273.

Fond za razvoj ekonomske nauke (2013) *Rodni jaz u platama u zemljama Zapadnog Balkana: nalazi iz Srbije, Crne Gore i Makedonije*. Online. Available http://www.fren.org.rs/sites/default/files/projects/attachments/Policy%20briefs_G PG_ser.pdf (accessed November 21, 2016).

Graham, Julie & Don Shakow (1990) 'Labor Market Segmentation and Job-Related Risk: Differences in Risk and Compensation between Primary and Secondary Labor Markets', *American Journal of Economics and Sociology*, 49(3): 307–324.

International Labor Organization (2016) *Labor Market Segmentation*. Online. Available http://www.ilo.org/global/topics/employment (accessed November 19, 2016).

International Labor Organization (2013) *Guidelines on Gender in Employment Policies*. Online. Available http://www.ilo.org/wcmsp5/groups/public/@ed_emp/documents/instructionalmat erial/wcms_103611.pdf (accessed November 26, 2016).

Kolin, Marija (2009) *Rodne nejednakosti na tržištu rada u Srbiji i podsticaj evropskih integracija*, Belgrade: Evropski pokret u Srbiji.

Leontaridi, Rannia M. (1998) 'Segmented Labor Markets: Theory and Evidence', *Journal of Economic Surveys*, 12(1): 63–101.

Nacionalna služba za zapošljavanje (2015) *Mesečni statistički bilten decembar 2015*, Belgrade: Nacionalna služba za zapošljavanje.

Nikolić, Jasmina, Vesna Nikolić-Ristanović, Sanja Ćopić, & Bejan Šaćiri (2012) *Diskriminacija žena na tržištu rada u Srbiji*, Belgrade: Viktimološko društvo Srbije.

Perišić, Natalija & Jelena Vidojević (2015a) *Challenging and Deconstructing Welfare Myths in the Socialist Serbia* (unpublished).

Perišić, Natalija & Jelena Vidojević (2015b) 'The Role of Public Policies in Supporting Female Employment in Serbia', *The South Slav Journal*, 34(1–2): 58–86.

Pokrajinski ombudsman (2012) *Žene i diskriminacija*, Novi Sad: Pokrajinski ombudsman.

Poverenik za rodnu ravnopravnost (2014) *Redovan godišnji izveštaj Poverenika za zaštitu ravnopravnosti za 2014 godinu*, Belgrade: Poverenik za zaštitu ravnopravnosti.

Republički zavod za statistiku (2016) *Stanovništvo*, Belgrade: Republički zavod za statistiku.

Republički zavod za statistiku (2015) *Anketa o radnoj snazi u Republici Srbiji*, Belgrade: Republički zavod za statistiku.

Republički zavod za statistiku (2014) *Žene i muškarci u Republici Srbiji*, Belgrade: Republički zavod za statistiku.

Tanasijević, Jelena (2016) *Politike usklađivanja porodičnih i profesionalnih obaveza u Srbiji*, Disseration Fakultet političkih nauka, Belgrade: Univerzitet u Beogradu.

Vlada Republike Srbije (2016) *Nacionalna strategija za rodnu ravnopravnost za period od 2016 do 2020* godine. Online. Available http://www.mgsi.gov.rs/lat/dokumenti/nacionalna-strategija-za-rodnu-ravnopravnost-za-period-od-2016-do-2020-godine-sa-akcionim (accessed April 19, 2016).

Vuković, Drenka (2009) *Socijalna sigurnost*, Belgrade: Fakultet političkih nauka.

Wachter, Michael L. (1974) 'Primary and Secondary Labor Markets: A Critique of the Dual Approach', *Brookings Papers on Economic Activity*, 3: 637–693

CHAPTER XVI

Socio-cultural Factors Structuring Women's Access to Land and Natural Resources in Northwest Cameroon

Ngambouk Vitalis PEMUNTA

1. Introduction

In the agrarian economies that characterize most of Africa including Cameroon, land is a critical natural resource and the main factor of production. It is at the heart of socioeconomic development (Nkankeu & Bryant, 2010) and a key resource for women and most of the rural masses living in poverty. In the predominantly agrarian and agricultural local and regional economies of Cameroon, it is the driving force (Mope Simo & Bitondo, 2010: p. 226) for sustainable development since access to land 'increases the ability of communities to feed themselves, earn a livelihood, adapt to climate change, and exercise their social, political and cultural rights' (ActionAid Online). In Sub-Saharan Africa and in Cameroon in particular, land is the main resource underpinning the survival of rural people, and on which the present generations are counting to improve their living conditions in the face of the acute short fall in the number of industrial jobs. Under such circumstances, there is an accentuated competition for the appropriation of land over time consequent upon increasing demographics, urban-rural migration due to the economic crisis, and the scarcity of white-collar jobs in cities (Nkankeu & Bryant, 2010). The problem of access to land for women and communities has been worsened by a conjuncture between the land grabs perpetuated by multinationals and society's wealthy and powerful, climate change, and resource use conflicts between farmers and grazers (Pemunta 2014). Yet an interplay between socio-cultural factors, legal ambiguities between modern and customary land tenure regimes, the unfettered and gendered effect of the Structural Adjustment Programme (SAP), population explosion, and climate change is undermining the ability of the poorest and the most marginalized [and vulnerable] people, especially women, 'to exercise their basic human rights, including the right to food' (ActionAid Online). Women constitute 52% of Cameroon's population of 23,636,676 people[1]. Although they produce 80% of Cameroon's food needs,

---

1   Source: Online data basis available at: http://countrymeters.info/en/Cameroon (accessed May 2016).

they own just 2% of the land and benefit only 5% of the total agricultural inputs (Cameroon Gender Equality Network, 2011). Women's rights to land which is the focus of this chapter is broadly conceptualized and in the light of international human rights law to encompass their:

'… ability to own, use, access, control, transfer, inherit and otherwise take decisions about land and related resources. They also encompass women's rights to secure land tenure and to meaningfully participate at all stages of land law, policy and programme development, from assessment and analysis, programme planning and design, budgeting and financing, implementation, to monitoring and evaluation. Women's land rights must also be understood in the context of intersecting forms of discrimination.'

(UN Human Rights and UN Women, 2013: p. 1)

According to the 2016 Africa Human Development Report the cost of economic and social discrimination against women in Sub-Saharan Africa stands in the tune of a staggering $100 billion annually. Closing the gender gap, the report argues will be an additional incentive for Africa's economic and social prospects since African women are denied the same rights that men enjoy in all spheres of national life. They are victims of harmful traditional practices that affect their health and certain social norms that hinder upward social mobility in society (United Nations Development Programme 2016, Scalise 2013). Gender disparity and patriarchy relations are intertwined on the one hand as well as the repeated occurrence of conflicts over land and resource rights. Simultaneously, custom, tradition, patriarchal relations and deeply engrained religious norms 'have perpetuated women's oppression, vulnerability and powerlessness over decision-making processes about land and resource rights' (Mope Simo & Bitondo, 2010: p. 223). Would women's rights to land continue to be upheld with the increase in population, land grab by local political and economic elites, climate change and increased demand for land that has implications on land values? The aim of this chapter is to examine the socio-economic, cultural and political factors that structure women's access to land and natural resources in a context of legal dualism in the Ndop plain of Northwest Cameroon.

2. Legal Pluralism and Women Rights in Cameroon

This section demonstrates that in Cameroon, the co-existence of seemingly gender neutral laws alongside customary laws (legal pluralism) regulating marriage and property ownership, including those over the ownership of land and natural resources instead tends to subvert women's rights. These laws are based on the biased and discriminatory notion of male-headed households, women as subordinates and parts of the man's estate as well as women as inefficient managers of property.

Cameroon is a former German and later Franco-British colony, three colonial legacies that have influenced the country's land tenure system. Following the defeat of Germany in World War I, the British and the French portioned out Cameroon into French and English speaking Cameroon. The former is comprised of eight regions while the latter is made up of two regions – the Northwest and Southwest Regions (then designated as the Southern Cameroons). In Cameroon like in most of Africa, access to land, ownership and the enjoyment of associated rights is influenced by a concatenation of three colonial legacies – German, French and English, a multiplicity of customary practices as well as by post-independence land reform measures. Additionally, with over 240 ethnic groups, a conjuncture between the huge ethnic diversity and therefore traditional tenure systems has led to a multiplicity of customary land tenure regimes. The colonial masters instituted the notion of private property through land registration as 'effective development'. In the process, collective parcels of land were taken over by the colonial masters and registered as titled land. Land is presently the bone of contention between individuals, community and State which claims monopoly over all parcels of land. Simultaneously, there is male hegemony over land and the predominance of customary land tenure. Men enjoy a hegemonic advantage in customary land tenure arrangements since 'women too are perceived and referred to as assets or chattels' (Scalise 2013; Pemunta 2011).

Like in most of Africa, 'received law regulated land rights on alienated land and customary law on land used and occupied by Africans' (Adam & Turner, 2005: p. 3). Similar to other British territories where indirect rule was adopted, customary land rights were respected, including the traditional land administration responsibilities of local leaders. This suggests that tenure arrangements in most territories remained largely intact (Adam & Turner, 2005; Mamdani 1996) including in the Southern Cameroons. Cameroon and other African countries were embroiled in an internecine economic crisis and the Bretton Woods institutions imposed Structural Adjustment Programme (SAP) on the country in the late 1980s. Against the backdrop of the economic crises, social safety nets including the existing rural crop cooperatives and farm groups were dismantled without being replaced. Cooperative organizations, their workers and dependents were left on their own and without any compensation. In the face of this new reality, women and most of the rural poor ingeniously turned to the land (Nebasina & Mbih, 2010: p. 206). The government of Cameroon lays monopolistic stewardship over the management of the country's land and the natural resources on them.

The legal system of African countries, including Cameroon's, is characterized by socially institutionalized patriarchal domination. Feminist analyses have demonstrated that nation-states like Cameroon are inherently gendered in their constitution and objectives (Mbilinyi 1988). Section 27(1) of the Southern Cameroons High Court Law, 1955 for instance, provides that:

'The High Court shall observe and enforce the observance of every native law and custom which is not repugnant to natural justice, equity and good conscience nor incompatible with any law for the time being in force, and [that] nothing in this law shall deprive any person of the benefit of any such native law or custom.'

According to the Cameroon chapter of the International Federation of Female Lawyers (FIDA), under Cameroonian customary law, the wife is defined as the property of the husband (Pemunta 2011: p. 85, UN Human Rights & UN Women, 2013). Gender inequalities with regards to the ownership of land and other natural resources are underpinned by assumptions that as heads of household (male-headed households), men are entitled to the efficient control and management of productive resources. Such an assumption implicitly suggests that women lack the capacity to effectively manage such productive resources:

'… productive resources given to women are "lost to another family" in the event of marriage, divorce or male death and that men will provide for women's financial security. Challenging these discriminatory ideas is critical.'

(UN Human Rights & UN Women, 2013: p. 2).

The marriage gift transaction [which is] distinct from that used for the payment of goods (e.g., lobola, bogadi, bohali) (Burman 1990 in Mifumi, 2004: p. 30) has been misinterpreted and misrepresented. 'A woman was free to (and often did) walk out of an abusive marriage and return to her parents and relatives' (Mifumi 2004: p. 30). In the same light, Ngwafor (1993) concedes that in Cameroonian customary law, a wife is regarded as property of her husband and members of his kinship group once bride-price has been paid. Due to the fact that husbands pay bride price, women are regarded as part of the man's acquired property and cannot inherit land (thus the oft-cited Ugandan adage, 'property cannot own property') (Landesa Rural Development Institute Online). As such, a woman cannot lay claims to property upon divorce or death of her husband no matter what her financial contributions have been towards the acquisition of such immovable property, as customary law does not countenance the sharing of matrimonial property. With specific reference to the case of *Achu v Achu*, FIDA took exception to the court's ruling. The verdict reached by the court was that 'customary law does not countenance the sharing of property, especially landed property between husband and wife on divorce. The wife is still regarded as part of her husband's property' (Pemunta 2011: p. 85). Most often, exclusion from property inheritance usually results in the expulsion of the widow from the marital home of her late husband. This is particularly the case when a widow refuses to remarry from within her late husband's kinship group. The Cameroon Chapter of the Inter-African Committee for the Fight Against Harmful Traditional Practices (IAC) has rightly characterized this inheritance law as a 'harmful traditional practice' (Pemunta & Fubah, 2016).

As rural leaders, the powers of traditional rulers derive not only from their command over their communities and their natural resources, but is also firmly rooted in postcolonial policies of direct rule or what Mahmood Mamdani (1996: p. 37) calls decentralized despotism. Rural rulers/Chiefs are called auxiliaries of the administration. Although land registration with its attendant developmentalist ethos was adopted by the postcolonial state, it co-exists with customary tenure arrangements. As I shall demonstrate later on, the co-existence of customary and statutory land tenure arrangements and matrimonial practices as well as the contradictions inherent in these two competing registers is bad news for women's land tenure rights. The government of Cameroon (GoC) rejects customary land holding –thereby turning citizens into squatters who could be evicted at any time. The co-existence of customary and statutory tenure arrangements infused with the colonial developmentalist paradigm of 'effective occupation' of land as evidence of development has led to contradictory rules, laws, customs/traditions, perceptions and regulations governing people's rights to use, control and transfer landed property (Gyau et al., 2014: p. 24; Mope Simo & Bitondo, 2010). The contradictions between customary and statutory land tenures often culminate in competing claims over the same piece of land by different actors with different quantities of rights and powers. The end result has been the exclusion of women and the poor from enjoying their constitutionally guaranteed land tenure rights. The multiplicity of overlapping tenure regimes and therefore governmentality regimes and power fields embedded in the 'co-existence of state law, traditional (precolonial), colonial and national land codes' is often appropriated by corrupt traditional and modern authorities for their own self-interests. In Cameroon, women and the poor (small holders) are increasingly being dispossessed by a national and international capitalist alliance comprised of urban elites, politicians and large scale agro-business consortiums. In fact, smallholders are gradually being pushed to the most arid land which is a bane on their productivity and livelihood by powerful and better connected local, national elites and their transnational partners who have higher stakes and leverage in 'negotiation' processes. According to Pauline E. Peters (2002: p. 56):

'The positive aspects of ambiguity and indeterminancy in Africa's "land question" may be overemphasized to the point of ignoring or deflecting research and policy away from growing inequality in access to land and use of land.'

Natural resources (farmland, wetland, pasture, rangeland, fishery, forest, as well as harvesting and hunting territories (UN Human rights & UN Women, 2013: p. 1), like other public resources of the state constitute part of the symbolic and material resources state elites can easily lay hands on for their own selfish interests (Pemunta 2013: p. 10).

In theory, Cameroon's constitution recognizes women's property rights on equal terms with men. The 1996 Cameroon Constitution is gender neutral and provides a legal framework for the sexes (individually or in association with others) to enjoy equal access to, and control over land and other properties. It states that no individual can be deprived of property unless it is taken in the public interest, in accordance with applicable law, and subject to the payment of compensation as required by law (GOC Constitution 1996). This seemingly gender-neutral provision of the law is however antithetical to women's welfare. Its implementation is stymied by 'socio-cultural norms and women's lack of knowledge of their entitlements' (UN Human Rights & UN Women, 2013: p. 8). All over Cameroon, customary law opposes the equality of rights between men and women. It explicitly favors male children through the inheritance law. The Cameroon Land Tenure Ordinance No. 74–1 of 6 July 1974, guarantees all persons and corporate bodies with landed property the right to freely enjoy and dispose of such lands. Article 9 of Decree No. 76–165 of April 1976, which modified the Ordinance of 1974, establishes the conditions for obtaining land certificates. It provides that customary communities and their members, or any other person of Cameroonian nationality, shall be eligible to apply for land certificates for national land, which they occupy and develop if they can show proof of effective occupation or exploitation before 5 August 1974. Any land registered becomes unassailable (Art 1(2) of 76–165 of April 1976), thus making the occupant the landowner (Samalang 2005: p. 134). By this article all members of any community, irrespective of gender, class or ethnicity have equal rights to access and own land. However, because of the high level of legal illiteracy and poor effort by government to sensitize its citizens about their rights, it is not clear if all the rural dwellers, the poor and women, are aware of these provisions or can afford the basic costs of obtaining land titles. Besides, how many women can withstand the cultural prejudices, which prevent them from pursuing their land rights?

3. Gender and the Control of Land in Northwest Cameroon

The Ndop plain Chiefdoms found in the Ngoketunjia Division of today's Northwest Region of Cameroon have had their own fair share of land-related conflicts in which women and children are often the most affected victims. The thirteen patrilineal Chiefdoms are comprised of ten Tikar ethnicities of Chamba origin. The former Chiefdoms are made up of- Babungo, Baba 1, Babessi, Bangolan, Bamali, Bambalang, Bafanji and Bamukumbit. Although each Chiefdom has its own distinct language, they have similar cultural patterns and claim a common ancestral homeland – Refum. The latter Chiefdoms who speak Mungaka include Bali Kumbat, Bali Gamsin, and Bali Gashu (Mope Simo & Bitondo, 2010; Nkwi 1987). The hereditary Fon who is the representative of the royal family, and is the central figure in whom 'all forms of customary power relations, social control mechanisms, accumulation and distribution' (Mope Simo & Bitondo, 2010: p. 226) as well as the management of natural resources including land are vested in him. He is assisted by a complex network of Palace institutions that are associated with royalty. He wields significant political, symbolic and spiritual powers in the highly stratified socio-political, economic and religious structures that constitute the social organization of the Chiefdom (Nkwi 1987).

As subsidiaries of the administration, Chiefs/Fons manage tribal lands which were communal property and have increasingly been privatized and commoditized. The land owned by each family within every village falls under the tutelage of the Fon (Nebasina & Mbih, 2010: p. 204). Despite the existence of legal dualism (Adam & Turner, 2005; Mamdani 1996), the delimitation of power and responsibilities between traditional authorities (customary law) and public authorities (modern law), traditional rulers sometimes fail to obtain the consent and act without the knowledge of public authorities. For instance, they grant farmers (mostly women) permission to cultivate in grazing areas as well as grazers to graze on fallow farmland (Elong & Nji, 2010: p. 218). This legal dualism has led to a conflict of laws and raised the question of who actually administers the land. For example 'strangers' including the Aku often evoke government ownership of all land to justify their claims over the land that they have bought. Customary land owners have found themselves in a state of illegality and insecurity given the government's institutionalization of land certificates as a mechanism of securing land (Elong & Nji, 2010).

The Northwest Region is characterized by communal land use and land use systems have been the source of livelihoods. Individualism has led to individual claims of ownership for agricultural land, grazing land or settlement. Beyond the hierarchical national and tribal superstructure, the ancestors are believed to be the first custodians and guardians of land, which gives land an intergenerational property. The chief represents them in a sense and holds the land in trust for the living and 'those yet to be born' (Nebasina & Mbih, 2010: p. 205; Mbiti 1970). 'Outsiders'/'Strangers' are either included or excluded when tribal or family land arrangements are considered. 'Outsiders'/'Strangers' encapsulate people from other places, settlers as well as women who are considered as temporal members of the family since most groups practice exogamy. Infringements or any encroachment into this family land is likely to generate conflict and can lead to confrontation. Among settled 'outsiders'/'non-natives' are the Fulani, Bororo and Aku cattle rearers who migrated from Nigeria into the region in the decades between the 1930s and 1950s. They practice transhumance but often trespass into crop fields, destroy crops (Nebasina & Mbih, 2010: p. 205). Women who are market gardeners or out-of-season vegetable or crop growers have often been drawn into confrontation with native crop growers and the Fulani, Bororo and Aku land title holders.

Intense commodification of land is going on in the Chiefdoms of Bamessing (Nsei), Bamunka, Babungo, Baba 1 and Babessi. While customary landowners are requesting money in exchange, female cultivators are pushed back from their precolonial positions of unfettered access to land. Today they lack power in land transactions and the Consultative Board for the management of natural resources and the settlement of conflicts is a gendered – male institution where women are underrepresented (Pemunta 2016; Mope Simo & Bitondo, 2010).

4. Gender and the Control of Land

In Cameroon, men own most of the land. In 2009, 60% of land titles on record were held in urban areas. Fifty percent of titleholders were male civil servants, while women held only 3.2% of certificates registered in the populated Northwest Region (Javelle 2013: p. 4). Most recent figures on land registration suggest that the percentage of titled women land holders varied from 3% in the Northwest to 15% in the Centre region (Endeley 2010). Data adduced from the Northwest and Southwest regions of Cameroon (Anglophone Cameroon) suggest that between January 1980-June 2010, 12,224 applications for land certificates were received. A total of 11,796 land certificates were issued to men (86.6%). Furthermore, out of 11,796 land certificates granted, 1,128 were issued to women (9.6%). Simultaneously, 452 land certificates were issued as joint ownership to applicants, giving a total of 3.8% land certificates controlled by applicants (Fonjong 2012: p. 97). Between 2005-2014, the gender inequality gap in access to land in Northwest Cameroon ranged from at least 55 % (55.24%) to a maximum of about 66%. Stated differently, the share of land titles issued to women was on average, 62% less than the share that went to men (Njoh 2017: p. 22).

Unequal and gendered access to land is deeply entrenched in these regions in particular and in Cameroon in general. Although most smallholder farmers are women, they own less than 10% of the total number of land certificates (Cameroon Gender Equality Network 2011). The gender blindness of the land tenure legislation seems to be the greatest obstacle to the enjoyment of women's land rights. It has instead led to the superimposition of customary practices that determine rules of land access at the expense of women.

5. Method and Theoretical Framework

Qualitative interviews were conducted with women, village elders and other male respondents in Northwest Cameroon to determine how and why women are refused formal land ownership and how they are challenging this act of dispossession. Qualitative techniques were considered more appropriate because they explore the 'how' and 'why' of a phenomenon and are capable of generating multiple perspectives on a phenomenon, providing an in-depth elucidation of a limited number of cases and for conducting cross-case comparisons and analysis. Data analysis was thematic and consisted of identifying differences and similarities across cases (Stake 2005; Miles & Huberman, 1994).

Gender is a socially and culturally constructed reference to 'differences between women and men within the same household and within and between cultures' that are subjected to change over time. Both men and women have different socially defined roles, responsibilities, access to land and other natural resources, constraints, opportunities, needs, perceptions and views, that have been inculcated into their habituses through the process of socialization. Without being a synonym for women, gender considers both women and men and their independent relations on the basis of the specific gender roles laid down in a given society. In other words, gender is a social and cultural phenomenon that is independent of biological characteristics. It underlines socially acquired and culturally-specific attributes that distinguish women and men. One's environment (society) plays a preponderant role in the development of gender roles through various agents of socialization. Socially established gender roles, social norms, and social control mechanisms inhibit women's property rights as well as their efforts to achieve economic autonomy and opportunities to break out of poverty and expose them to domestic violence and HIV/AIDS especially during crises (Scalise 2013; Mope Simo & Bitondo, 2010: p. 224).

6. Factors Structuring Women's Exclusion from Land Ownership

This section will examine the factors that structure women's exclusion from land ownership.

'Land law is the system of codified rules that are enforced through institutions that govern land tenure. Other types of law, for example marriage and family law, are also relevant to the protection of women's land rights'.

(UN Human Rights & UN Women, 2013: p. 1)

Despite legal dualism in both the official and customary land tenure and matrimonial systems, there is the privileging of statutory law over customary law. In fact, the conjuncture between the apparently gender-neutral land tenure legislation, accentuated by the gender insensitivity of the land tenure legislation, patriarchal socio-cultural norms embedded in the institution of marriage, the high cost of the land titling procedure and women's lack of social capital, farmer-grazer conflicts, demographic dynamics and land scarcity, the influence of economic liberalization and large scale agribusiness development structure their lack of access to land tenure and property ownership.

6.1 Uncertainty between statutory and customary tenure regimes

The legal dualism in place in Cameroon and most African countries has led to the selective appropriation of the rules governing several domains of life including family relations (marriage), ownership and inheritance including land tenure. Whereas the traditional land tenure systems exclude women from land ownership, the confusion and ambiguities of the modern land tenure system affect women's access and rights to land as well as the quantity and quality of household production and consumption, patterns of rural differentiation and accumulation. The legal dualism characteristic of Cameroon's land tenure 'has further weakened the rights and security of those who [women] face progressive marginalization' (Mope Simo & Bitondo, 2010: p. 224). The customary land tenure which initially granted land access to women is rapidly eroding; conflicts are flaring up over land and the natural resources on them, while market forces continuously discriminate against women thereby pushing them into deeper poverty and human insecurity. Adams and Turner (2005: p. 4) mention that:

'[Bridging] the divide between land tenure systems based on the imported concept of absolute private ownership and systems based on more complex indigenous frameworks of nested individual and group rights is a step forward in improving rural livelihoods.'

While colonial regimes instituted legal and but left in place existing customary tenure leading to legal dualism, they simultaneously reinforced settler interests and adopted minimalist approaches to land tenure and management by indigenous people. Concurrently, the roles of traditional authorities were simplified and strengthened while women's land tenure rights were typically suppressed. Customary law has however remained the dominant force in fields such as family relations, economic relations and – often spanning the two –land tenure. In patrilineal societies in general, men gained rights to land through membership in a lineage or clan while women gained usufruct rights/access rights only through their husbands. Spinsters gained access to land for the cultivation of foodstuffs either through their fathers or brothers. Men were obliged to allocate land to their wives to use for the cultivation of foodstuff to feed their families. This led to the so-called male-headed household thesis, even when women were largely responsible for provisioning the household with food. This prevented women from growing crops for sale and from the market economy as a whole. The male-headed household thesis has endured for a pretty long time and recent changes over the past four decades in Sub-Saharan Africa are the outcome of economic hard times including the SAP. According to Adams and Turner (2005), they also:

'… reflect the marginalization of women in development policy generally. Land policies have been typically blind to the gendered nature of property and its consequences. Consequently, women are losing out as a result of the process of "development". Furthermore, they do so from an already inferior position. Commercialization of production and individualization of tenure systems and formal titling schemes have all worked in the same direction; women's tenure rights have been – and are still being – eroded.'

(Adams & Turner, 2005: pp. 4-5)

6.2 Gender insensitivity of land tenure legislation

Cameroon's 1974 Land Ordinance laid down the rights and obligations of individuals, communities, the state and other entities in access to land, forests, water, and other natural resources as well as the distribution of benefits accruing from these resources. The Ordinance led to the institutionalization of freehold land rights or private land rights. However, customary tenure arrangements still hold sway in most Chiefdoms. It neither addressed women's land tenure rights nor guaranteed their access to the legal system particularly as customary tenure cancelled individual property rights in favor of group rights. The contention, in line with English Law, 'was that the right to individual property… did not extend to "usufructuary" or "communal" rights' (Adams & Turner, 2005: p. 4). Furthermore, the land

342

tenure legislation failed to address the 'power dynamics within (male-headed) households that often impair most women from asserting their land ownership rights' (Mope Simo 2002 in Mope Simo & Bitondo, 2010: p. 226). Paradoxically, although most of the rural masses who are mostly women rely on the land for their livelihood, they are the same social actors enjoying the least power in the hierarchical power structure of patrilineal societies. Women's land rights are undermined by: (a) hierarchical socio-economic and political relations resulting from gender inequalities and patriarchal ideologies. In this regard, several interlocutors constantly asked us: 'How can a woman who is also property own land? What will happen when she gets married and the husband divorces her?'; (b) wrong policies and institutions; (c) meddling by powerful self-interested individuals (both modern and traditional elites); (d) unrecognized customary tenure practices; (e) the gender-bias of some community organizations (Mope Simo & Bitondo, 2010: p. 226) including the male dominated Land Consultative Board in which women's voices are unrepresented.

Additionally, customary land tenure pays scant attention to power relations in the countryside and their implications for social groups, such as women, who are not well positioned and represented in local level power structures and who are more affected by the contemporary shift from land abundance to high levels of land scarcity (Whitehead & Tsikata, 2003: p. 79):

'This is because women suffer systematic disadvantages both in the market and in state-backed systems of property ownership, either because their opportunities to buy land are very limited, or because local-level authorities practice gender discrimination, preventing women from claiming rights that are in theory backed by law. Women also encounter problems in both the statutory and customary systems for resolving land struggles and disputes – who does the adjudicating and how – or in wider aspects of gender relations.'

This point is clearly articulated in the Convention on the Elimination of All Forms of Discrimination against Women[2] (CEDAW) mentioned by Landesa Rural Development Institute 2016.

'[Rural women's] lack of participation in decision-making processes at the community level . . . often lack [of] effective access to the ownership of land, despite the existence of legal provisions providing for such access, as reflected in the low percentage of women who own land; [and] about women's limited knowledge of their property rights and their lack of capacity to claim them.'

(para. 43, CEDAW/C/TZA/CO/6, 16 July 2008)

---

2   The CEDAW Convention defines discrimination against women as '... any distinction, exclusion or restriction made on the basis of sex which has the effect or purpose of impairing or nullifying the recognition, enjoyment or exercise by women, irrespective of their marital status, on a basis of equality of men and women, of human rights and fundamental freedoms in the political, economic, social, cultural, civil or any other field'.

6.3 Budgetary shortfalls

Administrative authorities are alleged to lack the necessary logistics (financial resources) to assist them in the resolution of land disputes as articulated in the land tenure legislation. Although the 1970 decree laid down the modalities for the adjudication of land disputes including funding as inscribed in the budget of the Ministry of State Property and Land Tenure, they have never been availed of such funds. The lack of financial resources for adjudicating land disputes has played into the hands of 'big men'. These traditional and modern elites ('big men') often meddle in land competition and in thwarting the course of justice when it comes to the impartial adjudication of land disputes. The liberalization of the economy gave them an undue advantage – they amassed huge swathes of land through both purchase and outright extortion and expansionism. This is in addition to the leverage they have over ordinary lands in every Chiefdom. Their inordinate expansionism led to 'tribal wars in the Northwest' (Kum-Set 1995 in Mope Simo & Betondo, 2010: p. 229) such as that between Bali Kumbat and Bafanji over a disputed piece of land on their common border. In the Region violent clashes have since been recorded during which full-grown crops were chopped down and over 3,000 people including women and children were displaced from their homes.

6.4 The African family and the institution of marriage

In Cameroon civil or religious authorities are mandated to celebrate marriage. In customary law, it is however, the payment of the bride price (a combination of goods, services and cash) that constitutes the cultural seal for the solemnization of marriage. Bride price is sometimes erroneously interpreted as the 'purchase price' of the wife by the husband and his kinship group. The woman therefore becomes their chattel because 'property cannot own property'. A woman therefore has only usufruct rights to land and is perceived as 'a factor of production for the husband's farm' which she has to continue to work in order to ensure access to her husband's land, but never as an equal who can own land in her own right (Scalise 2013: p. 163) (the case *Ekema J in Kumbongsi v Kumbongsi*). Although in most of Cameroon 'women are considered as property and property cannot own property' (Pemunta 2011: p. 86), they often control crop production and any income accruing thereof, but they however remain largely land users. Similarly, Goheen's (1996) analysis shows that women's labour in the production of both crops and children has long been the incontestable basis of male status and power. According to her, although Nso men obviously dominate their society at both the local level and nationally, women have had power of their own by virtue of their status as women.

A woman's access to her husband's land is seen as a privilege, not a right. In the same light, the female spouse's contribution to the acquisition of the property is not considered as a right to that property (the case of *Teneng Lucas v Nchang Irene*). Independent of matrimonial regime, women may still run into problems when their husbands die and in-laws move in to assert ownership rights over the woman and her husband's property (Pemunta & Fubah, 2016). This has often resulted in acrimonious legal battles and even ostracism, should the woman win. Customary law rarely countenance property ownership by women in their capacity as daughters or wives. In the case of *Zamcho Florence Lum v Chibikom Peter Fru & Others*, the Bamenda Court of Appeal maintained the customary law position. The verdict was however later quashed by the Supreme Court on two grounds (a) violation of the preamble of the 1996 constitution; (b) that it was repugnant and antithetical to natural justice, good conscience and equity. This case comes with far reaching repercussions on women's land tenure rights and ought not to be limited to instances of inheritance (Pemunta 2011).

In most of Cameroon, land is considered as a communal property often entrusted to male authorities: Chiefs or village elders or family/lineage heads, usually have males as custodians. Males are therefore vested with control over land at the detriment of women who are simply considered as 'strangers'. The contention is that unlike males who are considered as permanent members of the kinship group, as non-permanent members of the lineage group, women will be married off into other lineages. In many communities, the lineage authorities allocate land to the male household head. Women on the other hand have secondary cultivation rights that they obtain through male family members. In general therefore, the hierarchical nature of rights and responsibilities over land that emerge as a result of gender differentiated rights and roles are skewed against women and girls in favor of men and boys. As one interviewed elder stated: 'Women's limited access to land and natural resources is because women move out of the family for marriage. You can cultivate whatever you want on the land but you (woman) cannot sell the land'.

Social embeddedness is therefore important for understanding women's land rights. Both male and female genders have differentiated positions within the kinship systems that constitute the main organizing order for land and natural resource access. Marriage comprises one significant site for women's claims to land (Whitehead & Tsikata, 2003). 'The question of who gains access to land and on what terms can only be understood by seeing how control over land is embedded within the broader patterns of social relations' (Toulmin & Quan, 2000: p. 6). In the Ndop plain, women gain access to land from husbands' kin group, through loan or from a wider network of social ties. Economic changes have resulted in women's diminishing access to land. Concurrently, privatization and concentration negatively affect women's land and property rights, 'rather than national registration schemes *per se*' (Whitehead & Tsikata, 2003: p. 79).

The family or the male-headed household is a site of oppression and dispossession for women by virtue of their gender. The notion of the family in Africa is broad and goes beyond the restricted Euro-American meaning, consisting only of members of the nuclear family and the living. In its extended meaning, it brings together the dead and those still to be born, the ancestors and their descendants-the so-called communitarian view of human society (Mbiti 1970: p. 141). Such a socio-cultural conception of land makes it an indispensable, a resource that is the object of contention as evidenced by the intense ongoing land-use conflicts.

Land is further associated with a religious dimension. It is perceived as an intergenerational property linking both the worlds of the living and the dead (Mbiti 1990) and males are customarily regarded as custodians. This perception has led to son preference, thereby undermining both women's property rights and the rights of young girls to education. Women will eventually get married, and only sons are perceived as being capable of guaranteeing protection, and granting access to land. There is, for instance, the reluctance to sale land in Kom, Cameroon, to married native women because of fear of their husband's wrath. In Kom, women are capable of inheriting family land insofar as they are single-divorced/separated (Fombe et al., 2013: p. 79). While women face cultural and administrative bottlenecks, some women circumvent obstacles by using male relatives to stand as a front for them to buy land.

By ascribing 'double outsider' status to women within the family and in the larger community, women are excluded from property ownership. According to Pierre Bourdieu (1990), the insider is someone whose mental and bodily dispositions (habitus) have allegedly been acquired from within and, thus, fit into a specific space whereas women are 'outsiders' again when they marry into another kinship group because they do not have the power of sacrifice and owe their membership of the group to their husbands and their husband's lineage or kinship group. In this sense, gender discrimination serves as hidden structure or conceals son preference, contributes to the negation of women's access to education and curtails their opportunities in life including dispossession from natural resources including land. As a social construct, the expectations, capabilities and responsibilities of men and women are not always biologically determined. Rewards for different genders are structurally and culturally skewed in ways that 'create, reinforce, and perpetuate relationships of male dominance and female subordination'. Glaring policy gaps, legal templates and investment opportunities prevent women from performing to their optimum in the social, economic and political spheres. Inequalities are embedded in politico-judicial structures and in cultural-ideological productions. 'Values, norms, and practices enshrined in the domains of social interaction may contribute to fostering inequalities, reinforce gender related differentials or increase violence against women' (United Nations Development Programme 2016; Njogu & Orchardson-Mazru, 2008: p. 2).

6.5 Farmer-grazer conflicts

Women who constitute the majority (over 75% of the rural farming work force) of market gardeners or out-of-season vegetable or crop growers have been drawn into conflict with native crop growers on the one hand, and on the other with the Fulani, Bororo and Aku land title holders. In the face of the SAP imposed on Cameroon and other African countries in the late 1980s by the Bretton Woods institutions, existing systems, including the rural crop co-operatives and farm groups, were dismantled without being replaced. Co-operative organizations, their workers and dependents were left on their own and without any compensation. Faced with this new reality, which constrained their socioeconomic life chances, they ingeniously turned to the land. As Nebasina and Mbih (2010: p. 206) note:

'...and [they] got into the fast, double out-of-season vegetable and other crop production, this time to face and compete with urban returnee elites, who are financially well-to-do. These newcomers rent or invade just any available fertile, well-watered spots, thus increasing competition for the land, water and other natural resources that are part of the production process. In the process, there is encroachment onto land which was hitherto regarded as common property for ancestral rites (and therefore not anybody's land) or for community nature preservation.'

In the event of conflicts that have erupted over the multiple exploitation of a piece of land by many end users, the state has oftentimes drafted in the forces of law and order. Apart from leading to outright deadly confrontations, there have also been protests and the withholding of the sale of foodstuff from the open local market by women. In some extreme instances, women have been alleged to attack and wound or kill the horses or cows of grazers in protest. In one extreme case that occurred in October 2006, locals in Bali allegedly poisoned Fulani cows leading to massive losses. On one occasion, local women stripped and marched to the administrative offices to register their protest against the unilateral granting of grazing permits over their land to 'strangers' (Nebasina & Mbih, 2010: p. 207). As a result of significant crop destruction in 1972-1973, Aghem women marched from Wum to Bamenda (a distance of 80 km) to seek solutions to their problem from the local administrative authorities (Elong & Nji, 2010: p. 220). The instigators of land and natural resource conflicts are 'politicians and some ambitious chiefs (*fons*) seeking territorial aggrandizement and the spoils of power'. Simultaneously, land violence and 'bush wars' over land and other natural resources are taking place 'in the face of rapid population growth, economic and political liberalization, the institutionalization of private property rights in land and an irrevocable democratization process' (Mope Simo & Bitondo, 2010: p. 223).

6.6 High cost of land certificates and women's lack of social capital

The high cost of establishing land certificates (about 129,700F CFA) is beyond the reach of most peasant farmers, mostly women. The long complicated and bureaucratic procedures for the establishment of land certificates, with both official and unofficial additional fees (corruption) along the administrative ladder discourages villagers from acquiring them while benefitting rich traditional and modern elites ('big men'), politicians and other influential personalities who have acquired and registered large swathes of land (Elong & Nji, 2010: p. 213). Compounding women's situation is their lack of the financial wherewithal to engage in defending their rights in the court of law, should they choose to do so. Many women human rights activists also talked of women's fear of 'tradition' in challenging male hegemony especially over landed property that have continued to be seen as male prerogatives. Even when help with legal fees is readily available, women are unwilling to take advantage because of societal stereotypes that they will be styled as 'bad women' and will be isolated by other family members.

6.7 Demographic dynamics and land scarcity

The Northwest region's population is estimated at 1.82 million. Subsistent agriculture is the people's main activity, mostly undertaken by elites and retired elites who are involved in dairy farming. They have snapped up hundreds of hectares of arable land. Concurrently, there is intense competition for scarce land between farmers and grazers. An estimated 500,000 herds of cattle are reared across this part of the country (Nebasina & Mbih, 2010). Some Fons have adopted an expansionist policy thereby trespassing across natural and colonial frontiers. Simultaneously, land is facing unprecedented degradation and depletion owing to over-use and climate change.

Population explosion has led to conflicting claims over land that used to be a communal property. Information compiled by Ngwa Nebasina and Achia Mbih shows that between 1994 and 1995 alone, 781 farmer-grazier conflicts were reported in Mezam Division, 56 of these conflicts were from

Sabga (Ndop Plain). Farmer-grazer conflicts have led to 'conflicting, uncoordinated land use for grazing, agriculture and settlement, the manifestations of these conflicts become evident in various forms and at various levels' (Nebasina & Mbih, 2010: p. 204). Grazers and crop cultivators are struggling over land, host and 'stranger communities': cultivable land, water, grazing resources, urban and rural settlement land by various stakeholders-ushers in conflict, vulnerability of each community's socioeconomic and political structure (Nebasina & Mbih, 2010: p. 203).

6.8 The Influence of economic liberalization

The economic liberalization, which was imposed through the SAP, transformed the national, regional and local political economy, undermined the subsistent economy and led to a pattern of agrarian capitalism. The institutionalization of formal private property rights through the promulgation of the 1974 Land Law led to the commoditization of land. The local elites (traditional and modern) are now increasingly buying up and transforming what used to be a communal property into a private resource. A conjuncture between population explosion, environmental degradation, commodification and individualization (Mope Simo, 2010) has not only made land scarcer, but has reinforced gender inequality and rural differentiation. The liberalization of the economy led to tenure insecurity for women, land that used to be a communal property became increasingly commodified and a spectre of inter-Chiefdom conflicts rocked the Northwest Region.

6.9 Large scale agricultural development

The main agro-industrial consortium in the Ndop plain is the Upper Nun Valley Development Authority (UNVDA), a parastatal charged with transforming the swamps and marshy areas of the Ndop plain into an irrigated rice project that grows and markets paddy rice. The corporation has developed 2500 hectares for rice production involving 8500 farmers. Water from the Bamenjim dam and from numerous rivers and streams are used to irrigate UNVDA-developed farms (Cheo & Nkwain, 2015). Between 1971 and 2012, the total surface area of rice production rose from 33ha to more than 3000ha with more than 6000 farmers involved in its cultivation in the Ndop plain and its environs (Mbih et al., 2014). The ravaging economic downturn of the 1990s that negatively affected Cameroon and other African countries and led to the adoption of the SAP, forced many women to turn to rice production, the cultivation of cash crops, and other income generating activities as the means of supplementing family incomes that greatly transformed traditional gender roles. Additionally, rice production has afforded women with an opportunity to challenge and transform their traditional domestic/reproductive roles into becoming major actors in performing productive and community roles (Fonjong & Athanasia, 2007: p. 143). Arable land taken up by the corporation and conflicts over water often flares between the corporation and farmers and grazers (Pemunta 2014). Some women however reported that they are surreptitiously investing in landed property as well as owning land to invest and produce more rice in, for the future of their children.

Mary Ngeng who now farms over 15 hectares of land comfortably feeds her family and sells the surplus of the rice she grows to wholesale buyers and to the UNVDA to raise her family income. In the past, she could only cultivate on limited rented land and could therefore not do commercial rice farming. She has however been able to own land over time, increased her yields and supports her family's income. She concedes that unlike before when excessive rains and floods destroyed her vegetable farm, and harvest on the rented land was poor and her family's income constantly dwindling, large scale commercial rice farming on her newly acquired land has tremendously improved her family's livelihood and transformed her relationship with her male relatives.

7. Conclusion

In Cameroon, the co-existence of gender neutral laws alongside customary laws regulating marriage and property ownership tends to violate women's rights to and undermine their ownership of both movable and immovable property including land. Climate change aside, agricultural and agrarian livelihood systems (largely in the hands of women) are seriously threatened by the co-existence of state law, traditional, precolonial, colonial and national land codes (Mope Simo 2010; Mamdani 1996). The multiplicity of land tenure regimes in most of Africa and Cameroon that is anchored on power inequality-class, gender and ethnicity excludes women despite the usufruct rights that they enjoy. Women's marginal land ownership rights significantly prevents them from accessing credit and savings, exposes them to gender-based violence and to the scourge of the HIV/AIDS pandemic. Women's marginality due to discrimination goes along to prevent the sustainable development of agriculture and translate into food insecurity and deeper poverty. It has deeper implications for national development. Ambe Njoh has uncovered a negative link between gender inequality and per capita GDP. This speaks to the fact that economic growth is liable to address some dimensions of gender inequality. It further suggests that macroeconomic gains in each sector of the economy leads to 'lowering the gender gap prevalent in formal land ownership status' (Njoh 2017: p. 27).

Land and other natural resources are imbricated in unequal, gendered and power relationships that tend to disproportionately stall women's socioeconomic development. A gender lens provides the understanding of gender roles, ideologies, gender identities and other intersecting factors including class as well as gender relations instead of gendering the impact of resource use conflict on women. Social and cultural traditions and structures of domination that lead to unequal power between men and women and discrimination against women greatly inhibit and limit women's property rights (Mope Simo & Betondo, 2010: p. 230).

It is very clear that guaranteeing women's land and resource rights goes beyond the reformation of existing laws and includes the provision of effective avenues that oversee and ensure the implementation of women's human rights in general. It requires a holistic development approach that involves changes in the matrimonial law and the effective adoption and implementation of Cameroon's stalled family code. It further implies a purposeful, sustained adoption and implementation of a wide range of measures and participatory approaches that will ensure gender equality and justice, women's empowerment, the promotion of economic growth and the eradication of gendered poverty, gender-based violence and the enhancement of values of citizenship and human rights as the bedrock of sustainable development.

Gender considerations and the inclusion of women's voices in the Land Consultative Board and in all public consultations will energize Cameroon's boarding democratization process. For example, women constitute the highest segment of the country's population and are the main actors involved in small scale agricultural activities, are also the greatest users of land and other natural resources (Mope Simo & Betondo, 2010: p. 232).

Apart from changes in patriarchal cultural norms that disadvantage women, laws and policies to ensure that gender equality should be promoted and enforced or enacted and implemented are required at all levels of decision-making and policy. Such an approach will contribute to achieving the Sustainable Development Goals (SDGs) which African governments and other world leaders have pledged to for the coming 15 years (UNDP 2016). Women are reconfiguring the negative aspects of culture by challenging patriarchal norms that dispossess them of land ownership. By asserting their agency, they are demonstrating that identities are simultaneously shaped and performed within the context of culture (Njoku & Orchardson-Mazrui, 2008). Culture becomes an arena of contestation, debates and a polyphonic concept, not a unitary one. Women's contestation of the status quo of dispossession in matters of land and property ownership is illustrative of the multiple workings of power, of power as multiply deployed by both the powerful (men) and women simultaneously and of spaces for both resistance and agency (Crampton & Elden, 2007: p. 334).

Bibliography

Adams, Martin & Stephen Turner (2005) 'Legal Dualism and Land Policy in Eastern and Southern Africa', UNDP-International Land Coalition *Land Rights for African Development: from Knowledge to Action*. Online. Available www.undp/drylands (accessed July 23, 2016).

Bourdieu, Pierre (1990) *In Other Words: Essays towards a Reflexive Sociology*, translated from French by Mattheu Adamson, California: Stanford University Press.

Cameroon – Gender Equality Advocacy Network (GEADNET) (2011). Online. Available http://www.ahgingos.org/documents/Documents/CAMEROON.pdf (accessed June 20, 2016).

Cheo, George F. & Sama J. Nkwain (2015) 'Profit and Profitability of Rice Production in Ndop Plain, Cameroun'. Online. Available https://www.grin.com/document/316390 (accessed May 23, 2016).

Crampton, Jeremy & Stuart Elden (eds.) (2007) *Space, Knowledge and Power: Foucault and Geography*, Adershot: Ashgate Publishing Limited.

Elong, Joseph Gabriel & Michael A. Nji (2010) 'Farmer Grazier Land Conflict in Wum Central Sub-division, Menchum Division, North-West Region of Cameroon', in François Nkankeu & Christopher Bryant (2010) *Regards multidisciplinaires sur les conflits fonciers et leurs impacts socioéconomico-politiques au Cameroun*, Montréal: Laboratoire Développement durable et dynamique territoriale, Département de Géographie, Université de Montréal, pp. 213-220.

Endeley, Joyce (2010) 'Politics of Gender, Land and Compensation in Communities Traversed by the Chad-Cameroon Oil Pipeline Project in Cameroon', in Dzodzi Tsikata & Pamela Golah (eds.) *Land Tenure, Gender and Globalization, Research and Analysis from Africa, Asia and Latin America*, New Delphi: Zubann, International Development Research Center.

Fombe, Lawrence, Irene Sama-Lang, Lotsmart Fonjong & Anastasia Mbag Fongkimeh (2013) 'Securing Tenure for Sustainable Livelihoods: A Case of Women Land Ownership in Anglophone Cameroon', *Éthique et économique/Ethics and Economics*, 10(2): 74-86.

Fonjong, Lotsmart (2012) (ed.) *Issues in Women's Land Rights in Cameroon*, Bamenda: Langaa Research and Publishing Common Initiative Group.

Javelle, Anne-Gaelle (2013) *Focus on Land in Africa Brief: Land Registration in Cameroon*, Washington DC: World Resources Institute.

Goheen, Miriam (1996) *Men Own the Fields, Women Own the Crops: Gender and Power in the Cameroon Grassfields*, Madison, Wisconsin: The University of Wisconsin Press.

Gyau, Amos, Awah Faith, Divine Fondjem-Tita, Nji Ajaga & Delia Catacutan (2014) 'Small-holder Farmers' access and Rights to Land: the Case of Njombé in the Littoral Region of Cameroon', *Afrika Focus, Special Agroforestry Issue*, 27: 23-39.

Landesa Rural Development Institute (2016) *Supplementary Information Concerning Women's Land Rights in Tanzania Submitted to the 63 Session (15 Feb 2016 - 04 Mar 2016) of the Committee on the Elimination of All Forms of Discrimination against Women.*

Mamdani, Mahmood (1996) *Citizen and Subject: Contemporary Africa and the Legacy of Late Colonialism*, Princeton: Princeton University Press.

Mbih, Richard, Stephen Ndzeidze, Steven Driever & Gilbert Bamboye (2014) 'The Bamendjin Dam and Its Implications in the Upper Noun Valley, Northwest Cameroon', *Journal of Sustainable Development*, 7(6): 123-132. Online. Available:
http://www.ccsenet.org/journal/index.php/jsd/article/viewFile/41075/23202)
(accessed July 23, 2016).

Mbiti, John (1970): *African Religions and Philosophies*, New York: Doubleday and Company.

Mifumi Nonprofit Organization Management (2004) *International Conference on Bride Price 16th – 18th February*, Held at Makerere University, Kampala, Uganda Conference Report. Online. Available
http://mifumi.org/admin/publications/1430826417MIFUMI%20Bride%20Price%20Conference%20REPORT.pdf (accessed June 20, 2016).

Miles, Matthew B. & Michael A. Huberman (1994) *Qualitative Data Analysis*, Thousand Oaks, CA: Sage Publications.

Mope Simo, John & Dieudonne Bitondo (2010) 'Gender and an Assessment of the Impacts of Land Violence in Ndop Plain (Northwest Region of Cameroon)', in François Nkankeu & Christopher Brayant (eds.) *Regards multidisciplinaires sur les conflits foncieres et leurs impact socio-économico-politiques au Cameroun*, Montréal: Laboratoire Développement durable et dynamique territoriale, Département de Géographie, Université de Montréal.

Ndop, Plain (2015) 'Cameroon: A Value Chain Analysis Approach', Research Paper. Online. Available http://www.grin.com/en/catalog/business-economics/business-economics-trade-and-distribution/ (accessed June 20, 2016).

Nebasina, Ngwa E. & Achia R. Mbih (2010) *Settlement, Grazing or Agricultural Land: A Platform for Integration or Conflicts in Mezam Division (North West Cameroon)*, Grassfields.

Nebasina, Emmanuel Ngwa & Richard Achia Mbih (2010) 'Settlement, Grazing or Agricultural Land: A Platform for Integration or Conflicts in Mezam Division (NorthWest Cameroon)', in François Nkankeu & Christopher Bryant (eds.) *Regards multidisciplinaires sur les conflits fonciers et leurs impacts socioéconomico-politiques au Cameroun*, Montréal: Laboratoire Développement durable et dynamique territoriale, Département de Géographie, Université de Montréal.

Ngwafor, Ephraim N. (1993) *Family Law in Anglophone Cameroon*, Regina, Saskatchewan, Canada: University of Regina Press.

Njogu, Kimani & Elisabeth Orchardson-Mazrui (2008) 'Culture, Gender Inequality and Women Rights in the Great Lakes', in Kimani Njogu (ed.) *Culture,*

Performance and Identity: Paths of Communication in Kenya, Nairobi, Kenya: Twaweza Communications, pp. 1-39.

Njoh, Ambe (2017) 'Effects of macro-economic factors on women's formal land ownership status in Cameroon', *Women's Studies International Forum*, 62: 132-160.

Nkankeu, François & Christopher Bryant (2010): *Regards multidisciplinaires sur les conflits fonciers et leurs impacts socioéconomico-politiques au Cameroun*, Montréal: Laboratoire Développement durable et dynamique territoriale, Département de Géographie, Université de Montréal.

Nkwi, Paul N. (1987) *Traditional Diplomacy: A Study of Inter-Chiefdom Relations in the Western Grassfields, North West Province of Cameroon*, Yaounde, Cameroon: Publication of the Department of Sociology, University of Yaounde.

Pemunta, Ngambouk V. & Mathias F. Alubafi (2016) 'The Social Context of Widowhood Rites and Women's Human Rights in Cameroon'. Online. Available http://dx.doi.org/10.1080/23311886.2016.1234671 (accessed July 23, 2016).

Pemunta, Ngambouk V. (2014) 'New Forms of Land Enclosures: Multinationals and State Production of Territory in Cameroon', *Studia Sociologia*, LXI(2): 35-58.

Pemunta, Ngambouk V. (2011) *Culture, Human Rights and Socio-legal Resistance against Female Genital Cutting Practices: An Anthropological Perspective*, Saarbrücken: VDM Verlag Dr. Müller GmbH & Co.KG.

Peter, Pauline E. (2004) 'Inequality and Social Conflict over Land in Africa', *Journal of Agrarian Change*, 4(3): 269–314.

Scalise, Elisa (2013) 'Indigenous Women's Land Rights: Case Studies from Africa', in *Focus on Land Rights and Natural Resources. State of the World's Minorities and Indigenous Peoples 2012.* London: Minority Rights Group International.

Stake, Robert (2005) 'Qualitative Case Studies', in Norman K. Denzin & Yvonna S. Lincoln (eds.) *Qualitative Research* (3rd ed). Thousand Oaks, CA: Sage Publications.

Toulmin, Camilla & Julian Quan (eds.) (2000a) *Evolving Land Rights, Policy and Tenure in Africa*, London: IIED with DFID & NRI.

Whitehead, Ann & Dzodzi Tsikata (2003) 'Policy Discourses on Women's Land Rights in Sub-Saharan Africa: The Implications of the Re-turn to the Customary', *Journal of Agrarian Change*, 3(1-2): 67-112.

United Nations Development Programme (2016) *African Human Development Report 2016: Accelerating Gender Equality and Women's Empowerment in Africa*, Nairobi: UNDP Regional Bureau for Africa.

United Nations Human Rights and UN Women (2013) *Realizing Women's Rights to Land and Other Productive Resources*, New York & Geneva: United Nations. Online. Available http://www.ohchr.org/Documents/Publications/RealizingWomensRightstoLand.pdf (accessed July 23, 2016).

NOTES ON CONTRIBUTORS

ADAMIAK Marzena is a philosopher, Assistant Professor at the Institute of Philosophy and Sociology of the Polish Academy of Sciences in Warsaw, board member of the Polish Phenomenological Association, and lecturer at the postgraduate Gender Studies, the Institute of Philosophy of the 'Nicolaus Copernicus' University. She is the author of a book entitled *Of a Woman Who Comes to Mind. The Woman as a Figure of Otherness in the Concept of Subject of Emmanuel Lévinas,* published in Polish (2007): *O Kobiecie, Która nawiedza mysl. Kobieta Jako figura innosci w konepcji podmiotu Emmanuela Lévinasa,* Warsaw: WAIP. Her interests focus on theories of subjectivity and identity, especially from the perspective of feminist philosophy and phenomenology. She was responsible for the part on 'Phenomenology and Feminism' within the project 'Issues in Contemporary Phenomenology' (2012-2017) under 'The National Programme for the Development of Humanities'.

ANDAYA Barbara Watson is a Professor of Asian Studies at the University of Hawai'i and formerly Director of the Center for Southeast Asian Studies. Between 2005-2006 she was President of the American Association of Asian Studies. Educated at the University of Sydney (B.A., Dip. Ed.). In 1966, she received an East West Center grant and obtained her M.A. in history at the University of Hawai'i. She subsequently went on to study for her Ph.D. at Cornell University with a specialization in Southeast Asian history. Her career has involved teaching and researching in Malaysia, Australia, New Zealand, Indonesia, the Netherlands, and since 1994, Hawai'i. She maintains an active teaching and research interest across all Southeast Asia, but her specific area of expertise is the Western Malay-Indonesia archipelago. In 2000 she received a Guggenheim Award, which resulted in (2006) *The Flaming Womb: Repositioning Women in Southeast Asian History, 1500-1800,* Honolulu: University of Hawai'i Press (a Choice Academic Book of the Year in 2007). Her current project is a history of religious interaction in Southeast Asia, 1511-1900, with a focus on Christianity and gender.

ANDAYA Leonard Y. received a B.A. in History from Yale University, an M.A. and a Ph.D. in Southeast Asian history from Cornell University. He has held positions at the University of Malaya, the Australian National University, the University of Auckland, and the University of Hawai'i at Manoa, where he has been a professor of Southeast Asian history since 1993. He has written extensively on the early modern history of Southeast Asia, particularly on Indonesia and Malaysia. He has published: (1993) *The World of Maluku: Eastern Indonesia in the Early Modern Period* Honolulu: University of Hawaii Press; (2008) *Leaves of the Same Tree: Trade and*

Ethnicity in the Straits of Melaka, Honolulu: University of Hawaii Press; and with Barbara Watson Andaya (2015) *A History of Early Modern Southeast Asia,* Cambridge: Cambridge University Press; (2016) (Third Edition) *A History of Modern Malaysia,* London: Palgrave.

BIANCHERI Rita is an Associate Professor of the Sociology of Cultural Processes at the Department of Political Science of the University of Pisa (Italy). As a Principal Investigator of the TRIGGER Project (*Transforming Institutions by Gendering contents and Gaining Equality in Research*), co-funded by the EU's 7th Framework Programme, she coordinates the research group of the University. In her research, she has always adopted a gender perspective to analyze the socialization process, families and their transition, health and the labor market (with special focus on academic careers). She has authored several monographs and books, chapters and articles on these topics. More recently, she has edited a special issue of the Italian Review (2016) *Health and Society*, 'Culture di Salute ed Ermeneutiche di Genere', Milano: Franco Angeli; co-edited (with Patrizia Tomio) the book (2015) *Lavoro e Carriere nell'Università*, Pisa: ETS; co-edited (with Elisabetta Ruspini) the book (2015) *Interpretare il genere*, Pisa: Pisa University Press.

CERVIA Silvia is an Assistant Professor of the Sociology of Cultural Processes at the Department of Political Science of the University of Pisa (Italy). She is also a member of the team of the TRIGGER European Project (*Transforming Institutions by Gendering contents and Gaining Equality in Research*), and of the ReGED group (a thematic research group on Gender Equal Opportunities), for which she is Junior Coordinator of the sections 'The Methodology of Social Research' and 'The Participatory Approach & Consensus Method'. She combines methodological aspects in her work, while focusing on gender roles as social constructions, which she has researched at both a *micro* and *macro* level. She has authored a number of monographs and several chapters and articles on the latter, including, more recently, (2016) 'Sistemi locali di Network Governance in Sanità secondo una prospettiva di genere', *Salute e Società*, 3: 43-60.

CRUSMAC Oana is a Ph.D. candidate in political theory at the National University of Political Studies and Public Administration, Bucharest, Romania. Her Ph.D. thesis focuses on the current debates on distributive justice theories, approached from a feminist perspective. She holds a B.A. in communication and public relations, an M.A. in sociology and an M.Res. in political theory and political analysis from the same university. Her main research interests are gender equality, social justice and feminism. Recent publications include: 'Gender Mainstreaming and Work-Family Reconciliation. An Analysis of Family Policies in Romania and Germany' (co-authored, 2006), *Romanian Journal of Society and Politics*, 2: 49-74; (2015) 'Why Gender Mainstreaming is not Enough. A Critique to Sylvia Walby's The Future of Feminism', *Romanian Journal of Society and Politics*, 1: 102-117; (2014) 'Democracy, Deliberation and Exclusion. A Brief Case Study on Romanian Deliberation Regarding the Civil Partnership', *Analize – Journal of Gender and Feminist Studies*, 3(17): 137-158.

FALUDI Cristina is a Lecturer at the Social Work Department of the Faculty of Sociology and Social Work from Babeş-Bolyai University (BBU), Cluj-Napoca, Romania. She authored and co-authored academic publications and research reports, mainly related to sexual, reproductive, and risk behaviour of youth and the quality of life among the elderly. She holds a Ph.D. in Sociology from BBU. Since 2006, she has been a member of the European Association for Population Studies. She worked as a researcher in national and international research projects. In 2013, she published the book *Debutul vieţii sexuale şi contraceptive la studenţi. România în context European*, Cluj: Cluj University Press. She also published: (2015) (co-author: Csaba Laszlo Dégi), 'The Effect of Sexual Debut and Health Risk Behaviours on Baccalaureate Performance of Romanian Adolescents', *Croatian Journal of Education*, 17(2): 333-352; (2015) 'Contraceptive Prevalence', in Mehmet Odekon (ed.) *The SAGE Encyclopedia of World Poverty*, London: Sage Publications; (2016) (co-author: Csaba Laszlo Dégi) 'Psycho-social Predictors of Satisfaction with Intimate Life in Romanian Cancer Patients', *Cognition, Brain, Behavior. An Interdisciplinary Journal*, 20(4): 239-257.

FILIPOVÁ Petra has obtained a Master's degree in British and American Studies at 'Pavol Jozef Šafárik' University in Košice, Slovakia, where she is currently teaching gender studies. At present, she is involved in a European double degree doctorate programme at the same university, as well as the University of Balearic Isles in Palma de Mallorca, Spain. Her doctoral thesis focuses on the explorations of the representation of asexuality in the American media, most prominently in American television shows.

FÖRTSCH Silvia is a Senior Researcher at the Women in Computer Science Equal Opportunities Office, within the Faculty of Information Systems and Applied Computer Sciences, the University of Bamberg. She studied educational sciences (B. Sc.) at the University of Hagen and empirical educational research (M. Sc.) at the University of Bamberg. She worked as an assistant of the Women in Computer Science Equal Opportunities Officer and organized a mentoring program for female students in computer science. Between 2012 and 2015, she was a research associate at the project 'Alumnae Tracking'. Since 2015 she has been working as a Ph.D. candidate in the project 'Career Coaching in STEM. Her research interests include longitudinal research on educational and professional pathways, career aspirations, life course research, and gender studies.

MANOLACHE Viorella is a Scientific Researcher, Ph.D., at the Institute of Political Sciences and International Relations 'Ion I.C. Brătianu', Romanian Academy, Bucharest, Romania. She is the author of articles, studies, coordinator of international collective volumes and author of books – the latest ones being: (2016) *Philosophical-Political Hecate-isms. The Rule of Three*, University of Cambridge: Cambridge Scholars Publishing; (2016) *Ecce Philosophia Politica. 'Diferenţa' lui Roberto Esposito*, Bucharest: ISPRI Publishing House; (2013) *Repere teoretice în biopolitică*, Bucharest: ISPRI Publishing House; (2013) *Signs and Designs of the Virtual(izing) E@ST*, Saarbrücken: Lambert Academic Publishing. She is a member of several national and international societies and associations, editorial teams and editorial boards. She is also a peer-reviewer of scientific national and international journals.

MOLDOVEANU Daniela is a Lecturer in English and Intercultural Communication at the Military Technical Academy of Bucharest, Romania. She obtained her B.A., M.A. and Ph.D. in philology at 'Lucian Blaga' University of Sibiu, the Faculty of Arts and Letters. Her Ph.D. thesis 'Confession and Identity in the Feminine Romanian Poetry from the 70s and 80s' was published in 2014 under the title *Confessional feminine poetry*, Bucharest: Muzeul Literaturii Române. That same year she also published *The Identity of Metaphor – The Metaphor of Identity. Discourse and Portrait*, Frankfurt am Main, Bern, Bruxelles, New York, Oxford, Warszawa, Wien: Peter Lang, 2017. Poet and essayist, her research interests lie in the fields of comparative literature, intercultural communication, discourse analysis, feminine and identity studies, poetics, stylistics, philosophy and aesthetics. She has also published an award winning poetry book entitled 'Paper Clips' (2008), and her poems have appeared in various poetry anthologies.

MONTLIBERT Christian de is a French sociologist, Professor Emeritus at 'Marc Bloch' University in Strasbourg. He is the founder of the journal *Regards sociologiques* and its director starting from 1991. Between 1998 and 2004, he was the director of Centre de recherches et d'études en sciences sociales (CRESS) and, between 1996 and 2009, of the publication *Cahiers du CRESS (1996-2009)*. Relevant books: (2012) *Enjeux et luttes dans le champ économique, 1980-2010*, Paris: L'Harmattan, collection 'Questions sociologiques'; (2004) *Savoir à vendre. L'enseignement supérieur et la recherche en danger*, Paris: Éditions Raisons d'agir; (1997) (ed:) *Maurice Halbwachs 1877-1945. Colloque de la faculté des sciences sociales de*

Strasbourg, Strasbourg: PUS; (2001) *La violence du chômage*, Strasbourg: Presses Universitaires de Strasbourg.

MURRU Sarah, Ph.D., works at the Interdisciplinary Research Center on Families and Sexualities (CIRFASE) at the University of Louvain-la-Neuve (UCL) in Belgium. She is also an Associate Researcher at the Centre for the Study of International Cooperation and Development (CECID), at the Université Libre de Bruxelles (ULB). She has specialized in the conceptualization of resistance, in particular through the study of everyday forms of resistance as well as in the implementation of feminist epistemologies and methodologies. Past research projects include a study of Single Moms' resistance in Vietnam. Currently, she is working on the resistance performed daily by children in the context of divorce and shared custody agreements – a comparison between Belgium and Italy.

NIMU Andrada is a Fellow at The *Research Institute of Bucharest.* She holds a Ph.D. in Political Science at the National School of Political Science and Public Administration (2015), with a thesis on women and sexual minority movements from Central and Eastern Europe. Currently, her research interest is focused on LGBTQI mobilization in Central and Eastern Europe. She has written a series of articles in national and international journals, chapters in books and has co-edited a book on civil society in Romania with Cristian Pârvulescu and Arpad Todor: (2016) *Societate civilă, democraţie şi construcţie instituţională*, Iaşi: Polirom. She is a collaborator at Questia Group, a public-opinion polling company in Bucharest.

PEMUNTA Ngambouk Vitalis holds a Ph.D. in Sociology and Social Anthropology from the Central European University (CEU) Budapest, Hungary. His career has involved teaching at the Universities of Yaounde1 (Cameroon), Central European University (Hungary), and University College Dublin (Ireland). He has recently completed his postdoctoral research at Linnaeus University, Växjö, Sweden. He is also a consultant for several NGOs in both his native Cameroon and abroad-thereby cross-pollinating between the fields of anthropology and development. He is a country expert on asylum for Cameroon for the United Kingdom-based Rights in Exile Programme. He has conducted extensive ethnographic fieldwork in, and published on Cameroon, Chad, South Africa and Sierra Leone. His research interests include gender, reproductive health, HIV/AIDS, environmental policy, ethnography, medical sociology/anthropology, social science and medicine, colonialism and postcolonialism.

PERIŠIĆ Natalija, Ph.D., is an Associate Professor at the Department of Social Policy and Social Work at the University of Belgrade – Faculty of Political Sciences. Her primary scientific and research interests lie in Serbian and European social policies, as well as in the impact of EU social policy on national policies. She has participated at national and international conferences and projects related to social policy and has published numerous articles related to social welfare, pensions, older people and migrants.

PÎRJOL Florina-Elena is an Associate Lecturer at the University of Bucharest with a Ph.D. Dissertation on autofiction in Romanian post-communist literature. Her current project deals with the gastronomic imaginary and 'food habits' in the 19th century, but also during the communist period, as reflected in fictional texts. The project combines various perspectives: anthropological, sociological, historical, literary, and aims to recover/re-read two centuries of culture through gastronomical details found in literature. Main interests: contemporary mutations of autobiography (the self-fictionalization in literature), food history and literature. Recent book: (2014) *Carte de identități*, Bucharest: Cartea Românească.

RADU Daniela, currently a psychotherapist, has a Ph.D. in Political Science (International Relations). She has been involved in academic research and teaching for over 15 years. Her professional experience has benefited from research and documentation fellowships at University of Lille, University of Trieste, University of Geneva and the United Nations Office in Geneva. As member or coordinator of national and international research teams, she has implemented research projects concerning vulnerable categories of persons. Her professional interests are focused on the normative structure of international politics, peace-building processes, transitional justice, humanitarian crises and are reflected by studies and publications such as: (2012) 'A Constructivist Perspective on EU's actions within the International System', in Cecilia Tohăneanu, *Teorii versus ideologii politice* Bucharest: European Institute Publishing House; (2016) (first author) 'The Lack of Women's Inclusion in the Process of Peacebuilding' paper presented at IPSA World Congress – Poland; (2017) (first author) 'No more Victims? The Latin American Truth Commissions and their Implications in the Investigation of Past Violence against Women and Child Soldiers', paper presented at ECPR General Conference – Norway.

SCHMID Ute is a Professor of applied computer science and head of the cognitive systems group at the University of Bamberg. She holds a diploma in psychology and a diploma in computer science. Her research interests are mainly in the domain of high-level learning on structural data. Due to her function as a wome's equal opportunity officer, she has been organizing workshops for female high-school students for about ten years with the intent to raise the number of female students in computer science. From 2012 to 2015, she conducted the research project 'Alumnae Tracking' that compares career choices and paths of female computer scientists with criteria-matched males. Since 2015, she has been the head of the research project 'Coaching in STEM'. The objective of this project is to develop a coaching program that will support especially women after their reintegration into the workforce or in the context of professional reorientation.

STOICAN Adriana Elena, Ph.D. in Literary and Cultural Studies, University of Bucharest, is an Associate Lecturer at the Bucharest University of Economic Studies. She is specialized in English and Hindi philology with a focus on postcolonial and transcultural studies. She has published articles on Romani identity, Indian diasporic fiction in English, Romanian literature of migration and comparative approaches to Indian and Romanian women's writing. She is the author of the book published in 2015, *Transcultural Encounters in South-Asian American Women's Fiction. Anita Desai, Kiran Desai and Jhumpa Lahiri*, University of Cambridge: Cambridge Scholars Publishing. Her articles appeared in: (2016) *American, British and Canadian Studies*, 27(1): 94-116; (2016) *Transnational Literature*, e-journal, 8(2); (2013) *Between History and Personal Narrative. East European Women's Stories of Migration in the New Millennium*, Münster: LIT Verlag, pp. 69-81; (2013) *Muses India: Essays on English-Language Writers from Mahomet to Rushdie*, Jefferson, North Carolina: McFarland & Company, pp. 113-124; (2012) *Humanicus-Academic Journal of Humanities, Social Sciences and Philosophy*, 7; (2009) *The University of Bucharest Review. A Journal of Literary and Cultural Studies*, XI (2): 87-93.

TANASIJEVIĆ Jelena, Ph.D., a Social Work Practice Teacher at the Department of Social Policy and Social Work at the Faculty of Political Sciences, University of Belgrade, Serbia, and counselor at the Centre for Foster Care and Adoption in Belgrade. Her scientific and research interests are in national social policy and social work practice, especially in work-family reconciliation policy. Her practical expertise has been primarily within the challenges of empowering foster families to take care of children. Recently, her professional activities have focused on foster care of migrant children. She has co-authored and performed trainings for foster care and trainings for professionals working with students. She has been publishing on child and family welfare.

ZAMFIRA Andreea has a Ph.D. in Political and Social Sciences from the University of Bucharest and the Université Libre de Bruxelles. She is an Assistant Professor at 'Lucian Blaga' University of Sibiu (Department of

International Relations, Political Sciences and Security Studies), an Associate Researcher at the CEVIPOL (Center for the Study of Political Life, Brussels) and CEREFREA Villa Noël (Centre Régional Francophone de Recherches Avancées en Sciences Sociales, Bucharest). She is the author of the book (2012) *Une sociologie électorale des communautés pluriethniques*, Paris: L'Harmattan, collection 'Questions sociologiques' and of several articles and book chapters on interculturality, ethnic stereotypes, political parties and voting behavior. Recent publications include: (2015) 'Methodological Limitations in Studying the Effect of (Inter)ethnicity on Voting Behaviour, with Examples from Bulgaria, Romania and Slovakia', *Erdkunde*, 69(2): 161-173; (2015) 'Altérité, identité, interculturalité. D'un concept réifié et réifiant à une approche interdisciplinaire et dynamique de l'ethnicité', in Rodica Zane & Philippe Claret (eds.) *Les sciences humaines et sociales dans les sociétés en transition. Recueil d'études et témoignages en hommage à Pierre Bidart*, Bucharest: Editura Universității din București, pp. 407-421.

Index

H

I

J

Surviving historical trauma

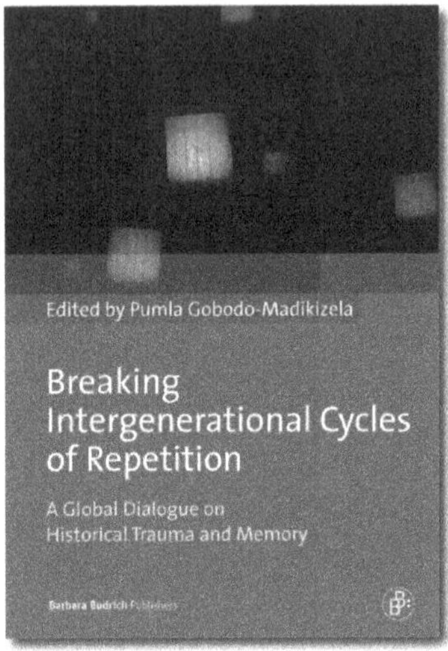

Pumla Gobodo-Madikizela (ed.)

Breaking Intergenerational Cycles of Repetition

A Global Dialogue on Historical Trauma and Memory

2016. 365 pp. Pb. 39,90 € (D),
GBP 36.95, US$58.00
ISBN 978-3-8474-0613-6

The authors in this volume explore the interconnected issues of intergenerational trauma and traumatic memory in societies with a history of collective violence across the globe. Each chapter's discussion offers a critical reflection on historical trauma and its repercussions, and how memory can be used as a basis for dialogue and transformation.

Order now:

Verlag Barbara Budrich
Barbara Budrich Publishers
Stauffenbergstr. 7
51379 Leverkusen-Opladen

Tel +49 (0)2171.344.594
Fax +49 (0)2171.344.693
info@budrich.de

www.budrich-verlag.de

CPSIA information can be obtained
at www.ICGtesting.com
Printed in the USA
LVHW051114121218
600106LV00002B/7/P